PRAISE FOR

AGENT SONYA

NAMED ONE OF THE BEST BOOKS OF

THE YEAR BY *KIRKUS REVIEWS* • *LIBRARY*

JOURNAL • *FOREIGN AFFAIRS* • *CRIMEREADS*

"We have at last, in Ben Macintyre's *Agent Sonya,* the tale of a fully fleshed-out female spy. . . . [Macintyre] has found a real-life heroine worthy of his gifts as John le Carré's nonfiction counterpart. . . . An enthralling account." —*The New York Times Book Review*

"With *Agent Sonya*, Ben Macintyre, the author of several popular works about espionage, has written a lively account of Kuczynski's remarkable career. . . . [A] fascinating portrait of a Soviet spy who never recanted her belief in communism, even as the system for which she had risked her life disintegrated."—*The Wall Street Journal*

"[An] immensely exciting, fast-moving account . . . Macintyre [is] one of the finest writers on spies and international espionage . . . a connoisseur of spy craft." —*The Washington Post*

"In his latest entertaining nonfiction spy thriller, Macintyre tracks Sonya's numerous audacious exploits during her prolific career. . . . The author crafts a narrative that serves as both an engrossing historical tale and a compassionate portrait of Sonya as a complex woman with distinctly modern sensibilities for her time. . . . An absorbing study of a remarkably accomplished twentieth-century spy." —*Kirkus Reviews* (starred review)

BY BEN MACINTYRE

AGENT SONYA

CROWN
NEW YORK

AGENT SONYA

THE SPY NEXT DOOR

BEN MACINTYRE

2021 Crown Trade Paperback Edition

Copyright © 2020 by Ben Macintyre Books Ltd.
Book club guide copyright © 2021 by Penguin Random House LLC
Excerpt from *Prisoners of the Castle* copyright © 2022 by Ben Macintyre
Excerpt from *The Spy and the Traitor* copyright © 2018 by Ben Macintyre

Published in the United States by Crown, an imprint of Random House,
a division of Penguin Random House LLC, New York.

CROWN and the Crown colophon are registered trademarks of
Penguin Random House LLC.

RANDOM HOUSE BOOK CLUB and colophon are trademarks of
Penguin Random House LLC.

Originally published in hardcover in the United States by Crown,
an imprint of Random House, a division of Penguin Random House LLC,
New York, in 2020.

Simultaneously published in Great Britain by Viking, an imprint of
Penguin Random House Ltd., London, and in Canada by Signal, an imprint
of Random House of Canada, a division of Penguin Random House
Canada Limited, Toronto.

Photo credits are located on page 355.

LIBRARY OF CONGRESS CATALOGING- IN PUBLICATION DATA

NAMES: Macintyre, Ben, 1963– author.

TITLE: Agent Sonya / Ben Macintyre. Description: First edition. |
New York: Crown, 2020 | Includes bibliographical references and index.

IDENTIFIERS: LCCN 2020019326 (print) | LCCN 2020019327 (ebook) |
ISBN 9780593136324 (paperback) | ISBN 9780593136317 (ebook)

SUBJECTS: LCSH: Werner, Ruth, 1907–2000. | Spies—Soviet Union—
Biography. | Spies—Great Britain—Biography. | Espionage, Soviet—
Great Britain—History—20th century. | Nuclear weapons—History—20th
century. | Soviet Union. Glavnoe razvedyvatel'noe upravlenie. | Cold War. |
Women spies—Soviet Union—Biography. | Spies—Germany (East)—
Biography.

CLASSIFICATION: LCC UB271.R9 M29 2020 (print) | LCC UB271.R9
(ebook) | DDC 327.12470092 [B]—dc23

LC record available at https://lccn.loc.gov/2020019326

Printed in the United States of America on acid-free paper

crownpublishing.com

randomhousebookclub.com

9 8 7 6 5 4

Book design by Barbara M. Bachman

Tinker, tailor, soldier, sailor . . .

What will my husband be?

A TRADITIONAL COUNTING AND
DIVINATION GAME PLAYED BY YOUNG
WOMEN TO FORETELL THE FUTURE

CONTENTS

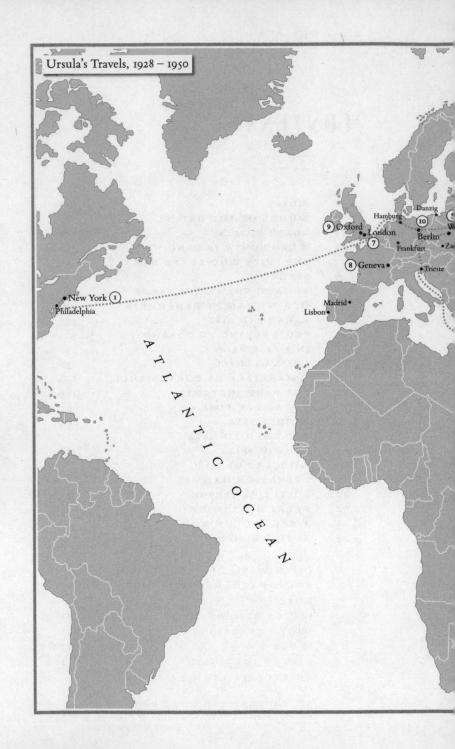

Ursula's Travels, 1928 – 1950

Hamburg
Danzig
⑤
⑨ Oxford
London
⑩
W
⑦
Berlin
Frankfurt
Za
⑧ Geneva
Trieste
New York ①
Madrid
Philadelphia
Lisbon

ATLANTIC OCEAN

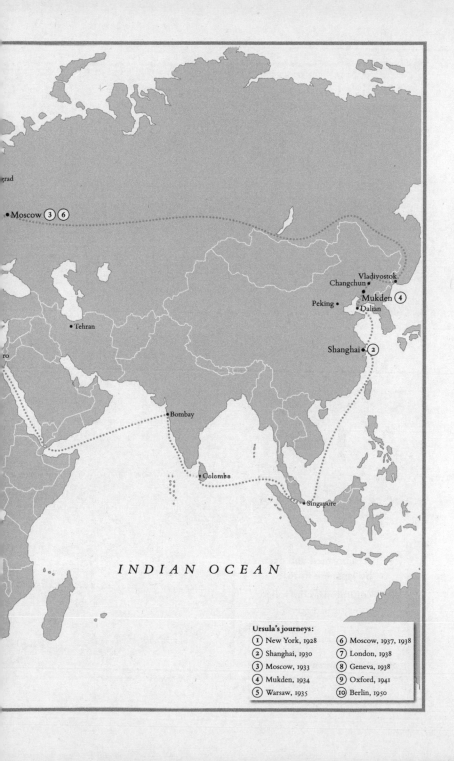

grad

• Moscow ③ ⑥

• Tehran

ro

• Bombay

Changchun
Peking • Vladivostok
• Mukden ④
• Dalian

Shanghai • ②

• Colombo

• Singapore

INDIAN OCEAN

Ursula's journeys:

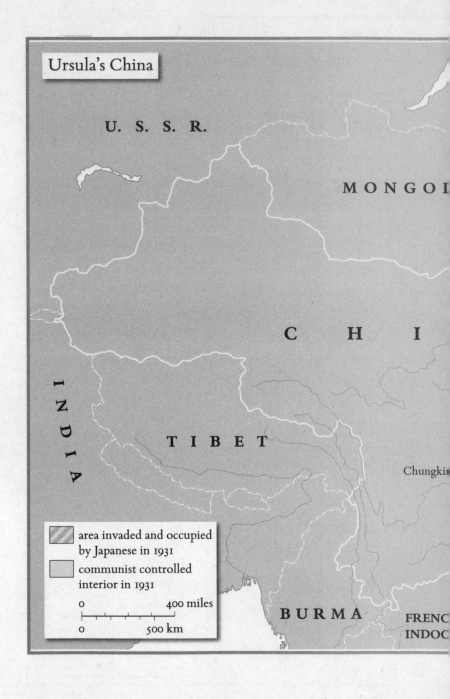

Ursula's China

U. S. S. R.

MONGOI

INDIA

C   H   I

TIBET

Chungki

area invaded and occupied
by Japanese in 1931

communist controlled
interior in 1931

0   400 miles

0   500 km

BURMA   FRENC
             INDOC

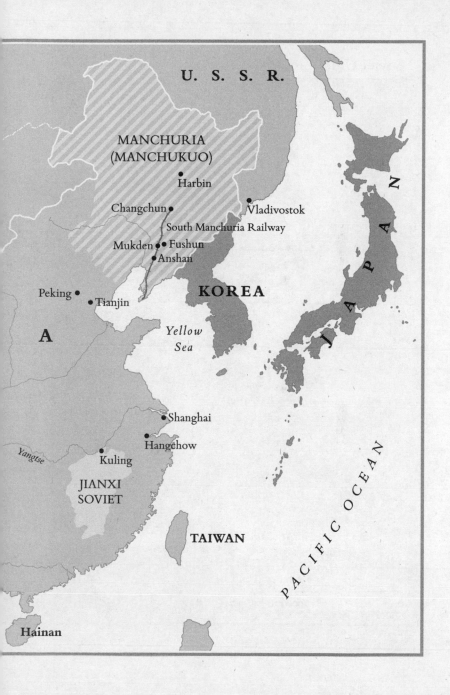

U. S. S. R.

MANCHURIA
(MANCHUKUO)

Harbin

Changchun

Vladivostok

South Manchuria Railway

Mukden Fushun
Anshan

KOREA

Peking

Tianjin

Yellow
Sea

A

Shanghai

Yangtse

Hangchow

Kuling

JIANXI
SOVIET

TAIWAN

PACIFIC OCEAN

J A P A N

Hainan

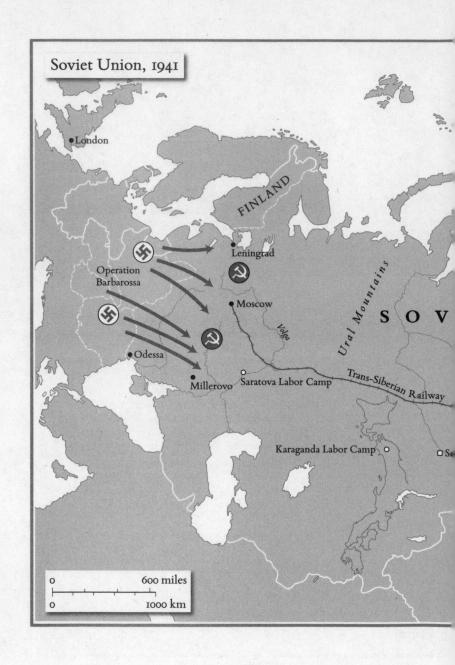

Soviet Union, 1941

London

FINLAND

Operation
Barbarossa

Leningrad

Moscow

Odessa

Volga

Ural Mountains

S O V

Millerovo

Saratova Labor Camp

Trans-Siberian Railway

Karaganda Labor Camp

S

0   600 miles

0   1000 km

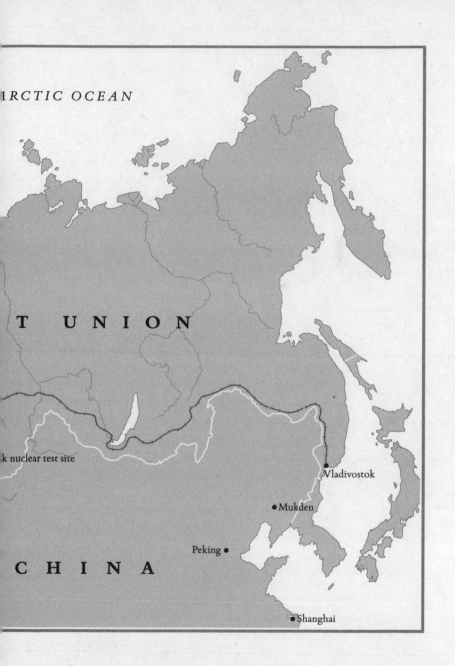

ARCTIC OCEAN

T U N I O N

k nuclear test site

Vladivostok

• Mukden

Peking •

C H I N A

• Shanghai

INTRODUCTION

I F YOU HAD VISITED THE QUAINT ENGLISH VILLAGE OF GREAT Rollright in 1945, you might have spotted a thin, dark-haired, and unusually elegant woman emerging from a stone farmhouse called The Firs and climbing onto her bicycle. She had three children and a husband, Len, who worked in the nearby aluminum factory. She was friendly but reserved, and spoke English with a faint foreign accent. She baked excellent cakes. Her neighbors in the Cotswolds knew little about her.

They did not know that the woman they called Mrs. Burton was really Colonel Ursula Kuczynski of the Red Army, a dedicated communist, a decorated Soviet military intelligence officer, and a highly trained spy who had conducted espionage operations in China, Poland, and Switzerland, before coming to Britain on Moscow's orders. They did not know that her three children each had a different father, nor that Len Burton was also a secret agent. They were unaware that she was a German Jew, a fanatical opponent of Nazism who had spied against the fascists during the Second World War and was now spying on Britain and America in the new Cold War. They did not know that, in the outdoor privy behind The Firs, Mrs. Burton (in reality spelled Beurton) had constructed a powerful radio transmitter tuned to Soviet intelligence headquarters in Moscow. The villagers of Great Rollright did not know that in her last mission of the war Mrs. Burton had infiltrated communist spies into a top secret American operation parachuting anti-Nazi agents into the dying Third

Reich. These "Good Germans" were supposedly spying for America; in reality, they were working for Colonel Kuczynski of Great Rollright.

But Mrs. Burton's most important undercover job was one that would shape the future of the world: she was helping the Soviet Union to build the atom bomb.

For years, Ursula had run a network of communist spies deep inside Britain's atomic weapons research program, passing on information to Moscow that would eventually enable Soviet scientists to assemble their own nuclear device. She was fully engaged in village life; her scones were the envy of Great Rollright. But in her parallel, hidden life she was responsible, in part, for maintaining the balance of power between East and West and (she believed) preventing nuclear war by stealing the science of atomic weaponry from one side to give to the other. When she hopped onto her bike with her ration book and carrier bags, Mrs. Burton was going shopping for lethal secrets.

Ursula Kuczynski Burton was a mother, housewife, novelist, expert radio technician, spymaster, courier, saboteur, bomb maker, Cold Warrior, and secret agent, all at the same time.

Her code name was "Sonya." This is her story.

AGENT SONYA

CHAPTER 1

WHIRL

O N MAY I, I924, A BERLIN POLICEMAN SMASHED HIS RUB-
ber truncheon into the back of a sixteen-year-old girl, and
helped to forge a revolutionary.

For several hours, thousands of Berliners had been trooping
through the city streets in the May Day parade, the annual celebration of the working classes. Their number included many communists, and a large youth delegation. These wore red carnations,
carried placards declaring "Hands Off Soviet Russia," and sang communist songs: "We are the Blacksmiths of the Red Future / Our
Spirit is Strong / We Hammer out the Keys to Happiness." The government had banned political demonstrations, and police lined the
streets, watching sullenly. A handful of fascist brownshirts gathered
on a corner to jeer. Scuffles broke out. A bottle sailed through the air.
The communists sang louder.

At the head of the communist youth group marched a slim girl
wearing a worker's cap, two weeks short of her seventeenth birthday. This was Ursula Kuczynski's first street demonstration, and her
eyes shone with excitement as she waved her placard and belted out
the anthem: *"Auf, auf, zum Kampf,"* rise up, rise up for the struggle.
They called her "Whirl," and, as she strode along and sang, Ursula
performed a little dance of pure joy.

The parade was turning onto Mittelstrasse when the police charged.
She remembered a "squeal of car brakes that drowned out the singing,
screams, police whistles and shouts of protest. Young people were

thrown to the ground, and dragged into trucks." In the tumult, Ursula was sent sprawling on the pavement. She looked up to find a burly policeman towering over her. There were sweat patches under the arms of his green uniform. The man grinned, raised his truncheon, and brought it down with all his force into the small of her back.

Her first sensation was one of fury, followed by the most acute pain she had ever experienced. "It hurt so much I couldn't breathe properly." A young communist friend named Gabo Lewin dragged her into a doorway. "It's all right, Whirl," he said, as he rubbed her back where the baton had struck. "You will get through this." Ursula's group had dispersed. Some were under arrest. But several thousand more marchers were approaching up the wide street. Gabo pulled Ursula to her feet and handed her one of the fallen placards. "I continued with the demonstration," she later wrote, "not knowing yet that it was a decision for life."

Ursula's mother was furious when her daughter staggered home that night, her clothes torn, a livid black bruise spreading across her back.

Berta Kuczynski demanded to know what Ursula was doing, "roaming the streets arm in arm with a band of drunken teenagers and yelling at the top of her voice."

"We weren't drunk and we weren't yelling," Ursula retorted.

"Who are these teenagers?" Berta demanded. "What do you mean by hanging around with these kinds of people?"

" 'These kinds of people' are the local branch of the young communists. I'm a member."

Berta sent Ursula straight to her father's study.

"I respect every person's right to his or her opinion," Robert Kuczynski told his daughter. "But a seventeen-year-old girl is not mature enough to commit herself politically. I therefore ask you emphatically to return the membership card and delay your decision a few years."

Ursula had her answer ready. "If seventeen-year-olds are old enough to work and be exploited, then they are also old enough to fight against exploitation . . . and that's exactly why I have become a communist."

Robert Kuczynski was a communist sympathizer, and he rather admired his daughter's spirit, but Ursula was clearly going to be a handful. The Kuczynskis might support the struggle of the working classes, but that did not mean they wanted their daughter mixing with them.

This political radicalism was just a passing fad, Robert told Ursula. "In five years you'll laugh about the whole thing."

She shot back: "In five years I want to be a doubly good communist."

THE KUCZYNSKI FAMILY WAS RICH, influential, contented, and, like every other Jewish household in Berlin, utterly unaware that within a few years their world would be swept away by war, revolution, and systematic genocide. In 1924, Berlin contained 160,000 Jews, roughly a third of Germany's Jewish population.

Robert René Kuczynski (a name hard to spell but easy to pronounce: *ko-chin-ski*) was Germany's most distinguished demographic statistician, a pioneer in using numerical data to frame social policies. His method for calculating population statistics—the "Kuczynski rate"—is still in use today. Robert's father, a successful banker and president of the Berlin Stock Exchange, bequeathed to his son a passion for books and the money to indulge it. A gentle, fussy scholar, the proud descendant of "six generations of intellectuals," Kuczynski owned the largest private library in Germany.

In 1903, Robert married Berta Gradenwitz, another product of the German Jewish commercial intelligentsia, the daughter of a property developer. Berta was an artist, clever and indolent. Ursula's earliest memories of her mother were composed of colors and textures: "Everything shimmering brown and gold. The velvet, her hair, her eyes." Berta was not a talented painter but no one had told her, and so she happily daubed away, devoted to her husband but delegating the tiresome day-to-day business of childcare to servants. Cosmopolitan and secular, the Kuczynskis considered themselves German first and Jewish a distant second. They often spoke English or French at home.

The Kuczynskis knew everyone who was anyone in Berlin's left-wing intellectual circles: the Marxist leader Karl Liebknecht, the artists Käthe Kollwitz and Max Liebermann, and Walther Rathenau, the German industrialist and future foreign minister. Albert Einstein was one of Robert's closest friends. On any given evening, a cluster of artists, writers, scientists, politicians, and intellectuals, Jew and gentile alike, gathered around the Kuczynski dining table. Precisely where Robert stood in Germany's bewildering political kaleidoscope was both debatable and variable. His views ranged from left of center to far left, but Robert was slightly too elevated a figure, in his own mind, to be tied down by mere party labels. As Rathenau waspishly observed: "Kuczynski always forms a one-man party and then situates himself on its left wing." For sixteen years he held the post of director of the Statistical Office in the borough of Berlin-Schöneberg, a light burden that left plenty of time for producing academic papers, writing articles for left-wing newspapers, and participating in socially progressive campaigns, notably to improve living conditions in Berlin's slums (which he may or may not have visited).

Ursula Maria was the second of Robert and Berta's six children. The first, born three years before her in 1904, was Jürgen, the only boy of the brood. Four sisters would follow Ursula: Brigitte (1910), Barbara (1913), Sabine (1919), and Renate (1923). Brigitte was Ursula's favorite sister, the closest to her in age and politics. There was never any doubt that the male child stood foremost in rank: Jürgen was precocious, clever, highly opinionated, spoiled rotten, and relentlessly patronizing to his younger sisters. He was Ursula's confidant and unstated rival. Describing him as "the best and cleverest person I know," she adored and resented Jürgen in equal measure.

In 1913, on the eve of the First World War, the Kuczynskis moved into a large villa on Schlachtensee lake in the exclusive Berlin suburb of Zehlendorf, on the edge of the Grunewald forest. The property, still standing today, was built on land bequeathed by Berta's father. Its spacious grounds swept down to the water, with an orchard, woodland, and a hen coop. An extension was added to accommodate Robert's library. The Kuczynskis employed a cook, a gardener, two more house servants, and, most important, a nanny.

Olga Muth, known as Ollo, was more than just a member of the family. She was its bedrock, providing dull, daily stability, strict rules, and limitless affection. The daughter of a sailor in the kaiser's fleet, Ollo had been orphaned at the age of six and brought up in a Prussian military orphanage, a place of indescribable brutality that left her with a damaged soul, a large heart, and a firm sense of discipline. A bustling, energetic, sharp-tongued woman, Ollo was thirty in 1911 when she began work as a nursemaid in the Kuczynski household.

Ollo understood children far better than Berta, and had perfected techniques for reminding her of this: the nanny waged a quiet war against Frau Kuczynski, punctuated by furious rows during which she usually stormed out, always to return. Ursula was Ollo's favorite. The girl feared the dark, and while the dinner parties were in full swing downstairs, Muth's gentle lullabies soothed her to sleep. Years later, Ursula came to realize that Ollo's love was partly motivated by a "partisanship with me against mother, in that silent, jealous struggle."

Ursula was a gawky child, inquisitive and restless in a way her mother found perfectly exhausting, with a shock of dark, wiry hair. "Unruly as horsehair," Ollo would mutter, brushing ferociously. Hers was an idyllic childhood, swimming in the lake, gathering eggs, playing hide-and-seek among the rowanberry bushes. Part of each summer was spent in Ahrenshoop on the Baltic coast in the holiday home of her aunt Alice, Robert's sister.

Ursula was seven when the First World War broke out. "Today there are no more differences between us, today we are all Germans who defend the fatherland," her school headmaster announced. Robert enlisted in the Prussian Guards, but at thirty-seven was too old for active service and instead spent the war calculating Germany's nutritional requirements. Like many Jews, Alice's husband, Georg Dorpalen, fought bravely on the Western Front, returning with a patriotic wound and an Iron Cross. Wealth cushioned the Kuczynskis from the worst of wartime privations, but food was scarce, and Ursula was sent to a camp on the Baltic for malnourished children. Ollo packed a bag of chocolate truffles made from potatoes, cocoa, and saccharin, and a pile of books. By the time Ursula returned, an avid reader and several pounds heavier from a diet of dumplings and prunes, the war was over. "Take your elbows off the table," her mother admonished. "Don't slurp." Ursula ran out of the dining room and slammed the door.

Germany's defeat and humiliation marked the beginning of the end of the Kuczynskis' halcyon existence. Great crosscurrents of political violence swept the country. A wave of civil disturbance triggered the kaiser's abdication, and a leftist uprising was brutally suppressed by remnants of the imperial army and the right-wing militias, or Freikorps. On January 1, 1919, Rosa Luxemburg and Karl Liebknecht founded the German Communist Party (the Kommunistische Partei Deutschlands, or KPD), but were captured and murdered within days. Thus was ushered in the Weimar Republic, an era of cultural efflorescence, hedonism, mass unemployment, economic insecurity, and roiling political conflict as the polarized forces of the extreme right and radical left clashed with growing fury. Robert Kuczynski's politics shifted further left. "The Soviet Union *is* the future," he declared after 1922. Though he never joined the KPD, Robert declared the Communist Party to be the "least insufferable" of the available options. In his journalism, he advocated a radical redistribution of German wealth. Right-wing nationalists and anti-Semites took note of Robert's politics. "He is not only against us," one German industrialist remarked darkly. "He is also extremely impudent."

The tumultuous fourteen-year period between the fall of the kaiser and the rise of Hitler is seen as a time of mounting menace, the backdrop to the horror that followed. But to be young and idealistic in those years was intoxicating, edgy, and exciting, as the world went mad. War debts, reparations, and financial mismanagement triggered hyperinflation. Cash was barely worth the paper it was printed on. Some people starved, while others went on lunatic spending sprees, since there was no point keeping money that would soon be valueless. There were surreal scenes: prices rose so fast that waiters in restaurants climbed on tables to announce the new menu prices every half hour; a loaf of bread costing 160 marks in 1922 cost 200,000,000 marks by the end of 1923. Ursula wrote: "The women are standing at the factory gate waiting to collect their husbands' pay packets. Every week, they are handed whole bundles of billion-mark notes.

With the money in their hands, they run to the shops, because two hours later the margarine might cost twice as much." One afternoon, in the park, she found a man lying under a bench, a war veteran with a stump, a pitiful bag of possessions clutched to his breast. He was dead. "Why do such awful things happen in the world?" she wondered.

Though life at Schlachtensee continued much as before, with its cultured conversation and fine furniture, millions were politically radicalized. In 1922, the foreign minister, Walther Rathenau, was assassinated by ultranationalists after signing a treaty with the Soviet Union. Every day Ursula witnessed the grotesque disparity between the urban poor and the wealthy bourgeoisie, of which she was a part. She devoured the works of Lenin and Luxemburg, the radical novels of Jack London and Maxim Gorky. She wanted to go to university, like her brother.

Jürgen was already a rising star of the academic left. After studying philosophy, political economy, and statistics at the universities of Berlin, Erlangen, and Heidelberg, he gained a doctorate in economics before embarking for the United States in 1926 to take a postgraduate degree at the Brookings Institution in Washington. There he would meet Marguerite Steinfeld, a fellow researcher in economics, whom he married two years later.

Berta put her foot down: her wayward daughter did not need more education; she needed some womanly skills, and then a husband. In 1923, at the age of sixteen, Ursula was enrolled in a trade school to study typing and shorthand.

At night, she wrote: poems, short stories, tales of adventure and romance. Denied an academic education, she poured her energies into her imagined world. Her childish writings reflected a craving for excitement, a sense of theater, a love of the absurd. Ursula was always the central character in her own stories, and she wrote of herself in the third person, a young woman achieving great feats through determination and a willingness to take risks. Of one character she wrote: "She had overcome the physical weakness of her childhood, she had toughened up and was strong." Her little sisters called her "Fairy Tale Whirl." Her diary reflected the usual sulky teenage preoccupations, but also an irrepressible optimism. "I am in a bad mood," she wrote. "Grumpy and growling, I am a hot-head, a cross-breed with a black mane of hair, a Jew's nose, and clumsy limbs, bitching and brooding . . . but then there is blue sky, a sun that warms, drops of dew on the firs and a stirring in the air, and I want to stride out, jump, run, and love every human being."

The year Ursula's formal education ended, Hitler launched the Munich beer hall putsch, a failed coup d'état that turned the future führer into a household name and landed him in prison, where he dictated *Mein Kampf,* the Nazi bible of bigotry.

Absorbing her father's political instincts, shocked by the human degradation she had witnessed, appalled by fascism, and entranced by these swirling new ideas of social equality, class war, and revolution, Ursula was drawn inexorably to communism. "Germany's own Socialist revolution is just around the corner," she declared. "Communism will make people happier and better." The Bolshevik Revolution had proven that the old order was rotten and doomed. Fascism must be defeated. In 1924, she joined the Kommunistischer Jugendverband Deutschlands, the Young Communist League, moving into the ideological home she would occupy for the rest of her life. She was sixteen years old. Like other communists from affluent families, Ursula played down her privileged background. "We lived much more modestly than one might have supposed," she insisted. "One great-grandfather sold shoelaces from a barrow in Galicia."

Ursula's fellow young communists came from all corners, classes, and communities of Berlin, united in a determination to overthrow capitalist oppression and usher in a new society. In that heady atmosphere, friendships bloomed swiftly. Gabriel "Gabo" Lewin was a middle-class boy from the suburbs. Heinz Altmann was a handsome apprentice, whose urging had given Ursula the "final impetus" to join the party. These were the young foot soldiers of German communism, and Ursula was thrilled to be one of them. The May Day demonstration of 1924 left her with a lifelong appetite for risk. The bruising from the policeman's truncheon eventually faded; her outrage never did.

On weekends, the Young Communist League ventured into the countryside to explain Marxism-Leninism to the German peasantry, who frequently responded by setting their dogs on the youthful evangelists. One evening, in Löwenberg, north of Berlin, a sympathetic farmer allowed the group to sleep in his hayloft. "That evening we were particularly cheerful," Ursula wrote. "As soon as we lay down, someone began to imagine the place twenty years later. Löwenberg in 1944: it has long since become communist. For a long time we argued over whether money would already have been abolished. We would then unfortunately be very old—in our mid-thirties!" They fell asleep, dreaming of revolution.

Ursula was one of nature's missionaries. She was never preachy, but she loved to convert, and tended to chip away at unbelievers until they saw the world as she saw it. She set to work on the family nanny. "I tried to explain things to her. She found what I said made sense," Ursula claimed. Olga Muth was not remotely interested, but allowed the girl to believe she was listening.

The Kuczynskis did not approve of their daughter being beaten up by policemen and spending her nights in haylofts with a bunch of young communists. Observing that "reading was her only field of interest," Robert arranged an apprenticeship in the R. L. Prager Bookshop on Mittelstrasse, specializing in law and political sciences. Berta bought her a pair of heels, a dark blue dress with a white collar, gloves, and a brown crocodile leather handbag. Mother and nanny inspected Ursula as she set off for her first day at work.

"Nothing in front and nothing behind," said Ollo. "You still look like a boy."

"But the legs are quite nicely shaped," said Berta. "You can only see that if you take small steps."

Ollo agreed: "Ursel will never be a lady."

Like everything Olga Muth said, this was tough but true. With her long nose, thatch of hair, and forthright manner, there was nothing ladylike about Ursula. "I'll never turn into the famous beautiful swan," she wrote in her diary. "How could my nose, my ears and my mouth get smaller all of a sudden?" Yet even as a teenager, she gave off a powerful sexual allure that many found irresistible. She giggled when the worker mending the roof of the Dresdner Bank wolf-whistled at her as she cycled to work: "He blows a kiss, and spreads his arms wide." With her bright eyes, slender figure, and infectious laugh, she was never at a loss for a dance partner at the teenage parties in Zehlendorf. At one of these, she wore "bright red scanty shorts and tight-fitting shirt with stiff collar," and danced until half past six in the morning. "There are those who say I kissed twenty boys," she told her brother. "It can't have been more than nineteen."

Working at Prager's was boring and exhausting. The manager was a chain-smoking tyrant with a large, bald, slightly tapering head, devoted to inventing fresh indignities and pointless tasks for his employees. Ursula nicknamed him "the Onion" and pronounced him a capitalist exploiter. Her time was spent "shaking out the dust cloth, standing in windowless niches." She was not permitted to read on the job. "Surely there are other professions," she reflected. "Lumberjack, for example. Could I become a female lumberjack?" Her small salary was rendered almost worthless by the raging inflation. She would remember her teenage years in the Weimar Republic through a series of politically tinted images: "The wealth of the small, privileged circles and the poverty of the many, the unemployed begging at street corners." She resolved to change the world. For Ursula was ambitious and confident: she would transform society in more radical ways than her father, and she was determined to be a better mother than her own. These twin ambitions would not always sit comfortably together.

Robert and Berta Kuczynski gave up trying to rein in their daughter's politics. In 1926, Robert took a temporary position at the Brookings Institution, alongside Jürgen, researching American finance and population statistics. He and Berta would visit America periodically over the next few years, leaving Ursula and Olga Muth to run the household together, reinforcing the bond between them. "Our Ollo, who never had anyone to love. Ollo, the hysterical, grey little creature, always dissatisfied, that is besotted with each one of us, Ollo who walks through fire for us, does everything for us, lives only for us, knows nothing of the world but her six." Ursula's letters to her part-time parents reflected her wry resentment: "Dear Mummy, I trust your maternal feelings will sustain your keen interest in all our little trivia." Another letter urged: "We are unanimous in our hope that Mummy will soon stop coming up with bright ideas on household matters, recommendations on how to cook cabbage, how to clean the house, and other advice."

While Ursula spent her days dusting books, her brother was writing them. In 1926, twenty-two-year-old Jürgen Kuczynski published *Return to Marx* (*Zurück zu Marx*), the opening rumble of an avalanche of print he would unleash over the coming decades. Jürgen loved the sound of his own voice, but even more the sound of his pen. His lifetime output was prodigious: at least four thousand published works, including acres of journalism, pamphlets, speeches, and essays, on politics, economics, statistics, and even cookery. Jürgen would have been a better writer had he been able to write less. His style became less florid with age, but he simply could not bring himself to say in a few words what might be said in many. His study of labor conditions eventually ran to forty volumes. *Return to Marx* was a comparatively slim work of five hundred pages. With typical grandiosity, he told his sister that he "hoped the workers would read it with pleasure." Ursula offered some editorial suggestions: "Write easier, short phrases. You should strive for simplicity of presentation, so that everyone can understand. Sometimes the text is only complicated when, for greater persuasiveness, it is repeated in two or three places, changing only the form and structure of the phrase." This was excellent advice, which Jürgen ignored.

At home and at work, Ursula was a drudge; outside those places, she was a revolutionary.

A few weeks before her nineteenth birthday, Ursula joined the KPD, the largest Communist Party in Europe. Under its new leader, Ernst Thälmann, the party was increasingly Leninist (later Stalinist) in outlook, committed to democracy but taking orders and funding directly from Moscow. The KPD had a paramilitary wing, locked in escalating conflict with the Nazi brownshirts. The communists prepared for battle. On moonlit nights in a remote corner of Grunewald forest, her earliest friends from the Young Communist League, Gabo Lewin and Heinz Altmann, taught Ursula to shoot. At first she consistently missed the target, until Gabo pointed out she was closing the wrong eye. She proved to be an excellent shot. Gabo gave her a Luger semiautomatic pistol, and demonstrated how to take the gun apart and clean it. She hid the weapon behind a beam in the attic at Schlachtensee, concealed inside a torn cushion. When the revolution came, she would be ready.

Ursula joined the anti-fascist demonstrations. "Terribly busy," she wrote. "Preparing for the Anniversary of the Russian Revolution." During lunch breaks she sat in Unter den Linden, the tree-lined boulevard running through central Berlin, reading *Die Rote Fahne* (*The Red Flag*), the communist newspaper. Often she sought out the working-class cabdrivers and fruit sellers, many of whom were communists, and avidly discussed politics with them. In her diary she wrote: "So many starving, so many beggars in the streets . . ."

One afternoon Ursula joined a group of young leftists, members of the Social Democratic Party as well as the KPD, for an afternoon of swimming and sunbathing at a lakeside outside Berlin. Ursula later recalled the moment. "I turn around, and there is a man in his mid-twenties, well groomed, with a soft slouch, a clever, almost beautiful face. He looks at me. His eyes are wide, and dark brown, he is a Jew." The young man asked if he could sit with her and chat. "I have no time," she said. "I have to go to a Marxist workers' class." He persisted, asking if they might meet again. "I could consider it!" Ursula said, and skittered away. A few days later, the young man with the brown eyes was waiting outside the building where her Marxist class was held.

Rudolf Hamburger was an architecture student at Berlin Technical University. Four years older than Ursula, Rudi turned out to be a distant relative—his mother and Berta Kuczynski were second cousins—and from a similar background. Hamburger was born in Landeshut in Lower Silesia, where his father, Max, owned textile mills manufacturing army uniforms. The second of three sons, Rudi was brought up in an atmosphere of liberal politics and lightly worn Jewish intellectual culture. Max Hamburger built a model housing estate for his 850 workers. The family was politically progressive, but far from revolutionary. Rudi was already a passionate advocate of architectural modernism and the Bauhaus movement. His fellow students, he wrote, included "an Austrian aristocrat, a Japanese who designed interiors in meticulously co-ordinated pastel shades, an anarchist and a Hungarian girl with a completely unjustified belief in her own genius." Another contemporary was Albert Speer, "Hitler's architect," the future Nazi minister for war production and armaments.

Ursula felt a surge of attraction, and on an impulse invited Hamburger to a communist meeting. They got on well. She invited him to another. "Finally time to be with Rudi again," she wrote in her diary. "He helps me make the tea. He doesn't realize I have put the gas on low so it boils slowly. . . . My winter coat is too thin, Rudi says. He wants to try to make me a little vain." She bought a new coat and then reproached herself for the extravagance when others were dying of starvation. "I long for Rudi," she wrote. "Then I am angry that such a person can turn my head. And that I need him so much. And then I fall asleep, sobbing." One night, as they walked home from a concert, Rudi paused under a streetlamp. "He stood against the light. His thick hair was still unruly in the same surprising way, his dark eyes never lost their melancholy and veiled expression, even when he laughed or was deep in thought." That was the moment she fell in love. "Can a second, a sentence, the expression in the eyes of a person suddenly change everything previously felt into something new?" she wondered. Rudi walked her home. "That night he kissed me," she wrote. "I was sad because my lips were so dry. Such a small thing, but I had been thinking of the kiss all afternoon, with quiet rejoicing."

Rudi Hamburger was almost the ideal boyfriend: kind, funny, gentle, and Jewish. Both sets of parents approved. If she became too serious, he softly teased her. And when he talked about his ambition to become a great architect, the large brown eyes danced with light. He was generous. "Rudi gave me a bar of chocolate," she told her brother. Sweets were rare, and she was keen to stress that this was not some bourgeois self-indulgence. "He did not spend money on it. We do not do such nonsense. But if someone gives him something, he always shares with me."

Rudi hinted at marriage. Ursula held back.

Because there was only one problem with Rudolf Hamburger: he was not a communist. They might share a Jewish heritage, cultural interests, and chocolate, but Ursula's lover was not a comrade, and he showed no signs of converting.

Hamburger's politics were liberal and progressive, but he drew the line at communism. Their disputes followed a pattern.

"You question socialism in general and our beliefs in particular," she would remonstrate. "Your views on communism are determined by emotions and lack the slightest scientific foundation."

Rudi listed his objections to communism: "The exaggerations in the press, the primitive tone of some articles, the boring speeches filled with jargon, the arrogant dismissal of opposing views, the ham-fisted behaviour towards intellectuals, whom you isolate instead of winning over, insulting opponents instead of disarming them with logic and recruiting them."

Ursula dismissed this as a "typical petty bourgeois attitude." But privately "she knew that a kernel of truth lay in what he said." This made her even crosser.

The fight usually ended with Rudi cracking a joke.

"Let's not quarrel. A world revolution is no reason to shout at each other."

Rudi joined Red Aid, a workers' welfare organization linked to the communists. He read some Lenin and Engels, and declared himself a "sympathizer." But he flatly refused to join the KPD, or participate in Ursula's activism. Beneath his placid nature, Hamburger was remarkably stubborn, and no amount of cajoling could persuade him to join up. "There are things about the party that disturb me," he said. "Perhaps I'll get there slowly, if you give me time."

After one particularly vehement argument, Ursula wrote: "When Rudi questions the viability of socialism itself, I get upset and answer back. For him it's as if we are having a difference of opinion about a book or a work of art, while for me it's about the most vital problems, our whole attitude to life. At times like this he seems like a stranger to me." But Ursula was not about to give up. She copied out a list of communist quotations and presented them to Rudi, an unlikely sort of love token. "I believe that, if we stay together, it is only a matter of time until he joins the party," she told Jürgen. "But it could well take another two years."

In April 1927, Ursula quit Prager's and the hated Onion, and took a job as archives assistant at the Jewish-owned Ullstein publishers, one of Germany's largest newspaper and book publishers. One of her first acts on taking up the job was to write an article for *Die Rote Fahne* about inadequate working conditions in her new workplace. "One thousand two hundred free copies were distributed at the entrance here and made quite an impression." It certainly made an impression on the management.

After less than a year at Ullstein's, Ursula was fired. She was a troublemaker, and at a time of political upheaval and intensifying anti-Semitism the publishers wanted no trouble.

"You have to quit," Hermann Ullstein told her.

"Why?" asked Ursula, although she knew the answer.

"A democratic enterprise can offer no prospects to a communist."

With a patchy job record, little experience, and unemployment still rising, Ursula found she was unable to get another job. She refused to accept handouts from her parents. She wanted a challenge, somewhere unfamiliar, and some space to think and write. She needed an adventure, on a different stage. She chose America.

The great Lenin had written: "First we will take Eastern Europe, then the masses of Asia. We will encircle the last bastion of capitalism, the United States of America. We will not need to fight. It will fall as a ripe fruit into our hands." America was ready for revolution. Besides, Jürgen was still living there, and she wanted to see him. Her mind was made up: she would go to the United States and return when Rudi completed his architecture studies. Or possibly not. It was a quixotic decision and, for an unmarried woman of twenty-one who had never been abroad, a remarkably bold one. Ignoring her mother's entreaties and rejecting her father's offers of financial support, in September 1928 she boarded an ocean liner bound for Philadelphia. Rudi waved goodbye, wondering if he would ever see her again.

America on the eve of the Great Depression was a place of roaring vitality and grinding poverty, opportunity and decay, bright hope and impending economic calamity. Ursula was independent for the first time in her life. She found a job teaching German to the children of a Quaker family, and then as a maid at the Hotel Pennsylvania. Her English, already good, improved rapidly. After a month, she took the train to New York and headed to Manhattan's Lower East Side.

The Henry Street Settlement, founded by the progressive reformer and nurse Lillian Wald, provided medical care, education, and culture to the city's immigrant poor. Immigrants could stay there rent-free, in return for a few hours of social work every week. Wald was the animating spirit of the settlement, a campaigner for women's and minority rights, suffrage and racial integration, a feminist ahead of her time, and to the latest arrival at Henry Street Settlement a revelation and an inspiration. Ursula left her first and only meeting with Wald deeply impressed by the American woman's personality and philosophy: "The task of organizing human happiness needs the active cooperation of man and woman; it cannot be relegated to one half of the world," Wald declared. Ursula moved in and got a job at Prosnit Bookshop in upper Manhattan.

Ursula would stay in the United States for almost a year. The experience shaped her profoundly, beginning a love-hate relationship with the capitalist West that would endure for the rest of her life. The political and economic extremes of America at the end of the Roaring Twenties were comparable to those in Weimar Germany. New York had surpassed London as the most populous city on earth, with more than ten million inhabitants, and the city was exploding with energy, creativity, and wealth, an obsession with new technology, cars, telephones, radio, and jazz. Yet, beneath the glittering surface, disaster was brewing, as investors, large and small, poured money into an overheating stock market in the belief that the boom would never bust.

Unlike the Onion, Prosnit was happy to have a bookworm as an employee. Ursula already knew her Marxist-Leninist literature; she could quote chunks of it from memory, and rather too frequently did. Many of Prosnit's customers were American communists, and the shelves offered new left-wing horizons in the form of the proletarian literature movement: books written by working-class writers for a class-conscious readership. Ursula was swept up by the intellectual vigor of the American left. One new book in particular spoke directly to her heart. April 1929 saw the publication of *Daughter of Earth* by the radical American writer Agnes Smedley. Thinly disguised autobiography, the novel tells the story of Marie Rogers, a young woman from an impoverished background who struggles with relationships, and takes up the causes of international socialism and Indian independence. "I have no country," declares Smedley's protagonist. "My countrymen are the men and women who work against oppression. . . . I belong to those who die for other causes— exhausted by poverty, victims of wealth and power, fighters in a great cause." *Daughter of Earth* was an instant bestseller, and Smedley was hailed as "the mother of women's literary radicalism." For Ursula, the book was a call to arms: a woman fiercely defending the oppressed, demanding radical change, and prepared to die for a cause that sounded romantic, glamorous, and risky.

A few weeks after arriving in New York, Ursula joined the American Communist Party. That spring she attended a socialist holiday camp on the Hudson River, where she met Michael Gold, an acquaintance of her parents and at that time America's most famous radical voice. Gold was the pen name of Itzok Isaac Granich. The son of immigrant Romanian Jews brought up in poverty on the Lower East Side, he was a committed communist, founding editor of the Marxist journal *The New Masses,* and a ferocious polemicist. Gold liked to pick fights. When he described Ernest Hemingway as a "renegade," Hemingway sent back a curt reply: "Go tell Mike Gold, Ernest Hemingway says he should go fuck himself." Ursula declared Gold's novel *Jews without Money* "one of my favourite books."

Both entranced and repelled by New York, Ursula missed her home, her comrades, and her family. Above all, she missed Rudi.

In the autumn of 1929, Ursula sailed for Germany. A few weeks later, the American stock market crashed, hurling millions into poverty and ushering in the Great Depression.

It was only when she saw Rudi waiting at the dockside that Ursula realized how much she loved him. Her doubts about Rudi's politics had eased during her American sojourn. He would see the light eventually. Ursula Kuczynski and Rudolf Hamburger married in October, in a simple ceremony attended by family and close friends.

The newly married couple were happy, jobless, broke, and, in Ursula's case, extremely busy fomenting rebellion. As a point of principle they refused to accept money from their parents, and moved into a tiny, one-room apartment without heating and hot water. She whirled around Berlin, writing articles for *Die Rote Fahne,* staging agitprop theatrical productions, and arranging radical book exhibitions. The party leadership instructed her to set up a Marxist Workers' Lending Library, where members could borrow improving left-wing literature. With the help of Erich Henschke, an Orthodox Jew from Danzig working as a gravedigger, she wheeled a handcart around Berlin, collecting communist books from radical publishers and sympathetic comrades. When a newspaper published a photograph of Ursula with her book barrow, her parents were appalled. "I was allowed to pull the cart through town, I just wasn't allowed to be photographed doing it." Henschke was a communist bruiser, who would rather have been beating up brownshirts than collecting books he had no desire to read. Finally they amassed a stock of two thousand volumes and arranged them on makeshift shelving in a former pigeon cellar in the Jewish working-class district. Rudi painted a sign in large red letters: "Marxist Workers' Lending Library. Loans 10 Pfennigs per book." The first customer was an elderly factory worker: "Do you have something very straightforward about socialism for my wife, without foreign words in it?" Business was slow, not helped by the faint but persistent odor of pigeon droppings.

Ursula was manning a stall at Berlin's Revolutionary Book Fair when an elegant dark-skinned foreigner began browsing the titles. She recommended he read *Daughter of Earth*. A little mournfully, the man explained he had already read it, since Agnes Smedley was his estranged wife. Ursula was stunned: this was the Indian revolutionary Virendranath Chattopadhyaya.

Promoting Marxist literature was enjoyable and ideologically laudable, and wholly unprofitable. Rudi was now qualified, but frustrated at the paucity of architectural work. A friend of Ursula's employed him to decorate (entirely in red) the interior of the communist Red Bookshop near Görlitz railway station. He planned an extension to his father-in-law's library and worked on the designs for a new hotel. But as the worldwide Depression worsened, the commissions dried up.

Help came from far away. Helmuth Woidt, a childhood friend of Rudi's, was working in Shanghai as an employee of Siemens, the German manufacturer. Early in 1930, Woidt sent a telegram alerting Rudi to a job advertisement in the Shanghai newspaper: the British-run Shanghai Municipal Council was seeking an architect to build government buildings in the Chinese city. Rudi applied and received an immediate reply: if he paid for his own passage to China, the job was his. Woidt offered them free accommodation in the apartment at the top of his house in Shanghai.

Ursula was initially uncertain. Would she be deserting her comrades by leaving Germany again? Then again, the revolution was worldwide, and China sounded impossibly romantic. Ursula informed KPD headquarters she was going to Shanghai and intended to join the Chinese Communist Party, as she had previously joined the American party. "Communism is international, I can also work in China," she naïvely told the comrades.

Ursula had no notion of the political firestorm she was marching into. There was indeed a Chinese Communist Party in Shanghai, but it was outlawed, persecuted, and facing annihilation.

CHAPTER 2

WHORE OF
THE ORIENT

URSULA DEPARTED BERLIN FIRM IN THE CONVICTION
that the communist revolution in Germany was only a matter
of time, and a short time at that. She was sorry to be missing it. The
Nazi Party had been trounced in the presidential elections, and Hitler's fascist thugs already seemed a grotesque irrelevance, a nasty little historical anomaly. She could not have been more certain about
the shape of the future, or more wrong. Within three months the
Nazis would be the second-largest party in Germany, the rise of Hitler unstoppable, and the destruction of German communism under
way.

On a warm July evening in 1930, Ursula and Rudi boarded the
train for Moscow with one-way tickets. They had sufficient money
to get to Shanghai, but not enough to get back. Their worldly possessions consisted of two suitcases of clothes, some hard sausage,
bread, soup cubes, a small spirit stove, and a chessboard. In Moscow,
they boarded the Trans-Siberian Express and continued the slow
journey east. Ursula lay on her bunk and watched the vastness of
Russia slip past the window, an undulating ocean of birch forest
stretching to the horizon. The train made an unscheduled stop between stations and the passengers alighted, grateful to stretch their
limbs. "An accordion sounded and people began to dance. Soon
hands grasped ours and we danced too." In a meadow, somewhere in
Soviet Siberia, Ursula and Rudi whirled to the music of a Russian
accordion.

In Manchuria, they boarded the Chinese Eastern Railway to Changchun, and then switched to the Southern Manchuria line for the long train ride south to Dalian, where they boarded a steamer to complete the final, six-hundred-mile leg of the trip, across the Yellow Sea to Shanghai.

The first thing that struck Ursula was the smell, the pure, hot stink of poverty that wafted up from Shanghai harbor, a miasma of sweat, sewage, and garlic. She had witnessed plenty of human suffering during the economic crisis of the Weimar Republic, but nothing on this scale. "Encircling the ship in floating tubs were beggars, moaning cripples with stumps for arms and legs, children with festering wounds, some blind, some with hairless scab-encrusted heads." Straining, emaciated porters formed a "human conveyor belt" from ship to shore.

Waiting on the dockside was Helmuth Woidt, clad in a dazzling white drill suit and pith helmet, his wife, Marianne, alongside him clutching a huge bunch of flowers. A short rickshaw ride whisked them to a spacious villa on a tree-lined avenue in the French Concession, where most of Shanghai's business community chose to reside, far from the stench and hubbub of the port. A Chinese butler in white gloves poured chilled drinks. Bowing servants served trays of food. Their dusty suitcases were removed, and Ursula and Rudi found themselves wearing crisp kimonos and sipping cocktails on a wide verandah overlooking a neatly tended garden. In a matter of moments, she had moved from one world into another.

Shanghai in 1930 had a good claim to be the most socioeconomically divided city on earth, a place where the distance between rich and poor was not so much a gap as a yawning gulf. Part colony, part Chinese city, it was home to fifty thousand foreigners surrounded by almost three million Chinese, most living in abject squalor. The international community included British, Americans, French, Germans, Portuguese, Indians, White Russians, Japanese, and others, some of them penniless refugees, others new-minted plutocrats of staggering wealth. Political upheaval and famine in the Chinese interior combined with the impact of the Depression to force fresh waves of humanity into the city, desperate for work and food. Rickshaw pullers could be found hanging dead between the shafts, while shiny new American cars cruised the streets driven by uniformed chauffeurs. Shanghai was the largest city in China, the commercial center of East Asia. Businesses and banks competed to build ever larger buildings along the Bund, the stylish waterfront. But behind the flashy commercial district and the foreigners' enclaves lay another Shanghai, a place of sweatshops, textile mills, and tenements, rife with disease and despair, and pullulating with political resentment. Shanghai was home to China's only industrial proletariat and the birthplace of the Chinese Communist Party (CCP). America, as Ursula discovered, had not been ripe for revolution, but China was.

In the wake of the nineteenth-century Opium Wars, the Chinese empire had granted extraterritorial "concessions" along the Yangtze to foreign powers—British, French, and American—self-ruling districts with their own laws and administrations. Only seven of the city's twenty square miles were under direct Chinese rule. The largest enclave, the International Settlement, a merger of the British and American concessions, contained roughly half the city's population, and as additional foreign powers entered into treaties with China, their nationals joined in its administration. Germany had surrendered its extraterritorial rights after the First World War, rendering the fifteen hundred German residents of Shanghai subject to Chinese law. The International Settlement was governed by the Shanghai Municipal Council, a body elected by foreign residents but dominated by the British, who chaired every department except the municipal orchestra, which was run, naturally, by an Italian. Driving from one side of the city to the other required three different driving licenses. Three police forces—French, Chinese, and the British-run Shanghai Municipal Police—competed, overlapped, and struggled to contain a burgeoning crime wave.

The "Paris of the East," Shanghai was also the "Whore of the Orient," where fashionable boutiques rubbed shoulders with opium dens, cabarets, ancient temples, movie houses, and brothels. The Shanghai-born British author J. G. Ballard recalled a city where "anything was possible, and everything could be bought and sold." Simultaneously glamorous and seedy, shiny and grotty, Shanghai was home to a teeming international throng of beggars, millionaires, prostitutes, fortune-tellers, gamblers, journalists, gangsters, aristocrats, warlords, artists, pimps, bankers, smugglers, and spies.

The expatriate German community in Shanghai had its own church, school, hospital, and club, the Concordia, a hideous, turreted Bavarian-style *Schloss* on the Bund, complete with ballroom and bowling alley. Here the Germans of Shanghai gathered to play cards, drink, sing patriotic songs, gossip, wax nostalgic for the Fatherland, and complain about their Chinese servants. Presiding as a mini-potentate over this small corner of Germany was the consul general, Heinrich Freiherr Rüdt von Collenberg-Bödigheim, a veteran diplomat and enthusiastic Nazi who would end up as Hitler's ambassador to Mexico.

The Hamburgers' first evening in Shanghai was spent in the club. A slew of social invitations followed: tea with Constantin Robert Eginhard Maximilian von Ungern-Sternberg, a Baltic nobleman, descended from Genghis Khan, who had narrowly escaped the Bolshevik Revolution (his older brother, Roman, a ferocious White Russian warlord known as the "Mad Baron," had invaded Siberia before being captured and executed by a Red Army firing squad); dinner with Hans Stübel, a professor of ethnology and an expert in Chinese tattooing; a swimming pool party at the home of a businessman, Max Kattwinkel; cocktails with Karl Seebohm, representative of the chemicals firm I. G. Farben, who had a glass eye, a large private income, and three hundred gramophone records. A club stalwart was Johann Plaut, the most important, and most self-important, journalist in the German community.

Two exotic birds to be found fluttering around the Concordia were Rosie Goldschmidt and Bernardine Szold-Fritz. The daughter of a German Jewish banker, Goldschmidt had already gained some celebrity through her travel writing, and a great deal more on account of her vagina. Rosie had been married to Ernst Gräfenberg, a Berlin gynecologist who made his name studying the female orgasm: the "G-spot," the erogenous point in the vagina, was named after him. In spite of this discovery, Rosie divorced Gräfenberg after five years to marry the sixty-three-year-old Franz Ullstein (scion of the publishing house where Ursula had worked), a liaison considered so unacceptable by his family that they falsely accused her of being a French spy. Rosie would become a war correspondent for *Newsweek,* a successful novelist, and a countess through her marriage to a Hungarian aristocrat. Bernardine Szold-Fritz was Rosie's close friend and bitter social rival: part of the New York circle that included Dorothy Parker and F. Scott Fitzgerald, Bernardine was married (pro tem) to Chester Fritz, a wealthy American metals trader nicknamed "Mr. Silver." Bernardine threw parties of legendary excess, wearing enormous hooped earrings, a breastplate of Balinese silver, and a turban. "She spent her afternoons pacing her red and black painted apartment using a telephone with an absurdly long cord to arrange buffet suppers, teas, and meetings of her amateur dramatics company." She told absolutely no one that she was really from Peoria, Illinois.

Such socialites were class enemies, but Ursula was dazzled nonetheless, and fascinated. Their lives and interests could not have been further from her own, yet she made friends easily, studying each of these new people as another story, and writing pen-portraits in her letters and diaries. "We went to a very fine cocktail party given by Mrs. Chester Fritz: she has a fabulous apartment, turban-like hats, and earrings the size of tennis balls, noble curved eyebrows and so many friends who are artists and intellectuals." In another letter she wrote: "We went to the Ungern-Sternbergs for cocktails. Both are highly intelligent and super-sophisticates." Rosie and Bernardine took her shopping for clothes, and vied to dress their young protégée in the latest fashions.

But the glitter of expatriate life soon palled, and after just a few weeks in Shanghai's superficial social spin Ursula was ravenous for intellectual stimulation. In one letter she wrote: "The women are like little lapdogs. They have neither professions nor household duties, nor do they show any interest in scientific or cultural affairs. They don't even bother with their children. The men are a little better because at least they have a job, and do a little work." Tea with Bernardine Szold-Fritz and Rosie Gräfenberg became a chore: "It's always the same. First a bit of gossip over bridge and mah-jong, then yesterday's dog-racing or the latest film . . . the other day we played miniature golf, very popular in Shanghai." Most of her fellow Germans were uninterested in the China beyond their enclave and ferociously racist toward the Chinese. Ursula kept her political views securely hidden. In the Concordia and the Rotary Club, and around the Kattwinkels' swimming pool, Hitler was spoken of with admiration, the coming man.

As wife of the Municipal Council's new architect, Ursula was expected to play hostess to Rudi's British colleagues. The most important of these was Arthur Gimson, the commissioner of public works responsible for the settlement's roads, bridges, drainage, sewers, and new buildings. A pillar of the Engineering Society of China, a war veteran, and a spectacular bore, Gimson was the proud author of *Foundations of the Szechuan Road Bridge with Some Reference to the Bearing Value of Piles,* the definitive work on the subject. Ursula described him as "a crazy bachelor" who sent her bags of garden fertilizer as thank-you presents. Then there was Charles Henry Stableford, head of the planning department, who was building a new concrete abattoir, later described by *The Architectural Review* as "an Art Deco masterpiece and one of the earliest attempts at combining stunning animals with stunning architecture." Ursula could not get excited by the bearing values of piles or the merits of poured concrete in the butchery-building business. Hosting dinners for Rudi's British colleagues was like wading through social glue.

Bernardine, with her dreadful parties and ludicrous outfits, the stultifying Gimson and his compost, the complacent, racist bores at the club: these people did not drive Ursula to outright rebellion, but they helped.

While the expats danced and dallied, below the surface of Shanghai society a brutal, semisecret spy war was under way. For in addition to commerce, narcotics, and vice, the city was the espionage capital of the East. Foreigners needed no passport or visa; they came and went without residence permits and were often subject only to the laws of their own countries. Like criminals, spies slipped anonymously from one jurisdiction to another. They usually maintained contact with the outside world using shortwave radios, and so many were in operation that tracking down the illegal transmitters was all but impossible. Agents of China's Nationalist government spied on homegrown and foreign communists. The underground communists spied on the government and on one another. The Soviet Union deployed an army of secret agents and informers throughout the city. The British, with American help, spied on everyone, all the time.

The central espionage battle in Shanghai pitted the ruling Nationalists under Generalissimo Chiang Kai-shek against the Chinese communists, backed by the Soviet Union—combatants in a civil war that would continue, intermittently, for the next two decades. In 1923, Sun Yat-sen, founding father of the Chinese Republic and leader of the Nationalist Party, the Kuomintang (KMT), had forged an alliance with the Soviet Union. A team of Soviet officials, led by the Bolshevik revolutionary Mikhail Borodin, arrived in Canton to dispense advice, money, and military aid. But after four years the fragile pact between the KMT and the CCP fell apart and the forces of Chiang Kai-shek, Sun's successor, launched a merciless purge of communists. Borodin and his advisers were kicked out.

No one knows exactly how many perished in the "White Terror" unleashed by Chiang's forces and their gangster allies. The killers did not keep count, but an estimated three hundred thousand people were hunted down and murdered. The bloodletting was particularly horrendous in Shanghai. Otto Braun, a Soviet agent active in the city, wrote: "Chiang Kai-shek's henchmen, supported by the international police, were combing the textile factories by day and the Chinese quarter by night in search of communists. Those who were caught faced a horrible choice: become traitors or be killed. . . . This systematic extermination campaign forced the communists into deepest secrecy."

The Soviet Union saw China as the cradle for the next phase of world revolution, and to achieve that end Moscow now turned to espionage, on a grand scale, in support of the persecuted Chinese communists.

Soviet spies in Shanghai came in a bewildering array of guises, representing various branches of Soviet intelligence and government, sometimes collaborating but frequently overlapping and occasionally competing.

The Communist International, or Comintern, founded in 1919 to foster revolution worldwide under Moscow's guidance, was used as a front for espionage in China. Its Liaison Section, the OMS, collected and disseminated secret intelligence, smuggled weapons, transferred funds and instructions, and ran multiple underground communist networks. The Comintern had a "Far Eastern Bureau" with an annual budget of $55,000 in gold, Reichsmarks, yen, and Mexican dollars, to spend on fomenting communist revolution in China, Japan, the Philippines, and British Malaya.

Then there was Stalin's civilian intelligence service, the NKVD (forerunner of the KGB), which maintained its own network in Shanghai to collect political and economic secrets, assassinate Moscow's enemies, and prevent potential counterrevolution from taking root in China.

But the most important Soviet spy network in Shanghai was run by the military intelligence service, formally the "Fourth Department of the General Staff of the Workers' and Peasants' Red Army." (In 1942, Stalin changed its name to the Main Intelligence Directorate, Glavnoye Razvedyvatel'noye Upravleniye, or GRU, the name by which it is still known.) Highly disciplined, obsessively secretive, and entirely ruthless, the Fourth Department's role was to defend the Soviet Union and protect the revolution by gathering, buying, or stealing military secrets. Its Moscow headquarters was known, simply, as the "Center."

Since the Shanghai Massacre, these spies worked as undercover "illegals" rather than accredited diplomats, posing as journalists, businessmen, or teachers. Rivalry among the different Soviet spy organizations would eventually erupt in internecine carnage. But as far as the Chinese Nationalist government was concerned, the Russian spies were all the same: communist seditionists sent to stir up trouble who should be extirpated in the same way as native Chinese revolutionaries.

Ursula never doubted that the communists would eventually emerge victorious from the terrible secret war being fought in Shanghai. As an obedient Marxist, she saw history as preordained: the oppressed Chinese proletariat would inevitably rise up and, under communist leadership, overthrow the capitalist order, sweeping away the bourgeois classes and their imperialist backers. Even so, Chinese communism seemed alien and unfathomable. In Berlin, she had been part of a mighty movement; here she was a bystander to events she only dimly understood. "Apart from the heat, the tedium and my problems with adjusting to Shanghai 'society,' I was tormented by not making immediate contact with the Chinese people. I found the dirt, the poverty and the cruelty repugnant. I asked myself if I was only a communist in theory." Like many born to privilege, she wondered if she had the stomach for the grimy, morally contradictory, and frequently violent reality of revolution. Could one be a revolutionary and still enjoy good things, like new clothes? Ought she to wear only the hair shirt of communist orthodoxy? She discussed politics with no one except Rudi, who was working too hard at the Shanghai Municipal Council to pay much attention.

Homesick, she wandered around Jessfield Park, which reminded her of the Tiergarten in Berlin. As always when her spirits dipped, she preferred to be alone. The Shanghai summer was stifling. "The pavement began to melt again yesterday, so that it stuck to my shoes in long black strips, and the cars left deep ruts in the road." She lay limply on her bed in the Woidts' spacious top-floor apartment. Life as the wife of a colonial official, she reflected, was an exercise in sloth. "You can't do a thing, because it's all done by the boy, the cook and the coolie." Waiting for the next cocktail party, the next round of mini-golf, she became listless, too exhausted even to read. She put her lethargy down to the climate. "The heat saps all your energy . . . one perspires incredibly, not in drops but in rivulets." Finally she went to see a doctor, who told her she was five months pregnant.

Ursula and Rudi were overjoyed. But she was determined not to spend the next four months merely gestating and being pampered by servants. "I had to find an occupation."

Opportunity appeared in the tubby and bumptious shape of the journalist Plaut, Far East correspondent of the Wolff Telegraphic Bureau and boss of the Transocean Kuomin Telegraph Agency, a semiofficial Chinese news agency that pumped out pro-Nationalist propaganda. "Plaut is urgently looking for a clever secretary, so I went to his office and asked if I could help him a little, which he was very delighted with. Of course I said that I was expecting a child, he said I could come and go when I wanted."

Plaut put Ursula to work organizing his press cuttings. "I read everything and learnt a lot," she wrote. A Shanghai resident for two decades, Plaut was an authority on Chinese politics and frequently delivered long disquisitions on the subject, peppered with the names of important people he knew. "He often interrupts my work in order to tell me interesting things," wrote Ursula. "Plaut was full of his own self-importance but he really was one of the leading experts on Asia, and on China in particular."

One afternoon, midway through yet another interminable lecture, Plaut dropped a name that made Ursula sit up with a jolt: Agnes Smedley.

The American writer was in Shanghai, it seemed, working as a correspondent for the *Frankfurter Zeitung,* one of the biggest German newspapers. Ursula described the deep impression that Smedley's novel had made on her, telling Plaut she was "keen to make her acquaintance but felt inhibited about approaching someone so outstanding." With a flourish, Plaut picked up the telephone, dialed a number, and handed over the receiver. Agnes Smedley was on the line. The two women arranged to meet the next day in the café of the Cathay Hotel.

Smedley asked Ursula how she would recognize her.

"I'm twenty-three years old, one metre seventy tall, jet black hair and a big nose," said Ursula.

Agnes Smedley laughed, a big booming guffaw. "Well, I'm thirty-four years old, middling height, nondescript."

The newly built Cathay Hotel was a grand capitalist citadel and statement of Western commercial clout, eleven stories high, with a green pyramidal tower and Tudor paneling. A few months earlier, while staying at the hotel, Noël Coward had written the first draft of *Private Lives.* The most luxurious hotel east of Suez, the Cathay was an unlikely setting for a rendezvous between America's foremost radical woman writer and a young German communist, but the date was apt: November 13, the thirteenth anniversary of the Bolshevik Revolution. Both women carried bunches of red roses to mark the occasion: Ursula intended to arrange hers in the Woidts' sitting room as a discreet avowal of her sympathies; Smedley was planning to present her bouquet to the correspondent of TASS, the Soviet news agency, in a more overt commemoration of the anniversary. The floral coincidence was a good omen.

Smedley was far from nondescript (she had also misrepresented her age; she was thirty-eight). With her short-cropped hair and masculine clothing, she cut a distinctive figure, in deliberate contrast to the overdressed women expatriates. "Agnes looks like an intelligent, working-class woman," Ursula wrote in an excited letter to her parents. "Dressed simply, thinnish brown hair, very lively large grey-green eyes, face in no sense pretty, but well-formed. When she smoothes back her hair, you can see the enormous sweep of her brow."

Ursula had never met anyone like this before; but then, there was no one quite like Agnes Smedley.

The two women bonded over English tea served in bone china. Ursula's hopes and anxieties tumbled out in a chaotic rush. She spoke of her loneliness and boredom, the distressing scenes of poverty she witnessed daily, her alienation from the other Europeans. "I talked freely about my political views for the first time since arriving in Shanghai." She described her upbringing in Germany, her decision to join the party, and how much *Daughter of Earth* had meant to her. She spoke of Rudi: his kindness and calmness, but also his political apathy, his stolid rejection of communism. Smedley listened intently, smoking and nodding. When Ursula had finished, Agnes related the story of her own life, a tale even more extraordinary in reality than the fictional version published a year earlier.

Smedley was born in 1892 in a two-room cabin without electricity or running water, and then raised in a hardscrabble Colorado coal town. Her part-Cherokee father was a sometime cattle broker, cowboy, traveling herbalist, and coal teamster, an alcoholic drifter with "the soul and imagination of a vagabond"; her mother was an abused depressive; her aunt a part-time prostitute. As a child she witnessed the Colorado Labor Wars, bloody pitched battles between striking miners and the hired enforcers brought in by the coal companies. When her mother died at the age of forty, her father "fell to his knees and wept dramatically, then rifled her old tin trunk. With the forty dollars he found hidden between the quilt patches, he went to the saloon and got drunk with the boys." Her education was gleaned from whatever she could find to read, "from trashy romances to a ghastly book on law and one called *Behaviorist Psychology*," a sparse selection far removed from the great library available to the young Ursula. Agnes wrote poetry, told fortunes using apple seeds, and learned to ride, shoot, and throw the lasso. She adopted the Navajo name Ayahoo, and espoused a ferocious form of feminism. If anyone dared suggest "that a woman's intellect or capacity to build was inferior to that of a man . . . she jumped out of her seat like a wounded lioness and almost clawed him red in the face."

After stints as a laundry worker, teacher, and traveling saleswoman, Agnes drifted to California, where she mixed with left-wing bohemians. Her politics grew more radical. Smedley never espoused a coherent philosophy, for hers was the politics of anger, a scattergun rage against the capitalists, mine owners, imperialists, and colonizers who kept the poor, the nonwhite, and the working class enslaved. She had no time for political theory: "Who cares if I read all that trash? I know who the enemy is, and that's enough."

In California she encountered the circle of Indian nationalists demanding independence from imperial Britain, and embraced her first cause. With the First World War raging, she became deeply implicated in the so-called Hindu-German Conspiracy, Germany's secret campaign to undermine the British Empire by bankrolling and arming the Indian independence movement. In March 1918, she was arrested under the Espionage Act, imprisoned for two months, and finally released despite being, in the words of her biographer, "guilty as hell." She moved to Berlin, met, married, and then left the Indian communist revolutionary Virendranath Chattopadhyaya, known as Chatto, and continued to conspire with the Indian rebels. She witnessed the human degradation of Weimar with horror and declared the Soviet Union to be "the grandest, most inspiring place on earth."

Agnes was several times larger than life, but even her closest friends found her quite trying. As one remarked, she saw the world as "a harsh morality play in which 'good' was pitted against 'wicked,' " and seldom dismounted from "the glorious white charger of her imagination." She was in her teens when she had her first nervous breakdown. She suffered what she called "insane spells," and began a course of psychoanalysis with a German Jewish analyst named Elisabeth Naef, a former student of Sigmund Freud in Vienna. Dr. Naef persuaded Agnes to write down her experiences in fictional form. The result was *Daughter of Earth,* with its angry, ambitious heroine, socially alienated and yearning for self-expression. Critics sang the book's praise. Michael Gold, in *The New Masses,* described it as "bitterly, beautifully drawn from the fiber of life." By the time the plaudits began to land, Agnes was already in Shanghai. She arrived in the city in May 1929, ready to charge into battle on behalf of the oppressed Chinese masses.

Agnes Smedley was an extraordinary bundle of contradictions. She was bisexual, but believed homosexuality a curable perversion. She professed to disdain men and insisted women had been "enslaved by the institution of marriage." Yet she loved many men and married twice: she treated her first husband abominably, and was physically and emotionally abused by her second. She considered sex degrading, but was an enthusiastic advocate, and energetic exponent, of free love. "Out here I've had chances to sleep with all colours and shapes," she wrote to a friend, shortly before meeting Ursula. "One French gunrunner, short and round and bumpy; one fifty-year-old monarchist German who believes in the dominating role of the penis in influencing women; one high Chinese official whose actions I'm ashamed to describe, one round left-wing Kuomintang man who was soft and slobbery."

She was a communist who never joined the party; a violent revolutionary and romantic dreamer; a feminist in thrall to a succession of men; a woman who inspired intense loyalty, yet inflicted enormous damage on many of her friends; she supported communism without considering what communist rule involved in reality. She was passionate, prejudiced, charismatic, narcissistic, reckless, volatile, lovable, hypercritical, emotionally fragile, and uncompromising. "I may not be innocent, but I'm right," she declared.

Ursula was entranced. Agnes Smedley seemed to embody political passion and energy, the very antithesis of the smug complacency she found in the bourgeois boudoirs of Shanghai. "Your very existence is not worth anything at all if you live passively in the midst of injustice,"

Smedley insisted. Agnes was everything Ursula admired: feminist, anti-fascist, an enemy of imperialism and defender of the oppressed against the forces of capitalism, and a natural revolutionary.

She was also a spy.

In 1928, Agnes Smedley had met Jakob Mirov-Abramov, the press attaché at the Soviet embassy in Berlin, a Lithuanian Jew and a veteran Bolshevik. Nominally a diplomat, in reality he was European chief of the OMS, the intelligence-gathering arm of the Comintern. Mirov-Abramov (occasionally, and confusingly, Abramov-Mirov) was on the hunt for recruits to establish new espionage networks in the Far East, and this radical woman writer with a license to ask impertinent questions seemed ideally suited. Agnes needed little persuading that the logical next stage of her one-woman revolution was to become a spy: she got a job as Shanghai correspondent for the *Frankfurter Zeitung,* saddled up the white charger of her imagination, and galloped off to China.

By the time Agnes and Ursula met eighteen months later, Smedley was already an important cog in the machinery of Soviet espionage, supporting the Chinese communists in their desperate struggle to survive the White Terror, the Nationalist government's continuing campaign of political extermination: she recruited other writers and intellectuals sympathetic to the cause, used her home for covert meetings and mail drops, and passed secret information back and forth between the CCP and the Soviet Union. Her reports and instructions were sent by radio, or via the Soviet vessels sailing in and out of Shanghai. Back in Moscow, she enjoyed a "very high standing."

Smedley would end up working for both the Comintern and the Fourth Department, but she did not know, or much care, which branch of Soviet intelligence she was serving, so long as she was fighting for ordinary Chinese workers. "The revolutionary movement out here is not a romantic idea or theory," she wrote. "It is either rebel or die." Her newspaper reporting was often indistinguishable from pro-communist propaganda. Her mental health continued to deteriorate. "I have a duty heavier than personal things," she declared.

Smedley knew she was being watched by the British Secret Service (whom she referred to contemptuously as "George and Mary"), along with the Americans, French, and Chinese. She was on the Chinese government's blacklist of dangerous subversives, and expected to be shot in the back at any moment. Her letters were messianic in tone: "George and Mary etc. are again hot on the trail [but] were Jesus Christ living in China today, he would also be in the bad books of the British and other secret services."

Ursula was unaware of her new friend's covert activities. She did not know that Agnes's handbag contained a loaded pistol. She knew only that she had found a sister of the heart. From that moment, they were inseparable. "There was hardly a day when we did not telephone or see each other," wrote Ursula. "Agnes was alone; her whole life had been devoted to the revolutionary struggle. I was a communist but had grown up without material worries and was now looking forward to my first child. I lived a sheltered and painless life. I was also quite inexperienced."

Smedley revealed to Ursula a very different Shanghai. They ate in local restaurants with Agnes's Chinese friends, secret communists all. Agnes explained how she had helped to found the League of Left-Wing Writers, a group of Chinese thinkers set up at the instigation of the CCP to promote socialist realism—an astonishingly dangerous enterprise given the government crackdown. The league was banned almost as soon as it was founded, but it continued a precarious underground existence. Through Agnes, Ursula now found herself mixing with some of the leading lights of Chinese leftist literature: Lu Xun, the celebrated Chinese poet, the twenty-eight-year-old novelist Ding Ling, and her husband, the poet and playwright Hu Yepin. On Lu Xun's fiftieth birthday, a party for one hundred artists and intellectuals (representing "dangerous thought," as Agnes put it) was held at a Dutch restaurant. Ding Ling addressed the guests. Agnes guarded the door. Ursula returned home flushed with excitement from the adventure. She did not tell Rudi where she had been.

Agnes also introduced Ursula to Chen Hansheng, alias Geoffrey Chen, a diminutive, bespectacled social scientist who spoke perfect English, having attended Harvard and the University of Chicago before moving to Berlin (where he studied the writings of Robert

Kuczynski). Chen would become one of the most celebrated academics in China. He was also a dedicated secret communist, recruited by the Comintern in 1924. By 1930, Chen was teaching at Shanghai University and working part-time as Agnes's "secretary." He and his wife were linchpins of Smedley's burgeoning spy network. Chen was also, briefly, one of her lovers.

Ursula was flattered by Agnes's attention, dazzled by her personality, and intrigued by her radical Chinese friends. But she was also a little daunted. "During the early days of our friendship, which was so precious to me, I could not understand why a person of Agnes's stature should want to spend her time with me, or why I should have become her confidante."

Their relationship may have gone beyond friendship. Agnes's sexual appetites were undoubtedly broad enough to include a pregnant married woman fifteen years her junior, but there is no firm evidence that Ursula had lesbian leanings. They certainly shared a bed on numerous occasions. But, as Smedley's biographer observes, "at this time . . . there was no hard and fast line separating the different kinds of attachments that existed between women." It is entirely possible that their relationship was passionate, romantic, and all-consuming without ever becoming physical. "I was always at her disposal," wrote Ursula.

Whether or not there was a sexual element to their blossoming attachment, Smedley had another motive for cultivating this clever, impressionable young communist who told her she "yearned to live an active, useful existence." Immediately after their first meeting at the Cathay Hotel, Agnes sent a message to Moscow requesting permission to arrange the recruitment of young Mrs. Hamburger.

Three weeks later, Agnes told Ursula to expect a visit at home from someone she could "fully trust." At the appointed hour, the Woidts' butler announced that "Mr. Richard Johnson" had arrived, and ushered in a man of about thirty-five. Ursula was immediately struck by his extraordinary good looks: "A slender head, thick wavy hair, his face already deeply furrowed, his intense blue eyes framed by dark lashes, his mouth beautifully formed." The stranger had a pronounced limp and a strong German accent. Three fingers of his left hand were missing. He radiated charm, and danger.

His real name was Richard Sorge. He was Agnes Smedley's principal partner in espionage and her current lover, the most senior Soviet spy in Shanghai, an adept seducer and an officer of the Red Army intelligence service.

Sorge did not stay long. But, in that brief half hour, Ursula's life was changed irrevocably.

CHAPTER 3

AGENT RAMSAY

IAN FLEMING ONCE DESCRIBED RICHARD SORGE AS "THE most formidable spy in history." Despite being German and communist, and approaching middle age, in 1930 Sorge bore a distinct resemblance to the fictional James Bond, not least for his looks, appetite for alcohol, and prodigious, almost pathological, womanizing. Even Sorge's sworn enemies acknowledged his skill and courage. After China, Sorge would move on to Tokyo, where he spied, undetected, for nine years, penetrating the innermost secrets of the Japanese and German High Commands and alerting Moscow to the Nazi invasion of the Soviet Union in 1941. When he met Ursula, Sorge was just setting out on his espionage career in the Far East, a journey that would lead, eventually, to a place in the small pantheon of spies who have changed the course of history.

Born in Baku in 1895 to a German father and Russian mother, Sorge joined a student battalion in the kaiser's army at the outset of the First World War and passed directly, as he put it, "from the schoolhouse to the slaughter block." Most of his brigade was wiped out within days of arriving at the front. He was first wounded in 1915, then again a year later, and finally, almost fatally, in March 1916, when shrapnel tore into both legs and removed much of one hand. The young Sorge's wartime experience turned him into a die-hard communist, convinced that only worldwide revolution would "eliminate the causes, economic and political, of this war and any future ones." A strange mixture of bibliophile and brawler, pedantic scholar and hard-nosed functionary, he worked his way up through the Soviet secret world and finally into the ranks of the Fourth Department, the Red Army intelligence service, an organization described by its chief as a "puritan high priesthood, devout in its atheism . . . the avengers of all the ancient evils, the enforcers of new heaven, new earth."

Sorge was a dissolute warrior-priest: self-indulgent, belligerent, and unquestioning of the brutal regime he served, a born liar equipped with lethal charisma, boundless conceit, and almost unbelievable good luck. He possessed a "magical facility for putting people at their ease," and getting women into bed. He was rigorously disciplined in his espionage and exceptionally messy in his personal life. He was also snobbish, nit-picking, and frequently drunk, a loud and louche habitué of fast motorbikes and loose company.

In 1930, the Soviet exporters of communist revolution were looking east. To bolster the beleaguered CCP and spy on the Nationalist government, the Fourth Department envisaged a new network of illegals, spies operating under civilian cover. Agnes Smedley was one; Sorge, code-named "Ramsay," was another. On orders from the Center, he secured a job as China correspondent for the thrillingly titled *German Grain News* and proceeded to Shanghai. Five months before Ursula's arrival, Sorge set up home in the YMCA on Bubbling Well Road, bought himself a powerful motorbike, and paid a visit to Agnes Smedley, as instructed, to seek her help in "establishing an intelligence gathering group in Shanghai." Agnes happily agreed to work with Sorge and then, with equal alacrity and gusto, slept with him.

Posing as a news-hungry journalist, Sorge joined the Concordia and Rotary Clubs, and went drinking with the German military advisers to the KMT. The German community ("all fascists, very anti-Soviet," in Sorge's estimation) eagerly embraced this convivial newcomer, "a good bottle man," regarding him as one of their own. Agent Ramsay "gutted them like a fat Christmas goose," wrote another Soviet spy. Smedley placed at his disposal her expanding network of Chinese communist intellectuals, writers, soldiers, academics such as Chen Hansheng, and a young Japanese journalist, Hotsumi Ozaki, who would become one of Sorge's most valuable informants. Communism was on the run in the cities, but in the remote regions of the southeast it was gaining ground. In the mountains, the insurgents would soon establish the Jiangxi Soviet, a self-governing state within the state. The fifty thousand peasant soldiers led by Mao Zedong were as merciless as the Nationalist forces, hunting down and executing enemies of the revolution: missionaries, land-rich peasants, officials, and gentry. On her journalistic trips to the interior, Agnes reported on the bloody progress of China's Red Army and declared herself as "hard and ferocious as many Chinese, filled with hatred, ready to fight at a moment's notice, without patience of any kind for the comfortably situated in life, intolerant of every doubting person."

Aided by an expert radio technician sent from Moscow, Sorge began providing the Center with a steady stream of information on Nationalist troop movements, command structures, and weaponry.

While Sorge respected Agnes Smedley's "brilliant mind," he was less complimentary in other respects: "As a wife [by which he meant sexual partner] her value was nil. . . . In short, she was like a man." Agnes, however, had fallen in love with the dashing master spy she called "Sorgie" or "Valentino." She could often be seen on the back of his motorbike, tearing up the Nanking Road, an experience that left her feeling "grand and glorious." In breathless letters home, she extolled the virtues of this "rare, rare person."

"I'm married, child, so to speak," she wrote to her friend Margaret Sanger, the American birth control pioneer. "Just sort of married, you know; but it's a he-man also and it's 50-50 all along the line and he helping me and me him and we working together in every way. . . . I do not know how long it will last; that does not depend on us. I fear not long. But these days will be the best in my life. Never have I known such good days, never have I known such a healthy life, mentally, physically, psychically. I consider this completion, and when it is ended I'll be lonelier than all the love in the magazines could never make me." The incoherent letter is testament to the riot of Agnes's feelings. Each new agent she recruited was a service to the revolution, and a love gift for Sorgie. In November 1930, with Moscow's approval, she gave him Ursula, now six months pregnant.

Years later, Ursula recalled her initiation into Soviet espionage.

Having received Ursula's assurance that the house was empty save for the servants, Sorge carefully closed the door to the sitting room and sat beside her on the sofa.

"I have heard that you are ready to support the Chinese comrades in their work?"

Ursula nodded eagerly.

Sorge then launched into a short but impassioned description of the monumental difficulties facing the Chinese communists. "He spoke of the struggle against the country's reactionary government, of the responsibilities and dangers involved in even the smallest degree of help for our comrades."

Again, she nodded.

Then he paused, and looked into her eyes.

"I want you to reconsider. At this point, you can still refuse without anyone holding it against you."

Ursula was slightly affronted. She had already vouchsafed her commitment. And implicit in Sorge's question was a threat that if she opted to play her part now but attempted to back out in the future, it would be held against her in a way that might be very unpleasant indeed.

Her "somewhat curt" response was framed in communist cliché: regardless of the danger, she was "prepared to take part in this work of international solidarity."

Sorge smiled. Her contribution would be strictly logistical, he said. Her apartment in the Woidts' residence would be used as a safe house, where Sorge could conduct meetings with revolutionary comrades. Rudi never came home during the day. She would let the visitors in, provide refreshments, warn if anyone approached the house, and otherwise stay out of the way. "I was simply to let them have the room, but not to attend the discussions."

Before departing, Sorge remarked that in a few days' time workers and students would be staging a demonstration in downtown Shanghai. She might like to go and observe the protest.

Then Mr. Johnson was gone. Ursula still did not know his real name.

A few days later she was standing on Nanking Road, outside the Wing On department store, her arms filled with shopping bags. The shopping, she calculated, would make her presence there on the day of the demonstration appear coincidental; she had also found a rather beautiful silk skirt in Wing On that fitted her figure perfectly. Crowds of students and workers were filing down the street in silent protest, flanked and observed by long lines of expressionless police. The tension was palpable, the atmosphere reminiscent of the May Day demonstration in 1924 when she had been hit by a policeman's truncheon. In Shanghai, the mere act of marching was a provocative statement of rebellion. Suddenly the police surged forward, batons and fists flying. They dragged one man into the doorway of a shop and began systematically beating him. Dozens of protestors were herded into side streets, where they were kicked and punched onto waiting trucks. They offered no resistance, wearing the blank-eyed look of the condemned. "I looked into the faces of young revolutionaries, whose death sentence had been pronounced at that moment, and I knew—if only for their sake—that I would carry out any task asked of me." If they could face certain death with equanimity, then she would try to do the same.

As she hurried away from the violent scenes on Nanking Road clutching her parcels, Ursula did not spot the balding, bespectacled man standing on a corner, watching her closely.

Gerhart Eisler was a senior figure in the German communist hierarchy: he would eventually move to the United States, where he was rumored to be the covert leader of the American Communist Party. In 1929, after a stint in Moscow, he was acting as a liaison between the Comintern and the CCP, and "purging the party of spies and dissidents." He had earned himself the nickname "the Executioner." Eisler was checking up on Sorge's latest recruit, observing her reactions to the demonstration. In the world Ursula had now entered, snooping on friends was as important as spying on enemies. Eisler was satisfied with what he saw. His only reservation was that Mrs. Hamburger did not appear sufficiently bourgeois. She should "look more ladylike on such occasions," said the Comintern enforcer, because the more feminine she appeared, the less she would be an object of suspicion. Eisler had strong views on the sartorial aspect of spying: "She should at least wear a hat."

A pattern for clandestine meetings was swiftly established. Richard Sorge would arrange a time to come to the house when Rudi and the Woidts were out. He always arrived first, followed, at staggered intervals, by his "guests," usually Chinese, occasionally European, and never identified by name. After a few hours, they would leave again, at different times. Ursula asked no questions. She did not tell Agnes when a meeting was planned. If the servants or neighbors noticed that the same handsome gentleman paid frequent afternoon calls on the lady lodger in the upstairs apartment, they said nothing. This was 1930s Shanghai.

Ursula knew Richard Sorge was a Soviet spy, but not what sort, or the true nature of the regime they served. The cause of revolution and the military interests of the USSR were indistinguishable in her mind: whatever benefited Moscow also advanced the march of communism. "I knew that my activities served the comrades of the country in which I lived. If this practical solidarity was an initiative of the Soviet Union—so much the better."

Ursula trusted Sorge, yet she was reserved in his presence, and not just because she knew he was Agnes's lover. He lingered awkwardly for a few minutes after each meeting, clearly wanting to chat. Beneath the charm, she detected "a sadness within him." "There were days when—in contrast to his usual vitality, his humour and his irony—he was withdrawn and depressed." She tried to appear businesslike. "The desire not to appear inquisitive made me diffident in talking to Richard." Sorge was unsettled by Ursula's manner. On one occasion, as he loitered in the hall, hat in hand, she said: "It's time you left." He looked hurt. "So, I'm being thrown out?" Sorge was not used to women telling him to go away.

Happy, prosperous, and elated at the prospect of fatherhood, Rudi was wholly unaware that his wife was now part of a Soviet spy ring, and that their home was being used as an espionage rendezvous. He doted on his pregnant young wife ("Rudi calls me his lemon tree," she told her mother, "because I flower and fruit at the same time"). He was enjoying expatriate life, designing costumes for the annual festival at the German club and producing a play with the amateur dramatics society. The work at the Shanghai Municipal Council was plentiful and absorbing: he drew up plans for a nurses' home and then an incineration plant, followed by a girls' school and a prison. Agnes Smedley asked him to design the interior decoration of her new apartment on the Route de Grouchy in the French Concession. On the side, he set up a business, the Modern Home, building chic Art Deco furniture for the foreign residents of Shanghai.

Rudi was pleased to make the acquaintance of Ursula's new friends, Richard Johnson (as he knew him) and Agnes Smedley, though he sensed that their politics were well to the left of his. He still rejected communism. A cultured, left-leaning, upper-middle-class liberal, he was as determined in his moderation as she was fierce in her radicalism. "I realize how rotten and corrupt the capitalist system is," he told her.

> I am for freedom and the equality of all races. I am interested in and admire Russia, even if I reject some of the things that happen there. You know that communism is the right thing for you. With me it's different. Except for what I suffer as a Jew, I live in harmony with my environment. German humanism, bourgeois culture and art mean a lot to me. Even if I condemn much of capitalism, and see it falling apart, I am a pacifist. I hate destruction, I shy away from it. I love to preserve. I just can't accept a world view in its entirety, I have to think it through piece by piece, and retain the freedom to decide what aspects I can accept and which I reject.

During dinner one night Ursula remarked, with false nonchalance, that she would like to work for the Chinese communist underground. Rudi was aghast and uncharacteristically angry. "I am trying to establish myself in a new country," he snapped. "I am responsible for the child we are expecting. If it comes to it, you will not be able to bear the cruelty and brutality communists are subjected to. You don't seem to have any idea what the child you are carrying will really mean to you." They had been lovers for three years, husband and wife for one. Rudi found her vitality and certainty both attractive and profoundly alarming. His anger reflected a creeping awareness that something beyond his control was coming between them. Ursula resolved that she could not and would not reveal the truth about her covert activities to her husband, whose levelheaded caution had no place in her new world. Ursula was committed to communism, but also increasingly addicted to danger, the romance of risk, the addictive drug of secrecy. "I took part in the resistance struggle, yet my most intimate companion warned me against the idea and stood on the side-lines."

The deception inside their marriage had begun.

Ursula was living a double life: one with Rudi, as the wife of a colonial official, dull, dutiful, and comfortable; the other with Sorge, Smedley, and their communist collaborators, a thrilling existence of secret meetings, comradeship, and intellectual stimulation. She often visited the novelist Ding Ling, whose short story "Miss Sophia's Diary" had caused a sensation three years earlier with its radical depiction of a young Chinese girl who rejects the stifling conformity of her upbringing. Like Smedley's *Daughter of Earth,* the story was painfully autobiographical, written at a time when Ding Ling was "miserable, drinking heavily, dispirited by the national tragedy of political counter-revolution, and exhausted by her impoverished, often squalid life in boarding-house rooms." She was on the government blacklist of dangerous subversives, as was her shy and unworldly husband, the poet Hu Yepin.

Ursula was no longer lonely. She wrote to her family: "As for friends—quite apart, and above all the rest for me—there is Agnes." She helped Smedley translate her articles into German for the *Frankfurter Zeitung.* The two women watched Buster Keaton films together, and Agnes introduced her to the more exotic forms of Chinese food: squid, snail meat, shark fin. "It doesn't taste too bad," Ursula reported. "But you have to summon up your courage."

Friendship with Agnes Smedley was stimulating, but demanding. The older woman's mood swings were abrupt and violent. When drunk, Smedley tended to dance wildly, often in public places. Sometimes she lay in bed for days. "Agnes had outstanding qualities," Ursula later wrote. "At the same time she was emotionally unstable. While she was frequently full of fun, infecting everyone with her sense of humour, more often she was depressed and subject to a melancholia which affected her health. If she felt lonely, I went to see her. If she felt depressed, she would ring me at three in the morning and I would get up to be with her." Occasionally, they argued. Agnes was scathing about marriage, men, and motherhood. If Ursula challenged her, the older woman responded with rising fury, before storming out. "A few hours later she would telephone as though nothing had happened and I would be glad that we were friends again." When Agnes was depressed, Ursula moved in with her, leaving Rudi to fend for himself: "I have been sleeping at her flat," she wrote. "She feels better when someone is there at night."

For Ursula these were days of extraordinary excitement, eager anticipation as the birth drew near, and considerable peril. The KMT government intensified its communist eradication campaign, aided by Shanghai's criminal underworld. In a secret deal, the generalissimo appointed Du Yuesheng—"Big-Eared Du," boss of the Green Gang and controller of the city's opium trade—as "Chief Communist suppression agent for Shanghai." The Chinese Public Security Bureau (PSB) ruthlessly hunted down communists, foreign as well as Chinese, often with the help of the British and French authorities, eschewing due process in favor of torture, intimidation, and murder. One woman communist, a rare survivor, described what happened when she was detained at the PSB barracks at Longhua. First she was beaten, methodically and wordlessly, by two guards. Then they performed on her "the tiger's bench," a variety of torture in which the ligaments under the knee are pulled apart until the victim passes out. "This place is the high command for massacring people," she wrote. "They have the power to kill anyone they wish, so oftentimes we can hear the shooting as prisoners are executed not far away."

As an American, Agnes had some legal protection and could appeal to the U.S. consul for help if the Chinese arrested her. But, as German citizens, Ursula and Sorge enjoyed no extraterritorial legal rights. The fascist consul general, Heinrich von Collenberg-Bödigheim, would be the last person to come to the assistance of two communist spies. If they were caught, they'd be at the mercy of the Chinese secret police.

Inspector Patrick T. Givens, known as Tom, was the International Settlement's chief spycatcher, for the British administration also saw communism as a dangerous threat. A "charming Irishman from Tipperary," with a military moustache and a good line in dirty jokes, Givens had joined the Shanghai Municipal Police back in 1907, rising to become the chief of Special Branch, the police unit responsible for security and intelligence. Givens's job was to track down communists within his jurisdiction and turn them over to the Chinese. On his retirement in 1936, he would receive a medal of honor and a commendation from the Shanghai mayor noting that "in the course of his duties in securing evidence against communists, he frequently worked in close cooperation with the PSB." As one commentator noted, Givens was an executioner at one remove: "Hounding down communists and suspected 'reds' and bringing them to justice in the vast majority of cases has meant death."

Givens was caricatured as Shanghai's police chief "J. M. Dawson" in the Tintin comic book *The Blue Lotus,* where he is depicted by Hergé as a greedy and corrupt arms dealer. Dawson attempts to have Tintin beaten up by prison guards, pointing out that the boy reporter has no papers permitting him to be in the International Settlement. He then tries to kill Tintin by planting a bomb on his plane.

In fact, the jovial Inspector Givens was incorruptible and implacable. He knew there were communist subversives operating on his bailiwick, backed by foreign agitators and bankrolled by the Soviet Union, and he intended to root them out.

On January 17, 1931, Givens received a tip-off that thirty-six communists, including five young leaders of the League of Left-Wing Writers, were holding a meeting in the Eastern Hotel. Special Branch swooped in, arrested the lot, and handed them over to the PSB. Among those detained was Hu Yepin, the gentle poet married to Ding Ling. News of the arrests spread swiftly through the communist underground. Not until many years later did it emerge that Special Branch had probably been tipped off by Wang Ming, the new leader of the CCP, who regarded the league as a cover for "dissenting comrades" and wanted them liquidated. As so often in the history of communism, the bloodshed came not from external forces but through vicious infighting. Ding Ling was frantic, but powerless to lobby for her husband's release. On February 7, 1931, twenty-three of the arrested communists, including three women, were executed at PSB headquarters at Longhua. Hu Yepin was said to have been buried alive.

Ursula had little time to mourn, or worry whether Hu, under torture, had identified her or other members of the group. Five days after the executions, her water broke and she was rushed to the Paulun German Hospital in the International Settlement. She arrived groaning in pain, which prompted the midwife, "a Nazi type," to wag her finger and offer an anti-Semitic admonishment: "You should be strong, like a good German woman." On February 12, 1931, Ursula gave birth to a boy: he was named Michael, after Michael Gold, the American Marxist she had met in New York three years earlier.

"I am in heaven over this child and then again appalled by how I have succumbed to him," she wrote to Jürgen a few days after giving birth. "I think only of the child, and everything else only in relation to the child." When Misha, as she called him, was eleven days old, she wrote home again, and this time only half the letter concerned baby matters, while the rest was about the new Soviet five-year plan and the writings of the communist leader Karl Radek. At night she read *Infant Feeding and Care* but also, "for balance," Boris Pilnyak's novel *The Volga Flows into the Caspian Sea,* a paean of praise to forced industrialization in Soviet Russia. The tension between the twin demands of politics and parenthood began the day Ursula became a mother, and continued for the rest of her life.

Rudi was instantly besotted with his son. The new parents proudly presented Michael to their friends. Agnes was supportive, but Ursula noticed the "sadness" in her childless friend. "I sacrificed my children for the struggle," Agnes remarked pointedly. Arthur Gimson, the commissioner of public works, sent over some congratulatory compost. Chen Hansheng brought traditional Chinese birth gifts and "took a great interest" in the baby.

One of the first visitors was Richard Sorge. Again, Ursula felt the conflicting pull of clandestine work and her maternal instincts, "partly embarrassed to be involved in such private matters as having babies, and partly proud of my little son." Sorge brought flowers. "I led him to the baby's crib," Ursula wrote. "He bent over and gently pulled back the quilt with his hand. For a long time he looked at the infant in silence." From Sorge's ruthlessly pragmatic perspective, little Misha was a complication, but potentially an asset. He was ideal cover. Who could possibly suspect that a first-time mother with a newborn baby might also be a spy?

CHAPTER 4

WHEN SONYA IS DANCING

O N APRIL 1, 1931, RUDI AND URSULA HAMBURGER MOVED into their own home on a boulevard lined with plane trees running through the heart of the French Concession. Number 1464 Avenue Joffre was a detached two-story villa, rented from a British company and set back from the road behind a wide garden.

After nine months in Shanghai they were keen to put down roots. The Woidts' apartment was too small for a growing family. "In the hot season, with small rooms directly below the roof, it's not the right place for a child," she told her mother. But Ursula had another reason for moving house. With two or three secret meetings taking place every week, Sorge needed a more secure venue. Marianne Woidt sometimes returned home unexpectedly, and had once bumped into him on the doorstep. The comings and goings might already have attracted attention.

As a secret rendezvous, the new house on Avenue Joffre was ideal. The servants (cook, houseboy, and nanny, or amah) were housed in separate quarters across a small courtyard. "We have an open view, with no other buildings to block it," Ursula wrote. Anyone coming up the front path would be spotted long before they reached the front door. "Our new home is completely wonderful. Rudi has done a great job with the interior design, and everything is very tasteful. The gardens have beautiful lawns, flowers and a few tall, old trees. It is the first time we have ever lived on our own, and we enjoy it immensely." Rudi knew nothing of the real criteria on which his new home had been selected.

The meetings started up again immediately, following the same deliberately unpredictable pattern. Ursula would inconspicuously stand guard in the main room or, if the weather was warm, in the garden, nursing her baby and keeping a watchful eye on the front gate, while upstairs Sorge gathered in earnest conclave with men (and very occasionally women) whose names she never knew.

Ursula's letters home gave no hint of her clandestine life. Instead, she vividly described her daily existence, the sights and sounds of Shanghai, and her adored baby. "Michael's hair is still red, his mouth is similar to that of his grandfather, his eyes grow brighter every day, but his nose is still very Christian for the time being. He often greets us with his fist raised as if he is already a Red Front Fighter. But don't worry, since he cannot yet speak he has not yet expressed his political beliefs." Occasionally she described the murderous anti-communist violence sweeping China. In some areas entire families were wiped out. Ursula was fully aware that she could become the next victim. With a baby to care for, the stakes seemed, suddenly, immeasurably higher. She later wrote: "I had to be constantly on the lookout in case anybody was watching the house or, for that matter, me. Before and after meetings with the comrades, I kept a discreet watch on the streets."

"The White Terror is ghastly out here," Agnes Smedley wrote to the American writer Upton Sinclair. In the four years of bloodletting that followed the initial Shanghai Massacre, at least three hundred thousand people perished. Suspected communists were rounded up by the hundreds, or simply abducted and murdered by Du's gangsters. "Only a few returned from the prisons," wrote Ursula. "Most never even reached that far: they were shot, beaten to death, buried alive or beheaded. In provincial cities their heads were impaled on posts near the city gates to intimidate the people . . . the foreign powers, of course, strongly support Chiang Kai-shek in his large-scale Red suppression campaign. I've seen photographs, which are horrific, and genuine." But the communists themselves were also capable of astonishing brutality, particularly toward any of their own suspected of treachery.

Gu Shunzhang was a former professional magician, an experienced assassin, and head of the Communist Red Brigade, the so-called Dog Killer Squad, responsible for hunting down party traitors and murdering KMT secret policemen. In April 1931, the PSB arrested Gu, who agreed to cooperate in exchange for his life. "A living dictionary" of party membership, he revealed the identities of countless communists, most of whom were rounded up and executed. Surviving party leaders went into hiding in the various Shanghai safe houses. But not before they had exacted vengeance. On the orders of Zhou Enlai, the most senior communist left in Shanghai, who would go on to become the first premier of the People's Republic of China, thirty members of Gu's family were kidnapped, murdered, and then buried in a garden in the French Concession, not far from Ursula's new home. Only his twelve-year-old son was spared.

On a beautiful summer morning, when Michael was almost six months old, Ursula received a telephone call from Richard Sorge, not to arrange another meeting, but with an altogether different proposition.

"Would you like to go for a ride on my motorbike?"

Sorge was waiting for Ursula on the city outskirts, astride an enormous black Zündapp flat-twin K500 motorcycle. He showed her how to put her feet onto the footrests and told her to hold on. Then they roared off, at breathtaking speed. Sorge was a fantastically reckless driver. Soon they were beyond the city limits and flying through the Chinese countryside, past paddy fields and villages, Ursula's arms tightly wrapped around Sorge. "Thrilled by his breakneck driving, I urged him to go faster and faster." Sorge accelerated, and the motorbike seemed to take off. Ursula was in a state of petrified ecstasy.

"When we stopped," she later wrote, "I was a changed person. I laughed and romped about and talked non-stop." Her anxieties seemed to evaporate. "Shanghai's detested social life was forgotten, as were the constant pressures to conform to etiquette, the responsibilities of clandestine activities, and the unnecessary worries about my son. . . . I was no longer afraid." Many years later, she reflected: "Perhaps he had only arranged this ride to test my physical courage. If, however, he had been seeking a way to establish better contact between us, he had gone about it the right way. After this ride, I no longer felt inhibited."

Sorge understood the seductive power of a fast motorbike. Ursula shared his love of risk. He was undoubtedly testing her, though in a way that was more emotional than physical. Exactly when Ursula Hamburger and Richard Sorge became lovers is still a matter of debate. Years later, when quizzed about her relationship with Sorge, Ursula replied obliquely: "I was not a nun." Most sources suggest that their relationship ceased to be platonic soon after this exhilarating motorbike ride, and quite possibly somewhere in the Chinese countryside outside Shanghai that very afternoon.

A housewife-spy, Ursula had hitherto stood on the periphery of Sorge's network, keeper of a safe house, a discreet enabler who asked no questions. "I hardly knew what was going on in my own home." With their newfound intimacy she joined Sorge's inner circle, a trusted lieutenant in the conspiracy, a partner and confidante. "Our conversations were more meaningful," she wrote. Sorge described his childhood in Baku, his horrific wartime experiences, and his conviction that only communism could defeat the scourge of fascism. He told her of a daughter in Russia he had never seen, by a wife he had never mentioned before. There was no "sensational moment" when Sorge revealed who he was working for, but over the coming months it became clear to Ursula that her lover was the mastermind of an extensive intelligence operation coordinated and financed by the Soviet Red Army, of which she was now an integral part. Now, when the meetings in Avenue Joffre ended, she did not send Sorge away.

Sorge introduced her to the other members of his network. His chief shortwave radio operator, Max Clausen, was a former seaman in the German navy who had built a tiny 7.5-watt transmitter, small enough to be hidden in a cupboard but sufficiently powerful to reach the Soviet receiving station in Vladivostok. Clausen's deputy was Josef "Sepp" Weingarten, nicknamed "Sober," because he was usually drunk. "Flaxen-haired, rosy-cheeked, good natured" and remarkably incompetent, Weingarten had married a White Russian exile, but had not got around to telling her he was a communist spy, and lived in terror that she might find out. The group's photographer, responsible for copying documents onto miniature film, was a twenty-five-year-old Pole from Łódź named Hirsch Herzberg who went by the alias "Grigor Stronsky," or Grisha. Ursula was struck by his distinctive appearance and grave manner: "He had dark, wavy hair with a side parting, his forehead shone as if it were polished, his eyes were dark above his bold cheekbones." As cover, Herzberg ran a camera shop, for which Rudi did the interior design, unaware of its ulterior purpose. Grisha Herzberg became a regular visitor to Avenue Joffre, as Ursula's social and secret lives entwined. Ursula plunged into another chapter of the story, making little notes on this fresh cast of characters. That spring Herzberg took a photograph of her, drinking coffee from a bowl, peering over the rim. Handing her the developed print, the Polish photographer remarked: "Very well caught—just like you. Could be called 'Portrait of a Pirate.'" Ursula's expression, at once mischievous and debonair, is the look of a communist corsair.

Then there was Isa. Ursula was instantly drawn to Irene Wiedemeyer (sometimes Weitemeyer), a German Jew from Berlin with "freckles on her very fair skin, hazy blue eyes and unruly red hair" who ran the Zeitgeist bookshop near Soochow Creek. "There is a friend I must tell you about," Ursula wrote home. "A young girl arrived here one day, without kith or kin but with boxes full of books. . . . She is 23 years old. Plucky don't you think?"

The Zeitgeist was not just a bookshop, and "Isa" Wiedemeyer was more than just a gutsy bookseller. A German Communist Party member from her teenage years, Wiedemeyer had married a Chinese communist, studied at the Sun Yat-sen University in Moscow in 1926, left her husband when he became a Trotskyite, lost her baby daughter to meningitis, and wound up in Shanghai. Her bookshop was a branch of the Zeitgeist Buchhandlung group of Berlin, a chain of shops funded by the Comintern. The store was used as a dead-drop site and rendezvous point by the Comintern, Sorge's Fourth Department group, the NKVD, and all the other branches of Soviet intelligence operating in Shanghai. "Messages and information were conveyed to agents there on sheets of paper slipped between the pages of designated books." General Charles Willoughby, the American military intelligence chief, later described the Zeitgeist bookshop as "a recruiting station for the 4th Bureau of the Red Army." Soviet and other foreign communists literally tripped over one another in Frau Wiedemeyer's shop, which measured just eighteen feet by twelve.

The two women became instant soulmates and co-conspirators. "She was like a sister to me," wrote Ursula.

Ursula had found a new, secret family. "The comrades became my dearest friends," she later wrote. "I felt the same protectiveness towards them as I felt towards my little son . . . just as my child's smallest sounds would wake me in the middle of the night, so I was on my guard for the slightest incident or irregularity in the vicinity of my comrades." Sorge began to use her to pass messages between members of his group, a "cutout" in spy jargon, often via the bookshop. He handed over handwritten notes of information he had secretly gathered on military or economic topics, and she typed them up. Too long to be sent by wireless, these documents, sometimes hundreds of pages long, were sent to Moscow on Soviet ships.

As doorkeeper for Sorge's meetings, she developed a nodding acquaintance with some of his agents, including "a frail young Chinese girl with short hair, a pale complexion and slightly protruding teeth," the daughter of a KMT general with access to useful military information. Two of the callers at Avenue Joffre were government officials, polite young men working for the Institute of Social Sciences. She knew them only as Chen and Wang. They offered to teach her Mandarin. Sorge agreed that language lessons would be good cover for Chen and Wang's frequent visits to the house. A natural linguist, Ursula took delight in deconstructing the complex language. Even the name "Hamburger," she told her mother, could be broken down into its constituent parts: "Han-bu-ga: Han = a famous Chinese surname; Bu = fine artist; Ga = good character. Therefore: 'a first-class artist with good character from the family Han.' Doesn't that fit Rudi? And then Ursula: Ussu la = 'pure as an orchid,' which doesn't fit me at all."

One day Sorge lugged a suitcase filled with documents into the house and asked Ursula to keep it somewhere safe. She hid it in the built-in cupboard behind a heavy mothproof chest containing winter clothes. Ursula was now the keeper of records for the Sorge network, as well as printed communist propaganda and other incriminating material. A few weeks later, Sorge returned with a heavy locked trunk and two Chinese porters to carry it upstairs. She stashed it alongside the suitcase.

The expatriates whose company Ursula had once found so tiresome were now valuable sources of information. At Sorge's instigation she began to pay more attention to the gossip at the Concordia, around the Kattwinkels' swimming pool, and at Bernardine Szold-Fritz's tea parties. Constantin von Ungern-Sternberg and Karl Seebohm could be surprisingly indiscreet when discussing the business affairs of their employers, Siemens and I. G. Farben, German companies supplying military technology to the Chinese government. She listened closely to the long political lectures delivered by the journalist Plaut, who never suspected she was "ruthlessly squeezing everything out of him." Even the consul general, Heinrich von Collenberg-Bödigheim, enjoyed chatting with the attractive young wife of the municipal architect. "I did not have to torment myself by adopting the guise of a Nazi," she wrote. Instead she played the part of a curious, innocuous, and rather bored young housewife who liked to shop, without a political thought in her pretty head. Sorge encouraged her to make her own assessments of the information she gathered. "Facts were not enough for Richard. If I was too brief, he would say 'and what do you think of that?'" When she came back with a fuller report, he would congratulate her: "Good, a proper analysis." Almost unaware she was being trained, the tradecraft was seeping into her: the outward appearance and the hidden inner life, filtering out extraneous material, constant vigilance, and habits of deception. "Clandestine conduct became second nature," she wrote.

On any given evening, gathered around the Hamburgers' dinner table might be Gimson from the Municipal Council, Plaut of the Transocean Kuomin Telegraph Agency, Rosie Gräfenberg, owner of the first G-spot, journalists, military officers and businesspeople from the club, Agnes Smedley, and Professor Chen Hansheng from the university. Lubricated by Rudi's wine, the guests chatted freely, most of them unaware that some of the company were spies, notably the hostess. Richard Sorge was a frequent dinner guest. Rudi liked the hard-living German journalist with the fund of risqué anecdotes and the big motorbike. As she entertained her dinner party guests, Ursula could feel Sorge's eyes on her across the table, an erotic complicity running invisibly between them. "I liked watching Richard listen to me, and I could tell by his expression whether something was important to him or not." According to Sorge's biographer, "the table talk reported by Ursula began appearing regularly in his cables to the Centre."

In his messages to Moscow, Sorge allocated Ursula a code name: "Sonya."

Sonya is a Russian name, of course, but it also means "dormouse," an affectionate term for a sleepy person. Sorge was offering a sly compliment to Ursula's ability to hide in plain sight: a "sleeper" in intelligence jargon is a long-term, deep-cover agent. But in 1930s Shanghai the "Sonyas" were also the Russian hookers who lined the North Sichuan Road, and "whose stock phrase was 'my Prince, ples, you buy little Sonya small bottle vine?'" There was a song, popular in Shanghai's nightclubs: "When Sonya is dancing to a Russian song, you can't help falling in love with her. There is no more beautiful woman than she. In her blood runs the Volga, vodka and the Caucasus. Even Vladimir is crazy about her, sets aside a glass of vodka, just to see Sonya."

The code name carried a significance only Sorge and Ursula understood.

Like many spies, Ursula was becoming intoxicated by the thrill of her own duality, the entwining of danger and domesticity, living one life in public and another in deepest secrecy. "None of our acquaintances would in their wildest dreams have imagined that I, as the mother of a small child, would jeopardize my family and everything we had created for ourselves in China by contact with communists." Yet the thought of what might happen was invading her own dreams. In one of her nightmares, the police broke down the door, found incriminating evidence, and seized her child. Ursula would wake shaking, bathed in sweat. She knew she was putting her family into ever deeper jeopardy. That knowledge was not enough to stop her.

Spying is highly stressful. So are bringing up a child, running a household in a foreign country, and concealing an extramarital affair. The demands on Ursula required both a genius for compartmentalizing the different areas of her life and an intense psychological stamina, as she juggled her rival commitments to husband and lover, bourgeois social engagements and communist subversion, her baby and her ideology. "Underground work cut deeply into my personal life," she wrote. "Rudi was as good and considerate as ever, but I could not talk to him about the people who were closest to me or the work on which my life centred." Under the twin pressures of espionage and infidelity, her marriage was falling apart.

Rudolf Hamburger was gentle and trusting, but he was not a fool. He must have noticed that his wife was spending more and more time with her left-wing friends, the red-haired Isa, the somber Grisha. She urged him to invite officials to dinner. Did Ursula's sudden enthusiasm for socializing with people she had previously detested strike him as odd? Did he wonder why Johnson, the good-looking German journalist with the English name, was a fixture at almost every dinner party they hosted? Did he suspect that his wife might be otherwise engaged on her afternoons, while he worked at the office in downtown Shanghai? Most cuckolds are, often unknowingly, complicit. Did he refuse to see what he did not want to see?

Agnes Smedley certainly did know what was going on between Ursula and Sorge, and she was not happy. Agnes was an advocate of free love, so long as the freedom was hers. The romantic aspect of her relationship with "Sorgie" had already ended—as she had predicted it would—but the discovery that her young protégée was now her ex-lover's lover did not fit in with her plans. "When word of the affair reached Agnes, she took it badly." In private she was still affectionate toward Ursula, but when others were present, Sorge in particular, she made snide remarks and took every opportunity to put her down. She mocked Ursula's interest in clothes, cookery, and entertaining. Clausen, the radio operator, decided Agnes was a "hysterical, conceited woman." Sorge's switch of partners added a new and unpredictable element to an already combustible sexual and political mix.

One afternoon, Sorge arrived at the house accompanied by a large man with "a round, almost bald head, small eyes and a sudden, friendly smile." They were joined by two Chinese men Ursula had never seen before. Half an hour later, she entered the upstairs room with a tea tray and found the four men holding revolvers. "There were also weapons lying in the open trunk and spread out on the carpet": rifles, handguns, machine guns, and ammunition. "The two Chinese comrades were learning how to take the weapons apart and reassemble them." Sorge ushered her out of the room, but he had doubtless intended her to see the cache of weaponry. Here was further proof of her importance. There was enough evidence in her bedroom cupboard to get them all killed. She was now not only Sorge's lover, confidante, courier, secretary, secret agent, and archivist, but also custodian of the group's arsenal. "I was of greater use than I had realized," she wrote. And in even greater danger.

Toward the end of June, Sorge appeared at the house without warning, sweaty and anxious; two porters were waiting at the gate. "You need to pack a suitcase for you and Michael," he told her. "You may have to leave Shanghai suddenly and go into hiding with comrades in the interior." Sorge gave her the address of a safe house where she and the baby could hide and await exfiltration to the Jiangxi Soviet. There was no suggestion that Rudi would be going too. Sorge promised to telephone, with a prearranged signal, if the moment came to flee. The porters hauled the trunk and suitcase containing weapons and documents downstairs, and Sorge hurried away. With trembling hands, Ursula immediately packed a small case with diapers, baby clothes, sterilized water, powdered milk, and a change of clothing. Waiting for the telephone to ring, she tried to reassure herself that since "Richard knew of a specific danger and an opportunity to escape had been provided, the situation was no more precarious than before." At night she lay awake alongside Rudi, rigid with tension and awash with adrenaline, waiting for the signal to bolt. While the nurse played with Michael in the garden, she stayed in the house, never more than a few feet from the telephone. Soldiers often describe experiencing a jolt of pure excitement when they come under fire. Ursula was very frightened. She was also elated. Facing death, she had never felt more intensely alive.

Ursula knew the cause of the crisis without having to ask: the network had been compromised.

A few days earlier, on June 15, 1931, the Shanghai Municipal Police had arrested Professor Hilaire Noulens and his wife, Gertrude, at their home on Sichuan Road.

Noulens went by a baffling array of names, nationalities, and occupations, all of them false. He variously identified himself as Paul Christian, Xavier Alois Beuret, Paul Ruegg, Donat Boulanger, Charles Alison, Philippe Louis de Backer, Samuel Herssens, Ferdinand Vandercruyssen, Richard Robinson-Rubens, and Dr. W. O'Neil. He claimed, at different times, to be Belgian, Swiss, and Canadian, a professor of French and German, a wallpaperer, a laborer, a mechanic, and a pacifist trades union organizer. Not to be outdone, Madame Noulens sometimes used the names Sophie Louise Herbert (née Lorent) or Marie Motte. Noulens was a small, sharp-eyed, and "extremely nervous" man in his late thirties, "forever moving about and switching from one to another of his three languages apparently without noticing."

While Inspector Tom Givens might be unsure exactly *who* this twitchy little man was, he quickly established *what* he was: an important Soviet spy. The trail had started with the arrest in Singapore of a "suspicious Frenchman," Joseph Ducroux, a known Comintern courier traveling under the alias Serge LeFranc. On a scrap of paper, Ducroux had scribbled a telegraphic address—"Hilonoul Shanghai"—belonging to the mysterious Noulens. Givens kept the couple under surveillance for a week and then launched a "lightning raid" in the middle of the night. A key in Noulens's jacket pocket opened an apartment on Nanking Road, where police found three steel boxes containing hundreds of documents, many in double-encrypted code. A copy of *The Three Principles* by Sun Yat-sen on the bookshelf was found to contain the key to the code. When decrypted, the cache turned out to be an encyclopedia of Soviet espionage in Shanghai, including contacts with the CCP. Payroll records revealed "the names of couriers and agents throughout the region" and communist spies in every corner of the city, including, to Givens's astonishment, inside the police force itself.

The man Givens had arrested was clearly "the main fulcrum for subversive communist plotting," with six passports "stolen, 'borrowed,' or expertly forged," a staff of nine people, no fewer than fifteen safe houses around the Far East, ten bankbooks, eight post office boxes, four telegraphic addresses, two offices, one shop, and an enormous budget for subversion: in the preceding ten months he had dispensed a staggering £82,200 to communists in China, the Malay states, Japan, Burma, Indochina, Formosa, and the Philippines. Soviet cash was also funding Mao's Red Army in its war with the Nationalist government. The Noulenses, it seemed, were involved in "every phase of communist activity" in the Far East, with "Moscow as the controlling centre."

Noulens was really Yakov Matveyevich Rudnik, a Ukrainian Jew with an impeccable revolutionary pedigree who had taken part in the storming of the Winter Palace in 1917, before going on to work as a Comintern agent in the Crimea, Austria, France, and finally China. His wife, Nikolaevna Moiseenko-Velikaya, was the daughter of an aristocrat and a gifted mathematician who left her post in the economics faculty of the University of Petrograd to become a spy. They had arrived in Shanghai in March 1930.

Givens never discovered the real identity of the man in his custody, but he was triumphant: "These archives offered a unique opportunity of seeing from the inside and on unimpeachable documentary evidence the workings of a highly developed communist organization of the 'illegal' order."

Rudnik's arrest was a hammer blow to Soviet espionage in the Far East. Stalin himself immediately gave orders to the Comintern to "close all its extensive Shanghai operations and evacuate its staff immediately." Soviet spies began fleeing in anticipation of mass arrests. Agnes Smedley headed to Hong Kong, "leaving in such haste that she carried no luggage." Gerhart Eisler, the German enforcer who had insisted Ursula wear a hat, made for Berlin. Some did not escape fast enough, or had nowhere to go, and dozens of communists were arrested. The party organization in Shanghai, already fragile, was left in tatters. In Hong Kong, the British police picked up a young Indochinese cook named Nguyễn Ai Quốc, the son of a Confucian scholar whose embrace of communism had taken him to France, America, China, and Britain (where he worked as a pastry chef on the Newhaven–Dieppe ferry). As head of the Indochinese Communist Party, he had been in regular communication with Noulens and was sentenced to two years in prison by the Hong Kong Military Tribunal. After his release in 1933, Quốc went on to become the architect of Vietnam's independence movement, prime minister, and leader of the Vietcong during the Vietnam War. He is better known as Ho Chi Minh.

Armed with the Noulens documents, the Chinese authorities tracked down hundreds more communists in what was chillingly described by the British as the "resolute, timely and decisive application of repressive measures." The urban communist movement in China was shattered, its leadership dispersed, the survivors living in fear. The secret police combed the city, raiding one safe house after another. Zhou Enlai fled to the mountains of Jiangxi disguised as a priest. By the beginning of 1932, there were just two CCP Central Committee members left in Shanghai. A foreign journalist (writing before the Holocaust) described the White Terror as "having no parallel in history except perhaps the invasions and slaughters staged by the Huns in the fourth and fifth centuries."

Sorge remained undiscovered. None of his agents were on the Noulens payroll, and as yet the police had not made the connection. Sorge was now "the sole senior Soviet intelligence officer in the city," with the unenviable task of sorting out the mess and doing "everything possible to free the Rudniks." Ursula, Isa Wiedemeyer, Grisha Herzberg, and the rest of Sorge's team were told to stand ready to flee at a moment's notice. But as the days passed without the emergency escape signal, Ursula began to relax. The suitcase of documents and the trunk of weapons were returned to their hiding place in Ursula's cupboard. The meetings resumed. "From now on," she wrote, "I kept a suitcase ready packed for Misha and myself."

By repeatedly changing their identities, the imprisoned Rudniks were keeping the authorities at bay. It is very hard to prosecute someone if you do not know who they really are. Meanwhile, the "Noulens Affair" had become an international cause célèbre, with left-leaning celebrities, fellow travelers, intellectuals, scientists, and writers lining up to insist that the accused couple were simply peace-loving union organizers cruelly hounded by the fascistic Chinese government.

At this moment, Sorge asked Ursula to perform a task more dangerous than anything she had attempted before. "Will you hide a

Chinese comrade whose life is in danger?" This was an instruction framed as a request. It was also a calculated gamble. Concealing a communist fugitive in the house on Avenue Joffre would be impossible without Rudi's knowledge. Indeed, it required his active collaboration. Ursula knew that Sorge was testing both her resolve and the state of her marriage, but there was no choice. "I had to take Rudi into my confidence." She was under no illusions. Rudi was unlikely to react well to the discovery that his wife was a communist spy.

CHAPTER 5

THE SPIES WHO LOVED HER

DURING THEIR TIME IN SHANGHAI, URSULA HAD DETECTED a small but distinct shift in Rudi's politics. Like her, he was appalled by the White Terror, the grinding poverty, the complacency of the expatriate bourgeoisie growing fat on Chinese misery. Moreover, events in Germany were propelling him further to the left. In two years, the Nazi Party had been transformed from a rump group of extremists into the most powerful political force in Germany, combining terror tactics with conventional political campaigning amid a blizzard of racist, anti-communist, nationalist propaganda. The paramilitary brownshirts beat up opponents, staged mass rallies, and smashed the windows of Jewish shops, while Hitler toured the country whipping up anti-Semitic fury. In the elections of July 1932, the Nazis would win nearly fourteen million votes to become the largest single party in the Reichstag. Facing electoral oblivion, the KPD increasingly turned to violence.

For Ursula, the disturbing news from Germany was further proof that only communism could resist the rise of fascism, and to her satisfaction Rudi was coming around to the same view: "He moved closer to me politically," she wrote.

But there were limits: when Ursula told Rudi she wanted to shelter a fugitive Chinese communist under their roof, he exploded. "You are over-estimating yourself," he insisted, "and you're not as tough as you think. The risk for you, and for Misha, is just too great." She responded with equal force. "Your attitude could cause the death of a comrade, and for that I would never be able to forgive you."

The argument raged back and forth, until Rudi relented or, rather, bowed to an eventuality over which he had little control, and agreed to shelter the communist. He was now, against his will and better judgment, complicit in the conspiracy, a part of the Sorge network. This might have brought Ursula and Rudi closer. But something vital had broken.

Their secret houseguest arrived the next afternoon, a small, polite, evidently grateful, and extremely scared young Chinese man, who spoke no English at all. Hamburger tried to make the best of the strange situation: "Once he was actually living with us, Rudi was anxious to make our guest feel at home and was warm and friendly towards him, in so far as this was possible without a common language." The young communist hid in the upper floors of the house, emerging only at night to walk in the garden. When there were dinner guests, he lay motionless in bed, fearful his movements would be heard in the rooms below. Even the servants were unaware of his presence. After two weeks, he was gone, spirited into the interior and the safety of the Jiangxi Soviet area. The immediate threat was lifted, but a crackling tension lingered. "It was clear to me," Ursula wrote, "that our marriage could not continue like this much longer."

The secret meetings resumed, but less frequently. Sorge was affectionate and solicitous toward Ursula, but preoccupied with the Noulens case and going through one of his periodic bouts of extreme recklessness. He drove his speeding motorcycle into a wall and smashed his left leg. "What difference does another scar make?" he joked when Ursula dropped in on him in the hospital. The Noulenses, awaiting trial in Nanking Prison, had a five-year-old son, known as Jimmy. (His real name was Dmitri; even the children of spies have cover names.) Agnes Smedley had returned to Shanghai to coordinate the Noulens Defense Committee. She became Jimmy's temporary guardian, a role she fulfilled by "showering him with presents like a little prince." When Ursula suggested this was not a good idea, Agnes angrily retorted that Ursula should take the child into her own home. Ursula was tempted. "I would try to give him the maternal affection he needed and Misha would have a big brother."

But Sorge quashed the idea, since it would establish a direct link between Ursula and the imprisoned Soviet spies. "It meant giving up my illegal work and neither he nor I wanted that," she wrote. But Agnes did: having got Ursula into the spy game, she now wanted her out.

Determined to extend the Soviet sphere of influence in the Far East, Moscow increased its covert support for Chinese communism. A fresh cadre of Soviet agents arrived in Shanghai to rebuild the communist networks after the Noulens debacle and "maintain the combative spirit of party members and their sympathizers." Arthur Ewert, a veteran German revolutionary, appeared in 1932 and took over as the Comintern's chief liaison with the CCP, along with his wife, the Polish-born Elise Szaborowski, known as Szabo. The Ewerts would eventually meet a grisly fate: Szabo perished in a German concentration camp, while Arthur Ewert was captured in Brazil and tortured into insanity. The fat, bald, smiling man that Ursula had seen handling guns in her spare room a few months earlier revealed himself to be Colonel Karl Rimm, code-named "Paul," a Red Army veteran from Estonia and Sorge's deputy. Rimm ran a restaurant in the French Concession with his wife, Luise, a "buxom, motherly" Latvian woman who coded and decoded wireless messages to and from Moscow.

There was one more notable figure on the fringes of this group, a twenty-seven year-old Englishman named Roger Hollis, significant less for what he was in 1932 than what he would become many years later. The son of an Anglican bishop, Hollis had flirted with communism at Oxford before he dropped out, set off for China as a freelance journalist, and then joined British American Tobacco, the multinational company whose Shanghai factory manufactured fifty-five billion cigarettes a year. Hollis was sociable and socialist; he certainly knew some of the Sorge group, including Karl Rimm, and may have met Sorge himself. According to Sorge's biographer, Hollis was "one of the guests at the Hamburger house." Hollis's flatmate, Anthony Staples, later gave evidence that an American woman and a German man, believed to be Agnes Smedley and the new Comintern chief, Arthur Ewert, had visited Hollis at his home. There is even some evidence that the Englishman had a three-year affair with Luise

Rimm, Karl's wife. Ursula later claimed to have no memory of Roger Hollis.

The presence, or otherwise, of this shadowy Englishman in the Sorge circle would be irrelevant, had Hollis not made a significant career change on his return to Britain from the Far East. In 1938, he joined MI5, the British Security Service, and would go on to become its director general with direct responsibility for hunting down Soviet spies in Britain at the height of the Cold War. Many years later, the suspected links between Hollis, Ursula, and her communist friends would provoke a damaging internal mole hunt inside MI5, based on the unproven but persistent conspiracy theory that Hollis was a communist spy, recruited in Shanghai back in 1932.

Sorge's network forged close internal bonds, as secret societies always do. The group went on excursions to the Chinese countryside, sightseeing trips that were also espionage work outings. Rudi seldom accompanied his wife on these jaunts. "Generous and good hearted as always, he was pleased for me whenever I had a chance to get out of Shanghai, even if he could not come himself." Rudi insisted he had too much work—the Modern Home furniture business now had twenty Chinese employees and a backlog of orders—but in reality he was also holding back, unwilling to get entangled in Ursula's spy community. There is a poignant photograph from this time of Rudi and Ursula asleep in the sun during a picnic. He has his arm around her, as if trying to cling on. She sleeps at an angle to him.

They continued to make plans together. In May 1932, she wrote to her parents: "Rudi and I think more and more that once his contract finishes, we will make a new start in Russia. I'm pretty confident that we both will find work in R[ussia]. There are a hundred reasons for R[ussia] and against Shanghai—Unfortunately, not all of them writable." In another letter she wrote: "I'm going to study Russian here intensively for the next six months, I want Rudi to learn Russian too. You never know." She did not explain that many of her new communist friends spoke Russian, nor that her instructions from the Center were written in Russian, nor that Sorge had advised her to learn the language if she wished to continue working for Soviet military intelligence in the future.

Ursula's photograph albums contain numerous images of the

young communist and her spy friends at play: Ursula linking arms back-to-back with Karl Rimm to play "see-saw"; Agnes Smedley in earnest conversation with Chen Hansheng, the university lecturer and secret communist agent. On one occasion, Ursula and Agnes joined the rest of the gang for a three-day boat trip up the Yangtze. "Szabo cooked for us all in the houseboat kitchen . . . and Agnes told jokes." Sorge was carefully fostering team spirit. "It may have been unusual for comrades who worked illegally to meet for such a sight-seeing excursion, but it was not irresponsible," wrote Ursula. To outside observers, they looked like any other group of expatriate friends, an assortment of foreigners thrown together by chance in a strange land. Ursula would look back on those days as "something quite rare and precious." She was still only twenty-five years old: "I ran races around the meadow with Richard [Sorge] and Paul [Karl Rimm] until we all collapsed into the grass from too much running and laughing." Her zest for life was infectious. She would always cherish the memory of a simple game of tag, in a field, with her friends and her secret lover.

One evening early in 1932, Ursula joined Sorge, Rimm, and Grisha at a hotel room in downtown Shanghai to welcome another new arrival. "Our dark-eyed, dark-haired host was a vivacious man whom I had not seen before." He was introduced as "Fred." The party was bibulous and convivial. Fred told funny stories, and sang German and Russian songs in a fine baritone. "He had a beautiful voice," Ursula recalled. Two days later, Sorge asked Ursula to deliver a cardboard tube to him containing rolled-up documents. Fred invited her to stay for a drink. For reasons she could never quite explain, Ursula felt drawn to confide in this man she barely knew, describing her political alienation from Rudi and the strain her clandestine work was putting on their marriage. "Should we separate?" she asked. "Fred listened patiently and told me he felt honoured by my confidence." Sensibly, he offered no opinion on her marriage. After three hours of intense conversation, Ursula headed into the night, oddly elated. Later it occurred to her that the sympathetic Fred had been interviewing her, "probing my suitability for the work." Later still, she discovered who he was.

Fred's real name was Manfred Stern, one of the heroes of

twentieth-century communism and, almost inevitably, one of its victims. An early revolutionary, he had led a partisan unit of the Red Army against the "Mad Baron," Roman Ungern-Sternberg, whose brother, Constantin, was a fixture of Shanghai's German club. Stern joined the Fourth Department of the Red Army and was deployed to New York in 1929, where, from a safe house on Fifty-seventh Street, he ran a network of spies extracting America's military secrets, copying stolen documents in a photographic shop bought for the purpose in Greenwich Village, and shipping them back to Moscow. The sympathetic, sweet-voiced Fred was a rising star of Soviet military espionage. He was in China as chief military adviser to Mao and the CCP, and as a recruitment agent for the Center. Moscow was beginning to take an interest in Agent Sonya.

Michael was now a toddler and beginning to speak. "Misha is walking around in a white blouse with green flowered linen underpants," she told her mother. "For three weeks now he has been walking independently through the garden and all the rooms, smelling all the flowers, falling over, getting up again growling, trying to take the steps to the garden, tumbling down, screaming murderously, suddenly discovering a little bird on a tree and falling silent in the middle of a wail. Says 'Daddy, Daddy, Mummy' and especially 'money-money-money,' which, to my horror, the Amah has taught him. I made up for it by teaching him 'dirty'—and now he repeatedly chants 'dirty money.'"

On January 28, 1932, Japanese imperial forces attacked Shanghai. The previous autumn Japan had invaded Manchuria, occupying 1.3 million square kilometers of China and establishing a puppet government in the region the Japanese renamed Manchukuo. Next, the expansionist Japanese military turned its attention to Shanghai, where Japan had existing extraterritorial rights. Claiming to be defending its citizens against Chinese aggression, Japan assembled thirty ships, forty airplanes, and seven thousand troops around the Shanghai shoreline, and then attacked the Chinese areas of the city. The Chinese Nineteenth Route Army put up a fierce resistance. The conflict barely touched the international concessions, but it seriously alarmed Moscow, since Japanese incursions into China represented a potential threat to the Soviet Union. Sorge was instructed to find out what was going on. He dispatched Ursula Hamburger and Isa Wiede-meyer to the war zone.

"This not undangerous mission," Ursula wrote later, with ring-ing understatement, "was best undertaken by women." The two for-eign females were stared at but left alone, as they wandered through the burned-out and looted Chinese neighborhoods. "Japanese sol-diers are prowling everywhere," Ursula reported. "Whole streets are empty except for a few corpses and the only sound to be heard in the deathly hush is the rumbling of heavy armoured Japanese military vehicles. . . . The poor were left with their gutted houses, millions of unemployed and their dead." Ursula and Isa visited wounded Chi-nese soldiers in the hospital, gauged the morale of the troops, and assessed the impact of the Japanese attack. Sorge was "amazed" by the quality of the information gathered by his women spies, now operating more like war correspondents reporting from the front line. "I was also able to give Richard an accurate picture of the mood among Europeans," she later wrote. The fighting ended after a few weeks with a cease-fire brokered by the League of Nations, but not before Ursula had witnessed a sight that shook her soul.

"I found a dead baby in the street," she wrote. Ursula picked up the tiny corpse. "Its nappies were still wet." The child was around the same age as Michael. Here, with appalling clarity, was a measure of what was at stake. She might frame the Japanese action in political terms—"a clear and brutal lesson in the methods of capitalism"—but it was also a warning of the pitiless world she now inhabited. If Ursula was caught and executed, the next dead child lying in the street might be her own.

Rudi was appalled by the Japanese attack, and furious. "It is an outrageous and shocking thing to invade a weak country," he wrote to his parents. "What we are witnessing here is military aggression conducted solely for economic interests." Rudi was beginning to think and sound like Ursula. "This period contributed fundamen-tally to Rudi becoming a communist," she later wrote. Her husband was turning toward revolution. He was also trying to save their mar-riage. His conversion to communism was a desperate act of love. But it was too late. Rudi was caring and sweet, but in his deep-brown eyes Ursula now saw only a lifetime of conventional marriage. Richard Sorge had shown her another world of excitement, commitment, and danger. With Rudi she was comfortable and content. But with Sorge, tearing along on the back of a motorcycle, in furtive conclave or secret assignation, she was alive.

Agnes Smedley was working on a series of short stories set in China, while using her journalistic cover to pass information between Sorge, the Comintern, the CCP, and the Center. Sorge "made her a member of the Comintern headquarters staff." But the British were harassing her "like ferocious dogs," she said, and her behavior was increasingly erratic. Readers of the *Frankfurter Zeitung* complained that her reporting was "one-sided." The newspaper also received an intelligence report, probably British, claiming she had attended a meeting in a theater with a "group of young Chinese communists whom she caroused drunkenly with and offered herself sexually to." As a finale, it was alleged, she had appeared "stark naked on the platform, wearing only a red hat, and had sung the *Internationale*." The German newspaper was liberal, but not that liberal. Agnes was sacked.

In the summer of 1932, Agnes and Ursula took a working holiday together in the mountains of Kuling, in Jiangxi Province, just outside the communist-controlled area. As ever, the political and personal merged. The trip was an opportunity to escape the summer heat of Shanghai and rebuild their friendship, while conducting some light espionage. The CCP provided a holiday bungalow. Since Mao's forces were encamped in the nearby mountains, Agnes would conduct "interviews with the Chinese Soviets and their defenders, the Chinese Red Army," report some of what she discovered as journalism, and pass any secret information she gleaned back to Moscow.

The five-day boat journey up the Yangtze was "followed by a bone-shaking bus to the foot of the mountain [and] another three hours up steep paths in a swaying sedan chair." Initially, their relationship seemed to regain its former warmth. "Agnes and I go for long walks every afternoon," Ursula wrote, "with beautiful views down the Yangtze Valley and towards the Hubei mountain ranges, where the Reds are."

On the day Ursula wrote this letter to her parents, the Noulenses

THE SPIES WHO LOVED HER / 73

(their real names still unknown to the authorities) went on trial in Jiangsu High Court, accused of "financing Communist bandits, directing subversive activities, arms trading with the Communists, and conspiring to overthrow the republic of China." A few days earlier, Sorge met two couriers sent from Moscow, each of whom handed over $20,000 with which to bribe the Chinese judicial authorities.

In Kuling, Ursula and Agnes received word that the Noulenses had gone on a hunger strike. As they sat down to lunch, Agnes announced theatrically that out of solidarity she too would eat nothing until the accused couple were released.

"That will not help the Noulenses," Ursula responded tartly.

Without a word, Agnes rose and stalked out of the room. Ursula picked up Michael and went for a stroll.

When she returned to the bungalow, a letter was waiting on the table.

"I cannot stay under these circumstances, and have returned to Shanghai," Agnes had written. "You are too preoccupied with your own personal happiness and your family. Private matters play too great a role in your life. You do not have what it takes to make a real revolutionary."

Ursula was deeply wounded. "Agnes surely knew me well enough to know that I was ready to take any risk. Must I exhibit my emotions in order to prove them? How could such a close friendship be damaged like this? Where had Agnes got these ideas about me?" In reality, Agnes's diatribe was more personal than political: she was jealous of Ursula's relationship with Sorge and her friendship with Isa, envious of her baby, and angry that she had refused to step back from espionage by agreeing with her suggestion to adopt little Jimmy.

Ursula remained in Kuling, brooding on the ruptured friendship. "It was a heavy blow." Word arrived that the Noulenses had been condemned to death, but the sentence commuted to life imprisonment. Ursula credited Sorge with saving their lives by bribing the judge. She picked over the accusations leveled by a woman whose ideas and friendship meant so much to her. "Perhaps Agnes was right. I enjoyed life and could take enormous pleasure in everyday things. Did I perhaps attach too much importance to them? Every breath my son took was like magic to me, and I was determined to have more children, although I did not think my marriage would survive its present conflicts."

Soon the hurt gave way to anger. Agnes had misjudged her. She was perfectly capable of separating personal life from political duty. She would prove to Agnes, and the world, that despite the demands of motherhood she had exactly what it took to make a real revolutionary.

Back in Shanghai, she described the argument with Agnes to Sorge. He changed the subject. "Richard seemed to regard it as a quarrel about some matter of special concern to women, and showed no desire to get involved." A veteran womanizer, Sorge knew better than to get caught up in a fight between two of his conquests. (While Agnes and Ursula had been falling out, he had seduced "a beautiful Chinese girl," from whom he obtained the blueprints of a Chinese military arsenal.) Ursula and Agnes still met up from time to time, but the friendship was gone, and both knew it.

Smedley had inducted Ursula into the world of communist espionage; the American woman's fierce spirit of rebellion had inspired her. But, after two years of undercover work, Ursula was maturing into something the volatile, egotistical Agnes would never be: a professional, dedicated, and increasingly self-confident spy. "I was constantly aware of the possibility that I might be arrested, and so I hardened myself physically to improve my resistance. I didn't smoke, or drink alcohol. That way I would not suffer if I were suddenly deprived of them." Agent Sonya was growing into her role.

One morning in December, Ursula answered the telephone and heard the familiar voice of the Polish photographer Grisha Herzberg. "Come to my apartment this afternoon. Richard wants to meet you there." This was a prearranged signal to stand ready for a possible meeting. "I had hardly ever been to Grisha's home and, as I understood it, I was only to come if he phoned again." Ursula waited an hour for the backup call. When none came, she went shopping.

Seated around the Hamburgers' dining table that evening were Fritz Kuck, a teacher and keen Nazi, and two brothers, Ernst and Helmut Wilhelm, one an architect and the other an academic, and their wives. The dinner party was excruciating, the guests "tongue-tied and boring," and the opportunities for useful intelligence gathering negligible. Kuck was laboriously showing slides of his expeditions into the interior and Ursula had gone into a trance of tedium, when the telephone rang in the next room.

She picked up the receiver. The moment would remain frozen in memory. A framed photograph of her childhood home in Schlachtensee stood on the table by the telephone. The murmur of conversation was audible from the dining room.

"I waited two hours for you this afternoon," said Richard Sorge. "I wanted to say goodbye."

Ursula felt the room lurch. She sat down heavily in the chair.

"Are you still there?" Sorge's voice came faintly from the receiver, hanging limp in her hand.

"Yes," she said. "Yes, I'm here."

Sorge hastily explained that he was leaving the next day. He had been recalled to Moscow. There was, he said, no cause for alarm, but he would not be returning to China. The Center wanted him elsewhere.

"I want to thank you for always looking after me so well, and all the others. This is only a beginning for you. Much more lies ahead. You must keep a stiff upper lip"—he used the antique English phrase—"you must promise me that. But for now—all the best, the very best, and goodbye." The line went dead.

Ursula could not move. She stared blankly at the wall. Grisha had forgotten to make the second telephone call, a simple error of tradecraft. "I could not grasp that Richard had simply gone. Never again would he sit in this chair to talk to me, to listen to me, to advise me, to laugh with me." He had departed, and she had not even found the words to say farewell.

"What had I been thinking of? Had I only just realized how much he meant to me?"

Ursula never saw Richard Sorge again. Perhaps their romantic relationship was already over, but for Ursula it never really ended.

Ursula returned to her dreary dinner guests. No one noticed that her heart was broken.

WITH SORGE GONE, HER FRIENDSHIP with Agnes Smedley over, and her marriage to Rudi in a state of quiet crisis, Ursula succumbed to a bout of homesickness. Karl Rimm took over the reins from Sorge. He was an efficient spymaster, whose chubby frame and dozy manner belied a "revolutionary's strength and passion." But he had none of his predecessor's panache. She yearned for Sorge. Without him, Shanghai seemed drained of its glamour and color. "We now have a longing for another home," she wrote to her parents. "I feel an immense sympathy for the Chinese people. I already feel a quarter Asian. If I leave this country I know I will always long for it." Restless, she made plans to return to Germany in the spring and introduce Michael to the rest of his family. The hot, damp climate was affecting the baby's lungs, and the German doctor had advised her to take him on holiday in Europe. Some time apart from Rudi would be good for them both.

The news from Germany, however, was appalling.

Nazi Party membership was soaring, and the violence between fascists and communists reaching a climax. On January 30, 1933, Hitler was sworn in as chancellor, unleashing a campaign of violence and terror more brutal than anything seen so far. A month later, following the Reichstag fire, Hitler suspended civil liberties on the pretext of averting a communist putsch and then set about creating a "ruthless confrontation" with the KPD. The Nazis rounded up thousands of communists, closed down the party headquarters, and banned demonstrations. Most of the KPD leaders were arrested, though some escaped into Soviet exile. The once-powerful organization Ursula had joined was driven underground, its surviving members harried and terrorized. The Enabling Act, passed in March, gave Hitler the power to rule by decree. The Nazi dictatorship had begun, and tremors from the political earthquake reverberated to China. The Zeitgeist bookshop closed abruptly, as funds from Germany dried up. Even Ursula's optimism wobbled. "It was impossible for me to understand how the German working class could permit the fascists to take power," she wrote.

In Germany, many still misread the writing on the wall. The

Central Jewish German Organization declared that "nobody would dare touch our constitutional rights." Robert Kuczynski was not so sure. He had never been a communist, but as a prominent Jewish left-wing academic he was a marked man. Jürgen Kuczynski was in even greater danger. After returning from the United States with Marguerite he had joined the KPD in 1930. Since then he had written for various communist publications, and even visited the Soviet Union with an official KPD delegation. On February 27, while walking toward the *Rote Fahne* offices, he bumped into a friend who told him the Gestapo was raiding the newspaper at that very moment. Jürgen turned on his heel, avoiding arrest and almost certain death, by a matter of minutes.

"We are aghast at the developments in Germany," Ursula wrote home. "Only some of what is happening finds its way into the newspapers here. A heavy heart robs me of words, but we beg you to write as much as you feel able."

In March, a posse of black-uniformed Gestapo agents banged on the gates of the Schlachtensee villa and demanded to speak to Robert Kuczynski. Olga Muth told them he was out. The Gestapo vowed to return. Robert immediately went into hiding, first at the home of friends, then in a mental asylum. Ursula's parents-in-law, Max and Else Hamburger, owned a holiday chalet in Grenzbauden, a picturesque village just across the Riesengebirge mountain range dividing German Silesia from Czechoslovakia. The Hamburgers had already taken refuge there, and agreed to shelter Robert until he could find a way to go onward to Britain or America, where he had friends in the academic community. In April, he escaped across the border into Czechoslovakia. Displaying what he described as "an almost blind loyalty in the leadership," Jürgen remained in Germany, joined the communist underground, and continued to write, at excruciating length, for a variety of secret party publications. Even Ernst Thälmann, the KPD leader now in hiding, found Jürgen's prolixity a little wearing: "Too much 'cyclical crises' and not enough broken lavatory seats," he told the young statistician. Berta put down her paintbrushes, and never picked them up again. She and her younger daughters hunkered down in the old family house and waited.

Ursula knew that returning to Berlin would be suicidal, with her father a wanted man, anti-Semitism spreading through Germany like a rampant virus, and her comrades arrested, dead, or on the run. Her name was on the Gestapo's list of communist subversives. Refugees from Nazi violence were already pouring into Shanghai. Her journey home would have to be postponed. "The swastika is fluttering over the consulate here," Ursula told her mother and sisters.

While the Gestapo was hunting for Robert and Jürgen Kuczynski, the indefatigable Tom Givens of the Shanghai Municipal Police was closing in on the Soviet spy ring. Based on the "confessions" of captured communists, the Irish detective had drawn up a list of foreigners suspected of being Soviet spies. Richard Sorge was on it. So was Agnes Smedley. Soon after Sorge's departure for Moscow, Agnes also made tracks for the Soviet Union.

And so did Ursula.

CHAPTER 6

SPARROW

G ENERAL YAN KARLOVICH BERZIN, CHIEF OF THE FOURTH
Department of the Red Army, was pleased with Richard
Sorge. The spy code-named "Ramsay" had done all, and more, that
was asked of him: he had built up an effective web of agents, successfully navigated the fallout from the Noulens affair, and survived
three years in Shanghai unscathed, save for a broken leg.

General Berzin knew all about survival.

The son of a Latvian farmer, Berzin had led a revolutionary partisan detachment against czarist troops and escaped twice from Siberian prison camps before joining the Red Army. During Lenin's Red
Terror, he instigated the systematic shooting of hostages as an effective method of subjugation, and in 1920 he was appointed to head the
Fourth Department, the first Soviet military intelligence bureau.
Berzin was charming, articulate, ambitious, and astonishingly brutal, a brilliant organizer with the eyes of a wolf and a glacial smile
who had established a vast global network of "illegal" spies, working
undercover, in every major capital of the world. The Fourth Department demanded total fidelity, which it frequently repaid with extreme disloyalty: if an officer or agent made a mistake, if a network
was compromised, the spies were on their own; for anyone suspected
of treachery, the punishment was swift and lethal. The "cold-
bloodedness of the Centre" set it apart, according to one former
agent. "It was entirely ruthless. With no sense of honour, obligation
or decency towards its servants. They were used as long as they were

of any value, and then cast aside with no compunction and no compensation."

Berzin personally debriefed Sorge in his office at 19 Bolshoi Znamensky Lane, the Center's innocuous two-story headquarters a few hundred yards from the Kremlin, listening attentively as Agent Ramsay described the subagents in his Shanghai network: Japanese journalist Hotsumi Ozaki, Chinese academic Chen Hansheng, and red-haired radical Irene Wiedemeyer. Agnes Smedley had done "excellent work," Sorge reported. Then there was the German housewife Ursula Hamburger, an agent displaying particular promise. Manfred Stern had also reported positively on Sorge's recruit. Berzin liked the sound of Agent Sonya.

In Shanghai a week later, Ursula was summoned to a meeting with Grisha Herzberg and Karl Rimm, Sorge's successor. A message had come from the Center, a cross between an invitation, a suggestion, and an order. "Would you be prepared to go to Moscow for a training course?" asked Rimm. "This will last at least six months. And there is no guarantee you will return to Shanghai at the end."

Sorge's parting message—"This is only a beginning for you"—now became clear. He must have "reported fully to the Red Army intelligence branch" and recommended her for further training. This was flattering, but surely impractical. "What about Michael?" she asked.

"A condition of accepting this offer is that you must leave him somewhere else," Rimm said flatly. "You cannot risk taking him to the Soviet Union as he is bound to learn Russian there." There was an elementary, if cruel, logic at work. After training in Moscow, she must slip back into civilian life without anyone knowing where she had been. Michael was picking up languages quickly: German from his parents and pidgin, the Chinese-English hybrid spoken by many urban Chinese, from his nanny. If the child returned speaking even a smattering of Russian, the secret would be out.

Ursula had never faced such a painful decision: she was being asked, in effect, to choose between her child and her ideological vocation, her family and espionage.

"The thought of giving up my work never occurred to me," she later wrote. Like a religious zealot, she had found a single, unwavering faith around which to wrap her life. The rise of Hitler, mounting Japanese aggression, and the continuing slaughter of Chinese communists had redoubled her determination to fight fascism. A training course would underline her commitment. Perhaps she would be reunited with Richard Sorge. Under the Center's rules, agents and officers were forbidden to make contact with one another while on separate deployments. She could not write to him, nor he to her. But there was a chance he was still in Russia. Long before his departure from Shanghai, she knew that Sorge's relentlessly wandering eye had alighted elsewhere. She knew he probably did not love her, or any of his women. But she longed to see him one more time. Ambition, ideology, adventure, romance, and politics combined to make up her mind: she would go to Moscow, the capital of communist revolution. "My decision was quickly made," Ursula wrote. But where would Michael live? Berlin was out of the question. Leaving him in Shanghai was not an option, since she had been warned she might never return. After a long discussion with Rudi, they agreed that Michael would spend the next six months with his paternal grandparents at their chalet in Czechoslovakia, on the ostensible grounds that "a change of climate" would do him good. Leaving Rudi in Shanghai would not excite comment since "it was quite usual for foreigners in China to send their wives and children on prolonged home leave to Europe." Rudi believed his marriage could be saved. His own commitment to communism was growing. If the Soviet intelligence service wanted Ursula to go to Moscow, he would not (and probably could not) stop her. Misha would be well cared for by his parents, and once her training in Russia was complete, Ursula would collect their son, the family would be reunited, and they could make a new start. That was Rudi's hope. When the time came to say goodbye, he held his son tightly until the child wriggled free.

Separation from her two-year-old son would leave a permanent scar. Ursula defended that bleak decision for the rest of her life. But she never quite forgave herself.

On May 18, 1933, Ursula and Michael boarded a Norwegian freighter bound for Vladivostok. Just before the ship weighed anchor, Grisha appeared with a large locked trunk containing documents for delivery to the Center. During the long voyage she recited nursery rhymes to the little boy and told him stories. They spent hours talking to a canary that lived in a cage on deck. "The thought of the parting knotted my stomach," she wrote. The weather was warm, and the scent of the timber cargo filled the air. "Misha will be in his grandmother's loving care," she told herself. "The mountain air will be ideal for him."

At the Vladivostok docks they were met by a Russian naval officer and escorted to the Moscow train. On the first night in their little cabin Michael was restless, disturbed by the clatter of the tracks. "I lay down beside him on the bunk until he went to sleep in my arms, and I realized once again how difficult it would be to part from my son." Nine days later they arrived in Moscow and handed over the trunk to waiting officers, before boarding another train, to Czechoslovakia, followed by a taxi to the little village of Grenzbauden.

Max and Else Hamburger, now permanently resident in Czechoslovakia, warmly welcomed mother and child. Robert Kuczynski had left the chalet several months earlier, and was now in England. "I told Rudi's parents that we were considering a move to the Soviet Union," Ursula wrote. She explained that she would be spending several months in Moscow, exploring the possibilities. The Hamburgers were "not too happy about the plan," but agreed to care for their grandson as long as necessary.

Ursula's mother arrived from Berlin a few days later.

For Berta Kuczynski, this should have been a happy occasion, a long-awaited get-together with her eldest daughter and first grandchild. But the poor woman was utterly distracted. In the months since Robert's flight, Nazi harassment had escalated. The Gestapo returned to Schlachtensee, demanding to know where Kuczynski had gone. Jürgen's home was also raided and searched. The KPD leader Ernst Thälmann was captured at the home of a man named Hans Kluczynski, and the similarity of the names brought renewed attention to the Kuczynski family—spelling was never a Gestapo strong point. Jürgen himself was arrested, but released after two hours of questioning. Secretly, he began to smuggle the family library out of the country: about two-thirds of the fifty thousand volumes would be saved. Jürgen and Marguerite were now living an underground life, in constant fear of arrest.

In May the Nazis staged public bonfires of "Jewish and Marxist" literature, including subversive works like Agnes Smedley's *Daughter of Earth*. Every book in the Marxist Workers' Lending Library, created by Ursula in 1929, was put to the torch. Her friend Gabo Lewin, who had taken over as librarian, was beaten up and thrown in prison. Soon after, Berta Kuczynski performed a book burning of her own. Faithful Olga Muth stood beside the boiler furnace in the basement shoveling in left-wing books and papers, while the rest of the family carried down anything and everything the Nazis might consider incriminating, including many of Ursula's papers. When the moment came to destroy Robert Kuczynski's handwritten manuscripts, Ollo could be heard muttering angrily: "They call themselves the Workers' Party, and everything your father wrote was to improve the lives of the workers." A few days later the Gestapo reappeared in force, and this time they ransacked the house. "They just barged in," Brigitte recalled. "We were still in bed and had to quickly make ourselves presentable and go downstairs into one room where we were made to sit while they searched." Ollo stood by, "calm and collected," arms folded. As they left in frustration, one Gestapo officer turned and spat: "We'll get her yet." Ursula was now on the wanted list, along with Robert and Jürgen. It was time to get out. Berta put the old family house up for sale and prepared to flee.

The woman who appeared at the chalet in Grenzbauden was a pale, prematurely aged shadow of the glamorous mother Ursula had left three years earlier. Berta barely noticed her grandson. "She could not enjoy anything any more," wrote Ursula. After just a few hours, Berta announced she was going back to Berlin.

Two-year-old Michael picked up the strained atmosphere. "He began to cry bitterly and kept repeating: 'Mummy stay with Misha, please mummy stay with Misha.'" Knowing she would be unable to control herself if she had to say goodbye, Ursula packed her bag in the dawn light, embraced Max and Else, and then stole away, weeping silently, while her son was asleep.

The officers at the station in Moscow greeted her as "Sonya." It was the first time she had heard the code name conferred on her by

Richard Sorge, and she immediately recalled the bar song in Shanghai. The word brought memories of the man on the motorbike flooding back. "Perhaps that is why I liked it," she later wrote. "The name sounded like a last greeting from him."

The waiting car went south and up into the Lenin Hills, the low wooded range on the right bank of the Moscow River looking down over the city. Near the village of Vorobyevo, a name derived from the Russian for "sparrow," they pulled up at the gates to a large complex of buildings surrounded by a double metal fence and patrolled by armed military police and guard dogs. This was the "Eighth International Sports Base" and also, more secretly, the "Radio Training Laboratory of the People's Commissariat of Defence." Unimaginatively code-named "Sparrow," this was the domain of Jakob Mirov-Abramov, the Comintern master spy who had recruited Agnes Smedley back in 1926 and was now the head of communications for the Soviet intelligence services.

Sparrow was equipped with laboratories, workshops, and the latest wireless technology. The top floor was a broadcasting dome, with two transmitters (500 watts and 250 watts) and a powerful Telefunken receiver. Here some eighty handpicked trainees, of all nationalities and both sexes, studied the art of clandestine shortwave radio operations: constructing transmitters and receivers, assembling and concealing wireless equipment, and coding and decoding messages in Morse. Students were also taught languages, history, and geography, indoctrinated in Marxism-Leninism, and trained in unarmed and armed combat, sabotage, mixing and handling explosives, surveillance and countersurveillance, and all the arcane techniques of spycraft including dead drops, brush contacts, and disguises. Before being deployed around the world, graduates of the spy school were put through "arduous training at an army sports camp," a course so physically demanding they were afterward "sent to recuperate at a sanatorium in the Crimea."

Mirov-Abramov was a "friendly, competent and loyal comrade," but also a martinet and an obsessive technical boffin, who demanded dedication and total obedience from the handful of people he selected for training. One colleague wrote:

Candidates were accepted by Mirov-Abramov after careful scrutiny. He proved an excellent psychologist. He invited the candidate into his office and asked whether he [or she] wished to make himself available to take part actively in the fight against Hitler and Fascism. After several meetings, Mirov-Abramov asked the candidate to sign the written conditions for this training, thereby totally committing himself to the Soviet espionage system. The candidates selected were young, intelligent people with a special gift for languages or technical matters. Unsuitable candidates were eliminated by continual examinations. The trainees had to change their names and promise never to reveal their true identities, not even to their colleagues. During the training they had to break off all links with friends, were never allowed to leave the school alone, and were not permitted to take photographs or talk to anyone about the school and their curriculum. The betrayal of secrets was punishable by death.

Ursula passed the interviews with Mirov-Abramov, signed the contract, and pledged her loyalty, on pain of death, to Soviet intelligence.

Why did she do it? Ursula was a married woman (albeit unhappily) and a mother, a Jewish, bookish, tender, middle-class intellectual who enjoyed the ordinary pleasures of shopping, cooking, and bringing up a child. As the world slid into war, people of similar backgrounds were fleeing for sanctuary, but she deliberately turned in the other direction, running toward danger, relishing the risks. Although Ursula was open and direct by nature, her existence hereafter would be shaped by intense secrecy and deception, concealing the truth from people she loved as well as those she detested. Soviet espionage was a job for life, and, not infrequently, death. Ursula looked back on the shape of her life as if it had been preordained, depicting her choices as the logical consequence of political conviction. But there was more than ideology at work. In the internal theater of her psychology, espionage offered an opportunity to prove she was the equal of her favored brother, a player in world affairs like her father, a more effective revolutionary than Agnes Smedley. Sparrow spy school offered the education she had never had and the romance that comes with membership of a secret elite. Life with Rudi offered safety and certainty. She wanted neither.

Spying is also highly addictive. The drug of secret power, once tasted, is hard to renounce. Ursula had observed the babbling, inconsequential expatriates of Shanghai, knowing that she was not of them, but a person apart, with another, secret existence. She had faced extreme peril, for herself and her family, and she had got away with it. Survival against the odds brings with it an adrenaline high and a sense of destiny from cheating fate. Espionage is finally a work of the imagination, a willingness to transport oneself, and others, from the real to an artificial world, to seem to be one sort of person on the exterior but another, secret human on the inside. Since earliest childhood, in her writings, Ursula had used her rich imagination to explore an alternative reality, with herself at the center of every drama. Now, as a trained intelligence officer, she would have the opportunity to write her own story in the pages of history.

Ursula became a spy for the sake of the proletariat and the revolution; but she also did it for herself, driven by the extraordinary combination of ambition, romance, and adventure that bubbled inside her.

The "foreign group" of trainees included two other Germans, a Czech, a Greek, a Pole, and "Kate," an attractive Frenchwoman in her late twenties "of great intelligence and feeling" who would become Ursula's roommate and friend. The daughter of a French dockworker, Kate's real name was Renée Marceau. (She would later be dispatched to assassinate General Franco, the Spanish Nationalist leader, using a false British passport in the name of "Martha Sunshine." The plot failed, but she escaped from Spain and was awarded the Order of Lenin.) The recruits came from utterly different worlds; Ursula found them fascinating. The group was housed together in a large red-brick building on the Sparrow site, surrounded by cherry orchards.

Ursula threw herself into training: "All we had to do was learn." Under instruction from a former navy radio operator, she practiced assembling a wireless from parts available in civilian radio shops and learned how to send coded messages. With daily lessons, her Russian improved rapidly. Rather to her own surprise, she quickly picked up the technical skills, learning to build transmitters, receivers, rectifiers, and frequency meters. To Ursula's delight, the group was joined by Sepp "Sober" Weingarten, Sorge's bibulous radio operator, who had been sent back from Shanghai for a much-needed refresher course. (His wife, who accompanied him, had finally twigged that Sepp was a communist spy. She was furious.) The food in the compound was excellent. "I blossomed: my cheeks grew rounder and rosier, and for the first time in my life I weighed over ten stone."

At weekends Ursula went sightseeing with Renée, accompanied by a minder, polite but vigilant. They wandered the streets for hours. "I loved the cold of the Moscow winter," she wrote. She made discreet inquiries among her instructors about Sorge's whereabouts and was told only that he had departed to take up another assignment. She was not told where, and knew better than to ask. The rules were clear: agents and officers might fraternize in Moscow and when jointly deployed, but contact at any other time was strictly forbidden. Sorge was in Japan, laying the groundwork for his next feat of espionage. Ursula's lover had moved on, emotionally as well as geographically. Soviet espionage had thrown them together, and now held them apart. She wondered if she would ever see him again, and the thought made her heart twist.

Memories of Sorge came rushing back when, one afternoon in the lift of the Novaya Moskovskaya hotel, Ursula felt a tap on her shoulder and turned to find a beaming Agnes Smedley. "We fell into each other's arms," Ursula wrote. Agnes was preparing to return to China. Ursula believed the meeting was fortuitous; in fact, Agnes had almost certainly been instructed to "bump into" her friend and check up on her progress. Unsurprisingly, their friendship never quite rekindled, but together they called on Mikhail Borodin, the former adviser to Sun Yat-sen who was now editing the English-language newspaper *Moscow News*. In the autumn of 1933, she and Agnes were given tickets to the October Revolution celebrations in Red Square. In a dazzling display of Soviet muscle, an army of athletes marched abreast under Stalin's approving gaze, carrying tennis rackets, boats, flags, and soccer balls in what became known as the "Parade of a Hundred Thousand Singlets." Through Agnes, Ursula was introduced to other foreign communists, including the Hungarian Lajos Magyar, a journalist at the official newspaper *Pravda,* and Wang Ming, the chief Chinese delegate to the Comintern, who, unbeknownst to Ursula, had almost certainly sent Ding Ling's husband, Hu Yepin, to his death in 1931. "It was unusual for students at our school to meet so many people outside the collective," wrote Ursula. She was being naïve, perhaps deliberately: Agnes was spying on her; she was being introduced to foreign communist luminaries to reinforce her loyalty, observe her reactions, and keep an eye on her. She was under tuition, and also under surveillance.

Ursula was busy, stimulated, and healthier than ever before. But she was also continuously tortured by yearning for her little son. She found she barely missed Rudi, but the separation from Michael was agony, and getting worse with every day. Only Renée was aware of her private pain and guilt. She found herself trailing after groups of children "just to hear their bright voices." "My constant longing for him drew me to every child I came across. When I stood in front of shops and saw the prams standing outside I could understand how women could steal children, simply in order to change their clothes, feed them, and hear them gurgling." Michael's third birthday came and went. They had been apart for seven months. Ursula knew she would "never be able to recoup those lost months." Michael was growing up fast more than a thousand miles away, while she built radio transmitters in a guarded camp, making friends with people whose real names she did not know. Her duty, as a mother, was to be with Michael; but her other duty was stronger. Sometimes, late at night, she cried. But she never once thought of quitting.

A week after Michael's missed birthday, Ursula was summoned to the Center on Bolshoi Znamensky Lane. A major commended her progress and then abruptly informed her: "You are soon going to be sent away—to Mukden in Manchuria."

The region of northeast China and Inner Mongolia known as Manchuria had been invaded by the Japanese in 1931, who renamed it Manchukuo and installed a pro-Japanese puppet government. The Japanese occupiers were battling widespread Chinese resistance from citizen militias, peasant brotherhoods, bandit gangs, and partisan armies with names like the Big Swords and Red Spear Societies. The most vigorous insurgency was being mounted by the communist underground network, backed by the Soviet Union—which regarded expansion of Japanese power into China as a threat. Ursula's task in the city of Mukden (now Shenyang) would be to liaise with the communist partisans, provide them with material assistance, and transmit military and other intelligence to Moscow by radio. "The political situation in Manchuria was very interesting," she later wrote with studied nonchalance. "And Mukden was a focal point." It was also spectacularly dangerous. The authorities in Shanghai had rooted out thousands of communist rebels, but the Japanese Kempeitai, or secret military police, was in a different league: brutal, racist, and extremely efficient. This was an important mission, a mark of how high she had risen in the estimation of her spy bosses, but it was also one she might not survive. Ursula was now a captain in the Red Army, though no one informed her of the promotion, or told her she held any rank at all.

"I accepted this surprising task without hesitation," she later wrote. The major's next statement, however, pulled her up short.

"You won't be working there alone, a comrade with overall responsibility for the mission will go with you. It's important, for him, that you already know China. I would prefer to send you there as a married couple."

She was momentarily speechless.

"Don't look so shocked, Ernst is a good comrade, twenty-nine years old, and you'll get on well together."

"That's out of the question," she protested. "In Shanghai Rudi and I are well known, and people from Shanghai frequently go to Mukden. I'm officially taking home leave in Europe, so I can't suddenly turn up with a false passport as someone else's wife. It's completely unrealistic, unless I get a divorce from Rudi, and that would take time."

She was not ready for divorce. In addition, she was not sure she liked the idea of a fake marriage.

"What if we don't get on? We are going to be bound together for a long time in clandestine isolation."

The major grinned: "The work is vital. Wait until you meet him."

The following day she was briefed on the Manchurian mission by Colonel Gaik Lazarevich Tumanyan, the head of the Asian section. Tumanyan was an Armenian from Georgia "with a long, slender face, dark curly hair and dark eyes," a veteran Bolshevik who had risen up through the Red Army ranks despite his kind soul and gentle nature. "Tums" had spent several years working undercover in China and knew exactly how much he was asking of Ursula. "I soon realized that I was dealing with an intelligent person, an expert in his field, who had trust in me," she wrote.

Tumanyan greeted her with a broad smile: "The marriage idea has been abandoned," he said, "regrettable as this might be for the comrade concerned." His laughter was infectious.

The colonel explained that she should return to Shanghai to see Rudi. She had told him they would be parted for six months; she had already been away for seven. Once there, she should arrange a suitable job in Mukden as cover and then travel on to Manchuria with her new colleague. Ernst was a seaman from a working-class background, he told her, and an experienced radio technician.

Ursula had one more question. "Tell me, does he know that I have a son? Has anyone thought about the baby?"

Tumanyan smiled again: "You had better tell him about that yourself."

A few days later Ursula spotted a child's fur hat in a shop window and immediately bought it. "In Manchuria they have cold winters and this little hat could fit the boy. I imagined him wearing it over his blond hair, blue eyes and soft skin."

Later the same day, she found herself in a bare and unheated room in the Center, awaiting the comrade who would be her new partner in espionage. She wondered if it was the cold or the anxiety that made her teeth chatter.

Finally a man entered, tall and slim, with the broad shoulders of someone used to hard work. "We shook hands fleetingly. I felt my fingers, cold in his warm hand and took in his blond hair and large furrowed forehead, too big for his face, the strong, prominent cheekbones, blue-greenish eyes with sharply etched and narrow lids."

For a moment they appraised each other.

"You are shivering," he said. "Are you cold?"

"Before I could answer, he had taken off his coat and hung it around my shoulders. The coat reached almost to the floor and was very heavy, but inside I felt lighter."

Ernst's real name was Johann Patra. A thirty-four-year-old sailor from the port city of Klaipėda, he was Lithuanian by birth, German in speech and manner, and communist by adamant conviction. Highly intelligent but wholly uneducated, he spoke German, Lithuanian, Russian, and English, but struggled to read in any language. In the late 1920s, the young seaman had been talent-spotted by a Bulgarian officer in Soviet intelligence and began doing odd jobs for the Comintern, acting as a courier as he sailed between Hamburg, Riga, and other ports. In 1932, he was brought to Moscow to be trained, first in sabotage and then radio operations.

Ursula's first conversation with her new boss was exceptionally awkward. Patra spoke in monosyllables, demanding to know if she could operate an illegal transmitter. "It soon became clear that he knew more about radio operating than I did."

They were still standing up.

After another long silence he said: "That hat there you're screwing up in your hands is a bit small for you, isn't it? I don't think it would fit you at all."

"It's not for me, it's for my son."

Patra stared in surprise. "You have a son?"

"Yes. Michael is three years old and I'm taking him with me. Have you got any problems with that?"

She had already made up her mind: "I would not allow us to be split up again unless I were involved in a revolution or the armed struggle of the partisans. If he refused to accept the boy, I would not go." She had even prepared a speech: "If you think that a child would affect my independence and my ability to work, that as a mother I would be less likely to withstand the dangers, then we must talk with the boss and see if he can find you a different colleague."

She waited.

Suddenly Patra smiled for the first time.

"Why would I object to your son?" he said. "After all, the revolution needs a younger generation."

Ursula felt a flood of relief.

A week later, Ursula was ushered into the presence of General Yan Berzin himself, "clean-shaven, bright-eyed and youthful in appearance, but grey-haired, gruff and all business." Berzin told her to meet Patra in Prague, then collect her son and go south to Trieste on the Adriatic coast. He handed her a pair of tickets for an Italian liner sailing to Shanghai. When she encountered Patra on board, it must appear to be for the first time. They should pretend to have an affair, and then head to Manchuria together. "If not marriage, at least pretend you belong together," Ursula was told. "That's the best way for you to make your situation in Mukden seem believable. He'll be registered as a businessman and you will have to support him in that role."

Here was a cover story that might have come from Ursula's own pen: an unplanned meeting, an impulsive shipboard romance, and an elopement.

CHAPTER 7

ABOARD THE
CONTE VERDE

O N A CRYSTAL-COLD MARCH MORNING IN 1934, URSULA
left the Blue Star Hotel in Prague and set off to meet Johann
Patra. Beside the Vltava River, she wrote, "the bare branches of the
trees were coated in frost, misty clouds lay over the river and drifted
upwards into the blue where they became transparent, broken like a
very fragile veil." Ursula's excitement was tempered by a grinding
anxiety. The following day she would be collecting Michael from his
grandparents after a seven-month separation. Would he remember
her? Then there was Patra, her senior officer, her new partner, handsome but unreadable. "What if, with the best will in the world, we
are not suited to each other?" Ursula was not always easy to live
with, and she knew it. "Even some good people get on my nerves to
such an extent that I can't stand another hour with them, particularly humourless people, and those who are boring and thick-
skinned. On the other hand, it may be that others find I get on their
nerves." The first meeting with Patra, when he had draped his coat
around her, had contained a peculiar undercurrent, a flicker of tension. Perhaps he was doubtful about working with a woman. "He
needs to know that he's got a tough mate, who will do her share of
the work whatever happens," she reflected. But had she put him off
by being too "outspoken and hard-nosed"?

She spotted Patra sitting in the corner of the café near the market,
oddly conspicuous with his wide shoulders and shock of fair hair. He

was hunched in concentration over a newspaper, a finger tracing the words on the page.

As they rehearsed the details of the mission, Patra seemed as taciturn as before. But then, suddenly, he brightened. "Let's go to the cinema." This was not part of the plan. But he was the senior officer and, besides, she had seen posters for a French film she wanted to see, *La Maternelle,* showing at a nearby basement cinema. As they settled into their seats and the movie began to roll, Ursula realized that she had chosen the wrong sort of film. *La Maternelle* (*Children of Montmartre* in its international version) is set in an orphanage and tells the story of an abandoned child longing for a mother's love. For Ursula, emotionally fragile after the long separation from her own son, the drama was too much. Ten minutes into the first reel, she began to weep. "Tears were streaming down my face. I was powerless to stop them. I cursed myself for my own weakness. I gripped the arms of the chair tightly, but the tears poured down."

Mortified at what Patra must be thinking, she whispered: "I'm not usually like this."

He put a consoling arm across her shoulders: "I'm glad you're like this."

That evening, over supper, Johann opened up. Her eyes still swollen from crying, Ursula felt her emotions well up again as he described his own hardscrabble childhood. His father, a fisherman, had spent his wages on drink and frequently beat his wife and children. His mother, "stalwart and patient," had sacrificed happiness to bring up four children, of whom he was the eldest. "I never forgot the respect with which he spoke about his mother," she wrote. Patra recalled how his father had returned home one night, raging with drink. The fifteen-year-old boy had interposed himself to protect his mother, but he was no match for the older man, an experienced fighter. The fisherman beat his son to a pulp and threw him out of the house. Patra immediately signed on as a cabin boy on a merchant ship and never returned to Klaipėda. Over the next five years he worked first as a stoker, then a radio operator. He was introduced to communism by a shipmate. Gradually, word by painful word, he waded through the writings of Marx and Lenin. "While his mates played cards, went ashore, or relaxed between watches, he struggled with the foreign words and long complicated sentences he did not understand." For Ursula, surrounded by books and ideas, communism had come effortlessly. For Patra, it had been almost impossibly difficult. "There probably never was an easy way for Johann," she reflected. At the end of the evening, the Lithuanian sailor walked her back to the Blue Star, shook hands formally, and disappeared into the night.

The next day, as the train chugged toward Grenzbauden, Ursula's excitement and apprehension rose in tandem. "Every minute brought me nearer to my son."

Inevitably, the longed-for reunion was a disappointment. A three-year-old child understands when he has been abandoned. "A strange boy stood before me and I was strange to him too," she wrote. "My son did not even want to greet me. He ran to his grandmother and hid behind her skirts." For three days Michael refused to speak to her. When he did, he addressed her furiously in the Chinese pidgin English that was still his first language: "Me thinkee Grenzbaudenside much more nice than Shanghai-side, but me want she Mummi and Daddy by and by come too and stay plenty time topside-house which belong Grossmutti." Ursula felt a fresh stab of guilt. The boy wanted his mother and father back, here, in the hills of Czechoslovakia.

Finally she had to drag the screaming child out of the house and into a waiting car. To make matters worse, he had caught whooping cough. Every few minutes he "emitted a hacking cough, and his face turned blue." As the train rolled south to Trieste she wondered: "Will my puny sparrow die?"

The next morning they climbed up the gangplank of the SS *Conte Verde*. The great ocean liner was the pride of the Lloyd Triestino Line, accommodating 640 passengers in three classes. On their first day at sea, Ursula spotted Patra across the saloon. He was traveling as a privately wealthy businessman, with a cover job as representative of the Rheinmetall typewriter company. They avoided eye contact. The three-week voyage would take them south through the Adriatic and Mediterranean to Cairo, then via the Suez Canal to Bombay, Colombo, Singapore, and finally Shanghai. For the first few days on board, the sickly Michael was confined to their second-class cabin. In his feverish state, the little boy was "seized by sheer panic, imagining that the steamer could sink and he and his mother would drown." Ursula held him tightly, his damp little body shaking. The child remained wary, but slowly their relationship improved, along with his health. After they had read the illustrated book of children's verse for the thirtieth time, she decided cabin fever was more of a danger than whooping cough and brought him up on deck, though she carefully kept him away from any other children to prevent infection.

The *Conte Verde* was a floating palace, built in the Dalmuir shipyards in Glasgow, 180 meters long with a crew of four hundred. Four years after Ursula's voyage, the mighty ship began ferrying a different sort of passenger: between 1938 and 1940, as the Nazi persecution gathered pace, the ships of the Lloyd Triestino Line would transport seventeen thousand Jewish refugees to the safety of Shanghai.

The liner was passing through the Suez Canal when Michael dropped his ball, which bounced off down the deck. A passenger trapped it with his foot before it rolled into the water, and brought it back. Johann Patra raised his hat and introduced himself to the boy's mother as Ernst Schmidt, of the Rheinmetall typewriter company. Ursula was wearing a pretty blue sleeveless dress she had bought in Prague. They pretended to fall into conversation. That night they dined together. And the next. If the other travelers noticed that the elegant young German woman seemed to be getting on remarkably well with the rich businessman, that was hardly exceptional aboard the SS *Conte Verde*. "Affairs on board ship were as normal as they are in spa towns," Ursula wrote.

As they steamed south, the weather grew balmy. In the evenings, when Michael was asleep, they strolled the decks, deep in conversation. During the day, they splashed in the swimming pool, played cards, or lay in deck chairs.

"You are a good mother," Johann reassured Ursula.

Back in Czechoslovakia they had agreed not to discuss the mission on board, but Patra swiftly broke his own rule. Ursula had memorized the transmitting code to be used in Manchuria. "Have you remembered it?" asked Patra after breakfast one morning. She nodded, and recited the code. He asked the same question the next day. At the third time of asking, she snapped: "Stop it. You can rely on me." He shot back, in an undertone, "No. I don't know you well enough, and I am responsible for this mission."

An hour later she saw Patra and Michael happily building a bridge out of wooden blocks, and her irritation evaporated.

"In the evenings we would spend several hours on the deck under the starry sky leaning on the railing and just looking out at the sea, without saying anything or talking quietly about the very different lives we had led, but which had led us to the same world outlook." She told him about her own childhood, her three years in China, and her recruitment by Richard Sorge. He described his life at sea and his continuing struggle to understand the literature of revolution. He asked her about Rudi.

"Of course, you don't have to answer me," he added.

"He is a good man, we grew apart. Yes, he was my first lover. . . . How old was I then?"

"I didn't ask you that."

"No, no it's not a secret, I was eighteen . . . and, no, there is no one else on the horizon."

Patra had not asked her that either.

"The long voyage with its warm days and clear nights, the sun and the star-dusted sky created an irresistible atmosphere," she wrote. "When we stood leaning over the ship's rail looking down into the water, whispering or silent, I was no longer quite so sure about wanting our relationship to continue on a purely 'comradely' basis." Patra seemed to dote on her son. His rare, swift smile was breath-stopping.

Ironically, given their shared commitment to class war, they were sharply divided by class. "His tastes were garish, and his manners were not those of a businessman," Ursula observed. People traveling in first class, she pointed out crisply, did not stick half-smoked cigarettes behind their ears. "I don't care about such little things, but it's part of the cover story that you should act like a bourgeois businessman." His failure to adapt was endangering them all. Enraged, Johann stalked off, saying he would sit somewhere else so as not to "embarrass" her.

Ursula was dismayed. "How is this possible?" she reflected. "We've got enormous tasks ahead of us; we are the only communists on this ship; we know that we have to work together for a long time, and we have a dispute about something trivial like that!"

Patra was trying to read Hegel's *Science of Logic*. This is something no one should ever feel obliged to do. Ursula watched him as he waded through the dense German, his face contorted with concentration.

He appealed for help. "With your education and a professor as a father, you'll be able to understand all this without difficulty." Ursula replied that she had never read a word of Hegel and that an eight-hundred-page nineteenth-century book of German dialectical metaphysics was not her idea of deck-chair reading.

"It's much easier for you," he retorted, "but you are too lazy to put in the necessary work."

"I'm just as dedicated as you, but I don't have to prove it by ploughing through Hegel."

A little later, he proudly showed her a postcard he had bought for his mother in Lithuania, a hideously kitsch castle bathed in a pink sunset.

"It's the most expensive one the purser had," he said. "Don't you think that's beautiful?"

"No. It's gaudy," she answered truthfully, and immediately regretted it.

"I see," Patra hissed furiously, tearing up the postcard. "Well, I'm only a worker, and I don't understand these things. A barbarian with no culture . . . whereas you're an intellectual."

Now she was angry. "That's enough. I will no longer let you squeeze me into this role, I've worked as a communist too long for that, and if you continue like this, I will lose all respect for you."

Patra took a step back. "I didn't mean that," he mumbled.

They came from different worlds, the rough-edged Baltic seaman and the middle-class German Jewish woman of letters. "He seemed to be annoyed by any advantage I might have acquired in life; my education, my fluent English, my greater confidence in handling people."

That evening, after tucking Michael into his berth, she found Johann on the stern deck, gloomily smoking his pipe on a pile of rigging. She was determined to patch up the quarrel. "Spontaneously, I told him everything I admired about him: his ardour and sensitivity, his zeal, his enormous willpower and his greater experience."

"Shall I tell you what I think of you?" he replied.

He spoke fluently, as if narrating a bitter story from memory:

"Every morning she appears in a different dress, in order to show off her admittedly good figure, and every morning she smiles amiably to at least twenty people. She likes making new acquaintances, but she doesn't care that this lot here are all petty bourgeois. She sparkles with her knowledge of English and French, especially in the presence of her uneducated travel companion, who doesn't understand a word; and she takes pleasure in making him aware that he is only a prole who doesn't know how to behave. He didn't stand up when she came into the room—how embarrassing—and he spooned the sauce from his plate, and he kept his cigarette butts. When he makes such mistakes, she attacks him like a hawk. He is a communist, and has learned and learned, but not good manners. The Party has used him, the sailor, for courier services. Once, in Brazil, the police caught him. He had incriminating letters with him and managed to tear himself free. They fired at him, the shot grazed his shoulder, he escaped and hid for three days, missed his ship, was left without a penny, and all the time he forgot to ensure that he learned good manners. Now he's on this damn steamer, for the first time in bourgeois society, and knows he mustn't stand out; he is constantly watching the fine nincompoops, observing everything, what fork they shove into their mouths, how they do not eat sandwiches by hand, but cut them into small pieces and impale them on sticks. He sweats like a ship's boiler, he's so damned insecure, but what sort of understanding could an intellectual from a rich family have of that?"

No one had ever spoken to Ursula this way. She felt her anger rise. "Never before had anyone thought me stuffy, vain, pleasure-seeking or malicious." *Take a few deep breaths,* she told herself. Then she replied.

"May I answer your charges one by one? I don't think you have to wait until we have a classless society to be friendly with individuals from other classes. Being happy is the flip side of being friendly. And it does not mean superficiality. If I am depressed, I try to be alone so as not to influence others with my bad mood. You're right, I like getting to know people. People interest me greatly. They are whimsical, funny, sad, bad, admirable, everyone has their own fate, through society and through themselves. And now the ridiculous dress question: I have four of them. Of course I enjoy putting them on. Don't you feel how pleasurable it is coming out of a cold March to discard the old winter clothes and suddenly to be in a southern summer, to run around sleeveless and without stockings, to lie in the sun, to swim in the pool? I thought you were enjoying all this too. These are our pleasant hours. So, those are the little things, your other accusations are much more serious—"

Patra interrupted: "Before you go on talking, those are pleasant hours for me too." Then he walked away.

The next day the ship docked at Colombo. The three of them went ashore, the little boy screeching in delight at the sight of the monkeys in the trees. They sat in a hillside café, overlooking the sea, Michael on Patra's lap.

That evening at sundown, as the liner steamed out of port, they leaned on the rail again, side by side. "Our arms touched, as one's arm might brush a neighbour on a crowded train. I moved my arm a bit further away."

"You don't have to be afraid," said Patra.

"Don't I?"

A pause.

"It's late, I have to check on Misha."

"Are you coming back again?"

"It's late."

"I'll wait here."

When she returned, Patra was gazing out across the ocean. He did not hear her approach.

She thought: *Go and stroke back the hair that is blowing in his face.*

Instead, she quietly stood alongside him.

"Much of this is my fault," she said, "but I don't know how long I can endure it if you insult me like that."

"Would you leave if you could?" he asked.

"Why think about something that is impossible?"

"I wouldn't leave you."

Patra fell silent, staring down at the stern wake. But then "he looked up, gazed out over the water, looked at me and stroked the hair from my face."

A point had been passed.

But still she held back. She had loved and lost one fellow spy already. "I resisted succumbing to the atmosphere of an ocean voyage with romantic evenings and constant togetherness." They would soon be working together. He was her senior officer. In many ways, they were incompatible. She told herself: "Rather let there be no beginning than a tortuous path with no end, because the work will keep us chained together." She was powerfully drawn to him, the heady combination of physical desire, forbidden love, and the promise of adventure.

Patra was pressing but patient. "I know there is something serious between us, and if you don't see it that way yet, I can wait."

The two spies were sailing to China to fight an underground war in which both might well perish. The other passengers on the *Conte Verde* saw only a happy young couple, falling in love.

CHAPTER 8

OUR WOMAN IN MANCHURIA

RUDOLF HAMBURGER WAS WAITING ON THE DOCKSIDE WHEN the Italian liner steamed into Shanghai. The months without Ursula and Michael had been painfully lonely. Rudi had buried himself in his architectural work and the furniture business, fearful they might never return. And now here they were: his fair-haired son clutching a ball; his wife, lovely in a sleeveless white dress, even more beautiful for the weight she had gained in Russia. He took them back to Avenue Joffre, his "great happiness" overflowing. The family was reunited. Patra withdrew quietly to a hotel.

Rudi's happiness lasted just a few hours.

"It was not easy to tell him that we were only coming for a visit," Ursula later wrote. She and Michael would soon be heading north to Manchuria, she explained, as gently as she could, and they would not be traveling alone.

A different sort of man might have launched into recriminations and remonstrations, demanding that she leave Michael with him, flinging around crockery, threats, or lawsuits. Rudi absorbed the grim announcement without a scene. "He was very depressed but, as always, calm." But he flatly refused to accept that this separation might be permanent; he would not give up his son, or his wife. In his own way, Rudi was as obstinate as she was. "Rudi possessed a special kind of persistence which nobody would suspect beneath his gentle exterior," she wrote. "He did not reproach me in any way or make any difficulties; he even accepted that I might not be living alone in Mukden."

There was another factor in Rudi's stoicism. He knew Ursula would be carrying out "secret party work" in Manchuria. Before, he had resented and resisted her espionage, but now he wholeheartedly endorsed it. He was a communist, he declared, propelled to action by the force of history. Their families were in exile, on the run, or facing mounting persecution. His homeland was in the grip of fascism. Refugees were streaming into Shanghai, and the club had become a nest of Nazis where he, a Jew, was now unwelcome. Ursula observed the change in Rudi with wonder: "He was no longer just a sympathizer holding back from commitment, but a communist who was ready to work with us." She felt a surge of admiration for the remarkable man she had married. But it did not make her love him again.

Three days after her return, Ursula caught a rickshaw to a small restaurant on the city outskirts where Patra was waiting with a senior CCP official. The unnamed Chinese "comrade" explained that the invasion of Manchuria had brought Japanese forces to the border with Russia, threatening the Soviet Union itself. "Your task is therefore doubly important," he said. Communist partisans in the mountains were waging a ferocious guerrilla campaign against the Japanese occupiers: "Manchuria is in a state of semi-war." Ursula and Johann would be the resisters' point of contact with Moscow. They must purchase parts for a radio transmitter-receiver, travel by train to Mukden, and establish an operations base in the city. As the main Soviet intelligence outpost in Manchuria, they would be responsible for furnishing the rebels with money, weapons, and explosives, sheltering fugitives, identifying individual partisans for training back in Moscow, recruiting and training local radio operators, and passing messages and intelligence back and forth between the Center and the guerrilla leadership. The comrade described how to make contact with the partisans. As expatriate Europeans, they could move around more freely than Chinese, but the Japanese would keep them under close surveillance since "anyone who enters Manchuria from China may be part of the anti-Japanese movement and thus a potential enemy." Finally, he described the risks. "The Japanese couldn't simply make foreigners 'disappear' as they did with the Chinese," but if they were caught by the Kempeitai, they would be tortured and then killed.

Johann Patra went shopping for valves, rectifiers, and wiring. The homemade radio would need to be powered by two large iron transformers, weighing five pounds each. Since these were impossible to conceal in their luggage, they would have to be purchased on arrival in Mukden.

Ursula needed a cover job, something literary. She visited Evans & Co., an American bookshop in Shanghai, explained that she was moving to Mukden, and offered herself as the shop's Manchurian representative. She would purchase a stock of books at wholesale prices, sell them at retail price to English readers, and keep any profit. Evans & Co. agreed, happily providing her with a formal letter of appointment and a set of printed business cards. Ursula was now chief executive and sole representative of the "Manchukuo Book Agency," specializing in educational, medical, and scientific books. And espionage.

In mid-May 1934, shortly before they were due to depart for Mukden, Ursula left Michael in Rudi's care, explaining she would return in two days' time. She did not tell him where she was going. That afternoon, she and Johann caught the train to the ancient city of Hangchow (now Hangzhou), two hours to the southwest, and checked into a charming little two-story hotel, surrounding a pretty courtyard garden.

"It was a dreamy day," Ursula wrote. "Hand in hand we walked through the old alleys, teeming with vendors and crowds of people." They stopped to watch a porcelain mender skillfully piecing together broken rice bowls. The old man carried an ingenious audible advertising device, a bamboo pole with a gong and two chains that emitted a tinkling chime as he walked along. In the garden of a Buddhist temple, they sat on a bench beside a small lake. "We talked about Confucius, the Chinese Red Army, the lotus leaves on the ponds, the passersby, Misha, and the trip to Mukden. We did not speak of the night ahead."

Back at the hotel, Johann went to fetch green tea. The sound of the mah-jongg players rose from the courtyard, the bone tiles click-ing like muffled castanets. Cool air wafted through the paper win-dow blinds, ruffling a mosquito net on the wide four-poster bed. Ursula was suddenly chilly. She put on Johann's jacket, remembering the moment, a few months earlier, when he had wrapped his coat around her as her teeth chattered with cold and anticipation.

She put her hand in the jacket pocket and drew out a photograph.

Johann, with his arm around the hip of a Chinese prostitute. A photo with the date, taken five days earlier in Shanghai.

She was still staring at the picture when Johann entered with a tea tray.

Seeing the photo in her hand, Patra broke into a guilty mono-logue, "the usual trivial thousand words of thousands of men," self-justifying, urgent, and meaningless.

"It was just a souvenir, it meant nothing at all, a purely physical matter, long forgotten, it was your fault, you shouldn't have . . . and I wouldn't have . . . and it has nothing at all to do with my feelings for you . . . never again will I . . . Yell at me, hit me . . . you can't make such a little thing into . . ."

On and on.

She said nothing.

Later, they climbed into the big bed. "I only had to say 'leave me alone' once," she wrote.

Patra quickly fell asleep. Ursula lay awake, listening to the mur-mur of Chinese voices and the cold clatter of the mah-jongg tiles.

ON THE LONG TRAIN JOURNEY to Mukden little Michael sat be-tween Ursula and Johann, chattering away as the soybean fields and tiny villages slid past. The radio valves were hidden inside rolled-up socks at the bottom of the suitcase. Johann reached for her hand. "We can't let that stupid matter in Shanghai spoil everything. It doesn't matter. . . . Come on, be cheerful, like you used to be."

Ursula said nothing. "It seemed pointless to accuse him of being a completely different person from me, and of being unable to un-derstand how deeply he had hurt me."

At the border, Japanese guards emptied every suitcase and piled their contents onto the platform. Johann had already stuffed the valves between the compartment seat cushions.

The ancient walled city of Mukden was like a smaller, less glamorous version of Shanghai, a teeming warren of narrow streets and low brick houses, interspersed with grand municipal buildings. A vast shanty town sprawled out from the fortified walls. The foreigners lived in their own enclave. Here the expatriate population was more beleaguered, and the profits were fewer since foreigners had to compete with the incoming Japanese. A peculiar international flotsam had washed up in Mukden: adventurers, crooks, nomads trying to escape the past or looking for a different future. One more unhappy wife running away with her lover excited little curiosity. The city was awash with opium dealers, criminals, and prostitutes. There would be "plenty of opportunities for Johann to enlarge his photo collection," Ursula reflected bitterly.

At the Yamato Hotel, they unpacked and deliberately left out their printed business cards for Rheinmetall and Evans & Co., for the spies to find. That afternoon, Johann set out to find a hiding place for the radio parts. Ursula left one suitcase full and laid a small thread across the clasp. When they returned from dinner, the thread was gone. The snoopers had made an inspection. "In the hotel we didn't exchange a single word of importance." Every waiter was listening.

It had been agreed that liaising with the partisans, the most dangerous task ahead, would fall to Ursula. General Berzin was emphatic: Patra "should not be exposed to the greatest risk." Of the two-person team, she was the junior officer, and the more expendable. Initial contact was due to take place not in Mukden but in the city of Harbin, four hundred miles to the north. Johann suddenly announced that he would be going instead of her. Why, she demanded, was he changing the agreed strategy?

"Well, you are a woman and a mother, maybe it's too much for you."

"We knew that beforehand," she replied tartly. "I'll take Misha with me."

"You want to put the small child through that long journey and then leave him alone in a hotel for hours? It's out of the question. If you go, Misha will stay with me."

Johann rehearsed the child's daily routine: mealtimes, clothing, how much cod liver oil to spoon into him. "You can relax as far as Misha is concerned," he said. "Come back in one piece."

Ursula hated Harbin, the largest city in Manchuria and home to thousands of White Russians who had fled the revolution. These were the deserving victims of historical forces, of course, but the ragged exiles made a pitiful sight, reduced to penury, crime, pulling rickshaws, and prostitution. "Many stood at corners, begging," wrote Ursula. "Of all the cities I have known, Harbin in those days was the most sinister."

Ursula's instructions were to meet a partisan contact identified as "Li," at a cemetery on the outskirts of the city, an hour after sunset. She had always feared the darkness. "It was a burden for me, because in our work many things took place during the night hours." Two drunks passed, swaying and singing. A man sidled up and stared. She waited for the identifying code word, but his expression suggested he was not there for espionage. She ran and hid behind a gravestone. She waited an hour beyond the appointed time and then she returned to the welcome brightness of the hotel. She went back to the cemetery the next night, as instructed, but there was still no sign of the partisan. "Why hadn't he come? Had he been arrested?" Disconsolate, she caught the train back to Mukden.

At the Yamato Hotel, Johann was so engrossed with feeding the boy supper he did not notice Ursula entering the dining room. "He had put Misha onto a chair seat raised by a pillow, and tied a napkin around him, very carefully, so that his neck hair did not get caught in the knot. He tasted the soup, to make sure it wasn't too hot, and put the spoon up to Misha's mouth. He wiped some liquid off the boy's chin, completely absorbed in his work."

She felt an upwelling of love.

Only when she was standing behind him did Johann turn his head.

"I am so relieved," he said quietly.

"Oh, Johann, what am I going to do with you?" She put her arms around his neck. "He held me tight for a long time."

But later, when she told him of the failed rendezvous, Johann's temper flashed again. "You have a wonderful talent for messing up your opportunities," he snapped. The same was true of him. They slept apart again that night.

A backup meeting with Li was scheduled for a week later. This time Johann insisted on going to Harbin himself. To her own annoyance, Ursula felt her anxiety rise as the hour for his return approached, then passed. "Strange how quickly you get used to a person," she reflected. She paced the room, unable to read. "Had he been arrested? Had they tortured Li until he couldn't take any more and told them the location of the meeting?"

At midnight, Johann finally slipped into the room, looking drained. Li had not turned up.

He climbed into bed beside her. Relief brought a surge of passion that she no longer tried to resist.

"Everything else was good that night," she wrote.

An alternative rendezvous was in the city of Fushun, thirty miles east, to be used in case the first failed. Ursula packed up her book supplies, sold a grand total of five books in Fushan, but returned elated. The partisan contact had appeared exactly on time, "a tall, quiet northern Chinese with economical gestures" who explained, using simple Chinese, fragments of pidgin English, and pencil sketches, that he was the leader of an underground communist unit consisting of workers, farmers, teachers, students, and street traders. "Right, right, very good," he said, repeatedly. Li, he explained, had "taken fright." The man gave his name as "Chu" and explained that he urgently needed explosives for a planned attack on the South Manchurian railway line.

"Our work can finally begin," Ursula reflected back at the hotel, as she sewed the notes from the meeting into the hem of her petticoat.

Two major hurdles remained: they needed transformers to power the transmitter-receiver, and a safe place from which to transmit. The Japanese were on the lookout for illegal wireless transmissions. Erecting an aerial on top of the hotel would have been dangerous, and probably impossible. Ursula set off to find a permanent base that could serve as a transmitting station.

Patra, meanwhile, scoured every radio shop in Mukden without finding usable transformers. Reluctantly, he boarded the train back

Robert René Kuczynski, Ursula's father: statistician, bibliophile, and refugee.

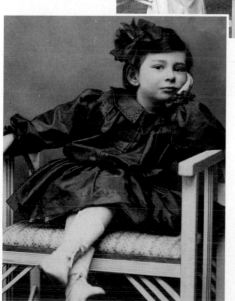

Olga Muth, the family nanny known as "Ollo" (left), with Brigitte, Jürgen, and Ursula Kuczynski, and their mother, Berta (second from right)

Ursula Maria Kuczynski, age four, in 1910.

The family home on Schlachtensee lake in the exclusive Berlin suburb of Zehlendorf.

Ursula as a teenager, reading a book in a tree on the Schlachtensee estate.

The six Kuczynski siblings (from right to left): Jürgen, Ursula, Brigitte, Barbara, Sabine, and Renate.

Members of the German Young Communist League marching in the May Day parade, Berlin 1925.

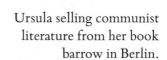

Ursula selling communist literature from her book barrow in Berlin.

Rudolf Hamburger, the ambitious young architecture student, at around the time he met Ursula.

Chinese communists executed during the "White Terror" in Shanghai, 1927.

A photograph taken by Ursula as she docked in Shanghai harbor: "Encircling the ship in floating tubs were beggars . . ."

Agnes Smedley: American radical, revolutionary, novelist, and spy.

"Portrait of a Pirate": a photograph taken by the Polish photographer and spy Hirsch Herzberg, alias "Grisha."

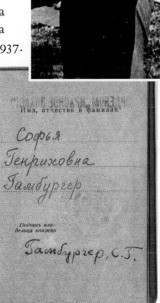

Playing "see-saw" with a fellow communist spy, probably Richard Sorge, during an excursion to the country outside Shanghai.

Certificate for the Order of the Red Banner, presented to Ursula in the name "Sophia Genrikovna Gamburger" at the Kremlin in 1937.

Имя, отчество и фамилия

Софья
Генриховна
Гамбургер

Подпись владельца книжки

Гамбургер, С.Г.

Richard Sorge, Ursula's recruiter and lover, who was described by Ian Fleming as "the most formidable spy in history."

Ursula with the Chinese academic and communist undercover agent Chen Hansheng and his wife.

Rudi and Ursula, sleeping after a picnic in the country-side, just before her departure for Moscow: the poignant last moments of a marriage.

Michael Hamburger talking to a canary on board the Norwegian freighter bound for Vladivostok in May 1933.

Ursula sunbathing on the deck of the SS *Conte Verde*.

The house in Mukden. The bamboo poles holding up the aerial for her transmitter can be seen at either end of the roof.

Ursula's homemade Morse code tapper, constructed from a metal ruler, a cotton reel, a strip of wood, and a length of copper wire.

Johann Patra, Ursula's lover and fellow spy in Japanese-occupied Manchuria.

A traditional Chinese porcelain mender. As a love token, Ursula gave Johann a gong, similar to the one hanging from the bamboo pole, visible at the left of the picture.

Mao Zedong, General Zhu De, and Agnes Smedley, Yunan Red Army base, 1937.

to Shanghai: he would have to buy them in the city and then work out how to smuggle the bulky metal objects back across the border. Ursula told him to consult Rudi, insisting that, despite the strangeness of the situation, her husband was completely trustworthy.

Japanese officials had requisitioned most of the available property in Mukden, but a few large houses had been abandoned by fleeing Chinese generals. One of these, a luxury villa behind high walls that had once belonged to a relative of the Manchurian warlord General Zhang Xueliang, stood next door to Mukden's German Club. Ursula took one look at the place and decided it was ostentatious, bleak, and way beyond their budget, but tucked in the corner of the grounds she spotted a smaller stone building. The servant explained, with a snigger, that this had been purpose-built for the owner's mistress. A tunnel led to it from the garden of the main house, providing the amorous general with swift and secret access to his concubine. The little building lacked running water and had only a wood-burning stove for heat, but otherwise it was ideal, with three small wood-paneled rooms on the raised first floor, a basement kitchen, an enormous bed for the general and his mistress, and a built-in escape tunnel. No one could see into the rooms from the outside, and proximity to the German Club was oddly satisfying: she would be fighting fascism next door to a building flying the swastika. For the first time in over a year, Ursula had a home, a nest: "It was a pleasure to roll out a straw mat, hang up a picture, buy a vase."

In Shanghai, Johann bought two heavy transformers eight inches long: the Japanese border guards would have to be blind to miss them. Rudi came up with a solution. They bought a heavy wing-backed chair with thick upholstery, "an ugly green-brown monster," and had it delivered to Avenue Joffre. Johann and Rudi turned the chair on its back, pulled out the tacks holding the sacking in place, and tied the two transformers to the internal springs with wire and cord. Then they pushed in the padding and tacked back the sacking. "Nothing was visible, and the extra weight in the armchair was imperceptible." The chair was then sent to Mukden as rail freight. Rudi was probably still unaware of the blossoming relationship between his wife and her superior officer; and if he knew, he was too civilized to make a fuss. Ursula's husband and her lover had completed their first joint mission, combining the spycraft of one with the soft-furnishings expertise of the other.

Back in Mukden, Ursula showed Johann around the new house.

"Perhaps our bedroom should be here in front," he said. "Then Misha next door, and the third could be our living room with the transmitter . . . why are you looking at me like that?"

She frowned. "I didn't know you thought we were moving in together."

"I took that for granted now that everything is clear and good between us. Everybody knows you're with me."

Ursula was adamant. Cohabitation was not in the cards.

"I will rejoice at every minute you are with me, and that will be most of the time, day and night."

"Then why not the whole time?"

"Because I have a different rhythm of life, and you demand that I should be completely incorporated into yours. Sometimes I need to be alone."

Ursula was falling in love with Johann: for his protective tenderness, his love of Misha, and his revolutionary zeal. But he was also irascible and domineering, an old-fashioned chauvinist who "granted men more opportunities than women" and found her independence an affront to his dignity.

In a towering huff, Johann moved into the spare room of a German businessman. But Ursula was sure her insistence on maintaining a separate home was right; like many touchy, assertive men, Patra's ego needed managing and massaging. "Gradually I overcame the offence. I showed him my love without reservation and I amazed myself by how tame, compliant and patient I became in all matters of work. But without the hours I had to myself I probably could not have managed it."

The ugly green chair duly arrived at Mukden station. When Ursula and Johann carried it into the house and turned it upside down, they saw "with horror" that one of the transformers was hanging halfway out: the jolting journey had snapped the wire, and the sharp edge had worn through the sacking. A single frayed cord held it in place. "A few more movements and the transformer would have fallen out, and even the most incompetent Japanese railway employee would have spotted it."

Johann set to work assembling the radio, a Hartley transmitter-receiver with a three-point system. He was a skilled technician, with nimble fingers, infinite patience, and phenomenal powers of concentration. "He never looked at his watch, and never took a break." Finally the set was assembled: a cumbersome, homemade monster of a machine with heavy rectifier and transformers, large valves, and coils shaped by winding thick copper wire around an empty beer bottle. The radio parts were hidden in the bottom of an old camphorwood clothes trunk, concealed under a false internal shelf built by Johann, with folded blankets laid over the top. The hiding place would not evade an intensive search, but it would keep the equipment from the prying eyes of the servants. She placed a feather under the lid. If it was opened, she would know. The final task was to erect a Fuchs aerial over the roof: to a casual observer this might "look no different from a reception antenna" for an ordinary radio, but if they were spotted putting it up, this would attract unwanted attention. It would have to be done at night. She told Johann to leave it to her.

Ursula waited until Michael was sound asleep. Then she climbed onto the roof, through a hatch in the attic, with two long bamboo poles, pliers, a rope, and a roll of antennae wire in a knapsack. She tied the first pole to one chimney, with the wire running through a hole in the top, as if through a bamboo needle. Then she shuffled along the apex of the roof with the other bamboo, similarly threaded, with the wire passing between, lashed that to the opposite chimney and looped the end securely around the base. "Treetops and roofs were visible in faint contours." Momentarily unbalanced, she "leaned against the chimney, which seemed comforting in its thickness." But then she made the mistake of "looking down into the endless obscure darkness." Suddenly she was terrified. "Coward," she told herself. "Scaredy-cat. There's no reason to fall at all, except in your imagination."

Then Michael began to scream. "Usually the boy slept deeply. Now he screamed without pause."

She shuffled fast back along the roof, flung the rucksack through the hatch, and dived in after it. The child's cries would surely wake the neighbors. Michael was sitting up in bed, sobbing. "I have fizzy water in my fingers," he wailed. The boy had pins and needles from sleeping on his arm: "Another argument against professional revolutionaries having children," she reflected ruefully and let out an involuntary giggle. She rubbed Michael's little hand and stroked the child's head until his breathing grew regular again.

Then she climbed back onto the roof.

The next night, the radio was ready for testing. By prearrangement, they would transmit only at night, at different times and on one of only two agreed wavelengths, to the Red Army receiving station in Vladivostok, code-named "Wiesbaden." Ursula sat at the desk, Johann linked up the batteries, and she tapped out a short coded message with nervous fingers. A few moments later, the acknowledgment came through, a faint patter of Morse code from distant Russia, a signal from the Center. "We smiled happily at each other."

The Red Army was not alone in listening out for Ursula's messages. Day and night, Japanese surveillance planes throbbed back and forth overhead, scouring the airwaves: if two of these picked up the signal simultaneously, they could pinpoint the location of the wireless. And if that happened, the Japanese secret police would pounce, and, quite soon, Ursula would be dead.

CHAPTER 9

VAGABOND LIFE

A NAZI MOVED IN NEXT DOOR.
Ursula had been living in the cottage less than a month when a new tenant took up residence in the main house on the estate. As a neighbor, Hans von Schlewitz was alarming in every respect: a German aristocrat, an arms-dealer, and a Nazi with senior contacts in the Japanese administration. He was also fat and drunk. Ursula was ready to loathe him on sight, and to quit the property at the first sign of danger.

Von Schlewitz turned out to be charming, gentle, and ironic, living proof that political and class enemies can be rather funny and very useful. An old-fashioned monarchist of ancient bloodline, von Schlewitz regarded Hitler as an oik and hated the Nazi Party, which he had joined strictly out of commercial expediency. He was potbellied, bald, convivial, canny, and very amusing, "a great story teller and full of wit." He walked with a limp, the legacy of shrapnel picked up at Verdun. "Thirty pieces of steel are in there," he liked to say, slapping his enormous thigh. He worked closely with the Japanese military in Manchuria and was exceptionally talkative, especially when plastered, which was often. "If you meet me somewhere and find I have had too much to drink," he told her, "do me a favour and take me home."

Von Schlewitz and Ursula became instant friends. "I so much prefer conversing with you than with the German philistines here," he said. He missed his own family back in Germany and took a shine to little Misha, encouraging him to slalom on his tricycle around the chairs in his vast dining room. He flirted extravagantly, more out of chivalry than intent, with the intelligent Jewish woman who lived in the garden cottage, and she flirted back.

Johann Patra, the Aryan typewriter salesman, was still welcomed by the other expatriate Germans, but there were unpleasant rumblings about his "Semitic girlfriend." Ursula forced herself to accompany him or von Schlewitz to the club and put up with the snide asides. The Japanese would be less suspicious of someone who consorted with Nazis. When von Schlewitz heard that Ursula had been subjected to racist remarks, he puffed up like a cockerel. "If any German here touches so much as a hair on your head, tell me immediately." So far from posing a threat, the new neighbor was a blessing in heavy disguise: if the Japanese came for her, they would have to go through von Schlewitz.

The attentions of the older man sparked Johann into a fit of jealousy.

"How old is this fascist?"

"In his mid-fifties, I think."

"He seems to impress you a lot."

She told him not to be ridiculous, pointing out that von Schlewitz was old enough to be her father. "He would never try anything on with me."

"You like to talk to that Nazi alcoholic, giggle over his compliments. If he knew what you were doing, he would shoot you. You should poison him instead of being nice to him."

"Johann, don't be so simple. We are not here to poison any Nazis. We have to get along with our fellow Germans. You do too, as part of our cover story."

In truth, Ursula thoroughly enjoyed her flirtation with von Schlewitz, who was excellent company, good cover, and a handy source of military information. She was not the first spy to use sexual chemistry as a tool of espionage.

Ursula's existence in Mukden was a bizarre mixture of danger and domesticity: a home life with Johann and Michael, a social life hobnobbing with fascists, and a third, hidden life as a Red Army officer coordinating communist paramilitary operations. "Every meeting with the partisans involved risk," she later wrote. "If our support for the partisans was discovered, we could expect the death penalty. How did we live with the dangers? Relatively calmly. If you are constantly in danger, there are only two possibilities: get used to it, or go crazy. We got used to it."

Ursula went shopping for bombs for Chu. The sabotage instructors at Sparrow had taught her how to mix explosives from ordinary household products, including ammonium nitrate, sulfur, hydrochloric acid, sugar, aluminum, and permanganate. These ingredients could all be sourced in Mukden but buying them together, or in bulk, would attract attention. At a downtown hardware shop, she asked for ten pounds of ammonium nitrate, the white crystal used as garden fertilizer, which forms an explosive when mixed with aluminum powder or fuel oil. Misunderstanding her Chinese pronunciation, the shopkeeper returned with a hundredweight sack. She wheeled away her bonanza in the baby carriage, Michael perched atop the makings for a hundred-pound bomb. Johann constructed timers and fuses. Chu came to the house to pick up the explosives. "Right, right, very good." He beamed.

The communist sabotage campaign intensified, with attacks on guard posts, Japanese-run factories, military convoys, and above all the railway system so vital to the Manchurian economy. Prearranged signals indicated whether an operation had been successful. "Only when I see the forked incision on the fourth tree on the right hand side of the first crossroad on White Moon Street, do I feel the burden taken off my shoulders," wrote Ursula. The Japanese-controlled press reported few details, but the repeated denunciations of "terrorists" and the savagery of Japanese countermeasures showed how effectively the underground war was being waged. "Last month anti-Japanese groups carried out 650 attacks in the Mukden province alone," she wrote to her family in July 1934.

Ursula did not reveal her own role in those attacks. She did not, in fact, tell her parents very much at all. They knew only that their intrepid and wayward eldest daughter had left her husband in Shanghai and was working as an itinerant bookseller in northern China. "I am busy from morn till night," she said, truthfully, before adding, a little less honestly: "On no account must you worry about me. There is absolutely no need to. I live exactly the life I want to live and am very satisfied. Don't worry, somewhere along the line this vagabond life must cease." She did not say that it might well end in a Japanese execution cell. She signed herself "your erring but contented daughter." She made no mention of Johann Patra.

Robert and Berta Kuczynski were now virtual vagabonds themselves.

Many Jews were slow to appreciate the virulence of Nazi anti-Semitism. But attacks on Jews and Jewish property in Berlin were escalating. Jews would soon be excluded from military service, Jewish actors banned from the stage, and Jewish students prevented from taking exams in medicine, pharmacy, and the law. The concentration camp system expanded rapidly. Elisabeth Naef, Agnes Smedley's brilliant Jewish psychoanalyst, wrote a brief note—"*Ich kann nicht mehr*" ("I have had enough")—and committed suicide. From Britain, Robert wrote to his sister Alice, urging her and her husband, Georg Dorpalen, to get out of Germany with their four children. Uncle Georg flatly refused, pointing out that he was a decorated war hero and a celebrated Jewish doctor. He would "remain in his homeland, which he loved."

In 1934, Berta finally sold the house on Schlachtensee at a much-reduced price, packed up the family's belongings, and fled to England with her younger daughters, Barbara, Sabine, and Renate. There they were reunited with Robert, who had obtained a post at the London School of Economics, researching colonial demography. A little later, Brigitte joined them. Olga Muth, the family nanny, was offered the choice of whether to stay or go. As an Aryan, she faced no threat in Germany and could find another job in Berlin. Moreover she spoke almost no English, and the Kuczynskis' prospects in Britain were at best uncertain. "But she chose to stay with the family" and duly squeezed into a small rented flat in North London with the rest of them. The Kuczynskis were now refugees.

Of Ursula's immediate family, only Jürgen remained in Berlin, dodging from one hiding place to another, writing unstoppably, the long-winded mouthpiece for an increasingly desperate Communist Party.

Ursula's radio traffic to Vladivostok included reports on sabotage, partisan morale, Japanese counterinsurgency measures, and military and political intelligence gleaned from fellow expatriates, including von Schlewitz. She was transmitting and receiving messages at least twice a week, taking down "the fastest incoming signals without making any mistakes." But it was frustrating, time-consuming work. The transmitter-receiver was weak. Frequently the Vladivostok signal was jammed, or unintelligible. The fragmented messages had to be repeated, time after time. She often sat down to begin the deciphering process at 3:00 A.M., working by a dim light behind shuttered windows, knowing that Michael would wake in a few hours. She dared not light the stove in case the smoke drew attention to her nocturnal activities. "I sat at the Morse key in my tracksuit, wrapped in blankets, with fingerless gloves on my hands. Aeroplanes circled over the house. One day they were bound to catch me. . . . I wanted so much to climb into my warm bed." Every transmission was a bout of Russian roulette.

But when the radio was working well, and the regulation five hundred letters of text, divided into batches of five, lined up like ranks of soldiers marching into battle, she felt a strange, secret elation. "My house with its closed shutters was like a fortress. Misha was fast asleep in the next room. The town slept. Only I was awake, sending news of the partisans into the ether—and in Vladivostok, a Red Army man was sitting and listening."

They needed a backup team. Chu agreed to provide someone to be trained in radio operations. A young Chinese couple duly appeared, bringing greetings from the partisan leader and a ready-made cover story: Wang would teach Ursula Mandarin, while his wife, Shushin, a skilled seamstress, would mend and make her clothes, and help with the housework and childcare. Wang was polite but ponderous, whereas Shushin possessed a hunger for knowledge, a decent command of English, and a visceral loathing for the Japanese. Despite her childlike looks, she had two children of her own, aged four and two, who were living with her parents. "Wang resembled Johann in his serious, thorough manner, and the amused, laughing Shushin was similar to me." The women struck up an immediate bond. "She was so delightful; when she practised Morse code, her fingers danced on the keypad." After each radio lesson, they would drink tea, complain about their menfolk, discuss politics, and tell the stories of their very different lives. Shushin made Ursula a wide summer coat with a concealed pocket in the lining, the size of two radio valves. One evening the conversation took a dark turn: What would it be like to be captured by the Japanese? Are men or women better able to withstand imprisonment and torture?

"Do you think that the extra worry of leaving children behind would wear a mother down?" Shushin wondered.

Ursula was still pondering the question, when Shushin volunteered her own answer: "I don't think whether or not you will be able to bear it depends on the amount of suffering. Perhaps it's the children who make us strong."

Michael was almost four years old, picking up Chinese from his playmates and expanding his vocabulary in three languages. Ursula delighted in his "intelligent, pensive questions" and his insatiable curiosity. "I would love to have four children like him," she wrote. Patra had started collecting traditional Chinese musical instruments, and took Michael with him on shopping expeditions. Ursula seldom accompanied them. "Both would have found me an intrusion." She loved to see this uncomplicated relationship developing, for Johann was an instinctive parent. She wondered if they might one day have children of their own.

Moscow did not know the partnership between the Mukden spies had become more than just professional, and she was happy to keep it that way. "We worked well together," she wrote. "He was more complicated than me, with his reserve, occasional anger, intolerance and nervousness, and I had, in the meantime, learned not to irritate him, to give in to him in almost everything." In espionage, she trusted him completely; in love, less so. A young Russian woman rented the room next door to Johann, "a slender, pretty doll, a pink bow in her yellow hair." Ursula was immediately suspicious. "Ludmilla is soon going home to her parents in Harbin," Johann reported, a shade too airily. She resented her own jealousy, but reflected: "I need to know where I am with this Casanova." Johann was irascible, demanding, and quite possibly unfaithful; yet he was also tender and, despite his insecurities, strong. He was a considerate lover. And he knew how to build an excellent bomb.

"We loved each other, lived in danger together, we were comrades, I loved that he muttered in his dreams, that he was proud of me when I looked good, worried when I stayed away too long, that we argued and then became reconciled, and longed for each other when the journeys separated us." She could talk to Johann about politics, revolution, and the funny remarks made by the little boy they almost shared. "We talked about what Germany would be like when the Nazi era was over, and what communist Germany would be like." Johann was disheartened that so many working-class Germans had supported Hitler as he tightened his grip on power and turned on the Jews. "I have lost confidence in my own class," he said. They agreed to celebrate when they sent the one hundredth radio transmission.

After a rendezvous with Chu in the city of Anshan, a two-hour train ride to the south, she went to the local market and spotted a porcelain mender like the one they had seen in Hangchow, "an elderly fellow with a thin white beard." She noticed that his hands were trembling as he reassembled a broken bowl. They fell into a halting conversation, and she asked about the little porcelain gong he carried on a pole. The old man picked up the object. "I'm working today for the last time," he said. "I have sons, grandchildren, great-grandchildren, and now in three days' time, I will lie down to die." Ursula was momentarily speechless. The old man pressed the porcelain gong into her hand. "Take it," he said. "You will live long."

That evening, back in Mukden, she told Johann the story of the porcelain mender repairing his last bowl, and handed him the little gong for his collection: a love token, promising longevity.

In January 1935, Rudi came to visit, bringing presents for Michael and spare parts for the radio. Ursula informed Moscow: "Rudi is now a convinced communist and does not want to stay politically inactive any longer." He returned a few months later, bringing bomb-making ingredients. Rudi spent hours playing with his son in the garden. Michael had grown close to Patra, but his father's sudden, unexpected, unexplained appearances were moments of the purest joy. Years later, in what he called "phantom mosaic fragments," he recalled his childish memories: being swung around by his father in the garden, the texture of Rudi's tweed jacket on his cheek, his mother reading aloud until he fell asleep: "The happy child of a happy German family in China."

Rudi did not inquire about Ursula's relationship with Johann, or demand to know when they were coming back to Shanghai. He exerted no pressure. But he had not given up on his family. Hamburger was a strange combination, a traditional-minded radical, a gentlemanly revolutionary. One friend later described him as "the last Victorian Communist." To keep up appearances, and for the sake of his son, he was prepared to play happy families, still hoping his own might be truly happy again one day.

Early in 1935, Moscow ordered Patra to construct a wireless for Shushin and Wang. Ursula took the train to Tianjin with Michael and bought more radio valves, which she smuggled back across the border sewn inside her son's teddy bear. A few weeks later, Shushin and Wang departed, taking with them the second radio set assembled by Johann. She did not know, and did not ask, where they were going. "I found the farewell to Shushin, my only friend, very difficult."

The Mukden mission was a time of happiness and fear, elation and exhaustion, love, jealousy, and occasional horror. After a meeting in the mountains with Chu, she was walking back to a nearby village, through a landscape "unspoiled and beautiful," when she spotted a baby's body lying on the path: the second dead child she had seen in as many years, and another shocking reminder of the threat to her own. Famine was driving starving peasants with large families to abandon children, usually girls. "Her body was still warm," wrote Ursula. "What sort of world was it in which a parent must sacrifice one child to save another?" Whenever her spirit quailed, she recalled Chu's simple gratitude. The young Chinese guerrilla leader "radiated calm and dignity." She told herself that the cause was worth any sacrifice: "We were fighting Japanese fascism."

The Japanese occupiers were convinced, rightly, that Moscow was behind the escalating guerrilla campaign. Foreigners were hauled in for interrogation. Ursula was "invited" to the Mukden police sta-

tion and ushered into an office with a Japanese officer. "His tightly
fitting uniform emphasized his bandy legs. Even though he stood
upright, he held his arms out from his body like handles." Casually
the officer said: "*Sadityes pozhaluyste,*" Russian for "Please sit down."
It was a trick to see if she spoke Russian and might therefore be a
Soviet spy.

"What did you say?" she replied.

After a short and desultory interrogation, Ursula was released.
But the Kempeitai were getting closer.

"The frequent use of our transmitter, the purchase of chemicals,
their storage in our house and transportation, my meetings with the
partisans—all took place under continuous Japanese surveillance."
Ursula claimed to have got used to the danger, but her sleep was
often interrupted by a recurrent nightmare in which the enemy
broke in before she had time to destroy the decoded messages. She
began to take sleeping pills.

Von Schlewitz noticed she was losing weight. "Madam neighbour, today I'm inviting you to dinner, we will order the most delicious and the best," he announced. Between huge mouthfuls of food
and draughts of wine, von Schlewitz "tried tactfully and unsuccess-
fully to find out what was wrong." Finally she said: "If a brick falls
on my head, you will have to look after Misha." Von Schlewitz said
he would happily do so and would adopt the boy if necessary. "That
was too much for me," wrote Ursula, who snorted at the grim irony
of a Nazi arms dealer raising the son of a Jewish communist spy. Still,
it was comforting to know her kindhearted neighbor would care for
her son if she and Patra were caught.

Von Schlewitz did not ask why she feared a "brick" falling on her,
nor why her son might need adoption, nor why she was so interested
in military matters. The boozy businessman probably knew a lot
more than he let on.

In April 1935, Ursula and Johann were eating supper in the stone
cottage when they heard a rap on the door. On the threshold stood a
breathless Chinese boy of about sixteen. He thrust a slip of paper
into Ursula's hand: a stranger had given him some money and told
him to deliver this "message about a serious illness."

Ursula closed the door and unfolded the note. It was written in simple English, in Chu's unsteady hand. She read it, and felt the room pitch sideways. Then she placed the paper in the ashtray, lit a match, and watched it burn. The embers were still glowing when she turned to Johann.

"They have arrested Shushin."

CHAPTER 10

FROM PEKING TO POLAND

A S SHE ENCRYPTED THE EMERGENCY MESSAGE TO MOSCOW, Ursula imagined what Shushin must be suffering. Were the delicate fingers that had danced over the Morse code tapper already broken? "We knew how they did it. First the thumb—'Give us the names!'—then the index finger—'Talk!'—one by one. If the victim still remains silent, they begin removing the fingernails." The Japanese must have arrested Wang too. She would not be able to withstand expert torture for long. Ursula tapped out the message, her one hundredth dispatch to the Center.

The response was swift and precise. "Cut off all contact with partisans. Dismantle and conceal radio. Leave Mukden. Relocate to Peking and set up new operating station."

The mission was over. The network, the equipment, and the life so carefully constructed over the last fifteen months must be destroyed immediately.

Ursula dismantled the radio and wrapped the pieces in plastic bags. The next morning, she and Johann boarded separate trains, changed twice, doubled back, and then met up on the edge of a forest on the northern outskirts of Mukden. Neither was followed. Johann dug a hole and swiftly buried the radio parts.

Then they sat in the spring sunshine in a little clearing.

"Let's talk for a while in the peace and quiet," Johann said gently. "Do Shushin and Wang have a good marriage?"

"A very good one."

The trail from the Chinese couple led straight to Ursula. "They have been in and out of your house for six months," said Johann. "You need to leave soon. Someone may be at your door right now."

He was right, of course. But if they both left the city with "undue haste" it would raise suspicions. They probably only had a few days, at most, before Shushin and Wang broke and the Japanese Kempeitai came for her.

"We need to have a cover story," said Ursula. "The first part is known to everyone: we met on the ship and fell in love. I followed you here from Shanghai. Now we add part two: we break up because you have a new girlfriend."

It was the first time she had alluded to Ludmilla, the Russian girl next door. Johann twisted his cap in his hands. For several minutes he was silent. Then he mumbled: "She admired me and listened to me as if I was a scholar."

Ursula stared at the ground. Between gnarled tree roots, tiny golden flowers sprouted out of the moss.

After a long silence she said: "I shouldn't say this, but if I come home and someone is waiting at my door, I would welcome it. At least then it won't always be others who suffer."

She wept. Johann stroked her hair.

As they were walking back to the station, Johann stopped and turned to her. "Do you remember how I told you on the ship that we would stay together forever? I meant it then, and today I know it even better. Despite everything, you gave me the porcelain seller's gong. It's almost as if the thing with the girl was necessary to show me something I don't need anymore, and that I need you."

Ursula felt numb.

On the train, they rehearsed their cover story. She would first leave for Peking (now Beijing), and word would spread that they had separated. Johann would follow in a few days. "Write me a farewell note—the usual stuff—you've met someone else, and we didn't understand each other that well. It bothered you especially that I kept secrets from you, a hint that you didn't know anything about my work. Add something about racial differences that cannot be bridged."

Johann looked stricken. "Don't you care about me at all anymore?"

"Johann, I am so terribly tired."

She told von Schlewitz she had been jilted and was leaving Mukden. The cheerful German arms dealer did not ask questions. If that was her story, he would stick to it when the Japanese turned up, as they soon would. Von Schlewitz waved them off at the station. She never saw him again.

As the train rumbled southwest, she reflected: "Months of intensive work suddenly broken off. So much remains unfinished."

URSULA LAY IN THE PEKING hotel bed, her jaw aching and her mind whirring. During the long journey, a dull toothache suddenly worsened and from the station she had rushed to the nearest dentist's surgery for an emergency two-hour root canal operation. Michael watched with interest as the dentist went to work with pliers. "So as not to give the child a lifelong fear of the dentist, I did not make a sound." The torture made her think of Shushin. As the anesthetic wore off, she felt the throbbing pain crawl up the side of her face and into her temple, along with a wave of guilt and nausea. Despite an "overwhelming tiredness" and several sleeping pills, she could not sleep. "We have abandoned our partisans," she thought. "Chu will come to the next meeting, and I will not be there." Perhaps Shushin was already dead. She hated Johann for sleeping with Ludmilla, but she needed him desperately. "We had only been separated a few days, and already I was longing for him." Without the radio she felt defenseless; it had become an integral part of her life, "as his rifle is to a soldier, a typewriter to the writer." Finally she fell into a drugged sleep.

Ursula and Michael were waiting at Peking station when the train from Mukden pulled in. Patra swung the boy around and kissed Ursula, long and hard. The next day, he gathered parts to build another radio. The first message from Moscow was surprising: "Hide the transmitter and take four weeks' leave." Red Army spies did not usually get holidays. In reality, the Center was trying to assess the damage to the Mukden network. That night they dined on roast duck skin, shark fin soup, and green tea. "We were tired, felt close and happy."

A strange honeymoon began. "Peking is heaven," she wrote to her parents. Gradually they relaxed, slowly discovering a "way to enjoy every hour of those rare days free of danger." The pain in her jaw eased, and the sickness she had felt before leaving Mukden subsided. She began to sleep again. They took Michael to the lake in the Summer Palace, climbed in the hills, wandered the city streets, and read books. Johann was sweetly attentive, the Russian doll a mere memory. "There were no sharp words," she wrote. "Johann was happy because we were living together. I think of that August in Peking as a time bathed in warm light."

After four weeks, they reassembled the radio. Johann was asleep when the message came through from Moscow, an abrupt command that made her heart jolt. "Sonya come to Shanghai with your luggage. Ernst remain in position and await new co-worker." From Shanghai, the message continued, she would be going to Moscow for further instructions and then on to Europe to see her family. After five years with the Shanghai Municipal Council, Rudi and his family were eligible for home leave. Ursula knew that she would not be coming back to China: her mission was over.

Ursula sat on the bed looking down at the sleeping Johann. "The furrowed forehead, the high cheekbones, the narrow nose, the restless, nervous mouth, the hands. I let the tears run." It was the third time she had wept over him. First in a Prague cinema, then in a forest outside Mukden, and now in Peking, while he slept, and she silently said farewell.

"That means goodbye forever," he said the next morning, when she relayed Moscow's orders. Then he brightened. "Our people are not inhuman, we'll be allowed to stay together. As soon as I get away from here we'll get married."

Ursula said nothing.

Johann accompanied them to the station, stowed the luggage, hugged Michael, and then stood, a little awkwardly, on the platform outside the compartment window. "I'll write to you again when I leave China," he said. "Definitely."

The doors slammed and the train whistle blew. Johann did not wave. Then he turned and walked away.

She had not told him she was pregnant.

COLONEL TUMANYAN, URSULA'S SENIOR OFFICER, greeted her
warmly at the office in Bolshoi Znamensky Lane and offered congratulations on her work in Mukden, and what had turned out to be
a narrow escape from Shanghai. In May 1935, Inspector Tom Givens
of the Shanghai Municipal Police had arrested another high-ranking
Soviet spy. "Joseph Walden" claimed to be a penniless writer, but
was in reality Colonel Yakov Grigoryevich Bronin of Soviet military
intelligence. In Bronin's apartment, police found evidence that his
typewriter had been purchased by one Ursula Hamburger. Rudi was
interviewed, and gave Special Branch "a convincing but untrue account of the typewriter's disposal." Givens was getting far too close
for comfort. Ursula caught the next boat out of Shanghai, knowing
she would not be coming back.

But the Fourth Department already had a new mission in mind:
"Will you go to Poland? With Rudi?" Tumanyan asked. The right-
wing Polish government had driven the Communist Party underground, and the comrades there were in dire need of an expert radio
operator. Since Rudi was now willing to work for Soviet intelligence
and she vouched for his commitment, they could operate as a team,
coordinating the Polish communist cells, gathering military intelligence, and reporting back to Moscow. Rudi's job as an architect
would provide cover. Though still head of the Asia section, Tumanyan would continue as her handler. Colonel Tums was still unaware
of the state of Ursula's marriage. She did not tell her commanding
officer she was pregnant with Johann Patra's child. "From his point
of view this was a logical, humane proposal."

From Ursula's perspective, however, the proposition was anything but straightforward. Obtaining an abortion in China was comparatively easy, but from the moment she discovered she was
pregnant, her mind was made up. "I yearned for a second child and
now that it was on the way I wanted to keep it."

The pregnancy created an extraordinary situation. Before leaving
Shanghai, she had told Rudi she was pregnant by Patra; stunned, he
urged her to have an abortion. When she wrote to inform Johann, he
too tried to persuade her to terminate the pregnancy. Bizarrely, let-

ters passed back and forth between Patra in Peking and Hamburger in Shanghai, discussing what she should do. "I said nothing while the two of them bargained over my future." She was keeping the child, and that was that. Finally, Rudi did the decent thing, as he always did, and "declared that he could not leave me on my own in this condition." He would follow wherever Moscow deployed her; he would continue to be her husband, in appearance if not reality, and a father to Michael; they would conceal from the world, the Center, and their own families that the child she was carrying was not his. Once the baby was born, she could decide her own future, with or without him. Patra's reaction to this plan was also noble, in its way: "If I can't be with you, then there is no one better than Rudi, and I shall feel much calmer if you are with him."

Tumanyan's suggestion of a joint mission cast this unconventional arrangement in a very different light. Rudi and Ursula would be living and working together. Hamburger was a good father, a skilled architect, and a kind man, but he was likely, she feared, to make a pretty hopeless spy. "His charm and perfect courtesy made him popular everywhere, especially with women, and opened many doors," but on the other hand, "he was in many respects naïve, and softhearted." Meanwhile, danger had become part of her daily life. As she had discovered, espionage involved not only risk, but also sacrifice, loss, and pain. She was pregnant with another man's child. She still loved Patra, though she knew there was little chance they could ever be a couple again. Was it fair to "expect Rudi and me to share a life together under present circumstances"?

Ursula told Tumanyan she would accept the assignment, take Michael to Britain to see her family, and then travel on to Warsaw. Rudi would come to Moscow separately to discuss the mission with Tumanyan. He could then decide for himself whether to follow her to Poland. If he chose not to, she would go alone. "I was not afraid to carry out the necessary work on my own." Before leaving Moscow she was introduced to a Bulgarian intelligence officer named Stoyan Vladov (real name Nikola Popvassilev Zidarov), who would be her main contact in Poland.

The entire Kuczynski family, accompanied by the faithful Ollo, was assembled on the dockside at Hay's Wharf in Gravesend when the SS *Co-Operatzia* from Leningrad pulled in on October 21, 1935. Ursula had not seen her father or siblings for more than five years.

Jürgen was now also in Britain. Ursula's older brother had clung on in Germany until the last minute, toiling for the communist underground, hoping the German working class would come to its senses and overthrow Hitler. Early in 1935 he even visited the Soviet Union, where he met numerous communist notables including Karl Radek, whose writings Ursula had read in Shanghai after the birth of her son. At thirty, Jürgen was seen by the Kremlin as a man of the future: Radek reported that Stalin himself had asked whether the young Kuczynski would be aided or hindered by being made a member of the Soviet Academy of Science. Jürgen sensibly turned down an honor which, if the Nazis found out, would give them yet another excuse to kill him. He returned to Berlin, as he put it, "completely convinced that I would soon be able to welcome my comrades back to Germany." That conviction was fantasy, and the reality was brought home when Jürgen was instructed to smuggle the KPD's remaining funds out of Germany and deposit the money in a Dutch bank. The Nazis were picking off his friends and political allies. Berta sent letters, beseeching him to come to Britain before it was too late. On September 15, 1935, following the annual Nuremberg rally, the Reichstag passed the "Reich Citizenship Law," rendering Jews ineligible for German citizenship. Aliens in their own country, with hope of a communist resurgence vanishing and Germany's anti-Semitic hysteria intensifying, Jürgen and Marguerite emerged from hiding and fled. Three days after reaching London, he contacted the British Communist Party.

The family was reunited, but under circumstances far removed from their old life: packed into a poky, three-room flat in North London. Their first full family gathering since 1929 was boisterous and loud, but suffused with sadness. "We all yearned for the house where we grew up, and for the landscape to which we belonged." When Ursula's parents and siblings learned she was expecting a second child, they assumed the father was Rudi. "There was no need to lie," she wrote later—an interesting way to excuse what she knew was a "detestable deception."

After the family gathering, she took Jürgen aside and told him the truth. The siblings were as close, and competitive, as ever. She explained that she had had an affair in China, though she did not say with whom, and that Rudi had not fathered the child inside her, and knew it. He told her she was "impossible," but promised not to tell anyone else. Jürgen might be unable to shut up on paper, but he was a good secret keeper, and she trusted him completely.

The Kuczynski children had all, to differing degrees, absorbed left-wing views. Brigitte, the next in age to Ursula, was already a member of the Communist Party. Expelled from Heidelberg University for slapping a student leader of the Hitler Youth, she fled to Britain in September 1935. Even the youngest, Renate, "proudly called herself a communist." The political sympathies of the refugees did not pass unnoticed.

MI6, Britain's foreign intelligence service, first opened a file on Jürgen back in 1928, when he began writing for communist newspapers. Robert, the paterfamilias now teaching demography at the LSE and conducting research for the government, was also suspected of Bolshevik sympathies. MI5, the Security Service, was taking a close interest in this family of German leftists newly implanted in the United Kingdom. Over the coming years, the British intelligence services would amass no fewer than ninety-four files on the Kuczynskis. The British immigration authorities noted Ursula's arrival from Leningrad, a first blip on MI5's radar.

Rudi landed in Britain a few weeks later. His meeting with Colonel Tumanyan in Moscow had not been entirely satisfactory. "My wish had been to take on independent [intelligence] work in the future, and to receive appropriate training for the purpose. This wish was not fulfilled, but I received promises." His decision to work for Soviet intelligence was a political choice, but also personal. Rudi still loved Ursula and "clung to the vain hope that they could be reconciled." He was not about to relinquish his son. Tumanyan instructed Rudi to accompany Ursula to Poland and provide her with assistance.

They set off in January 1936, with an important addition to the party. Olga Muth begged Ursula to take her too. Renate was nearly in her teens, too old for a nanny. In Poland, Ollo could look after Michael and help care for the new baby when it arrived. Ursula readily accepted. She had known Olga Muth since the age of three. "There was always a special bond between Ollo and me," Ursula wrote.

Poland was in turmoil. Józef Piłsudski, the country's autocratic, right-wing leader since 1926, had just died, leaving a government that was fiercely anti-Soviet and determined to root out communism, which had been forced largely underground. Polish anti-Semitism was on the rise. The Poles were attempting to negotiate a deal with Hitler to launch a joint attack on the Soviet Union. It was a bad time to be a communist spy in Poland or, from a different perspective, a very good one.

The Hamburgers rented a house in the Warsaw suburb of Anin, and Rudi found work with the help of two Polish architects. Ursula began learning Polish and building a transmitter-receiver, the first she had constructed alone, and hid it inside a wooden gramophone case from which she removed the innards. One night, she "first pressed the key under a dim light in our flat." Two minutes later, the response from Russia came back, with perfect clarity.

A senior officer in the Fourth Department, the Bulgarian Stoyan Vladov, had already established a network of Polish informants, code-named "Mont Blanc." A former musician in a cinema orchestra, Vladov had joined the Communist Party in 1914, served five years in prison for gunrunning, undergone military and intelligence training in Moscow, and was now working on a large horticultural farm, growing roses, spying for the Red Army, and supporting the Polish communists. Once a month, Ursula met him in Kraków to gather his intelligence haul, and then returned to Warsaw to pass it on to Moscow. "I was supposed to advise him," she wrote. Vladov neither wanted nor needed advice.

Ursula grew bored. After the excitement and danger of China, her existence seemed almost mundane: she was either commuting back and forth to take dictation from Vladov or stuck in the apartment coding, transmitting, and preparing for the birth of her second child. Rudi's espionage was even more limited. Occasionally he manned the transmitter, or carried out "general repairs and maintenance," but the Center balked at giving him greater responsibility. "On several occasions he insisted on transmitting his own messages, asking when he would be able to come to Moscow for intelligence training in order to be able to undertake intelligence work on his own account." The response from Moscow was "invariably dismissive." Rudi emphatically wanted to be a spy, but the Red Army, as yet, did not want him.

Nor did Ursula. "Rudi and I got on in a comradely way and there were no quarrels," but the relationship was as cold as the Polish winter. At the time little Michael felt only an "intense happiness that the family was together again"; much later he wondered how his father had endured "the mental burden of this masquerade." A husband in name only, Rudi made no pretense that the impending birth gave him pleasure. Ursula's thoughts were often with Johann Patra, wondering where he was, whether he was safe: "He won't be able to cope alone," she reflected. "He'll do something stupid." But as the months passed she found their separation easier to bear. They were fundamentally incompatible. Johann "needed a completely different sort of woman as a permanent companion; one who accepted him without criticism, without questioning or discussion." At the start of their relationship, she had been his subordinate; she was now his equal, perhaps even his superior in the eyes of the Center. Stubborn and old-fashioned, he would never have been able to accept that imbalance. Yet with Johann's child growing inside her, she felt his absence like a permanent, dull ache. Catching sight of her pregnant profile reflected in a shop window, Ursula thought: "How sad it was that my child was not being joyfully awaited by *two* people."

In truth, it was. Devoted Olga Muth, now fifty-five years old, was in her element preparing for the new arrival, looking after Michael, and discreetly supporting the family's espionage operations. Ollo was fully aware that her employers were spies working against the fascists, and she approved, without ever saying so. She knew that, late at night, the mistress of the house, the girl she still called Whirl, sent radio messages on an illegal transmitter hidden inside a gramophone with a record of Beethoven's *Egmont* Overture on the turntable. The collaboration between the two women was unspoken, based on personal loyalty more than politics, and not once overtly discussed. "I never mentioned the nature of my work," Ursula wrote.

"And Ollo did not ask about it." Olga Muth was a nursemaid; but she was also an assistant spy.

On April 27, 1936, in a clinic in suburban Warsaw, Ursula gave birth to a healthy girl. She named her Janina, or Nina for short. Eight hours later, she was back at the apartment, "sitting next to a shaded lamp at her illegal transmitter" and tapping out a message that began: "Please excuse my delay, but I have just given birth to a daughter."

Writing to her parents, she was more effusive: "What bliss it is to arrive home and find a little crib complete with occupant standing in front of our house in the woods. . . . Ollo is a wonderful help and crazy about Janina. Rudi is very busy."

Nina was six months old when the Center instructed Ursula to move to Danzig (now Gdansk) to support the embattled communist underground there. Rudi would continue to work in Warsaw to ensure the renewal of their residence permits. The Baltic port of Danzig was a "Free City," an autonomous city-state wedged between Poland and Germany and theoretically independent of both. In reality it was anything but free: the majority of inhabitants were German, its government was dominated by Nazis, and by 1936 there was a mounting campaign to absorb Danzig into the Third Reich. Ursula arrived in a city undergoing intensive Nazification: "The swastika hung from official buildings, portraits of Hitler decorated the walls of public offices, Poles were terrorized, Jews intimidated, persecuted and arrested." Karl Hoffman, a young communist with a "delicate face" and a racking cough from tuberculosis, had established a small resistance cell, sabotaging the U-boats under construction in Danzig's shipyards and laying plans to disable traffic lights to impede the expected Nazi invasion. Ursula was their link to Moscow.

Ursula, Ollo, Michael, and Nina moved into a sunny apartment in a modern block in the Oliwa district. During the day, Ursula went shopping with her baby in a carriage and collected reports from Hoffman's spies; in the evenings, when everyone else had gone to bed, she would take the transmitter-receiver out of the gramophone and pass messages back and forth to Moscow. As the mother of two small children, she no longer needed a cover job.

Michael tried to make friends with the local children. One day he asked his mother, "What does 'not welcome' mean?" She told him it meant "forbidden." The little boy persisted: "What is Jewish?" She tried to change the subject. Michael made up a chant: "Smoking forbidden, Jews forbidden, noise forbidden." She told him to be quiet. He changed his chant: "Spitting allowed, Jews allowed, singing allowed . . ." She slapped him, for the first and only time in her life. Tears welling, Michael ran from the room. Ursula was devastated by what she had done. The strain was getting to her. "What will happen to my children if I am caught?" she wondered. She tried to console herself with the thought that "they both have blond hair and blue eyes; that will protect them from any brutality." She knew it wasn't true.

The work was both dull and dangerous; unrewarding but not unrewarded.

Soon after Michael's sixth birthday, an incoming message unlike any before arrived from the Center. Addressed to her personally, it read: "Dear Sonya, the People's Commissariat for Defence has decided to award you the Order of the Red Banner. We congratulate you warmly and wish you further success in your work. The Director."

Established after the Revolution, the Order of the Red Banner was the highest Soviet military medal, awarded for courage and heroism on the battlefield. Stalin himself had been thus honored, as had Trotsky. She was initially embarrassed by the honor, wondering if her "value was being overrated," but then suffused with a quiet pride. Over the previous six years she had risked her life repeatedly in Shanghai, Manchuria, and Poland. A German Jewish communist spy under Nazi rule in Danzig, Ursula knew that arrest meant deportation to Germany, imprisonment, and death. She had underrated herself, for here, from the head of the Fourth Department, was recognition of her achievement as a secret soldier of the Red Army.

A few days later, on the street outside the apartment, she encountered the wife of a Nazi official who lived upstairs, a fascist busybody who had failed to spot Ursula was Jewish.

"Do you get a lot of interference on your radio?" the woman asked.

"I haven't heard anything," Ursula replied, feeling a sudden chill. "What time was it?"

"Around 11:00. . . . Last night it was quite bad again."

Ursula had sent a long message to Moscow the previous evening.

The woman prattled away: "My husband says there's someone transmitting quite near us. He's going to arrange for the block to be surrounded on Friday . . ."

That evening, after the lights went out in the floor above, she dashed off a message to Moscow, explaining that she was moving the radio to another location immediately and would be listening for a reply. At a safe house owned by a member of Hoffman's network, she set up the radio. Moscow's response was repeated several times: "Return to Poland." The Danzig mission had lasted three months.

Yet another message arrived after her return to Warsaw: a comrade would meet her at a designated rendezvous site in a few days' time. When Colonel Tumanyan himself appeared, grinning broadly, she had to restrain herself from kissing him. Decorated Soviet military heroes don't kiss each other. Tumanyan brought congratulations from General Berzin, who was back in Moscow as chief of Red Army intelligence after a year in Spain dispensing military advice to the Republicans locked in civil war. "The director is satisfied with your work," Tumanyan told her, but as they strolled through Warsaw the Armenian grew grave. "May I speak to you as a friend, not a superior? You no longer seem to radiate your former happiness. How are things with Rudi?"

To her own surprise, she unburdened herself to Colonel Tums: the state of her non-marriage, and the relationship with Johann Patra that had produced Nina. "I told him that I valued Johann highly and still missed him, but did not want to return to him." She described her frustration with the work in Poland. "I feel inexperienced," she said. "I don't know enough about the latest techniques in radio construction. Above all, I would like to receive further training."

Tumanyan nodded sympathetically: "Then you will come to Moscow for a few months, and afterwards return to Poland."

Without quite meaning to, Ursula had turned another page in her story.

CHAPTER 11

IN FOR
A PENNY

O N JUNE 15, 1937, IN THE HEART OF THE KREMLIN, ONE OF the oldest Bolsheviks pinned a medal on one of the youngest, a rising star of the Red Army.

Mikhail Kalinin, a former butler and early disciple of Lenin's, was the first president of Soviet Russia, a member of the Politburo, chairman of the Presidium of the Supreme Soviet, an obedient crony of Stalin, and to ordinary Soviet citizens a figure of almost inconceivable grandeur. The city of Kaliningrad was named after him. By 1937 he was a figurehead, taking little part in government but wheeled out for ceremonial occasions. On this day, he was presenting the Order of the Red Banner to some two dozen soldiers and sailors for sundry acts of courage, as he had done many times before. What made this occasion different was that one of the recipients was a thirty-year-old woman.

Earlier that morning, Ursula put on a gray suit and polished her shoes before climbing into an army truck. At the Kremlin, the medalwinners were led down long corridors and into the main auditorium. A few minutes later, "an elderly grey-haired comrade entered the room."

Kalinin held on to Ursula's hand, as he attached banner number 944 to her lapel. "The Red Army men applauded loud and long, maybe because I was the only woman." On the old man's face she saw an expression of "pure kindness." This was misleading, because Kalinin was a brute. Three years later, as a member of the Soviet

Politburo, he signed the execution order for twenty-two thousand Polish officers imprisoned in a forest near Smolensk: the notorious Katyn massacre.

Ursula had traveled from Warsaw to Moscow via Czechoslovakia, where she left the children with Rudi's parents, along with the ever-capable Olga Muth. Else Hamburger was ill and would die within the year. Rudi, who remained in Poland, had pleaded with Ursula "not to cause additional grief to his mother during these hard times" and so they stuck to the fiction that Nina was Rudi's child. Using a false Soviet passport supplied by Tumanyan in the name Sophia Genrikovna Gamburger, Ursula traveled on to Finland, before crossing the border into Russia.

The Red Army rolled out the red carpet. Tumanyan insisted she take a brief holiday at a special holiday camp in Alupka on the Black Sea, and then stay with him and his family in their Moscow apartment. The Red Army was rigidly hierarchical, but for Ursula nothing was more natural than to establish a close friendship with the tough old Soviet warhorse who was also her boss. Back at the Sparrow compound, she began another rigorous training course: operating a sophisticated "push-pull" transmitter, cooking up explosives, and constructing a variety of timed fuses using electric wire, ignition cord, and an acid that ate through a rubber seal to set off a detonator. In a field outside Moscow, she practiced blowing up railway lines. Some of the instructors were communists who had seen action in Spain, where civil war was raging between Franco's Nationalists (supported by Hitler) and the Republicans (backed by the Soviet Union). Others were experienced deep-cover agents, teaching "what a partisan operating behind enemy lines must know." Her colleagues and instructors treated her with respect. She wore the Red Banner, presented by the great Kalinin, pinned to her lapel.

In her spare time (and without telling her senior officers, who would have disapproved), Ursula wrote a short novel. Based on Sepp "Sober" Weingarten, it told the story of a communist secret agent who falls in love with a White Russian but conceals his true allegiance. The heroine of the story is so awed by the wonders of life in the USSR that she eventually converts to Marxism-Leninism, and they live happily ever after in the Soviet socialist paradise. "The manuscript was really worthless," she later admitted. But for a piece of clunking communist propaganda, it was surprisingly well written, the work of a natural storyteller.

Ursula felt the separation from her children keenly, the now-familiar combination of guilt and anxiety. At least the children have each other, she told herself. But would they reject her, as Michael had done after her prolonged earlier absence? She eagerly devoured every letter from Czechoslovakia. She was tormented by the knowledge that some of their earliest memories would be formed without her, but never once did she contemplate abandoning the work. Like every spy, she compartmentalized her different lives: Moscow was one world, motherhood another. There was much to distract her.

A message came from headquarters. "A good friend of yours is in Moscow and wants to see you, if you agree."

"God, you're as slim as ever," said Johann, as he threw his arms around her in the lobby of 19 Bolshoi Znamensky Lane. Patra had been brought back from China for a wireless refresher course. He would soon be returning to Shanghai.

Patra blithely expected their relationship to resume after almost two years apart, and immediately asked Ursula to return to China with him. She told him that this was impossible. They might share a child—she proudly showed him photographs of his daughter—but the romantic bond had gone. "In spite of his undoubted qualities, he was even more irritable, hard and intolerant than before." They parted as friends.

Many of her German communist comrades were now in Moscow, driven into exile, including Gabo Lewin and Heinz Altmann, who had taught her to shoot in the Grunewald forest back in 1924. Lewin now edited a German-language communist newspaper; Altmann was a journalist. Karl Rimm, Sorge's replacement in Shanghai, appeared one day at the compound wearing the uniform of a senior officer. She hugged him—"not exactly etiquette"—and they dined together that evening. The happiest reunion was with Grisha Herzberg, the Polish photographer from Shanghai with the dark eyes and mournful manner who was steadily ascending through the ranks of Red Army intelligence. They took a barge trip together on the newly opened Moscow-Volga Canal, their rediscovered friendship only slightly impeded by the restriction that, under the rules, neither could tell the other where they had been, what they had done, or what they might do next. They went swimming and then lay on the banks of the canal, "happy to bask in the unbroken sunshine."

Yet a dark shadow loomed across Ursula's happiness: her friends and colleagues were already being murdered at an astonishing rate.

Stalin's Great Purge was one of the most extensive serial-killing sprees in history. Triggered by raging paranoia and a conviction that the revolution was being undermined from within, between 1936 and 1938 the Soviet state arrested 1,548,366 people accused of disloyalty, counterrevolution, sabotage, and espionage. Of these, 681,692 were killed. Most of them were innocent. The NKVD (precursor to the KGB) extracted confessions by torture and forced each victim to name other "enemies of the people," creating an ever-expanding vortex of suspicion and destruction. The luckier victims were sent to the system of labor camps known as the Gulag. The rest were summarily executed: party officials, intellectuals, the wealthier peasants (kulaks), Poles and other minorities, Trotskyites, semi-Trotskyites, bureaucrats, scientists, priests, Jews, musicians, writers, and anyone else who might, however improbably, pose a threat to Stalin's authority. Signing off on the daily execution lists, Stalin was heard to remark: "Who is going to remember this riffraff in ten, twenty years' time? No one."

The Soviet armed forces were seen as a particular hotbed of treachery, and the military intelligence service, a rival to the NKVD, was accused of harboring fascist spies. The officer class of the Red Army and Navy was virtually wiped out, along with most of the Comintern. Spies were suspect; spies who had contact with foreigners, or were non-Russian, doubly so. And because the NKVD itself was composed of spies, it began to accuse, and then systematically kill, its own people.

General Yan Berzin's survival skills finally deserted him: the chief of the Fourth Department was sacked, arrested, and shot in the basement of the Lubyanka, the NKVD headquarters. His predecessor was killed too. His successor lasted just a few days before he, too, was executed. "Unfortunately, comrades in leading positions changed frequently at that time," Ursula wrote, with grim euphemism. "Unfortunate" does not begin to do justice to the arbitrary and unstoppable carnage. "The whole Fourth Directorate has fallen into German hands," Stalin declared in May 1937. Of the six military intelligence chiefs between 1937 and 1939, all but one perished. The fabled recruiters of the British communist spies known as the "Cambridge Five" were recalled to Moscow and fed into the grinder.

Many of the people Ursula most loved and admired were arrested and brutally murdered, one by one, some before her arrival, some during her stay in Moscow, and many more subsequently. German communists who had taken refuge in Russia were killed in the hundreds or sent back to Nazi Germany to meet the same fate. Gabo Lewin, her childhood friend, was convicted of counterrevolutionary activity and sent to the Gulag. Heinz Altmann, who had urged her to join the communist youth league back in 1924, preceded him into captivity. Manfred Stern, whom Ursula met in Shanghai in 1932, had gone on to lead the International Brigade in the Spanish Civil War under the nom de guerre "General Kléber." Stern was sentenced to fifteen years' hard labor, and died in the Gulag in 1954. Jakob Mirov-Abramov, Agnes Smedley's recruiter, who had admitted Ursula to the Sparrow training camp, was tortured into a confession and shot on November 26, 1937; his wife was executed three months later. Karl Rimm was liquidated in 1938 for membership in a "counterrevolutionary terrorist organization," swiftly followed by his wife, Luise. Richard Sorge survived because he wisely refused to return from Japan when summoned, and since his bosses were being replaced and killed so fast, he got away with it. The Hungarian journalist Lajos Magyar and the writer Karl Radek—people Ursula revered as the loyal intellectuals of revolution—were summarily dispatched into oblivion. Boris Pilnyak, whose novel Ursula read immediately after Michael's birth, was accused of being a spy and plotting to kill Stalin; he was tried on April 21, 1938, and executed the same day. Mikhail Borodin died in the Lubyanka after severe torture. Sepp Weingarten vanished. So did Isa Wiedemeyer. Foreign communists in Russia were swept up in the butchery: Agnes Smedley's ex-husband, Virendranath Chattopadhyaya, was sentenced on September 2, 1937, and immediately executed. Stalin's friendship was no protection. A year after Ursula received her medal from Mikhail

Kalinin, his Jewish wife, Ekaterina, was arrested, tortured in Lefor-
tovo Prison, and sent to the camps.

Ursula later claimed to have been ignorant of the purges, the scale
of the bloodletting, the flimsiness of the trumped-up charges, and
Stalin's personal agency in the criminal slaughter. She accepted the
myth that capitalist spies were sowing an atmosphere of distrust inside the Soviet Union, making it "no easy matter for those responsible to distinguish between the mistakes of honest comrades and
enemy actions." In the jargon of mass slaughter, "mistakes" was a
weasel word used to justify executions based on no real evidence.

But Ursula knew that her friends and colleagues were being an-
nihilated, and that they were innocent. She later wrote: "I was convinced that they were communists and not enemies." She did not say
so at the time. She did not inquire what they had been accused of, or
where they had gone, for to display any form of curiosity was itself
an invitation to death. Like millions of others, she kept her mouth
shut, uttered no word of remonstrance, and wondered who would
be next.

Grisha Herzberg disappeared, suddenly and completely, soon
after the idyllic day spent sunbathing with Ursula on the banks of
the Moscow-Volga Canal. The date and place of his execution are
unknown. Like so many others, the thirty-two-year-old Pole simply
vanished overnight. They had arranged to meet for dinner. Grisha
did not appear. Ursula did not inquire of the Center where he had
gone. It would be years before she dared to mention his name again.

Ursula was terrified, secretly. She had faced danger before, but
nothing like the insidious, pervasive dread of awaiting false accusa-
tion of treachery. As a foreign-born spy with links to many of those
liquidated, she was in mortal danger. The threat from the Soviet state
was far greater than anything she had faced from the enemies of
communism. Her gender was no protection, for Stalin was an equal-
opportunity murderer. A request to return to Poland might be seen
as an admission of guilt. Like many people faced with a horror too
unspeakable to name, Ursula chose to pretend it was not happening,
that her friends would return and that those who did not must have
made mistakes. She looked away, while constantly looking behind
herself.

How she survived is a mystery. She put it down to luck, but there was more to it than that. Ursula had a remarkable capacity to inspire loyalty. In a profession based on deception and duplicity, she was never betrayed. Victims of the purges were encouraged to identify other traitors, but Ursula was never denounced. Years later she concluded that someone must have "held a protective hand over me." That "someone" was Colonel Tumanyan, the Armenian-Georgian veteran who had steered Ursula's career through Manchuria and Poland. Tums had always watched Ursula's back, and he had faithfully guarded her secrets. He knew about her relationship with Patra and her troubled marriage, her struggle to balance espionage with daily domestic life. "He was the sort of person with whom you could discuss such things," and although he always "maintained the authority of his military rank," behind the dark eyes was a sensitive soul. She had come to see him as a friend. As long as Tumanyan was in command, she felt safe.

And then, like so many others, Tumanyan was gone.

Ursula was summoned to the Center, to find her boss's office stripped of his personal effects and a heavily built man in the uniform of a colonel seated at his desk, with shaven head and deep-set eyes, who stated impassively that Colonel Tumanyan had been given a "new assignment." She never discovered what had happened to Tums, and the expression on the face of her new boss suggested it would be extremely unwise to ask.

Khadzi-Umar Mamsurov, known as "Comrade Hadshi," was the son of Muslim peasants from North Ossetia, and one of the toughest fighters in the Red Army. During the Spanish Civil War he led a partisan unit behind Nationalist lines, where his reputation for ruthlessness won him literary immortality: Ernest Hemingway based Robert Jordan, the main character in *For Whom the Bell Tolls,* partly on Umar Mamsurov.

Colonel Mamsurov was a skilled office politician who had adapted the techniques of guerrilla fighting to the treacherous terrain of Stalinist bureaucracy, and would rise to become deputy head of Soviet military intelligence. Ursula came to admire his indestructible resilience, but he had none of Tumanyan's sensitivity. Comrade

Hadshi was not watching Ursula's back. He was too busy watching his own.

After five months in Moscow, the day before she was due to return to Poland, Ursula was granted an audience with the new director of the Fourth Department, Semyon Gendin, a decorated soldier and NKVD officer, the replacement for Berzin's replacement. He commended her work, instructed her to return to Poland, and asked her to pass on a message of thanks to Rudi. A few months later Gendin followed his predecessors to the execution cells.

The purges would eventually burn themselves out, leaving a permanent, unhealed scar on the Soviet psyche. Ursula's loyalty was undimmed, but it now came with an admixture of fear. A worm of doubt had lodged in her soul. Henceforth, she would never know whether a summons to Moscow was to receive a medal or a bullet.

Back in Poland, reunited with her children, Ursula was happy to plunge back into domestic life, at least for a while. Her letters home were filled with the details of raising children, having her hair done, Ollo's affection for baby Nina and her squabbles with Michael, the struggle to renew their residence permits. With Rudi she shared parental responsibility and espionage duties, but nothing else. They moved into a new home in Zakopane, a resort town at the base of the Tatra Mountains.

Michael would look back on this time with painful nostalgia in a series of interlocking childhood memories: learning to whistle, climbing trees, and making cardboard houses with cellophane windows with his father. He recalled his mother: "The warm brown eyes, the slightly tousled black hair, the laughing mouth under the prominent nose." What the seven-year-old Michael remembered as a "dream of paradise" was really the dying moments of a marriage.

Every two weeks she made radio contact with Moscow, passing messages back and forth from the Bulgarian florist and spymaster, Stoyan Vladov. In Moscow she had been taught to blow up bridges and run undercover agents; back in Poland, she was little more than a secret postman.

Elsewhere in the world, her fellow communists were fighting furiously as the Nazi threat escalated and Europe lurched toward war.

Johann Patra was returning to China to run a new network of agents and saboteurs against the Japanese. In Spain, the Republicans were in retreat. In Berlin, the last vestiges of Ursula's old life were being destroyed. By mid-1938, more than 250,000 Jews had fled Germany and Austria, while hundreds of thousands more were attempting to escape. The remnants of the communist underground prepared for armed resistance. In England, Jürgen was churning out anti-fascist tracts, and swiftly emerging as the de facto leader of the German émigré communists in Britain.

Ursula watched these events unfold with horror and frustration. "I felt I was not accomplishing much in Poland." She needed another adventure. In 1938, she requested permission to come to Moscow once more. By now, none of her friends and German comrades remained. She told Comrade Hadshi she was ready for a new challenge.

The Center had also concluded that Agent Sonya was being underused. It was agreed that her next mission should be in neutral Switzerland, the country with the world's highest per capita quotient of spies and a prime target of Soviet espionage. Ursula's father had contacts at the League of Nations in Geneva who might prove useful. Rudi could probably get work there as an architect. Switzerland was already providing sanctuary for thousands of fleeing Germans; one more family of Jewish refugees would easily blend in.

At her final briefing, Colonel Mamsurov informed Ursula that she had been promoted to major, which came as a shock since she had been unaware of holding any formal military rank. "I did not know how to salute, let alone march." She was flattered nonetheless. "I was proud to be a soldier of the Red Army." Before leaving Moscow, she was introduced to a young German named Franz Obermanns. Five years her junior, Obermanns was a former waiter and a member of the communist resistance in Berlin who had been arrested by the Gestapo before escaping to fight in Spain with the Thirteenth International Brigade. Mamsurov explained that the young man had completed his radio training and would be following Ursula to Switzerland, where he would act as her junior officer and assistant. Obermanns was enthusiastic, brave, and quite stupid. He would travel on a false Finnish passport, under the name "Eriki Noki"—an odd choice of cover since Obermanns had never been to Finland, knew nothing of the country, and spoke not a single word of Finnish.

Switzerland, peaceful land of cowbells and cuckoo clocks, has the oldest policy of military neutrality in the world, having successfully avoided involvement in any war since 1815. This made it ideal for spying, and exceptionally unsafe. Sandwiched between Nazi Germany and Austria, fascist Italy and democratic France, it was a hotbed of international espionage. The Germans, British, French, Soviets, and Americans all ran competing spy networks in the country, using Switzerland as a base to launch operations into enemy territory. The undercover war in Shanghai had been brutal but haphazard; in Manchuria, Ursula had dodged the murderously proficient Kempeitai; in Poland and Danzig, she was a courier to the communist underground. But in Switzerland the game was different. The country was riddled with espionage, an international hunting ground for spies of every stamp. Everyone spied on everyone else, and the Swiss security service spied, politely but insistently, on all the other spies.

The Soviet Union, fearful and distrustful of Hitler, needed information on the military buildup inside the Reich, and neutral Switzerland, sharing a 225-mile border with Nazi Germany, was the ideal place from which to gather such intelligence. Ursula was ordered to travel to Switzerland via Britain, settle somewhere near Geneva, construct an illegal radio transmitter-receiver, make contact with the preexisting Soviet intelligence networks, and establish a reliable wireless link with Moscow using a memorized set of cyphers. At the same time, the Center instructed her to recruit her own team of agents to be infiltrated into Germany to gather military information and conduct sabotage operations. For the first time, Ursula would be directly targeting Hitler's regime: she could hardly wait.

The Nazis had plenty of their own spies in Switzerland, and a number of informants inside Swiss intelligence. The police had developed a highly efficient system for detecting illegal wireless sets, and the Swiss government was strictly neutral and uniformly severe when it came to espionage: anyone caught spying, of whatever nationality or political allegiance, faced arrest and deportation. If Ursula was sent back to Germany she would be killed. Unless, of course, the Gestapo or its agents found out what she was up to and opted to murder her in Switzerland instead.

Before leaving Moscow, Ursula made a suggestion: might she find recruits in London on her way to Switzerland and send them into Germany as undercover agents? Numerous British communists had volunteered to fight in Spain in the International Brigade, and among the survivors might be some willing to continue the battle against fascism by being inserted into Germany as penetration spies. Britons still enjoyed a certain status in Germany, and despite the rising enmity between the two nations, Ursula pointed out, "it was not unusual for the odd, well-to-do Englishman" to turn up there on holiday, even in 1938. This was the first time she had taken the initiative and framed a plan of her own. She was no longer merely obeying orders. Ursula was making the transition from spy to spymaster. The Center agreed: while visiting her family in London she should try to enlist "one or two comrades who had given proof of their courage and reliability in the course of the Spanish Civil War," and then start for Geneva. She should avoid contact with the Communist Party of Great Britain (CPGB). Colonel Mamsurov finally handed over a sheet of paper and told her to sign it: "a statement that admitted the right of the Centre to have her shot if she disclosed her cypher to a third party without authorization." It was not a legal document, but a warning.

In Shanghai she had worked under Sorge; in Mukden, she had spied alongside Patra; in Poland, Rudi had been her designated aide. She would be taking off for Switzerland as a solo spy. She and Rudi had "come to realize that we could no longer live together." For the last two years their partnership had survived only on joint parenting and a shared ideology, but now the marriage was finally over, without rancor. Rudi announced he would be returning to Shanghai, where he wished to resume his architectural practice and begin working independently for Soviet military intelligence. He intended to pass the summer in America, spending time with his brother Victor (now professor of embryology at Washington University in St. Louis), and then complete a course in radio technology in Paris to ensure he was ready to take up full-time spying back in China. Mamsurov agreed, somewhat reluctantly: Rudi's plans for his future espionage career were more ambitious than anything Moscow had in mind.

Ursula's German passport was carefully doctored by the forgers of the Fourth Department, with blank pages stitched in "to replace the pages which had contained visas, stamps etc. of her sojourn in the Far East." It appeared to show she had spent the last two years in Germany. On June 10, 1938, she arrived in Britain, yet another Jewish refugee, indistinguishable from the flood seeking safety. She told the immigration authorities she intended to stay with her parents for about three months, and signed a formal undertaking to leave by September 20: "I understand that should I overstay the period allowed, steps will be taken to compel me to return to Germany, notwithstanding any pleas to the contrary." Despite the popular myth, Britain did not open its arms to all German Jews, especially communist ones.

The Kuczynskis were still living in Hampstead. Brigitte had married a Scottish communist, Anthony Lewis, and moved into the Isokon building two doors from her parents in Lawn Road—a modernist block of flats that would become infamous as home to a suspiciously large number of communist spies. Jürgen took up residence in nearby Upper Park Road. The British left had embraced these distinguished German Jewish intellectual refugees with enthusiasm. Indeed, as one historian puts it, "the Kuczynskis' list of friends and acquaintances reads almost like a *Who's Who* of British left-wing political, academic and literary life of the period": writers such as Cecil Day Lewis, Sidney and Beatrice Webb, Rosamond Lehmann, Rose Macaulay, John Strachey, and Stephen Spender; the publisher Victor Gollancz; Labour politicians Aneurin Bevan and Tom Driberg; the historian Arnold Toynbee; and many more. Jürgen even became friendly with Sylvia Pankhurst, the suffragette campaigner, and Lilian Bowes Lyon, the then queen's first cousin. It was quite hard to attend a Hampstead dinner party in 1938 without bumping into a Kuczynski.

Jürgen was the standard-bearer of German anti-fascism in Britain, chief among the swelling community of exiled German communists. He toured the country giving lectures, raised funds for refugees, held scores of meetings, nurtured contacts on the British left, and wrote, unstoppably: pamphlets, histories, reports, propaganda leaflets. He started work on his *History of Labour Conditions*, which he would continue to expand for the rest of his life. When not scribbling, he was soliciting funds for Freedom Radio 29.8, an anti-Nazi station broadcasting to Germany, for which Albert Einstein, Ernest Hemingway, and Thomas Mann wrote scripts, and helping to found the Free German League of Culture, a "German, anti–National Socialist, anti-fascist, non-party refugee organization with the aim of nurturing German culture." Jürgen Kuczynski was inexhaustible, and completely exhausting.

Secretly, Jürgen was also writing political and economic reports for the Soviet Union, which were couriered back to Moscow via the Soviet embassy. A frequent visitor to Jürgen's home was the Soviet press attaché, Anatoli Gromov (real name Gorski), in reality the chief of Soviet intelligence in Britain, code-named "Vadim." He flattered Jürgen, telling him his reports were valued in Moscow for their "ice-cold logic." Between his arrival in Britain and the Fall of France, Jürgen made trips to Paris "whenever the laws of conspiracy allowed," to take orders and pass information to the Comintern and the exiled KPD leaders.

Jürgen Kuczynski was a committed communist secretly sending intelligence to Stalin. He knew his sister was involved in Soviet espionage, though he did not know the extent. He believed it his comradely duty to pass valuable information to the Soviet Union. Whether that made him a spy was a matter of perspective.

The British secret services did not know quite what to make of the Kuczynskis. They were committed opponents of Nazism, to be sure, but they were also Germans, communists, and Jews, which made them triply suspect in the eyes of MI5, an organization with its fair share of anti-Semites. MI5 knew about Jürgen's communist activities and his trips to Paris, but nothing of his contacts with Soviet intelligence. The LSE professor Robert Kuczynski was considered more dubious than his son. Brigitte was known to be an active member of the CPGB (North London branch). The family was being watched, but as war with Germany drew closer, MI5 was more concerned with digging out Nazi spies than a handful of communist sympathizers in leafy Hampstead.

Ursula immediately set to work. At Moscow's suggestion, she contacted Fred Uhlman, a German poet, lawyer, painter, communist, and Spanish Civil War veteran, and asked him if any of his British former comrades in the International Brigades might be willing to undertake "illegal, dangerous work inside Germany." Uhlman passed on the inquiry to Douglas Springhall, a fellow International Brigader, who in turn contacted Fred Copeman, former leader of the British Battalion. Copeman recommended a young volunteer who had just returned to Britain.

Alexander Allan Foote is one of the most important, but also one of the most enduringly mysterious, figures in modern espionage history.

The son of a poultry farmer from Yorkshire, Foote was thirty-two, with receding fair hair swept back from a wide forehead and sharp blue eyes. He left school at sixteen to work in a garage before becoming a coal merchant and then, as he put it, a "restless sales manager" for a chicken feed business. He did not share his father's "single-minded passion for chicken farming." Foote was a strange mixture of parts: pleasure-loving, adventurous, opportunistic, and charming. While still a teenager he attended communist discussion groups, but it was the outbreak of the Spanish conflict in 1936 that provided him with a handy, albeit shallow, political philosophy. "The Civil War seemed to show everything up in black and white," he wrote. The Spanish Nationalists and their fascist allies were trying to destroy democracy, and the Republicans were defending it with the help of the Soviet Union. "It all seemed as simple as that." He did not join the Communist Party, but described himself as "a bit of a Bolshie."

Foote joined the RAF in 1935, but on December 23, 1936, "on the point of being thrown out," he deserted from Gosport barracks, bolted to London, and then embarked for Spain with several hundred other idealistic British volunteer fighters, most of whom would not return. Foote's motives were only partly political: he had got a girl pregnant, and decided the risk in Spain was less than that posed by her enraged father. The British Battalion, part of the Sixth International Brigade, assembled in Catalonia, consisting of British, Irish, and colonial citizens, a handful of Swedes, and a slightly baffled Ethiopian. Most were communists of one shade or another. Sergeant Foote was appointed transport officer. He remained in Spain for two years and ended up as batman to Copeman, a former Royal Navy heavyweight boxer. As battalion commander, Copeman left something to be desired; he was described by one of his men as "more or less insane, giving completely inconsequential orders to everybody in sight, and offering to bash their faces in if they did not comply." Nonetheless Copeman saw in Foote something more than just another angry young man looking to die for a cause. In the autumn of 1938, Foote was allowed to return to the United Kingdom to attend the Fifteenth Communist Congress in Birmingham Town Hall, which he found very boring. Soon afterward, Foote was invited to dinner with Copeman and his wife, Kitty, at their home in Lewisham.

"Springhall has asked me to recommend someone for an assignment," said Copeman, who had recently been invalided home from Spain after being shot in the face and neck. "We think that you might fit the bill. I know nothing about the assignment save that it will be abroad, and very dangerous." Foote immediately accepted despite, as he put it, having "no notion of whom I would be working for or for what purpose." Copeman scribbled down an address in Hampstead.

By this point Ursula had already departed for Switzerland, leaving Dover on September 24, 1938. So when Foote knocked on the green door in Lawn Road it was not Ursula who opened it, but Brigitte, now anglicized to Mrs. Bridget Lewis. Ursula's younger sister had become an accessory to Soviet espionage, and she knew precisely what to do if and when a man named Alexander Foote appeared.

Foote sat, a little nervously, in a chintz-covered armchair, while a "respectable housewife with a slight foreign accent" grilled him over tea and biscuits. "The whole atmosphere of the flat was one of complete middle-class respectability." After ten minutes the interview was over. "I was dealt with by the lady of the house as briskly and impersonally as she would have engaged a housemaid."

"You will proceed to Geneva," said Brigitte, handing him a £10 note. "There you will be contacted and further instructions will be given to you."

Her next words might have come straight from the pages of a second-rate spy novel.

"On Thursday next week, you must be waiting outside the General Post Office in Geneva at exactly midday. You must wear a white scarf and carry a leather belt in your right hand. At noon, you will be approached by a woman carrying a string shopping bag containing a green parcel. She will say, in English: 'Where did you buy that belt?' You will reply: 'I bought it in an ironmonger's shop in Paris.' You will then ask her where you can buy an orange like hers, and she will reply: 'You can have it for an English penny.'"

CHAPTER 12

THE MOLEHILL

URSULA WAS LIVING IN A SWISS PICTURE POSTCARD. The little farmhouse in the mountains above Lake Geneva, near the village of Caux-sur-Montreux, was surrounded by some of the most majestic scenery in the world. "Before us the meadows descended to the forest, and the forest to the valley, where the lake and the ribbon of the Rhône sparkled," she wrote. The Alps rose magnificently in the distance, and behind the house lush pastures led up to a pine-covered ridge beneath the summit at Rochers-de-Naye. The nearest neighbors were the farmer and his wife, a quarter of a mile distant. A narrow path led to the village of Caux, from which a winding road ran down to Montreux on the lake. At night, from the cowshed at the back of the building, came the sounds of gentle bovine breathing. In the evenings, Ursula played Lotto with Michael while Nina combed her doll's hair and Ollo sewed and sang. As the sun went down, Ursula stood by the open window, breathing in the serenity. "The air was cool. I had known many countries, cities, villages, apartments, hotels, boarding houses; never before and never since have I lived in such a wonderful landscape." The farmhouse had been advertised in the window of a Geneva rental agency: it felt like a refuge from a world falling apart.

The term "mole" as slang for a spy was not coined until the 1960s, but to modern ears the name of the farmhouse sounds distinctly apt: La Taupinière, the Molehill.

At night, when everyone was asleep, Ursula constructed her

transmitter-receiver from parts bought at hardware shops in Geneva, Vevey, and Lausanne: keypad, an antenna with banana plugs, and two heavy batteries "each the size of a dictionary," which she hid in the hayloft. At the back of the bottom shelf in the built-in wardrobe was a panel held in place by screws, behind which was just enough space to hide the assembled equipment. She drilled two small holes in the plywood partition and fed through the leads, enabling her to use the transmitter without removing it from the cupboard. When disconnected, the holes were concealed with wooden plugs resembling knots in the wood. The hidden transmitter might "evade a superficial house search" but she knew that "if it was located by taking radio signal bearings, even the best hiding place would be useless."

Ursula moved the large wooden bed alongside the wardrobe, "so that I could see the mountains," and communicate with Moscow while sitting up in bed.

On September 29, 1938, a clear, cool night, ideal for transmitting, Ursula tested her homemade radio for the first time. At 11:20, she established a good connection on a frequency of 6.1182 MHz and tapped out her call sign and a brief message, half a dozen "groups" comprised of five numbers each. She imagined the message as a shooting star. "With the speed of light my numbers streaked across the sky, where the half-moon was visible, arrived where they were expected, helped the comrades and gave them strength." Some 1,500 kilometers away, in the receiving station in Dymovka forest near the Polish-Ukrainian border, a Red Army operator picked up the signal and sent back a brief acknowledgment. From Dymovka, the news that Sonya's transmitter was functioning passed to the Center, and the desk of Major Vera Poliakova, the woman officer in charge of Swiss espionage.

Flooded with relief, Ursula stood at the open window: "I leaned my elbows on the ledge and looked out. Even the night air smelled of woods and meadows, and it was very quiet."

Too pumped with adrenaline for sleep, she lay awake for hours before turning on her transistor radio and tuning in to the BBC, quietly, so as not to wake the household. The news banished sleep that night: "The British Prime Minister has been hailed as bringing 'peace to Europe' after signing a non-aggression pact with Germany." The

Munich Agreement allowed Nazi Germany to annex the Sudetenland region of western Czechoslovakia in exchange for a promise of peace, soon to be broken. As Ursula put it, the deal "gave the green light to Hitler's expansionist aims." War was coming.

"He should be beaten with his own umbrella," declared Olga Muth, when Ursula told her of Neville Chamberlain's deal the next morning. "And if Hitler wants to take Switzerland too, what will become of us?"

The news grew steadily worse. In Spain, the "Munich Betrayal" removed the last hope of an anti-fascist alliance, destroying Republican morale. Franco's troops advanced swiftly, and Nationalist victory at the Battle of the Ebro signaled the end for the Spanish Republic and its band of international fighters. "How I wished I had been there with them," wrote Ursula, "instead of on my own front here with two children, an old woman and twelve cows." The fascist tide was rising on all sides. With horror, she read of the events on November 9, when Nazis went on the bloody rampage known as Kristallnacht, the night of broken glass, destroying Jewish businesses and synagogues, murdering and arresting Jews. *The Times* reported: "No foreign propagandist bent upon blackening Germany before the world could outdo the tale of burnings and beatings, of blackguardly assaults on defenceless and innocent people, which disgraced that country yesterday." The Kuczynski Bank, founded by Robert's father and the source of the wealth that had underpinned their former life, was confiscated and Aryanized overnight. So was Ullstein, the Jewish publisher for which Ursula had worked back in 1928: henceforth the company would be churning out Hitler's propaganda and *Das Reich,* the Nazi newspaper.

From her Molehill high on a Swiss hillside, Ursula wrote to her parents in London: "Our spirits, just like yours, have sunk to zero."

LOITERING IN THE CRISP autumn sun outside Geneva Post Office, Alexander Foote reflected wryly that every Swiss housewife seemed to have bought an orange for lunch that day. He had no clear idea what he was doing in Switzerland. During the train journey he wondered if he might be embroiled in a black-market smuggling operation, or perhaps "cast in some Scarlet Pimpernel–like role of rescuing prisoners from Dachau." This business was obviously clandestine, illegal, and in tune with his vaguely leftist politics, which was just fine with Foote. But he felt remarkably conspicuous standing around in a white scarf with a leather belt in his hand, eyeing up every passing woman as the clock ticked down. "I felt a self-conscious fool, at best self-doomed to embarrassment and at worst to a Swiss charge of accosting." The town bell was striking twelve when he spotted her. "Slim, with a good figure and even better legs, her black hair demurely dressed, she stood out from the Swiss crowd. In her early thirties, she might have been the wife of a minor French consular official." She was holding an orange, and a string bag containing a green parcel.

"Excuse me," said Ursula. "But where did you buy that belt?"

Over coffee in a nearby café, each sized up the other. "He was tall, and a bit overweight. His hair was reddish blond, the eyelashes were fair, complexion pale and eyes blue. To another Englishman, his accent would have betrayed a lower middle-class background, but in Germany this would not matter." She told him to call her "Sonya" and explained that henceforth, in all communications, he would be "Jim." Foote was drawn to her. "A pleasant person and an amusing companion, my first espionage contact was not as frightening as I had expected . . . she spoke English with a slight foreign accent and was, I should judge, a Russian or a Pole." Ursula observed him closely—"every word, cadence, gesture"—and noted that "he grasped things quickly and asked sensible questions." After an hour, she had made up her mind.

"You will go to Munich on a one-year tourist visa," she said. "There you will settle in, learn the language, make as many friends as possible, and keep your eyes open." He should read up about wireless technology and study basic photography. In Munich his primary task would be to cultivate workers and officials at the BMW factory, which, in addition to cars, manufactured aircraft engines for the Luftwaffe. When Foote pointed out that he knew nothing about Germany, her response was brusque: "Look up Munich in the public library." Once established, he could communicate his address via Brigitte in London by sending her a novel: on a specific page, he should write the address using an invisible ink made by adding cornstarch to water. When iodine solution was brushed over the page, the secret writing would appear. She then handed over 2,000 Swiss francs "for expenses" and told Foote to meet her, outside the post office in Lausanne, at midday exactly three months hence. She gave him some simple advice on how to detect if he was being followed. Finally she asked for a recommendation. The British Battalion in Spain had been disbanded, and its 305 surviving volunteers repatriated. Was there anyone else among Foote's former comrades, she asked, who might be suitable for a similar assignment to his? He thought for a moment and then suggested a communist friend who had fought alongside him during the Battle of Jarama, earning a reputation for fearlessness. This man, Foote said, was "the only one of his old comrades capable of carrying out a risky job on his own."

Ursula memorized the name: Len Beurton.

Alexander Foote boarded the train with a light heart, a full wallet, and only the faintest sense of what the future might hold. He had been told to expect a "difficult and dangerous" assignment; an expenses-paid holiday in Munich seemed to be neither. Clearly he was involved in some sort of espionage, but he had no clue who he might be spying for, nor, indeed, what spying might involve. Perhaps, he reflected, Sonya was part of the Comintern, a communist organization he had dimly heard of. Back in Britain, he collected his belongings from his sister in East Grinstead, applied for a German tourist visa, and paid another visit to Mrs. Lewis at Lawn Road to learn about "conditions in Germany" and confirm the secret arrangements for passing on his address. Brigitte was no longer so brisk and impersonal. They met twice more, for what he called "social occasions." An MI5 report later noted: "It is possible that F[oote] had a flirtation with Brigitte."

The snow fell early in Switzerland that year, blanketing the mountains. "The magnificent landscape seemed to have been specially created as a backdrop for this house," wrote Ursula. Every day, seven-year-old Michael skied down to the school in Caux. On Sundays they caught the little blue train that chugged to the top of the mountain, and then skied almost a mile to the house. Nina and Ollo spent the afternoons tobogganing. Ursula began to mix among the large expatriate community in Geneva, where the spies rubbed shoulders with diplomats, journalists, and sundry others who seemed to do nothing at all. As always, Ursula made friends both with people of like mind and others of quite different views. They were all interesting: Robert Dell, the correspondent for *The Manchester Guardian,* and his son-in-law David Blelloch, who worked for the International Labour Organization; an elderly Jewish woman named Lillian Jakobi, who had escaped an unhappy marriage to a rabbi; Marie Ginsberg, a librarian at the League of Nations. Diplomacy was the overriding topic of conversation in Geneva, gossip and secrets the chief currency of exchange. In this strange kaleidoscope, it was impossible to tell who was spying for whom. Many of Ursula's new acquaintances were well informed, and sometimes indiscreet, about the deteriorating international situation. She passed on whatever she gleaned to Moscow. "Was I deceiving people who were sympathetic towards me?" she wondered. Ursula also struck up a friendship with the wife of the local farmer, Frau Füssli, a kindly, exhausted Swiss woman with four children, a domineering husband, and "friendly brown eyes." Their conversations tended to focus on how much Frau Füssli would rather be married to the farmer on the other side of the valley, with whom she was conducting an affair.

One Spring afternoon, Johann Patra appeared at the door of the farmhouse. After their last meeting in Moscow, he had gone back to China to aid the communist insurgents (a lucky absence that probably saved him from Stalin's butchers), and was paying another brief visit to the Center before returning once more to Shanghai. He had found out where she was living, and decided to drop in on Ursula unannounced. She was pleased to see him, but struck by how naïve he now seemed and dismayed at how little interest he showed in his vivacious three-year-old daughter. "I did not blame him," she wrote. "But neither did I understand him." Perhaps they had never really understood each other. Their love affair now seemed a distant fantasy.

Ollo was an ever-present helpmate: cooking, cleaning, sewing, and caring for little Nina, with whom she had established a deep bond, occasionally referring to the baby as "my child." Nanny and child shared a bedroom. At times, Ursula wondered whether Ollo's attachment to her daughter was a little obsessive. With Michael, she was overly strict. Olga Muth knew that Ursula often worked late into the night, sending messages on the transmitter hidden in the bottom of her wardrobe. When Ursula came to breakfast drained from lack of sleep, Ollo sent her back upstairs. "I see how long the light burns in your room. . . . Stay in bed, I'll keep the children quiet." Their complicity was more open these days. Ursula even discussed what Ollo should do in the event of a police raid. "If something happens, you have seen nothing and heard nothing, and you stick with that story."

As in Ursula's childhood home, the rivalry between mother and nanny was unspoken, but intense. Ollo considered herself to be the better mother, and once even hinted that Ursula's espionage was impinging on her maternal duties. Stung, Ursula shot back: "Should I give up my work because I have them, or should I give up the children because of my illegal work? Both would be impossible for me." Ollo had touched a raw nerve. When Ursula needed to send a wireless message or attend a rendezvous, she ceased mothering and, as her own mother had done for rather different reasons, handed the job over to Ollo. She adored her children, but sometimes it was a relief to be able to pause being a mother and resume being a spy. She did not put her work ahead of her children; but she did believe she could have both a family and a career as a spy.

That winter, Foote installed himself in a furnished apartment at 2 Elisabethstrasse, Munich. A university student and SS officer named Eugen Lahr agreed to teach him German, and happily introduced Foote to other Nazis. As instructed, Foote bought a novel, wrote his address in secret ink, and posted it to Lawn Road. He forgot, however, to indicate which page the message was on, leaving Brigitte "to soak the entire volume in iodine to bring out the secret writing." Then he relaxed. Posing as an eccentric and wealthy British tourist, he had "enough pocket money and little to do, save enjoy myself"—something he was rather good at.

Foote dined out for every meal. One day, in search of lunch, he alighted on the Osteria Bavaria on Schellingstrasse, which offered a decent-looking set menu. Foote was tucking into his deep-fried trout with *Kartoffelsalat,* when there was a "flurry at the door and Hitler strode in."

By chance Foote had chosen to lunch in the führer's favorite restaurant, run by a former comrade from the First World War. Hitler always ate in the rear annex, separated from the other diners by a thin wooden partition, on which hung a coatrack. He was usually accompanied by his adjutant, SS Obergruppenführer Wilhelm Brückner, and several aides. Like most tyrants, Hitler was fussy about food, and his order never varied: "Eggs and mayonnaise, vegetables and pasta, and compote of fruit or a raw grated apple, and Fachinger Wasser," a faddish medicinal mineral water that claimed to cure stomach ailments. The führer farted frequently during meals. No one objected. In March 1935, Hitler dined at the Osteria Bavaria with the British Nazi-sympathizing Mitford sisters, Unity and Diana: one a substantially insane Hitler groupie, the other the mistress of Oswald Mosley, the British fascist leader. Over lunch, Diana admired Hitler's "greyish blue eyes, so dark that they often appeared brown and opaque." A year later, she married Mosley at the Berlin home of Joseph Goebbels, with Hitler in attendance.

Amused to be in such infamous company, Foote took to lunching regularly at the restaurant and noted that when in Munich Hitler ate there up to three times a week. "This triviality," he wrote, "was to have surprising consequences."

Foote and Ursula met again, as planned, outside Lausanne Post Office. Sonya was still only "moderately enlightening" about his role, but her financial generosity was enough to allay any qualms: he was now on the payroll, she explained, with a salary of $150 a month, plus expenses, in return for which he should compile reports on "political and economic conditions in Germany." More intriguingly, she said he would shortly be contacted by a "new collaborator." Together they should work on "a possible sabotage operation and keep it on ice until such time as the director authorized it."

Not much the wiser but quite a lot richer, Foote returned to a Munich "still full of tourists basking in the twilight of European peace" that would not last much longer. "Conversations with my SS friends and the evidence of my own eyes convinced me that it was only a matter of time before the military machine took control and the country went to war."

RUDI HAMBURGER CAME TO Switzerland to say farewell. Having completed a two-month radio course in Paris, he was keen to get back to China and begin working as a Soviet spy in his own right. Moscow had finally agreed to his request: he was ordered to sail from Marseilles to Shanghai accompanied by the Red Army's senior intelligence officer in the region, who was returning to China and would oversee Rudi's clandestine work.

The officer was Johann Patra.

For both men, the situation was, to put it mildly, odd. Johann would be working with the man he had cuckolded. Rudi would be taking orders from his wife's former lover, the biological father of the child everyone believed to be his. The Center was not known for its sensitivity, but even hard-bitten Umar Mamsurov had felt moved to ask Hamburger if he was prepared to work under Patra. As Ursula put it, "generous and principled as he was, Rudi had a high opinion of Johann, and agreed." Rudi was philosophical, or pretended to be. "There was no personal conflict between us on account of his earlier co-habitation with my wife. As men, we understood each other. The past was the past."

Rudi was determined to avoid a scene and stayed for only a few days, but the final parting from his family was supremely painful. Little Michael, deeply attached to his father, recalled the moment of separation with undimmed pain eight decades later. "I remember him saying goodbye, and saying he would return soon. My mother told me he would be coming back, but he didn't. She was not honest with me about that. One day he was there; the next he was gone. I waited and waited." Ollo was also upset by Rudi's departure, unwilling to accept that the marriage was really over.

Ursula accompanied him to the station at Montreux. Rudi had been her first love. They had been partners, in marriage, ideology, and espionage, since she was eighteen years old. She no longer loved him, but his departure was yet another severance. She had already lost so many people she loved: Sorge and Patra, her friends Agnes,

Shushin, and Grisha, and countless other colleagues and comrades, friends and family, destroyed by Stalin or Hitler. Her life seemed to have been measured out in painful railway station partings and dockside departures. Loyal and stubborn, Rudi was one of the few people she trusted wholly, and now he was leaving too. She "stood on the platform and watched the little blue mountain train until it had disappeared round the bend."

LEN BEURTON WAS SURPRISED to find himself outside the Uniprix shop in the Swiss town of Vevey on Lake Geneva, at exactly 11:50 on January 15, 1939, holding an apple in his left hand and a folded newspaper under his right arm, and scanning the crowd for a woman carrying a net bag of oranges. The weeks since his return from Spain had been full of surprises: a message from his former commander asking him to call a number in Hampstead, then the meeting with a posh woman "with a slight foreign accent" who gave him money, told him to go to Switzerland, and made him memorize all the complex arrangements involving fruit, newspapers, and peculiar passwords. He had felt reassured when Mrs. Lewis mentioned Alexander Foote, his former comrade in arms. If Footie was involved, it was probably some kind of "international swindle." It all sounded pretty dodgy. But Len didn't mind. He quite liked dodgy, and he certainly wasn't scared. Len didn't really understand fear.

Ursula observed the handsome young Englishman from a nearby doorway. "He was twenty-five years old, with thick brown hair, eyebrows that met and clear hazel eyes. He was lean and athletic, strong and muscular." Len turned, saw her watching him, and smiled.

"Do you like ice cream?" she asked.

"No, whisky," he replied.

As they walked around Vevey, Ursula explained that Len had been recommended for "dangerous work in Germany, a continuation of his fight on Spanish soil." When she warned that the job could be extremely dangerous, "his face lit up." Len should return to Britain, she said, and then head for Frankfurt, home of the industrial giant I. G. Farben, a vital cog in the German war machine. There he should begin teaching himself German. He must tell no one where he was going. Once settled in Frankfurt, Len should contact his old friend Alexander Foote in Munich and await instructions. The young man asked no questions. He did not want to know what organization he was working for, nor how long he would have to stay in Germany. He displayed no trace of anxiety, or even hesitation. He simply put the money she gave him in his pocket, shook Ursula's hand warmly without quite meeting her eye, and walked away, grinning.

Ursula was intrigued by this young Englishman, seven years her junior. "Half shy, half aggressive, he gave the impression of boyish immaturity." He struck her as "a nice, modest young man" but "extremely sensitive."

Len Beurton could not stop thinking about the woman he now knew as Sonya.

I was twenty-five, and my experience of falling in love had been limited to boyhood worship of distant film stars. That may explain why my instantaneous reaction to Sonya has left the recollection of what was said at our first meeting somewhat cloudy. I suspect she thought I had not quite recovered from the bombing in Spain. Of course, she could not know that *she* was the bomb.

Len fell for Ursula the instant he saw her standing on the pavement outside a Swiss supermarket, holding a bag of oranges.

Until this moment, Leon Charles Beurton (pronounced "Burton," and often spelled that way) had experienced nothing remotely resembling love. Len's life started in Barking in 1914, three weeks into his parents' shotgun marriage. His French-born father was a hotel waiter who joined the French army on the outbreak of war and was killed within weeks of arriving at the front. Florence Beurton paid for her six-year-old son to be fostered by a widowed railway clerk named Thomas Fenton. "I'll come back in the school holidays," she told him. "Every morning he woke up with the fresh conviction that his mother would definitely come today." Len never saw his mother again. Fenton had two sons already and ignored his foster son. "There was no affection. It was a purely commercial transaction," Len later wrote. At the age of fourteen, he ran away from home and found work as an agricultural laborer, then as a mechanic and truck driver in London. On weekends he learned to shoot at the Territorial Army gym, and during his lunch hour he boxed at the Blackfriars boxing ring. "Many of the most colourful boxers were Jewish," he later wrote. "To make good, a Jewish boy had to be twice as tough as the non-Jewish fighters. I developed a natural respect for them. This laid the foundations for my outraged contempt when Hitler's anti-Semitism became official doctrine."

At eighteen, he found work in a quarry on the island of Jersey, where he was befriended by an Irish American former seaman called Moriarty. A burly giant, mild in manner and fierce in politics, Moriarty introduced Len to the radical writings of Jack London, and the legend of Joe Hill, the American labor activist executed in 1915. "Moriarty taught me much more than how to cut granite with a seven-pound hammer. The revolution entered my life." Together, they listened to Radio Moscow. "We watched the rise of fascism and together firmly believed that the German working class would settle accounts with Hitler. We followed events in Spain and decided that the only place for an anti-fascist was in the International Brigades."

Beurton joined the British Battalion in Spain in January 1937 and three weeks later, on February 12, he went into action on the Jarama front. Many years later, he wrote up his memories of the action at "Suicide Hill," one of the bloodiest of the civil war, in which Nationalist forces sought to dislodge the Republican and international troops defending the road to Madrid.

That morning, the dawn came up cold, clear and bright. The world seemed young, and we too, as the battalion, 600 strong, climbed up to the ridge above the Jarama. By nightfall we were no more than 300. On the morning of 13th, we numbered 225. On the 14th, we were 140. That historic 14th broke the back of the Fascist offensive. The lifeline of the Madrid–Valencia road had been saved. The battalion buried its dead. From the British working class none ever died with greater honour. We held that front for four months. "Solidarity and

Unity," Old Moriarty had said, "are the two most beautiful words in the revolutionary's lexicon." The Jarama proved how right he was.

The battalion was the first family Beurton had ever known, and within a month of being adopted by it three-quarters were dead.

Len was, understandably, an insecure man, oversensitive and quick to complain. He was happiest on his own, behind the lines, wandering the Spanish countryside during lulls in the fighting. But he had one very remarkable quality: he was immune to fear. He was not brave, exactly, but he was nerveless at moments when others were terrified. An American psychologist interviewed him at the height of the fighting and declared "he had never met anyone so completely devoid of physical fear." In February 1937, Beurton was driving a truck from the battalion cookhouse with Captain George Nathan in the passenger seat when the vehicle took a direct hit from an artillery shell. Beurton emerged from the wreckage not only unscathed, but weirdly cheerful. He lost two more trucks to strafing, without registering a whiff of anxiety. "My nervous system, I had discovered, operated efficiently under stress," he wrote.

In April 1939, Len Beurton caught the train from Frankfurt to Munich and rang the doorbell of number 2 Elisabethstrasse. Foote was delighted (and not very surprised) to discover that the "new comrade" Sonya had referred to was his old friend Len. He suggested they have lunch at the Osteria Bavaria, in order, as he put it, to "have a look at Hitler." Sure enough, the Englishmen had scarcely sat down when they were told to put out their cigarettes as the fanatically anti-smoking führer was about to arrive. "We didn't have to give the salute because we were British subjects, but we stood up like the rest." Two women were also waiting for the führer's arrival: one was Unity Mitford, Hitler's British acolyte, and the other was his mistress, Eva Braun. "They clearly couldn't stand each other," Len observed. Hitler greeted his two female guests, bowing and kissing each by the hand, and then processed through the restaurant to loud applause. At that moment Len reached into the inside pocket of his jacket. He was searching for his cigarette case, but to Foote the movement looked "as though he was going to draw a revolver." He was horrified. "There must have been a fair sprinkling of trigger-happy Gestapo agents" among Hitler's entourage who would open fire at any hint of an assassination attempt. "Nothing whatever happened." The führer's goons stood around looking bored as Len pulled out his cigarettes, and Hitler disappeared into the back parlor. Foote breathed again, reflecting: "It's a wonder no-one tries to bump him off considering the lack of precautions taken on these informal occasions."

Sonya had told Foote and Beurton to identify sabotage opportunities inside Nazi Germany, some target that might be dramatically destroyed in a way that would impede German rearmament and attract the attention of the international press. Len believed he had already found the ideal objective. His friendly landlord took him to see the *Graf Zeppelin,* the mighty passenger-carrying, hydrogen-filled airship. In 1936, Goebbels sent the zeppelin on a tour of Germany, dropping propaganda leaflets and blaring loud martial music. The great flying machine had been decommissioned and was now on display in a huge hangar at Frankfurt airport, a proud symbol of German scientific prowess, military might, and national pride. Len suggested they blow it up.

Foote told him "not to be ridiculous," but the more they discussed it, the more feasible a sabotage operation seemed. Beurton insisted: "It would be perfectly easy to put a time bomb with a slow fuse in a cigarette packet under one of the seats and let it and the hydrogen in the envelope do the rest." He returned for another look, carefully inspecting the cushions and curtains, and the "impregnated canvas skin." If an incendiary device was planted in the gondola, the whole airship would go up like a giant firework.

At the next rendezvous with Ursula in Vevey, Foote outlined the plan. Sonya was "extremely excited" and explained that an effective bomb could be constructed from sugar, aluminum powder, and charcoal. "A moderately accurate time fuse was not difficult to make," giving the saboteurs ample time to escape before it went off. She invited Foote to come to the house the next morning "so that we could try out the mixture in peace and quiet"—an odd way to describe detonating a homemade bomb. Foote was pleased by the invitation to Sonya's home. "I felt it was a step forward in my initiation into the network." In the lean-to shed abutting La Taupinière, they mixed the bomb and inserted a time fuse. "The whole thing fitted inside a cigarette packet." Then they placed the incendiary device under a sofa cushion and took cover inside the house. "The only result was a large quantity of black smoke and an unholy stink." If it could not set fire to a cotton cushion, the bomb was extremely unlikely to ignite the thick leather upholstery of the zeppelin.

Over dinner, they agreed that the plan was probably unfeasible. The conversation turned to Foote's life in Munich. He told her how he had taken to eating at the Osteria Bavaria, where Hitler frequently lunched with his dozy bodyguards. "It would be easy to put a bomb in a suitcase beneath the coats and hats which hung on the partition wall separating Hitler from the main restaurant," he idly observed. Sonya's response stunned him.

"What an excellent idea."

"Just fancy," he later observed. "She expected me to assassinate Hitler."

Foote returned to Munich, and Ursula immediately sent a message to Moscow reporting that Agent Jim had "presented an opportunity for coming close to Hitler and assassinating him." The response came back: "The director is extremely interested in the report on Hitler"; Foote should "check up on his movements and habits."

"The snow melted," wrote Ursula, "and the spring had a fairy tale beauty." The warmer weather brought a flood of wild daffodils to the hills above the chalet, and no fewer than three spies to the Molehill. Alexander Foote and Len Beurton traveled separately to Switzerland and checked into a Montreux boardinghouse, the Pension Elisabeth, overlooking Bon Port on Lake Geneva. The next day, while the children and Ollo "made their way through a sea of flowers, picking arms full of daffodils," the three conspirators sat in Ursula's kitchen and discussed how to murder Hitler.

Foote was distinctly alarmed to discover that in the intervening weeks the ambiguous injunction to "keep an eye" on Hitler at the Osteria Bavaria "had burgeoned in the eyes of the Kremlin into a full-blown scheme for assassination, with Len and myself apparently cast for the principal roles." Beurton was enthusiastic. "What could be easier than to put a time bomb in an attaché case along with our coats and, having had an early lunch, abandon the lot in the hope that the bomb would blow Hitler and his entourage, snugly lunching behind the deal boarding, into eternity?" An alternative method— "assassination in its more traditional character"—would be to shoot Hitler as he passed through the restaurant and hope his inattentive bodyguards were too slow to intervene. The only problem with this second plan was that it was suicidal. Ursula and Beurton shared the conviction that killing Hitler was not only possible, but a moral imperative. "Neither of us believed in the effectiveness of terrorist attacks on individuals," she wrote. "But there were some people we considered so dangerous and bestial that we were both prepared to break the rules." Foote was not nearly so keen. He too wanted Hitler dead. He just didn't want to die himself. Beurton might be a stranger to fear, but Foote was not.

The next day they practiced assembling bombs, and Ursula gave her accomplices an initial lesson in wireless technology. How very different were these two Englishmen, Ursula reflected. Len was "intelligent, well-read and a keen observer" but he "did not possess Jim's self-assured poise." Foote was "resourceful and shrewd" with "a talent for organization," but she also detected a "tendency towards cynicism" and a taste for the high life: he seemed to be having rather too good a time in Germany. Beurton liked to wander alone in the mountains, whereas Foote was happiest in the fleshpots of Geneva. "I preferred the sensitive Len," she wrote. "Who loved nature and took an interest in my children."

Franz Obermanns, the deputy Ursula had been introduced to in Moscow, arrived in Switzerland several months later than expected. During training, the young German communist had set off a bomb prematurely and gashed his chin with flying glass. The Center insisted he would be too conspicuous in Switzerland with a face swathed in bandages, so he had delayed his departure until the wound healed. Ursula met him in Bern and instructed him to find lodgings in Fribourg in western Switzerland, build a transmitter, watch for any signs of surveillance, and await developments. Obermanns did not inspire confidence: he was enthusiastic enough, but still had a vivid red scar on his face—"not exactly an advantage in secret work." He seemed clumsy.

By the summer of 1939, Ursula had two working transmitter-receivers, two agents embedded in Germany, a willing assistant in Obermanns, and a plan to blow up the führer. To finance operations, Moscow transferred funds into a London bank account, disguising the origin, which she withdrew as required. The Center was pleased: Major Sonya's Swiss network was running like clockwork, and war was on the horizon.

In March, German troops had occupied Prague, the same month that Austria was annexed by Nazi Germany. Franco's Nationalists were supreme in Spain. "Would it be Switzerland's turn next?" Ursula wondered. Foreigners were already fleeing the country, fearful of a Nazi invasion. The Nazis had two separate intelligence organizations operating in Switzerland: the Abwehr (military intelligence) and Heinrich Himmler's powerful Reich Security Main Office, or RSHA, which combined the Gestapo and the Sicherheitsdienst (SD), the SS intelligence service. German spy hunters were combing Switzerland for enemies of the Reich. "Geneva was swarming with secret agents from many countries, and the Gestapo men came in droves," wrote Ursula. Her German passport, issued in Shanghai in 1935, would expire in May 1940, and as a Jew stripped of citizenship she was ineligible for a new one. Without a passport and residence permit she was liable to be deported, tantamount to a death sentence. Horrific accounts of what was happening to Jews in Germany were already circulating in Geneva. Marie Ginsberg, the librarian at the League of Nations, was a Polish Jew active in the underground network smuggling Jews out of Germany on false passports. She offered to help: for 2,000 Swiss francs, a Bolivian diplomat in Bern could provide Ursula with a Bolivian passport. It was some protection, but not much. What Ursula needed was legal citizenship of another country and a genuine passport to get her out of Switzerland in a hurry if the Nazis marched in.

Olga Muth returned from the village one afternoon bearing a worrying rumor: "Jews with expired passports would be put over the German border."

Ursula downplayed the danger. "There are many people without passports, and the deportations can only be isolated cases."

Ollo was unconvinced. "If they find out anything about your

work, it will be your turn. You know what will happen to you under Hitler. You won't survive."

But then the German nanny brightened. "I promise you one thing. I will keep the children with me, even if I have to hide them. When they send me back to Germany, I will take them with me. With their blue eyes and blond hair they won't attract attention. I can earn enough for the three of us. You won't need to worry about them. They'll have a good time with me."

Ursula did not like the direction this conversation was taking and brusquely put a stop to it. "I am still alive. My work may not be discovered, and even if they do arrest me they may not hand me over."

Olga Muth had intended to be reassuring. But her words carried a peculiar chill. The nanny had already framed a plan, should Ursula die, for adopting and raising the children herself, back in Nazi Germany.

CHAPTER 13

A MARRIAGE
OF CONVENIENCE

O N AUGUST 23, 1939, THE FOREIGN MINISTERS OF GERMANY
and the Soviet Union signed a diplomatic agreement in
Moscow—and Ursula's political universe imploded. Under the deal
agreed by Joachim von Ribbentrop and Vyacheslav Molotov, Nazi
Germany and the Soviet Union, hitherto sworn enemies, pledged
not to attack each other. In a secret protocol attached to the non-
aggression pact, they simultaneously agreed to carve up, into German and Soviet spheres of influence, Poland, Lithuania, Latvia, Estonia,
and Finland. This was power politics at its most cynical, a calculation
by both sides that, for the moment, they had more to gain from non-
belligerence than conflict. Hitler privately believed that war with the
Soviet Union was "inevitable," and he would make it so. But the führer, whom Ursula had so recently plotted to assassinate with the full
approval of the Red Army, was no longer the enemy.

The day after the signing of the Molotov-Ribbentrop Pact, Ursula received a radio message from Major Vera Poliakova at the Center: "Cease all activities against Germany. Pull all agents out and
break all contact with any remaining resident agents."

Ursula was shocked to the core. Without warning, Moscow had
suspended offensive operations against the regime that had forced
her family into exile, destroyed the German Communist Party, and
begun the systematic slaughter of her fellow Jews. She had fought
fascism all her adult life, in Germany, China, Manchuria, Poland,
and now Switzerland; she had repeatedly risked her life for the So-

viet Union; and now communism, the cause she loved, was in league with Nazism, the creed of racist violence and death she detested.

Ursula had never experienced such a crisis of political conscience. Stalin's purges had exposed the brutality at the core of the regime, but she had told herself this was the result of individual "mistakes." The Nazi-Soviet pact was a betrayal. For months, rumors had been circulating in Geneva that Germany and Moscow were in secret talks, but Ursula had dismissed this as "journalistic gossip." Throughout the trials of her early life she had been sustained by a belief that the party, directed by Moscow, was infallible. In time, Ursula would parrot the myth that the nonaggression pact had been a necessary, temporary truce, stymieing a Western capitalist plot to lure Nazi Germany and the USSR into a war of mutual destruction. In truth, like most intelligent communists of the time, she knew Hitler represented the polar opposite of everything she believed in; and Stalin had chosen, for reasons of expediency, to make peace with him. She was devastated, deeply disillusioned, and she was not alone. The Nazi-Soviet pact was greeted with dismay by communist parties worldwide, and with horror by Jews everywhere. It surprised Germany's allies, including Japan, and galvanized her enemies: two days later, Britain entered a treaty with France in defense of Poland. A day after that, the Swiss army was mobilized in anticipation of a German invasion. Caux, usually bustling with summer visitors, became a ghost town as the last tourists fled.

She might have been heartbroken at Moscow's pact with the devil, but Ursula remained a disciplined Red Army officer. Alexander Foote was in Geneva when the news broke. Ursula told him to stay where he was and get word to Len Beurton to leave Germany immediately and join them in Switzerland. She knew better than to defy Moscow, but she hinted at her misery in a message to the Center requesting a transfer from Switzerland to the United States. The stern message came back: "No more agents were needed in America." Sonya should remain at her post, await orders, and spend the time usefully training Foote and Beurton to operate a shortwave radio.

On September 1, Germany invaded Poland. The Free City of Danzig was incorporated into the Reich, and much of its communist underground wiped out overnight. Karl Hoffman, the delicate and tubercular leader of the group Ursula had worked with, was summarily murdered and his network liquidated.

Len was in Bavaria when he received Foote's telegram instructing him to "get out of Germany as fast as he could." Beurton crossed the border into Switzerland on September 3, 1939.

That day, Britain declared war on Germany.

Foote and Beurton checked into the Pension Elisabeth—they were the only guests—and the little spy trio hunkered down in the Swiss mountains. From the Center came an ominous silence. "During the first week of a Europe at war, we received no kind of instruction," wrote Foote. Hitherto Ursula had not specified the source of their orders, but now that they were no longer fighting fascism she owed her subagents a fuller explanation: Ursula told them her real name, described her work in China and Poland, and explained that she was an officer in the Red Army. The order to cease spying on Germany came directly from Moscow. Foote was wryly amused that all the preparatory work for assassinating Hitler had been "completely wasted," but he was not unduly perturbed to discover that he was an employee of Soviet military intelligence. Ursula tried to seem unruffled by the dramatic change of Soviet policy, but they could tell she was disgusted and distraught.

"The Russian-German pact," wrote Foote, hit her "like a thunderbolt out of the clear sky. Its effect on Sonya was shattering. She had always regarded the party line as being firmly and steadfastly directed against Fascism. At one blow, all this was changed and she, as a good party member, had now to regard the Nazis as her friends and the democracies as her potential foes. It was really too much for her."

So began a strange period of limbo. A few days after the outbreak of war, Ursula wrote to her parents in Britain: "Now it has happened, I can hardly believe it. Strange, how the sunsets are still as beautiful and peaceful as ever. It is lonely here." Every day, the two men walked up to La Taupinière for wireless tuition. Foote spent his afternoons sunbathing and his evenings in Geneva's bars and restaurants, courting the sister of the Romanian foreign minister. Ursula and Len took long walks in the countryside. Slowly the younger Englishman opened up, describing his abandonment as a child, his conversion to radical politics, and his experiences in Spain. Len's strange life had made him "oversensitive and introverted," she reflected, but there was also something special about this "shy, quiet man, intelligent, brave, and with high morals." He frequently stayed for supper, and played with the children before returning to the boardinghouse.

"Moscow was leaving us severely alone," wrote Foote. "Our usefulness to them was past for the moment, and the Red Army was content to allow the network to remain fallow until the time should come to revive it. Moscow had clipped our espionage wings." Ursula was going through the motions, supplying the Center with bland monthly reports on the political situation but, as Foote observed, "her heart was not in the work." That disillusionment was compounded when the Soviet Union invaded Finland in November 1939, an act of nakedly aggressive territorial expansion. Franz Obermanns, Ursula's number two, was equally disenchanted. "Shocked and bewildered, we talked for hours," she wrote. The Swiss had taken to carrying out spot checks on foreigners. During one of her conversations with Obermanns a policeman appeared, without warning, at the front door, panting from the exertion of the climb to La Taupinière. Ursula pretended the young man with the scarred face was one of her suitors (local gossips had noticed that men frequently called on the attractive single woman on the hillside), and the policeman departed satisfied, having inspected Obermanns's false papers and noted down the name, Eriki Noki.

The Nazi-Soviet pact theoretically precluded active espionage operations, but it did not prevent the Gestapo from continuing to hunt down communist spies and subversives both inside Germany and beyond her borders. Moscow maintained its support for what remained of the communist movement in Germany. In late October, Ursula was instructed to arrange collection of a large sum of money from a courier in Geneva and then transfer it across the border into Germany for Rosa Thälmann, wife of the imprisoned KPD leader, Ernst Thälmann. This was all very admirable as a "gesture of international solidarity," but Ursula, Obermanns, and the two Englishmen could not enter Germany without facing immediate arrest. She wondered whether to attempt the journey using Olga Muth's German passport. "If things turned out badly, she could say that I had stolen it from her." But no amount of disguise could make Ursula six inches shorter, age her by twenty-five years, and turn her eyes from brown to green. Ollo agreed to make the trip herself. No one would suspect the gray-haired nanny of being a communist money mule, and she could pretend she was visiting the military orphanage where she had grown up. Ollo's principal concern was Nina. "I'm an old woman, what can happen even if it turns out badly? But the separation from my child, I wouldn't survive that."

At twelve o'clock the following Sunday afternoon, Alexander Foote waited for the cash courier outside the entrance to Geneva's botanical gardens. As instructed, he wore a dark-blue felt hat, and held a furled umbrella in the crook of his right arm, a pair of leather gloves in his right hand, and a copy of the *Picture Post* in his left. The handover took less than a minute. Back at La Taupinière, Ursula prized off the back of her old clothes brush, folded the money tightly inside, and sealed it up with glue. Ollo, "innocent, small and mouse-grey," set off for Germany. If the Nazis discovered what she was up to, she would not be coming back.

Rosa Thälmann was initially suspicious of Nazi entrapment when an unknown woman appeared at her apartment door. But, once inside, Ollo convinced her that the money would provide "material aid to the starving families" of other victims of Nazism. The next day, in a Berlin park, Ollo handed over the clothes brush in a bag. The two women hugged and briefly wept. "I will never forget this," said Rosa.

"Everything's fine," Ollo called out, as she trotted back up the path to the Molehill. Ursula was relieved to see her, and profoundly grateful. But as the nanny swept up the three-year-old girl and held her tightly, Ursula could not help noticing "she only had eyes for Nina."

Switzerland, once a safe haven, was becoming a cage. The hunt for illegal radios intensified, and foreigners were subjected to increased Swiss surveillance. Himmler's spy hunters stepped up their pursuit. "As far as I could tell, I was not under observation," Ursula wrote. But whenever she turned on the transmitter she wondered if this would be the last time. The Swiss banking authorities clamped down on foreign transactions, and the money from Moscow dried up. Ursula was now supporting not only her family and Ollo, but also Foote, Beurton, and Obermanns. The Center promised to send more money. None arrived.

An officer of the Swiss security service appeared one morning, unannounced and inquisitive. Ursula parried his questions and then demanded: "Why does neutral, democratic Switzerland distrust Germans persecuted by Hitler, instead of concentrating on German Nazis, of whom there are more than enough in this country?" The officer replied sadly: "I would be a hundred times happier to do just that." The visit was unsettling. Len Beurton dug a hole in the woods and laid a board covered with earth and leaves over the top, a hiding place for the transmitter in an emergency.

Alexander Foote was fond of Ursula, but somewhat taken aback when she asked him to marry her.

Her reasons could not have been less romantic. When her German passport expired, she would be legally unprotected, save for a fake Bolivian document. But as the wife of an Englishman, she would be eligible for British citizenship and could apply to the consulate in Geneva for a British passport. Then, if the Nazis invaded Switzerland, she could flee to London and join the rest of her family.

The Center had approved the plan, and Foote accepted Ursula's marriage proposal. "Numerous *mariages blancs* [unconsummated marriages of convenience] were taking place in Switzerland at the time purely for the purpose of acquiring legal papers," he wrote. Ursula assured him that "a divorce would be possible at any time." The only problem was that she was still married to Rudi, who was somewhere in China. Foote was an opportunist, but he drew the line at bigamy. Again, the solution was brutally simple: Foote filled out a formal witness declaration for the Swiss divorce courts, stating that Rudolf Hamburger (present whereabouts unknown) had committed "adultery with one of Sonya's sisters in a London hotel." Rudi had done no such thing, but it is probable that Foote himself had, with Brigitte. Years later, Foote "made no bones at all about the perjury he had committed in the Swiss courts," but the subterfuge would come back to haunt Ursula. On October 26, 1939, Ursula's marriage was terminated on the grounds of Rudolf Hamburger's adultery. Seldom has a divorce ruling been more unjust.

In early December, Franz Obermanns failed to turn up for a scheduled meeting in Zurich; nor did he appear at a backup rendez-vous a week later. Ursula, seriously alarmed, broke every rule by telephoning his apartment in Fribourg. A voice she did not recognize said he no longer lived there.

It is a mystery why the Swiss police took so long to spot something fishy about Eriki Noki, a man with a distinctive facial scar traveling on a Finnish passport issued in Canada, who spoke neither Finnish nor English. A raid on his apartment uncovered a "litter of wireless parts," and Obermanns was arrested. Ursula knew that somewhere in the police files was a report that "Enoki" had been seen at La Taupinière. That night, she and Len extracted the radio from the cupboard, wrapped the individual parts against the damp, and buried them in the woods. Henceforth each contact with Moscow required digging up and reassembling the radio. There was no more transmitting in bed.

The police swiftly established Obermanns's real identity, and when the Gestapo discovered the convicted communist agitator was in Swiss custody, they issued an immediate extradition demand. This was rejected, on the basis that he was already being investigated by the Swiss authorities for alleged passport violations. The unlucky spy got lucky; Obermanns would spend the rest of the war in a relatively comfortable Swiss internment camp. "The whole affair shook Sonya severely," wrote Foote.

Meanwhile, Foote and Beurton were getting on each other's nerves. Apart from their shared experiences in Spain, they had little in common: Beurton was serious and sober, whereas Foote frequently behaved as if he was on some secret holiday, growing fat, literally and metaphorically, while Europe burned. Len complained that his partner was "an egoist, who set too much store by pleasure." Foote was also fickle. A few weeks after the divorce came through, he told Ursula he had a "confession" to make: he had gone to Spain to avoid marrying a woman he had impregnated in England. If he married Ursula "this affair would be stirred up again," so he was backing out. This was both highly inconvenient and ideologically troubling. If it was true, then Foote had fought in Spain for ignoble reasons rather than political commitment. And if it was a lie, he was trying to wriggle out of a direct command from the Red Army.

But Foote had an alternative suggestion. "Would you consider marrying Len instead?"

Ursula was happy with Plan B. Indeed, rather happier. Marriage to either Englishman was a passport to a passport, but she liked Len more. She put the idea to Beurton, reassuring him that the marriage was strictly pro forma. "You can trust me to divorce you as soon as you want."

Len retorted sharply. "I understand the meaning of a 'paper marriage' perfectly well," he snapped. But he agreed nonetheless.

Ursula was struck by Len's "unaccustomed belligerence." His sensitivity over the bogus marriage touched her. From that moment, their friendship took on a slightly different hue. At first, she could not put her finger on it. He was strange, this withdrawn young Englishman, but there was something appealing about his combination of shyness and courage, tenderness and toughness. The Swiss might be watching them. The Germans might invade. The Gestapo, if they found them, could kill them all. But the tension and danger barely seemed to touch him. At one point he even suggested that he volunteer to spy for the Germans, "in order to double cross them," an idea as brave as it was impractical. She was moved by Len's deepening relationship with Michael and his "cautious way of empathizing with the boy."

Olga Muth was shocked to discover Ursula was now engaged to Len Beurton.

"I thought you were only working with him," she protested. "And now he's going to live here?"

Ursula put a hand on the nanny's shoulder. "He is a good man. He has bonded with the children. This marriage is really very important because it finally gives me a useful passport."

"Are we going to be free of the worry that they will catch you and dump you over the border?"

Ursula nodded.

"Then that's the only reason you're marrying him—a sham marriage?"

Ursula nodded again, a little less convincingly. "The passport plays a part . . ."

Ollo sighed crossly and launched into a diatribe, as if ticking off a little girl. "That's typical of you. First you had a man, and there couldn't have been a better one. Then suddenly you claim that you have grown apart from Rudi and bury yourself with the little one in the furthest corner of China. We were all shocked. Your mother and I had the same suspicion: there was something political behind it. The next thing we heard, you're having a child. We never even got to see the father, and now—another man!"

Ursula was shaken. Ollo had always been blunt, and fond of Rudi. But there was something more to her beloved nanny's reaction, something darker and more dangerous. Olga Muth was not just angry; she seemed scared.

Word that Frau Hamburger had become engaged to the younger of the two Englishmen spread swiftly through Caux, as such news does in small communities. Though she did not know the strange subtext to the engagement, Frau Füssli, the farmer's wife, was delighted for Ursula, as was Lillian Jakobi, the elderly Jewish woman who had become a close friend.

The betrothed couple took to the slopes. Ursula was now an accomplished downhill skier, but Len was a dangerous combination of intensely enthusiastic, barely competent, and completely fearless. One afternoon, they caught the little train to Rochers-de-Naye, 6,700 feet above sea level. The view over the valley was spectacular. They skied down fast. In Len's case, far too fast: he lost control on a steep slope, slammed into a wall of ice, and broke both his skis. They trudged home on foot through the deep snow, holding on to each other to avoid sliding. Beurton laughed happily all the way down. Ursula wrote: "It dawned on me how much I liked Len." There was no romantic epiphany, no sudden tumble into love, just the slow realization that, although she had told Len he could divorce her whenever he wanted, she rather hoped he never would.

Beurton had never experienced a home life before. "Becoming part of our family, feeling warmth and care in a cheerful, harmonious atmosphere, was a decisive experience. We were comrades bound to one another through work and danger. We shared the same opinions about books and people. Every day we consciously enjoyed the beauties of the landscape. Len's understanding for the children was quite amazing."

They chose a politically auspicious date for their wedding: February 23, the anniversary of the founding of the Red Army, later known as "Defender of the Fatherland Day." The ceremony was so low-key as to be barely audible: two paper rings from the Uniprix in Vevey and some swift paperwork in the registry office at Geneva, with the porter and clerk as witnesses. Then Mr. and Mrs. Leon Beurton went back home to La Taupinière for a pancake lunch cooked by Ollo.

There is, of course, no record of when this arranged marriage ceased to be merely convenient, pro forma, and white. But it is entirely possible that it was consummated (and Len lost his virginity) that very evening, in the Molehill, exactly twenty-two years after the birth of the Red Army.

Ursula Kuczynski accidentally fell in love with Len Beurton, and by the most circuitous route. The fourth, and enduring, love of her life came about as the result of an illegal spy plot and a sham marriage.

Later they debated the precise moment their love affair had started. "When did you realize that you liked me?" she asked him.

"In novels they would say 'love at first sight.' At our first illegal meeting in Vevey, outside Uniprix."

"As early as that? I never had the slightest idea!"

"I didn't let on to myself for a long time," said Len.

But Ursula had also fallen for Len earlier than she admitted. In a letter to her mother, written soon after their engagement, she explained that she intended to marry this Englishman, seven years her junior. "I love him," she added.

Many years later, Len wrote an assessment of Ursula, as a wife, an intelligence officer, and a revolutionary.

Style, elegance, restraint, modesty and the initiative to carry the fight to the enemy, coupled with stability under stress. You may well say it is immodest to talk about one's boss and wife in such terms. Sonja [the German form of Sonya] was equipped with a command of the techniques of diversion, manufacture and use of explosives, theory and practice of radio communications and the ability to teach others. She never made demands that she would not make on herself. Her dedication to the destruction of Fascism was absolute. But she remained feminine and was the most devoted of mothers.

Like many successful marriages, this one was not entirely straightforward. Len sometimes accused his wife of being "dictatorial"—which she could be, particularly in matters of professional espionage. He was never in doubt that he had married his superior officer. She found him thin-skinned and liable to sudden, inexplicable changes of mood. "He fussed over things that I felt were unimportant." But Ursula provided Len with love, unconditional and absolute, something he had never known. For many years she had lived in danger and courted risk, while constantly accompanied and sometimes paralyzed by fear. What Len gave Ursula, in addition to lifelong loyalty and a marriage certificate, was a by-product of his own, strange character: he lent her some of his own stolid fearlessness.

Richard Sorge had offered glamour and peril. Johann Patra, the working-class seaman, was a creature from another world, jealous and competitive, an irresistibly romantic revolutionary. But Len was neither her boss nor her rival. He needed her as no one had ever needed her before, and loved her in a way that was simple, strong, and unquestioning. Ursula was no longer the headstrong adventure seeker, but a mature undercover agent and trained intelligence officer with two children, a spy network, and a heavy burden of responsibility. She no longer lived for fast motorbikes or political arguments that stretched into the early hours; she needed backup, emotional and professional. She did not want another firebrand or a sparring partner. She wanted a good husband. And she got one.

Ursula applied for a British passport the day after the wedding, and the consul duly wrote to the Passport Office in London, asking whether he should issue one. The reply came back on March 28, 1940: "We have no record on Mrs. Ursula Beurton and only a possible trace of her ex-husband with a communistic smell. On the face of it, I do not see how you can refuse to issue a British passport."

MI5 thought otherwise.

The British Security Service was by now profoundly suspicious of the Kuczynski family, and concerned to discover that yet another member might be en route to Britain. Fear of the "Red Menace" had intensified with the Nazi-Soviet pact. Both Robert and Jürgen Kuczynski had adopted the party line from Moscow and publicly condemned the war as a conflict between imperialists that communists had no stake in. Robert was described by MI5 as "spreading defeatism" with his "anti-war" attitudes. The family was deeply involved with the Free German League of Culture, which MI5 considered "a communist front organisation."

At the end of 1939, Jürgen Kuczynski was brought before the Aliens Tribunal, the body set up by the Home Office to rule on which of the seventy thousand German and Austrian "enemy aliens" in Britain should be locked up as potential enemy agents. MI5 submitted evidence that he was a communist (something he did nothing to hide), and on January 20, 1940, Jürgen was interned at Seaton Camp in Devon, a former holiday camp, along with 568 other "Category A" internees, most of them Nazis. Robert was designated "Category C" and remained at liberty, to MI5's annoyance: "Everyone knows, as the judge does, that he is a real Communist and professes everywhere his aversion against this Imperialistic War." MI5 was equally suspicious of Len Beurton, but as yet uncertain whether his sympathies lay with communism or Nazism. "Beurton is known to have been sufficiently interested in Germany to have bought a German Grammar and German readers, and was said to be in Germany in September 1939." He was placed on the Central Security War Black List as a possible subversive.

Jürgen Kuczynski's internment led to a tussle between MI5, which wanted him locked up, and the Home Office, which saw no reason to detain him. Numerous well-connected friends weighed in to demand Jürgen's release, insisting (wrongly) that he was completely innocent. Labour's leader, Clement Attlee, even raised the issue of Kuczynski's continued internment in the House of Commons. Lilian Bowes Lyon, the queen's cousin, wrote to Marguerite, sympathizing over her husband's incarceration. Sir Alexander Maxwell, permanent under-secretary of state at the Home Office, pointed out that being a communist was "not in itself a reason for internment" and insisted that "unless MI5 have some information beyond what appears in these files, Kuczynski ought to be released." Jürgen was freed on April 19, 1940, with a glowing commendation from the camp commandant, who described him as "a very able man intellectually, and a thoroughly good sort." MI5 was furious. It still had no idea just how deeply Jürgen was involved with Soviet intelligence, but nonetheless considered him to be "a very dangerous person," whose sister should not be granted citizenship.

MI5 tried to jam the brakes on Ursula's passport application. "We have now received further information with regard to Mrs. Ursula Beurton, and are strongly of the opinion that she should not be issued with a British passport." The reply came back: "We can do little now, as we authorized the issue of a passport on 24th of April."

Ursula collected the "precious document" from the consulate at 41 Quai Wilson in Geneva. Just in time, she had acquired the means to flee Switzerland if the Nazis attacked, as they fully intended to do.

A week after Ursula became a British citizen, Hitler launched his Blitzkrieg: activated by the code name "Danzig," German troops poured westward and north in an unstoppable armored tide. Denmark, Norway, the Netherlands, Belgium, and Luxembourg were overrun. On June 14, the Nazis occupied Paris, leaving only the southern "Free Zone" of France under Pétain's Vichy regime. German planning for the invasion of Switzerland started on the day France surrendered. Publicly, Hitler declared that "at all times, whatever happens, we will respect the inviolability and neutrality of Switzerland." Privately, he prepared to incorporate the country into the greater Reich, regarding the Swiss as a "misbegotten branch of our Volk" and "a pimple on the face of Europe."

As Ursula put it, "Switzerland was encircled by the fascists; only a single narrow passage through France remained open."

Foote later claimed that Ursula and Len were too preoccupied with each other to pay much attention to international events. This was not true, but they were certainly "acting like a honeymoon couple," wandering the Swiss Alps hand in hand, picking daffodils. "It was perfectly obvious that this was anything but a marriage of convenience," wrote Foote, who found their blooming love affair quite amusing. Olga Muth did not. She had been assured that this marriage was one of expediency, whereas it was plainly a reality. She brooded furiously. Ollo felt a fierce residual loyalty to Rudi, who had no idea that his wife had obtained a divorce, a new husband, a new name, and a new nationality.

But then, Rudolf Hamburger was hardly in a position to do anything about the situation, since he was being tortured in a Chinese jail.

CHAPTER 14

THE BABY
SNATCHER

EMILY HAHN, THE *NEW YORKER* CORRESPONDENT IN CHINA, was taking cover in the bomb shelter of the Press Hostel in Chungking when military police burst in and arrested one of her fellow guests. The man pulled a gun and was disarmed after a brief struggle, but not before he had attempted to swallow a piece of paper. He was tied up and led away. "It was just like the movies," Hahn wrote.

"Mickey" Hahn had seen plenty of drama in her thirty-five years: a cigar-smoking adventurer from St. Louis, Missouri, she had lived with a pygmy tribe, driven across America dressed as a man in a Ford Model T, and walked alone from one side of Central Africa to the other. She arrived in Shanghai at around the time Ursula left, and became notorious for smoking opium and attending dinner parties with "Mr. Mills," a pet gibbon she dressed in a diaper and tailor-made dinner jacket. She was befriended by Agnes Smedley, who used Hahn's Shanghai address as a "mail drop" for letters she did not want intercepted by the police. After the outbreak of war between Japan and China in 1937, Hahn moved with a posse of fellow journalists to Chungking, the wartime capital of the Chinese government under Chiang Kai-shek. The city was being pummeled by Japanese bombers. At the sound of the sirens, the international clientele of the Chungking Press Hostel, many still in their nightwear, crammed into a shelter constructed inside a cave in the garden. Here Chinese waiters served snacks and cocktails as incendiary bombs rained down.

It was during one of these gatherings that Emily Hahn witnessed the calamitous end to Rudolf Hamburger's first, short-lived spy mission.

It had all started so promisingly. On April 20, 1939, Rudi and Johann Patra boarded the *Katori Maru* in Marseilles. The boat was packed with Jews fleeing Europe and bound for Shanghai, "one of the few places in the world still open to them," as Hamburger wrote. In Shanghai, he rented a small house, while Patra took a room in the home of a wealthy Chinese family. Most of the people he and Ursula had known in the 1930s had gone, but two members of Rudi's immediate family were now resident in the city: his younger brother, Otto, a businessman, and his widowed father, Max. There was little architectural work to be found, and so he passed his days receiving instruction from Patra on operating radios and making explosives. They got on well. Ursula was seldom discussed. Hamburger was eager to begin work as a spy, but Moscow was still in no hurry to deploy him. Finally, after twiddling his thumbs for almost a year, he was dispatched to Chungking, in southwest China, with vague orders to recruit expatriate communists as informants. Patra built him a shortwave wireless concealed inside an ordinary commercial radio and told him to "keep in touch." He sailed to Hong Kong and then flew on to Chungking on March 9, 1940.

In the arrivals halls, Chinese police examined his luggage and confiscated the radio, telling Hamburger he could collect it in two days' time. A more capable spy would have fled immediately. Instead, Hamburger did as he was told. When the radio was duly returned to him "without comment," he wondered how the "incompetent" Chinese had failed to spot the illegal transmitter concealed inside. Rather later, he realized that "they knew very well that it was an espionage-grade receiving-transmitting device and were now alerted."

International crises attract a peculiar congregation, and journalists, writers, entrepreneurs, and spies flocked to the Chungking Press Hostel. Hamburger was surprised to bump into Agnes Smedley, whose friendship had played such a pivotal role in Ursula's life and, by association, his. Agnes was continuing her quixotic crusade on behalf of Chinese communism, marching with the Red Army, interviewing its leaders (including Mao), writing thinly veiled propaganda for Western newspapers, and spending more time on the front line of the Chinese war than any other correspondent, male or female. She inspired devotion and irritation wherever she went. When she turned up at the Chungking Press Hostel, following another nervous breakdown and more than a year in the war zone, she was suffering from malnutrition, malaria, hives, liver damage, and possibly typhus. Her toenails and teeth were falling out, but she remained a distinctive figure, as Hahn described her, "incongruous in a peach-coloured satin nightgown." Rudi knew Agnes was a spy, but Smedley was almost certainly unaware that her old friend's husband was now in the espionage game himself.

Keen to start spying, Rudi Hamburger went shopping for additional radio parts. All such purchases were closely monitored by Chinese intelligence. General Dai Li, the "Himmler of China," ran the "National Investigation and Statistics Bureau," a secret police force dedicated to rooting out spies. Rudi was a sitting duck.

Emily Hahn had spotted the "*soi-disant* German refugee" on arrival at the hotel, but made a point of avoiding the beret-wearing architect, "taking him to be one of those heavily Teutonic artists from Munich . . . he looked the part to perfection." On the night of April 21, 1940, the hotel guests were milling around the shelter "shivering and yawning" as they waited for the air raid to end, when the squad of Chinese soldiers burst in. As he was seized, Rudi "protested he had nothing to hide," but then somewhat undermined his assertion of innocence by brandishing a revolver, which he had no idea how to use.

Hahn could not believe her eyes:

He chewed up a paper and tried to swallow it. It had a code on it, exactly like the movies. Everybody was badly shaken by the scene. Hitherto we had accepted him as a perfectly pukka refugee. . . . He didn't seem surprised at the arrest, or even very indignant. "Let me get dressed, will you?" he said. The soldiers tied his hands with rope, and then marched him out past all of us, standing there in our pyjamas in a row, our mouths hanging open. He didn't look at any of us. We heard all sorts of other stories afterward, the most reasonable of which was that he hadn't been spying for the Nazis but for the Chinese Reds.

A search of Rudi's hotel room revealed the transmitter and other incriminating items. After a night locked in a wooden shed inside the police compound, the interrogations started: "Angry questions were asked—which country or organization did I belong to?—but to no avail." Rudi Hamburger might be a hopeless spy ("his naivety made him totally unusable for conspiratorial activities," as his son put it), but he was preternaturally stubborn. He refused to answer questions. "After eight days they resorted to torture. My arms were tied behind my back and I was pulled up with a kind of pulley system on the arms about two feet above the ground." He was left dangling, as the sinews in his shoulders slowly stretched and cracked. "I found myself hanging in a rather painful position," Rudi wrote, with typical understatement.

After four weeks of interrogation, he was driven twelve miles up the Jialing River to Bai Mansion, a large country house in the Geleshan region, a delightful valley rolling out beneath a range of pine-wooded hills. The mansion was a concentration camp and torture center for political prisoners, "surrounded with electric fences and guarded by armed patrols that shot intruders on sight." The locals called it "Happy Valley."

The mansion held around fifty male inmates. Hamburger was the only foreigner. His cellmate was Wong Pin Fong, a young man who spoke English and claimed to have been arrested for taking part in an illegal street protest. He had evidently been placed alongside Hamburger to find out who he was working for. Rudi treated the stool pigeon with extreme caution, but Wong reached his own, accurate conclusion: "In reality you must be a member of the American or Soviet secret services," he declared. For fifteen minutes every day, Hamburger was allowed to see the view from the front of the mansion through a barred window—thirty miles of lush, rolling landscape—before he was locked up again, an ingenious form of mental torture to accompany the physical variety. Every six weeks he was brought before an official and told to confess. Like every other prisoner, he contracted malaria. On a dwindling prison diet of rice, he began to waste away, physically and psychologically. "How long can they hold me?" he wondered. "Months? Years? The country is at war, and in war, everything is possible."

IN JUNE 1940, SOON after the Fall of France, Ursula received a message from Moscow instructing her to contact "Albert," a comrade in Geneva, and put a series of questions to him: "Does your office still function? What is your financial position? Can you get messages to the Centre via Italy? Do you require a transmitter?" The inference was clear, and most surprising: there must be another Soviet spy ring operating in Switzerland, run by this mysterious Albert. As instructed, she pushed a note through the mailbox of 13 Rue de Lausanne, arranging to return in a few days' time.

The man who opened the door was "thickset, verging on the plump, with dark hair, dark eyes, and a melancholy air." With his round glasses, heavy-rimmed eyes, and mournful expression, he resembled a corpulent and slightly depressed owl. "Greetings from Mr. Weber," said Ursula. The man nodded in recognition of the password, led her to an office "full of books and maps, the desk strewn with papers and journals," and cleared a space for her to sit down. Ursula wondered if he might be some sort of academic. The owl took in his visitor, "a tall, slender, almost fragile-looking woman in a closely-fitting woollen dress. I put her age at about thirty-five. Her movements were smooth, and a trifle languid."

"My codename is Sonya," said Ursula with a smile. They spoke German. "The director told me to get in touch with you. I was given your name and address and instructions to call on you and find out how things stand with your group. I'm supposed to report back to the director. You'll undoubtedly be receiving further instructions through me."

"Albert" was Alexander "Sandor" Radó, a Jewish Hungarian communist and an "obsessive cartographic scientist" by profession. He was also chief of a Soviet spy network that would become known as the Rote Drei (Red Three), the lynchpin in the wider anti-Nazi espionage ring that Himmler's spy hunters dubbed the Rote Kapelle

(Red Orchestra). A former commissar in the Hungarian Red Army, Radó had studied mapmaking in Berlin, run an anti-Nazi propaganda service in Austria, and fled to Paris in 1933, where he was listed by the Nazis as "Public Enemy Number 1." He was recruited by the Fourth Department in Moscow in 1935 and given the almost inconceivably stupid code name "Dora," a simple anagram of Rado. By 1940, the rotund and unassuming Hungarian geographer was running a cartographic agency in Geneva named Geopress, supplying maps to European newspapers. He was also the Soviet *rezident* (the Russian term for spy chief) in Switzerland with the rank of major general, conducting the most important section of the Red Orchestra: a web of spies in Italy, Spain, and Switzerland, and, most important, inside Nazi Germany. Radó typed his reports, used microphotography to shrink them to "microdots" the size of a period, and pasted them into books, which he sent, via courier, to Paris, where they were enlarged, enciphered, and transmitted to Moscow by the French branch of Soviet military intelligence. The Nazi occupation of northern France had blocked this avenue of communication. As Radó put it: "I was head of an intelligence group, there was a war on, and we had no contact."

"Important information is lying idle," he told Ursula. In theory active espionage against Germany had been suspended under the Nazi-Soviet pact, but Radó's team was continuing to collect critical military intelligence. "Geopress is a sound cover organization and the local authorities suspect nothing," Radó told Ursula. "We are still receiving information regularly but it is simply piling up because I have no means of passing it on to the Center. We need a transmitter, trained radio operators, and a flat or house to operate from. We need a code, and transmission and reception times. There are plenty of problems, as you can see, and they all need solving as a matter of urgency."

Radó wrote, "I knew precious little about Sonya. I had no idea where she lived, or whom she worked with, or what type of intelligence she collected. The rules of conspiracy forbade me to ask her. Our two groups—Sonya's and mine—operated independently and in complete isolation until circumstances forced us to contact each other."

Ursula hauled her radio out of the hole in the woods. Radó wrote out his reports in plain text, on tissue paper, and then drew a white cross in chalk on a street corner in Geneva. Ursula monitored the signal site, before picking up the package from a "dead-letter box," or "dead-drop site," spy jargon for a secure place to leave messages: a small cavity under the railings in the hallway of the apartment opposite. She then folded the tissue paper inside a large flashlight, which Len had adapted by taking out one of the two batteries, rewiring it, and installing a lower-wattage bulb: the flashlight still worked, a little dimly, while concealing several sheets of tissue. Back at La Taupinière, she enciphered the reports, transmitted them overnight to Moscow, deciphered the replies, and delivered them back to Radó at another dead-letter box in Geneva.

Radó's output was prodigious; Ursula felt useful again. "With so much work to do, I would have felt happy if other worries had been fewer," she wrote.

Switzerland was effectively isolated from the rest of Europe, its economy deteriorating under the threat of German invasion. The Swiss government warned that if a single German soldier crossed the border, the army would destroy the country's industrial infrastructure and retreat to the mountains to fight a guerrilla war. Radó wrote: "The bitter joke made the rounds that Switzerland was now the world's largest prison. Hitler and Mussolini had completely cut off four million people. Only a narrow corridor near Geneva remained open to traffic through to Pétain's unoccupied zone [and] it was expected that even the corridor through to Vichy France—and hence via Spain or Portugal to England or the United States—would one day be closed."

Ursula's other worries were closer to home. Olga Muth's behavior was becoming increasingly erratic. She refused to be separated from little Nina, barely spoke to Len, and bickered incessantly with Michael. Ursula wrote to her parents: "If anyone says something nice about Misha, Ollo immediately contradicts them and begins to talk about Nina." One afternoon, Ursula was idly chatting in the kitchen with her elderly friend Lillian Jakobi, while Ollo sat silently sewing in the corner. Lillian had just obtained a visa for Britain, where her son was already a refugee. She would soon be getting out of Switzerland and urged Ursula to do the same: "You are sitting in a mousetrap that will close when the Nazis come. Don't think they'll respect your papers. You have to leave for the sake of the children. In England you are ten times safer, despite the war."

At that moment Ollo jumped to her feet with a cry and ran upstairs, sobbing. Ursula found her lying on her bed, shaking and pale, staring at the ceiling.

"What's the matter, are you sick?"

"I am not sick, but I understand everything," she replied.

"What are you talking about?"

Ollo sat up and slapped the edge of the bed.

"You have taken me for a fool, but I won't let you. Don't act so innocent. You planned everything and thought I wouldn't notice until it was too late. But you were wrong!"

"I still don't know what you mean," said Ursula, amazed by the outburst.

"You know perfectly well: you wanted the new passport to get out of here with the children. You want to go with them and Len to England and leave me here alone, without Nina, because as a German I can't go with them. That's the thanks I get!"

Ursula calmly insisted she was not planning to leave Switzerland, and Ollo's hysteria slowly subsided. But the nanny's fears were not unfounded: if the Germans invaded, her family would flee with their British passports, and she would be left behind. War could drive a brutal wedge between Ollo and Ursula, and they both knew it. A few days later, Ollo took Ursula aside, tearfully declared "she could not live without Nina," and made a proposition. "Why don't you go to England, and leave Nina with me, wouldn't that be better? I won't need any money. I will work my fingers to the bone and the child would lack nothing. Do you really want to expose Nina to German bombs in England? Do you want to be responsible for dragging the little one into that danger? When times calm down, I will bring the child to you." From Ollo's perspective, the idea seemed entirely logical. Ursula was busy with her espionage and her new husband. She might read to her children and take them for long walks and skiing expeditions, but in Ollo's eyes she was as deficient a parent as her mother had been. It was Ollo who combed the nits from Nina's hair, shared her private toddler language, and soothed her to sleep with German lullabies. Nine-year-old Misha was rejecting her, but Nina was still her baby and she would not be parted from her.

Suddenly, Ursula was very scared. Adored Ollo, her family's rock for so many years, was trying to take away her child.

Ursula did not even address this outrageous suggestion. Instead, she changed the subject. "Why not take a holiday?" she said. "I'll find you a nice place, and in a few weeks you can come back."

Ollo snapped: "No. I won't be forced to leave here. I am not going to let you out of my sight. You can be sure of that."

The Molehill now crackled with tension. Ollo stopped eating, wept copiously, and barely spoke, exuding a "silent bitterness." At night, she locked the door to the room she still shared with Nina, fearful that Ursula might take the baby while she slept and steal away in the night. She obtained a pair of binoculars ("Where did she get them?" Ursula wondered), and whenever she was not working she perched on the hillside above the house, watching them. "When I talked to Len alone, she tried to listen at the door." The spy was being spied upon. Ollo began to steam open Ursula's letters.

One afternoon, Ursula returned from Geneva after collecting a fresh batch of Radó's reports from the dead-drop site, to find a letter from her parents. Even if the envelope had not been so clumsily re-sealed, Ollo's thunderous expression would have revealed that she had read the contents. The letter was an entreaty, urging Ursula to leave Switzerland. "If you stay there until Hitler invades the country, death is certain. If the work of your husband, whom we do not know, keeps you there, then at least send us the children. But if he understands the situation, he will see to it that you come here too." For Ollo, the letter was confirmation: she was about to be deserted and deprived of "her" child.

The next day, Olga Muth put on her hat and announced she was going to the hairdresser. Instead, she went at once to the British consulate in Montreux. Angry and determined, Ollo had framed a plot of her own: she would prevent Ursula from leaving with Nina by revealing to the British that her employer was a communist spy.

Ursula later depicted this as the work of an unhinged mind, but by Ollo's own lights her plan was perfectly rational. She had loved each successive child of the Kuczynski family, but her attachment to Nina carried an additional element of desperation, the infatuation of an aging, childless, terrified woman at the mercy of international events she barely understood. Ollo saw herself as the victim of a cruel betrayal. She had given everything to the family, and now Ursula had contrived an escape plan that excluded her. She would tell the British government that the newly minted Mrs. Leon Beurton was a spy who had married solely for the purposes of obtaining British citizenship. The king of England would then withdraw Ursula's passport, and they could all happily remain in Switzerland. After she had explained everything to the British, she would have her hair done and then visit Lillian. That was Ollo's scheme. It did not work out.

Olga Muth spoke only a few words of English. The official at the British consulate had French, almost no German, and very little time to spare. With so many people seeking refuge in Britain, the consulate was bombarded with requests, inquiries, "rumours and denunciations," some realistic, many frantic, and some simply mad. Ollo gave the official her name and address and then launched into a deafening torrent of what she thought was English, but was really German with odd shards of English thrown in. Like many people unable to speak a foreign language, Ollo believed that volume would compensate for a limited vocabulary. "Her ravings in broken English were so incoherent," Foote later wrote, that when she paused for breath, the official stood up and asked her, very courteously, to go away. He then "added her name to the list of lunatics who pestered the consulate daily."

Frustrated and surprised by this setback, Ollo confided in her hairdresser (as people, bizarrely, often do) and asked him which branch of Swiss officialdom she should go to in order to denounce her employer. The coiffeur, an anti-Nazi to his roots, wanted nothing to do with the business. He was also, she felt, "deliberately rough" with her hair. Ollo needed an English speaker who would explain the situation to the British on her behalf.

She arrived at the door to Lillian Jakobi's flat "agitated and confused," her hair in a mess. Lillian insisted she lie down and take some valerian drops, a natural remedy for anxiety.

"You must help me," Ollo repeated. "You must come with me. You know that I cannot live without Nina. Please, come with me, right now."

Lillian was baffled. Ollo continued to rant.

"I have known for ages they want to leave Switzerland, even though they act as if that isn't the case. They are evil people. They lied to me and want to abandon me. But I am not giving up Nina."

Ollo described how she had already tried to tell the British authorities that Ursula and Len were "communists who secretly ran a radio station at night so that England wouldn't let them in and they'd have to stay here." But for some reason "she had not been properly understood." That was why Lillian must "accompany her to the consulate and explain everything again properly."

Lillian was stunned to learn that Ursula was a spy, but horrified by Ollo's treachery in revealing this to the authorities.

"For God's sake, what have you done? They could be arrested at any moment."

The nanny's response was chilling: "Then I will have the child," she said and burst into tears.

Ollo had come to the wrong person. Lillian stood over the woman bawling on her sofa and delivered a ferocious rebuke.

"When your mind is clear, you will never be happy again. You will suffer forever from the terrible guilt you have burdened yourself with. Don't you realize what a betrayal you are committing? No decent person will forgive you if you plunge this family into misery. I regard your condition as an illness and want to help you. Of course I had no idea they were secret communists, but I tell you honestly, I can only admire that."

She told Ollo to go home and say nothing about the day's events to Ursula, who was due to come shopping in Montreux the next day.

The moment Ursula alighted from the train, Lillian steered her into a nearby park: "Something terrible has happened."

Ursula was astonished, livid, and very frightened. Who else had Ollo confided in? Would the hairdresser go to the police? Ollo knew nothing about Radó, so the network was probably safe for the moment. But she certainly knew the identity and whereabouts of Alexander Foote. Even Rudi, wherever he was, would be in danger if Ollo told the Nazis what she knew.

Ursula had evaded the Chinese secret police and the British authorities in Shanghai, the Japanese Kempeitai, the Swiss and Polish security services, MI5, and the Gestapo. No one had ever betrayed her: not Shushin, under torture, nor Tumanyan, and none of Stalin's other victims. Even Rudi had kept her secrets safe. But she now faced disaster after being denounced by a woman she had known and loved since the age of three.

"Everything that we had laboriously and illegally built up was now threatened with collapse. We had to act immediately."

Suddenly another terrible thought seized her. Ollo had arrived home late the previous evening, looking tired and anxious. She had gone straight to bed and was not up when Ursula left the Molchill that morning. Len would be out walking in the hills. "What was to stop Ollo from leaving the country with Nina?" She might already be on her way to Germany. "I had to get back immediately." Ursula caught a taxi to Caux, something she had never done before, and ran the last mile uphill to the chalet, her head spinning with terrible fears. If Ollo had taken the baby, she would have to inform the police, but if they intercepted her before the border, she would tell them everything. Yet again, her espionage and her family stood in direct conflict. "If the police found out, our work would be over, and that was exactly what could not be allowed to happen. But I had a duty to do everything I could to ensure that my daughter was not taken away from me, and placed in the hands of the Nazis, perhaps forever." Panting, she rounded the path above the woods and there, across the meadow, she saw Nina and Michael playing happily in the sun. "My knees went soft. I lay down in the grass, looked up at the sky and stayed there until my breathing calmed down."

That night, when the house was still, she told Len what had happened. They dismantled the radio, carried it though the darkness to the hole in the woods, and then crawled back into bed, "wet, dirty and tired."

The next morning, they sat on the bench outside the house,

drinking coffee in the cool sunshine while the children played tag. Ollo was still in her room. "The meadows were full of autumn flowers. Nina squeaked with pleasure, and Michael laughed."

Len turned to Ursula. "She has already spoken to too many people. We have to do something before she turns you and the others over to the police and kidnaps Nina," he said. "You will have to kill her."

CHAPTER 15

THE HAPPY TIME

URSULA LAY AWAKE, WONDERING WHETHER TO MURDER her nanny.

Len was firm. "During the Spanish Civil War he had looked death in the face many times." Unless Ollo was stopped, she could get them all killed. "Would she go to the Swiss authorities, or would she even go so far as to contact the German fascists?" Espionage is a lethal profession, as Ursula was well aware. "The past had required me to deal with death more than once." But the idea of "liquidating" Olga Muth, whatever her treachery, was more than she could bear. "We were not terrorists or criminals, neither unfeeling nor cruel." And Ursula loved her. She recalled Ollo's kindness to her as a child, her stalwart courage when the Gestapo ransacked Schlachtensee, her quiet discretion, her bravery in taking money to Rosa Thälmann in Nazi Germany. She "had adapted to the illegal atmosphere wonderfully and supported me as a matter of course." Ursula blamed herself for the appalling situation. "Her fear of losing us arose out of her love for the child and also for me. Ollo deserved my understanding, my patience." Ollo had risked her life for Ursula. They could not kill her, and she would not give Moscow the opportunity to order her to do so.

In the course of a long, sleepless night, Ursula formed a plan: she would smuggle the children somewhere beyond Ollo's reach, secretly rent a flat in Geneva, and install the transmitter-receiver there.

Then she would fire Olga Muth and send her back to Germany. After that they would explain to Moscow what had happened and await orders. None of this was possible, however, with Ollo under the same roof, observing their every move. Ursula discussed the situation with Alexander Foote, who expressed sympathy for "the faithful old thing," but agreed "she was a danger to us all . . . at any moment the faithful retainer might try another denunciation."

Sensing the stress, the children were fractious. During yet another quarrel with the nanny, Michael called Ollo a "witch." She slapped him across the face. Ursula exploded. "Right, that's enough, no one can live with you any more. The endless weeping, your imaginings, you are driving us all crazy. And now you have hit the boy. That's the end of it." With extreme reluctance, Ollo agreed to move in with the farmer's wife until the atmosphere was calmer. As she left the house, she muttered darkly: "I will not let you out of my sight; you can be sure of that." Early the next morning, a small figure sat hunched on the bench outside the Füssli farmhouse, her binoculars trained on the Molehill. "When one of us came out of the door, she lifted up the field glasses. If I went to the village, she focused them in my direction until I was out of sight." A few days later, Frau Füssli arrived to muck out the cow barn and took Ursula aside: Ollo had told her that Ursula was a spy. "I don't know anything about politics," Frau Füssli said. "But I understand that war and Hitler are disasters. I'm outraged at what she has done and still intends to do." Ollo was studying the timetable of trains to Germany and planning to go to the German consulate in Geneva. The farmer's wife promised to alert Ursula the moment Ollo left for the city. Frau Füssli was now spying on Ollo, who was spying on Ursula. And time was running out.

Les Rayons, a boarding school in a remote area above the lake near Gland, agreed to take in Michael and Nina at short notice, with payment in advance. The German owners seemed kind, and Ursula felt sure "they would keep the children for some time if we were arrested." Then she found a two-room apartment for rent in central Geneva, a place with "cold, mortared walls" far from the "warm, breathing house on the hillside." The thought of leaving La Taupinière was wrenching. "The mountain landscape had become part of my life. It was my daily joy."

"I will be lonely," said Frau Füssli, when Ursula explained she was departing. The farmer's wife did not need to ask why.

That night they packed and Len took the luggage to the village under cover of darkness, along with the exhumed transmitter. A thick mist blanketed the hill at dawn the next morning as Ursula bundled up the children and they walked down the track to Caux. Len stayed behind, ready to intercept Ollo if she spotted them leaving and attempted to follow. She did not. "The cold autumn fog was kind to us," wrote Ursula. Parting from the children was agony. "How long are you sending us away for?" asked Michael, at the gates of the children's home. Nina clung to Ursula and wept. "Would I ever see the children again?" she wondered. The moment took her back, with excruciating clarity, to the time when she had first left Michael in the mountains of Czechoslovakia: "Mummy stay with Misha, please mummy stay with Misha." Returning to the chalet, Ursula experienced what she called "one of my few moments of despair," followed by a fresh flash of anger. "All of this, not because of my work—I could be brave if that was the case—but due to a crazy old woman. Because of her we have to leave home, give away the children, interrupt the revolutionary work and perhaps even go to prison."

The nanny arrived at midday, to find Ursula in the empty hall.

"Where are the children?" she said. "Where is my Nina?"

"They are safe," Ursula replied. "They are in a place where you cannot reach Nina, even if something happens to me. And it does not matter what happens to me now. Do whatever you intend to do. You must know me well enough to know I am not afraid."

Ollo's face turned ashen and she collapsed onto the flagstone floor.

"What will become of you now, Ollo?" Ursula asked gently, as she cradled the older woman's head in her lap.

"I don't care about anything," Ollo sobbed.

"I can give you enough money for half a year."

"You don't have that much."

Ursula explained that she had sold her brooch, the last object of value she possessed.

"May I come with you to the station?" Ollo asked.

"That will only make it more difficult for you."

"Allow me this last request."

As Ursula climbed aboard the little train at Caux, Olga Muth wept silently on the platform. "She knew the farewell was final." Yet another departing train, another love gouged out of Ursula's life. The carriage pulled away, and the little woman trotted awkwardly alongside, stumbling and mouthing something through her tears. Ursula could not make out her words. Olga Muth, the loyal and loving traitor, was still standing on the platform as the train rumbled around the bend and out of sight.

MOSCOW'S ORDERS WERE BLUNT: get out of Switzerland.

Ollo's denunciation to the British authorities had compromised the network. Franz Obermanns was still in prison, and at least three people outside the network were aware of her espionage activities; Agent Sonya was now a liability, and the risk of exposure too great. Major Poliakova instructed Ursula to hand over the transmitter to Foote, install him in her place as Radó's radio operator, and then head for Britain via Vichy France, Spain, and Portugal, taking Len and the children with her.

Sandor Radó considered Ursula's impending departure to be "near desertion," but the owlish spy was impressed by her replacement, the Englishman "Jim." Foote struck Radó as "intelligent and determined" despite his "total lack of political education," and was clearly "a talented pupil of Sonya's" and an "outstanding radio operator with an extraordinary capacity for work." Ursula passed on Moscow's orders: Foote was to train another radio operator for Radó, construct another transmitter-receiver, and then move to Lausanne. She would be leaving the network in good shape. By the end of 1940, wrote Radó, "I had at my disposal two transmitters and three trained radio operators."

Len Beurton would be one of those operators, and a most unwilling one. Ursula obtained a visa to pass through Spain without difficulty, but Len's application was refused. As a former member of the International Brigades, his name appeared on a list of foreigners unwelcome in Franco's Spain. The Spanish consulate flatly refused to issue a transit visa. He was trapped in Switzerland.

Ursula packed her belongings into a single suitcase, collected the children from Les Rayons, and took leave of her few friends remaining in Switzerland. "It is even harder to say good-bye to people you love and respect when you know it may be farewell forever," she reflected. In one of her final messages to the Center, Ursula suggested a method for contacting Soviet intelligence once she reached the United Kingdom: "Wake Arms. Epping 1 & 15. GMT.3." Translated, this meant: meet at the Wake Arms pub near Epping Forest north of London (an inn once frequented by the highwayman Dick Turpin) on the 1st and 15th of each month, at 3:00 P.M. Greenwich Mean Time. Moscow, however, had a different rendezvous point in mind, a street corner south of Marble Arch in Central London. The Center also sent a new set of codes and call times, which she passed on to Foote.

Ursula was required to inform the British consulate that the United Kingdom was her intended destination. When the consul alerted the immigration authorities in London, a series of alarm bells went off.

Germans entering the United Kingdom were closely monitored, and Ursula ticked just about every suspicious box: the Kuczynski family was already under MI5 surveillance; she had been married to a man with a "communistic smell"; her communist brother, Jürgen, had been interned as a security risk; her father was an antiwar leftist intellectual; her new husband was a suspected subversive who had fought in Spain and visited Germany immediately before the outbreak of war. The marriage to Beurton itself seemed dubious, since "she clearly comes from an entirely different social strata [sic]."

"It looks as though the family is on the move and we should make provision for their arrival," MI5 concluded. "It seems fairly obvious that this is a marriage of convenience but being British subjects we cannot refuse to let them come. The husband is already on the Black List . . . and it seems best to get her name on the Black List so that we may keep a close eye on her activities."

On December 11, 1940, Ursula Beurton was formally designated a potential threat to British society.

At dawn a week later, Len Beurton accompanied her and the children to the bus station in Geneva and stowed their luggage on the roof rack. "Len was left standing at the side of the road" as the bus pulled out, a forlorn figure in the slush. Married for just ten months, they would not see each other again for two years.

On Christmas Eve, the little family finally arrived in Portugal after a hellish journey: twenty-eight hours by bus to Nîmes in southern France; an unexplained six-hour delay; another twelve hours to the Franco-Spanish border; more waiting while papers were checked and luggage searched, on leaving France and arriving in Spain; a night trip north through the Spanish countryside ("bright moonlight, little towns asleep . . . a few hills, and on our left the Mediterranean"); Barcelona at 3:00 A.M.; a train to Madrid and then finally, at 11:00 P.M. on December 23, a packed train to Lisbon. A friendly Lithuanian couple allowed the children to sleep in their bed, while Ursula stood in a corridor through the night. At midday, the train creaked into Lisbon station. Ursula found a cheap hotel, a doctor for Nina, whose temperature was soaring, and a doll and some wooden bricks for Christmas presents, and collapsed into a hard bed.

Then they waited. People were allocated passage to Britain by ship or plane in order of their importance to the war effort, and Ursula and her children, three more German Jews fleeing Hitler, were somewhere near the bottom of the list. Nina recovered quickly. Ursula tried without success to book Len onto a boat from Marseilles to Britain (circumnavigating Spain). Before leaving Switzerland, she had withdrawn what little money remained in the bank and was already running low on funds. She sent two telegrams and two letters to her parents, who had recently moved out of London to Oxford, but received no reply. In a letter dated January 4 (intercepted by MI5) she wrote: "I am here with the kids in Lisboa after rather a tiring trip. We will have to wait at least three more weeks. I do not know where we will land. . . . I am rather at a loss why I don't hear from you."

Finally, Ursula was informed she would be sailing on the SS *Avoceta,* bound for Liverpool.

MI5 read the passenger list and alerted the immigration authorities in Liverpool: "When she arrives please give us her destination, description and the part of the train on which she is travelling. I will then arrange for her to be picked up." Before setting foot on British soil, Ursula was being tailed.

On January 14, 1941, the SS *Avoceta* set sail with a convoy of fourteen merchant ships carrying iron ore, timber, and fruit, with a Royal Navy escort of eight vessels as protection against German submarines. The *Avoceta,* under the command of the convoy commodore, Admiral Sir Bertram Thesiger, was a seventeen-year-old, slow-moving, three-hundred-foot passenger steamer and a tempting target. U-boat captains referred to this as "the happy time," *die glückliche Zeit,* when they were still sinking large amounts of British shipping in the Atlantic, with few losses. For Ursula and the children, the three-week passage, via Gibraltar, was anything but happy, a stark contrast to Ursula's last sea cruise with Johann Patra aboard the *Conte Verde.* They were crushed into a tiny cabin, the porthole screwed shut and blacked out. The children were continuously seasick. Ursula's thoughts were crowded and claustrophobic. Would Len ever get out of Switzerland? What had happened to Rudi? In accordance with the rules, she was forbidden to contact him directly in China, but he had sent frequent letters and postcards to the children. In the spring of 1940 these had abruptly stopped, and she had heard nothing since. His silence was uncharacteristic, and deeply worrying. Ursula did not share her fears with Michael. In Britain, she would be spying inside a country at war with Germany. "What sort of work will the Centre want me to do?" she wondered. "Will I be capable of carrying it out? What if no one turns up?" The weather was foul, with squalling winds and rolling seas. The crew was tense. Bilious, fretful, and bored, Ursula braced for the impact of a German torpedo.

OTTO HAMBURGER WAS ANXIOUS. He had not heard from his brother in almost a year. After setting off for Chungking in the spring of 1940, Rudi had vanished. When Otto opened a suitcase left behind by his brother, he found it was "full of communist material." He feared the worst. But then, early in 1941, Otto received a telephone call from a German business acquaintance in Shanghai, Dieter Flatow, who suggested they meet on a street corner midway between their offices. Dieter explained that his brother Gerhard had sent a telegram from Chungking written in Rotwelsch (literally "rogues' jargon"), the semisecret language used by thieves and other covert groups in southern Germany. It read: "H's Bruder als Späher in Kittchen. Soll weggeputzt werden," which loosely translates as "H's [Hamburger's] brother is in the jug for nosing around [spying]. Faces being rubbed out [liquidated]." The message, meaningless to the Chinese authorities, could not have been clearer to Otto. He immediately called "Rudi's communist friend," Johann Patra, who got on the wireless to Moscow.

Relations between the USSR and the Republic of China had warmed since the signing of the Sino-Soviet Non-Aggression Pact in 1937, and Moscow was now providing substantial military aid to China's Nationalist government in its continuing war with Japan. In January 1941, the relationship further improved with the arrival in Chungking of General Vasily Chuikov as head of the Soviet military mission. The future victor of the Battle of Stalingrad, Chuikov was now the most senior foreign adviser to Chiang Kai-shek and in a position to ask for favors.

Three weeks later, Rudi Hamburger was taken from his cell in Bai Mansion and brought before the investigating magistrate. After nine months of captivity, half-starved, and ravaged by malaria, he looked like a ghost. Instead of being ordered, yet again, to confess, he was informed that he would soon be released and allowed to fly to Russia. "The friends had intervened," Rudi wrote. His imprisonment in Happy Valley was over.

At the beginning of February, Rudolf Hamburger arrived in Moscow and was taken to a heavily guarded dacha at Kuntsevo outside the city, near Stalin's personal residence. The "reception was enthusiastic," Rudi wrote in a letter to his father, describing his lodgings "in a lovely rest home on a beautiful wooded estate." Incarceration had done nothing to dim his enthusiasm for espionage; if anything, he was even more determined to excel at a job for which he was so singularly ill-suited. The dacha contained a large library, and after months deprived of intellectual stimulation Rudi gorged himself on the literature of communism. Once a skeptic, Hamburger was now a fully fledged communist believer. "Four men [Marx, Engels, Lenin, and Stalin] have achieved the greatest spiritual development of the last 50 years," he declared. Despite the unmitigated failure of his first mission, the Center had new plans for him. Rudi would be on the move to Turkey, the great borderland between East and West and, like all neutral countries, an espionage hothouse.

THE SS *AVOCETA* DOCKED in Liverpool on the afternoon of February 4, 1941, and Ursula and the children disembarked, "very cold and tired," but relieved to be beyond reach of German submarines. The foreboding she had felt on board was fully justified. A few months later, the captain of the German U-boat *U-203* spied the *Avoceta* through his periscope and fired four torpedoes into her port side. "She staggered like a stumbling horse," the captain wrote, and then sank swiftly, taking with her 123 passengers and crew, including 32 women and 20 children.

Immigration officer John Pease plucked Ursula out of the line waiting for passport control. The other passengers stared as they were led away. "Nina began to cry." The questions came fast: "Where is your husband? What are you going to live on? Why did you leave Switzerland?" After two hours, Pease gave the children a penny each, handed Ursula over to Major Taylor of MI5, and typed up his report.

> Mrs. Beurton is the subject of individual case No. 186 in Central Security War Black List. She is proceeding to her father, Professor Robert René Kuczynski, 78 Woodstock Road, Oxford. The reason given for leaving Switzerland is that she is afraid to stay any longer owing to her connection with a well-known anti-Nazi family—her father left Germany about eight years ago for the same reason and is now occupying a chair at the London University as an expert on population questions. Mr. Beurton is unable to leave Switzerland as he cannot obtain a Spanish visa.

Now it was Major Taylor's turn to grill Ursula. She had been trained to withstand interrogation, and politely answered his questions, one after another. But Taylor was also good at his job, and something about Mrs. Beurton did not ring true. "She was very vague as to her movements, and it was impossible to check up on her statements owing to the recent issue of her passport." Ursula told him she had met Len Beurton in Switzerland, where he was "recovering from tuberculosis," but when Taylor pressed her to describe exactly how and when they had met, she said she was "not sure"—an odd thing for a newlywed to forget. "She either could not or would not give even approximate dates. . . . She went on to say that Beurton has now recovered from his tuberculosis and had hoped to return with her to England." What was Len doing in Germany immediately before the outbreak of war? Her answer—"an unsuccessful attempt to secure money belonging to her which still remained there"— sounded like a lie. After two hours, Taylor told her she was free to go. Then he sent an urgent message to MI5 headquarters: "You may wish to cause Mrs. Ursula Beurton to be kept under observation."

Ursula checked into a cheap hotel. A few hours later they were woken by air-raid sirens and ushered into the cellar with other hotel guests as the Luftwaffe bombs rained down on Liverpool's docks.

They were homeless, virtually penniless, and under bombardment in a country at war. Her first husband had disappeared. Her second was trapped in Switzerland. Her nanny was in Nazi Germany, probably even now divulging her secrets to the Gestapo. But at least Ursula was no longer living in daily fear of capture, deportation to Germany, and the death camps. As the train trundled southward in the rain through the quiet English countryside, Ursula could feel the accumulated stress and fear begin to ebb. The Nazi spy hunters could not follow her here.

But the British ones could.

CHAPTER 16

BARBAROSSA

MOSCOW HAD CHOSEN A PARTICULARLY INAPPROPRIATE place for a rendezvous—smack in the middle of London's red-light district.

Loitering in Shepherd Market in the deepening dusk, Ursula felt painfully conspicuous. From time to time, a man sidled up from the shadows, and she would wave him away. The regular prostitutes were becoming suspicious of this soberly dressed woman who seemed determined to hang around, turning down good customers and undermining business.

Ursula's instructions were precise: at 7:15 P.M. on the first day of the month, she should make her way to this street corner east of Hyde Park, where she would be contacted by a military intelligence officer from the Soviet embassy. If he failed to appear, she should return on the fifteenth. Every fortnight, for three months, she caught the train from Oxford and waited among the whores, pimps, and drunks. The officer never appeared. One evening as she made her way through the blackout, the air-raid sirens sounded, and she was herded off the street into an Underground station, where thousands of Londoners were following instructions to keep calm and carry on. "They unpack their supper, their Thermos flasks of tea, the knitting and the newspapers," Ursula wrote.

The city was battered but unbowed. "Yesterday I wandered through London," she wrote to Len. "The debris of the great department stores bothers me less than a little home in ruins, a line of washing still hanging over the kitchen stove." Instead of cowing the city's inhabitants, the Blitz was having the reverse effect: "They hated Hitler and fascism," wrote Ursula. "The whole country rose to defend itself." For the first time she felt proud to be newly British, but frustrated: the battle against fascism was raging, and she was a spectator. She purchased parts for a transmitter, increasingly sure she would never have the opportunity to use it. Something must have happened in Moscow. Her spying career, it seemed, was over. "Little hope remained that anyone from the Centre would meet me."

Like so many refugee families in wartime Britain, the Kuczynskis were dispersed, distracted, and insolvent. With so many fleeing the Blitz to cities outside London, rental accommodation in Oxford was scarce: one landlady insisted she play cards and pray with her every evening; another threw her out after a few days, unable to endure Ursula's "foreign countenance." Over the next four months, she and the children moved four times. The Oxfordshire police tracked her movements and reported back to MI5: "She is now living at 97 Kingston Road with her sister," noted Detective Constable Charles Jevons. "The only people who visit her are her father and his wife. Kuczynski, I am informed, holds strong communist views." Robert Kuczynski had retired from the LSE at the statutory age of sixty-five. Despite his academic eminence, he had little paid work. "He is much too proud to be a good job-hunter," wrote Ursula. Jürgen, Marguerite, and their two small children were crammed into a flat in Hampstead, surviving on whatever he could earn from writing and giving lectures. Jürgen's welcome to his younger sister was distinctly tepid. Alexander Foote later claimed: "Jürgen was angry about Sonia's [sic] return to the UK . . . because her presence there as a Russian agent might compromise the rest of the Kuczynski family in their political work." Without employment or a permanent home, with few possessions, no husband to provide for the family, and no money coming in from the Center, she faced penury. "I was down to the last of my savings," she wrote. "I did not reveal these worries to my family. None of them had much to spare." Finally, in April 1941, she found a furnished bungalow for rent at 134 Oxford Road in the village of Kidlington, five miles outside Oxford. MI5 was intercepting her letters. They did not, however, spot the pattern of her trips to

London, and the way she lingered on a dubious street corner before returning to Oxford.

For the first time in her life, Ursula began to sink into depression. Her letters to Len were freighted with loneliness and longing. "There are so many small things I want you to share. I haven't found any friends yet. This morning I raced off with the pram to fetch a sack of coal. That means our first bath in weeks." Len was continuing to work as a radio operator for Sandor Radó's Rote Drei, but without enthusiasm. The Spanish still refused to issue a transit visa, and he was trapped in Switzerland indefinitely. "How much I counted on your coming," she wrote. "In a hundred ways—'We must do this walk together,' 'We must discuss this book.' . . . Now I shall have to get used to the fact that such things are not for us." She put on her best clothes, alone, for a man she had known as a husband for only a few months. "I am wearing a new dress; the first that you do not know. Red with little white polka dots on it, white belt and white collar." She wondered if he would ever see her wearing it.

In late May, she traipsed once more to Shepherd Market and waited disconsolately on the street corner, ignoring the hostile looks of the prostitutes. "I had all but given up hope." Then she saw him, "a tough looking man—thickset and balding, with big nose and big ears—who could clearly take care of himself in a fight." He was watching her intensely. "The man approached me, not the first in this accursed street, but this time he was the one I wanted."

Nikolai Vladimirovitch Aptekar, a thirty-two-year-old former tractor driver from Odessa, worked as chauffeur and secretary to the air attaché at the Soviet embassy. He was also an officer in the Red Army operating under the code name "Iris" and a key member of the large Soviet military intelligence presence in London. As it did throughout the world, Moscow ran two distinct species of spy in the United Kingdom: "legals," intelligence officers like Aptekar working under diplomatic cover out of the embassy, and "illegals," such as Ursula, living as ordinary civilians and therefore without diplomatic protection. Aptekar had graduated from the aviation school in Leningrad and served as an engineer in the RAF Bomber Command, before being seconded to military intelligence and sent to Britain. He might look like a prizefighter, but Aptekar was a formidable intelligence officer, with a good grasp of English and a firm grounding in spycraft and military technology.

Aptekar whispered the code word. Ursula responded with another. They immediately parted and walked in opposite directions. Ursula's spirits soared. "I glided down the street and along two more as if on wings to the place where we were to talk."

"Call me Sergei," said Aptekar, a few minutes later, in the cover of a shop doorway. She never knew his real name. He conveyed "greetings and congratulations from the Centre," handed over an envelope containing "enough money to allay all my financial worries," and apologized because a car accident had prevented him from coming sooner. "The Centre needs news," he said. Britain was not an enemy of the Soviet Union, but neither was she yet an ally. Moscow was hungry for information. "What contacts can you make? In the military? In political circles? You are to set up a new information network. When can you have a transmitter working?"

She told Aptekar that she could have her radio up and running within twenty-four hours.

Ursula was back in the game.

No sooner did she reestablish radio contact with Moscow than events more than a thousand miles away on the western borders of the Soviet Union transformed the war, and Ursula's role in it.

On June 22, 1941, Germany attacked Russia. Operation Barbarossa was the largest invasion in the history of warfare, some three million German troops advancing along an eighteen-hundred-mile front. This was Hitler's war of extermination, the long-planned operation to liquidate the Jewish and Slavic populations of the western Soviet Union, create Lebensraum (living space) for the German population, and destroy Bolshevism. "We only have to kick the door in and the whole rotten structure will come crashing down," declared the führer. Millions of dead and four years of brutal fighting would eventually prove him disastrously wrong. Soviet spies, including Richard Sorge in Tokyo and Sandor Radó in Switzerland, had sent warnings of the coming invasion, but Stalin refused to believe them, convinced that as long as Germany remained locked in battle with Britain, Hitler would never open up a two-front war by attacking Russia. His underlings were too terrified to tell him the truth.

For Ursula, her family, her husband, ex-husband, former lovers, and fellow spies, the outbreak of war on the Eastern Front changed everything. Britain and the Soviet Union were now allies, joined within six months by the United States after the Japanese attack on Pearl Harbor. The Nazi-Soviet pact, anathema to so many communists, was smashed overnight.

Ursula was both appalled and elated. The German armies advanced with a series of swift victories, occupying swaths of Soviet territory; it appeared that Moscow would fall, and communism itself might perish. Ursula described herself as "shattered" by news of the surprise attack. But she was also relieved, no longer burdened by the pretense of supporting Stalin's cynical pact with Hitler. Moscow had made contact at the exact moment her espionage could once again be devoted to destroying Nazism. She was now a combatant, no mere observer, and fighting alongside the British.

On the day of Operation Barbarossa, Winston Churchill gave one of the most stirring speeches of the war, broadcast live on the BBC, vowing to fight Hitler on land, air, and sea "until, with God's help, we have rid the earth of his shadow." Britain now stood shoulder to shoulder with America and the Soviet Union: "The Russian danger is our danger and the danger of the United States just as the cause of any Russian fighting for his hearth and home is the cause of free men and free peoples in every quarter of the globe."

Crouched over her radio, Ursula listened, rapt, to Churchill's towering oratory and pronounced it "brilliant." "Hitler's attack on the Soviet Union made a powerful impact on Britain," she wrote.

For several days after Operation Barbarossa, Moscow failed to respond to her messages. When she finally established radio contact, Ursula found the Center avid for intelligence about Britain. What were the politicians and generals really thinking? How sincere were Churchill's words? Would Britain support Russia? Robert Kuczynski, with his wide range of well-connected friends and acquaintances, was uniquely placed to answer such questions. Many of the left-wing economists and Labour politicians he knew were directly involved in the war effort. Ursula chose this moment to recruit her father as a Soviet agent. The professor agreed to supply whatever information he could glean, in the knowledge that she would somehow pass it on to Moscow; he did not know his daughter was an intelligence officer of the Red Army. Robert Kuczynski reported that "Britain's leading politicians and soldiers were counting on the Soviet Union's defeat within three months."

With the end of the Nazi-Soviet pact, Jürgen Kuczynski switched his position overnight, no longer attacking the war as an imperialist ploy but stoutly defending it as a moral imperative. MI5 observed his change of heart with approval, noting that the communist firebrand had stopped "spreading defeatist propaganda among refugees" and was now "advocating cooperation with the Allied war effort and active help to the USSR." Jürgen also passed on to Ursula everything he could gather that might be of interest or use to Moscow. Although never formally recruited by Soviet military intelligence, Jürgen Kuczynski now had his own code name, "Karo." Radio messages to Moscow from the London *rezidentura* (the intelligence section within a Soviet embassy), intercepted in 1941 and decrypted long after the war, show the high esteem in which he was held by Major General Ivan Andreevich Sklyarov, the chief of military intelligence in London: "I unhesitatingly recommend Jürgen Kuczynski. He is a brilliant scholar, a Jew, and an economist of deep Marxist conviction. I know him to be perfectly reliable. He knows not only Germany but the continent and England and would be more valuable and trustworthy for us than anyone I know. . . . He is tall, slender, dark, ugly, very brilliant and very stable politically." Unlike their father, Jürgen knew exactly where the intelligence he passed to Ursula was going.

Sonya's network, beginning with members of her own family, would gradually expand into a wide web of informants providing, consciously or unconsciously, a range of information useful to Moscow: economic, political, technical, and military. At dinner parties in Hampstead, Britain's left-wing intellectuals freely exchanged gossip and secrets, unaware that, via one Kuczynski or another, it was all being funneled back to Moscow through Ursula's wireless. One "fertile source of information" was Hans Kahle, a German communist and former fighter in the International Brigades who, as military correspondent for the American magazines *Time* and *Fortune,* had access to highly useful information.

A report from the London *rezidentura* to Moscow, sent on July 31, 1941, and partially decrypted in the 1960s, noted: "IRIS had a meeting with SONIA [*sic*] on 30 July." The note indicates she was sending daily messages to Moscow at hourly intervals during the night and passing on additional intelligence using microphotographs, the size of periods, attached to letters and sent to safe houses in neutral Spain or Portugal for collection by Soviet intelligence. The Center was paying her £58 a month, backdated to her arrival in Liverpool, a substantial sum in wartime Britain. Years later, MI5 was still puzzling over the identity of Iris: "Probably the English Christian name IRIS used as a cover-name for a woman. The Russian word IRIS means either the flower, or a kind of toffee; the word seems an unlikely choice as a cover name." Iris was, of course, Nikolai Aptekar, the burly Soviet intelligence officer, who would have been amused to be mistaken for a woman, or named after a toffee or a flower.

Every fortnight, Sonya caught the train to London to meet "Sergei," never at the same place twice, never for longer than fifteen minutes, and usually in the darkness she had always feared. "In that blacked-out city, without street lamps or even the glimmer of window light, I was afraid. There was hardly a soul on the streets and anybody who did pass by was invisible. I stood in the pitch dark, expecting somebody to grab my face or throat at any minute. Whenever I heard gentle footsteps, I would hold my breath in fear and be relieved if they belonged to 'our man.' "

MI5 continued to watch the Kuczynskis. A memo from February 1941 recorded that "various sources" had reported Jürgen Kuczynski was in direct contact with Soviet intelligence. But the Anglo-Soviet alliance had shifted MI5's focus: with the Russians on the side of the Allies, the Security Service was less concerned with monitoring communist subversives than catching Nazi agents. The surveillance of the Kuczynskis dwindled, and then almost ceased. In fact, there were no Nazi spies active in Britain: thanks to the code breakers at Bletchley Park, every single one was intercepted and either executed or turned. But there were Soviet spies aplenty: the Cambridge Five—Kim Philby, Anthony Blunt, Donald Maclean, Guy Burgess, and John Cairncross, all men in positions of authority in the British establishment—and one unobtrusive refugee housewife in Oxford-shire, Agent Sonya, the eyes and ears of Soviet military intelligence in Britain.

Ursula saw no contradiction in supporting Russia's allies and spying on them. And nor did her first husband.

Rudi Hamburger's new orders were to travel to Turkey overland via Iran, but as so often in the career of this hapless spy, the plan did not work out. He had got as far as Tehran when Operation Barbarossa redrew the map of war. He could not get a Turkish visa. In August 1941, the British and Soviets launched a joint invasion of Iran to secure the oil fields against seizure by the Germans. Tehran, hitherto a sideshow in the war, was suddenly a place of vital strategic importance, particularly after the Americans arrived to help build the transport infrastructure needed to maintain the flow of fuel and other supplies to Soviet troops on the Eastern Front. Hamburger wrote: "I received instructions to give up trying to get a visa for Turkey and to concentrate on tasks in Iran"—monitoring troop movements, arms shipments, and the military activities of the British and Americans. Hamburger settled down in the Iranian capital and began spying on the Soviet Union's allies, with characteristic ineptitude.

In Switzerland, Alexander Foote picked up the first message from Moscow after Operation Barbarossa: "Fascist beasts have invaded the Motherland of the working classes. You are called upon to carry out your tasks in Germany to the best of your ability. Director." Sandor Radó immediately expanded operations. For the next two years, from an apartment in Lausanne, Foote sent hundreds of messages to Moscow, distilled intelligence from spies inside Nazi Germany that provided astonishingly detailed insight into German military planning. As Foote put it, Moscow's generals were "virtually fighting their war on the material."

Len Beurton, by contrast, gradually lost interest in working for the Rote Drei and then fell out with Radó, who stopped paying him. "Len had only one desire," wrote Foote. "To return to England and rejoin Sonya." The corrupt Bolivian consul who had issued Ursula's false passport agreed to do the same for Len, in return for another 2,000 Swiss francs. The French consulate, however, spotted the fake in the name of "Luis Carlos Bilboa" and refused to issue a French transit visa. In Britain, Ursula enlisted the International Brigades Association to lobby the government to help Len get out of Switzerland, and wrote to the Labour MP Eleanor Rathbone, whose efforts on behalf of German exiles earned her the nickname "Minister for Refugees." Even Anthony Eden, the foreign secretary, was made aware of Beurton's plight. Nothing seemed to work.

"Inactive, missing his wife, short of money, down on his luck, and desperate to get back to the UK," Len was miserable. But the new alliance between Britain and the Soviet Union suddenly offered a glimmer of hope. The British consulate at Quai Wilson was just a few hundred yards from his apartment on Lake Geneva. Len popped in for a chat.

Victor Farrell was passport control officer. The fact that he was also an MI6 officer prepared to issue passports to deserving fugitives was "one of the best known 'secrets' in Geneva." Beurton offered to provide Farrell "with useful intelligence information," if the MI6 man helped him get back to Britain. Exactly what information Len passed to MI6 is unknown, and the relevant passages have been redacted in declassified documents. He revealed nothing about Ursula's activities and his own work on behalf of Soviet intelligence. But he certainly identified at least one of Radó's agents, a Chinese journalist named L. T. Wang accredited to the League of Nations. A frequent guest at Wang's home was General Alexander von Falkenhausen, a former military adviser to Chiang Kai-shek in China, who was now the Nazi governor of occupied Belgium. Wang was secretly spying on Falkenhausen and passing on information to Radó. Len introduced the Chinese journalist to Farrell, who found Wang "friendly and inscrutable" but also, in time, a rich source of intelligence. Since Britain and the Soviet Union were now allies, Beurton felt no qualms about passing Wang on to MI6. In return, Farrell agreed to furnish Beurton with a forged passport.

The plates of loyalty were shifting beneath the new political landscape. Ursula and Rudi were spying on Britain, Moscow's ally; a British intelligence officer, Victor Farrell, was using Soviet assets to spy on Nazis in Switzerland; Len, still a Soviet intelligence agent, was secretly aiding MI6, without telling Moscow. They might all be united in the wider battle against Nazism, but the Allies were spying on each other, as allies always do.

Hitler's invasion of the Soviet Union had one more momentous repercussion, by driving one of the most important spies in history into Sonya's net.

CHAPTER 17

THE ROAD
TO HELL

K LAUS FUCHS LIVED BY TWO SETS OF RULES: THE IMMU-
table laws of physics, through which he would help to unleash
a new science of terrifying power, and a second group of socio-
political laws, in which he believed no less profoundly, leading to
the inevitable triumph of communism. The combination of these
two parallel bodies of ideas, scientific and ideological, set off a chain
reaction in Fuchs that turned him from a brilliant physicist into
the world's most dangerous spy. In 1951, a U.S. congressional committee would conclude: "Fuchs alone has influenced the safety of
more people and accomplished greater damage than any other spy
not only in the history of the United States, but in the history of nations."

He really didn't mean to.

Fuchs was the third of four children born to a Lutheran pastor in
western Germany. His father, Emil, was a man of great courage, outspoken opinions, and towering moral arrogance, who taught his
children to follow the dictates of private conscience regardless of
consequences. Four years younger than Ursula, Fuchs had also come
of age amid the political and economic chaos of Weimar Germany.
Like the Kuczynskis, the Fuchs siblings embraced communism,
joined the KPD, and hurled themselves into the increasingly violent
student and street battles of the 1920s. Klaus was nicknamed Der rote
Fuchs, the Red Fox. Returning home after an anti-Nazi meeting he

was ambushed by brownshirts, badly beaten up, and thrown into a river with his front teeth shattered. The young physicist was studying at Kiel University in 1931 when his mother killed herself by drinking hydrochloric acid. His father was arrested two years later for speaking out against Hitler. His brother was imprisoned and driven into exile along with his younger sister, while his older sister was hounded by the Nazis and eventually committed suicide by throwing herself under a Berlin train. Klaus Fuchs understandably believed that fascism had destroyed his family. He saw politics as he understood science, an equation with only one correct solution, a world of black and white: "There were no half-tones . . . you had to be either a Nazi or a Communist," he said. Marxism replaced the religion he had grown up with.

Already a prodigiously talented scientist, at the age of twenty-two Fuchs enrolled at the Kaiser Wilhelm Institute for Physics in Berlin, but by now he was a marked man, a communist agitator liable to be arrested at any moment. At a secret meeting, the KPD leadership urged him to get out of Germany, continue his studies abroad, and await the revolution that would surely destroy Hitler. Fuchs arrived in Folkestone in September 1933, "white faced, half-starved, with a bundle of dirty linen in a canvas bag."

Like many academics fleeing Nazism, Fuchs was welcomed warmly by Britain's scientific community. The physicist Nevill Mott took him on as research assistant at Bristol University and in 1937, after obtaining a doctorate in physics, Fuchs moved to Edinburgh University, where he worked under another German refugee, the distinguished physicist Max Born, investigating electron behavior and electromagnetic radiation. A cursory investigation by MI5 concluded that he posed no security threat.

Fuchs was eccentric, even by academic standards. He occasionally socialized with others in the German exiled community, and met Jürgen Kuczynski at the Free German Club in London. But he remained a largely solitary, enigmatic figure, a chain-smoker and self-taught violinist, ferociously punctual, occasionally drunken, tall, myopic, gangling, with "a sensitive and inquiring face, and a mildly lost air." One colleague composed a clerihew:

Fuchs
Looks
Like an ascetic
Theoretic

The young German appeared to be the "perfect specimen of an abstracted professor." He never discussed politics, or much of anything else outside physics. People wondered what was really going on behind the thick round spectacles but no one doubted, least of all Fuchs himself, that here was a major scientist in the making. He had inherited his father's rigid sense of moral rectitude, and later remarked: "From time to time there have to be individuals who deliberately take on the burden of guilt because they see the situation clearer than those who have the power."

In 1939, on the eve of war, Fuchs applied for British citizenship, but before this could be granted he was interned, along with other German enemy aliens, first on the Isle of Man and then in Canada at a camp outside Quebec. He felt no bitterness at this treatment and continued to collaborate, long-distance, with Max Born, who pleaded for his release, insisting his colleague was "in the small top group of theoretical physicists in this country." The lobbying paid off and on January 11, 1941, two weeks after his twenty-ninth birthday, Fuchs landed back at Liverpool, where Ursula would arrive a month later.

On April 3, Jürgen Kuczynski hosted a party at 6 Lawn Road Flats in Hampstead to "celebrate Fuchs's return to the United Kingdom." The gathering included several German and British notables, a large number of communists, a few scientists, and a fair sprinkling of spies. Among the guests were Brigitte Lewis, now working as a secretary at the LSE, and the German communist Hans Kahle, who had struck up a friendship with Fuchs when both were interned in Canada. As well as providing intelligence for Ursula, Kahle was "a talent spotter for the Soviet Intelligence services." The party for Fuchs may have been his idea. The drink flowed, and the guest of honor fully partook. At one point, Jürgen introduced Fuchs to "a courteous, intelligent man, with perfect English [and an] interest in science," who introduced himself as Alexander Johnson. Their conversation turned to "the possibilities of atomic energy." Back in 1938, German scientists had discovered that fission in uranium liberates both energy and neutrons, enabling future fissions and potentially causing a chain reaction. The Danish atomic theorist Niels Bohr had established that fission occurs in the rare isotope U-235, a breakthrough offering the prospect of a new energy machine (a nuclear reactor) with, as Fuchs put it, "a long term possibility for the production of power." At the end of the evening, Fuchs agreed "to prepare for Johnson a short account about the possibilities of atomic energy." He then weaved off into the night and missed the train back to Edinburgh.

"Johnson" was really Colonel Semyon Davidovitch Kremer, an officer in Soviet military intelligence with the code name "Barch."

A year earlier, two more exiled German physicists working at Birmingham University, Otto Frisch and Rudolf Peierls, had drawn up a secret scientific paper that would change the world and eventually threaten its existence. The Frisch-Peierls memo was a terrifying leap forward in nuclear science: the first practical exposition of how to build a nuclear weapon, a "super-bomb" that could harness the energy in atomic nuclei and unleash an explosion at "a temperature comparable to that in the interior of the sun." The initial blast "would destroy life in a wide area," the scientists concluded, and the subsequent cloud of radioactivity would kill many more.

Peierls recommended that the atomic bomb be developed as a matter of urgency. "While there is no evidence that the Germans realise the potentialities of a U-235 bomb," he warned, "it is quite possible that they do, and for all we know they may have completed its production." The British government set up a top secret committee, code-named "Maud," to explore the feasibility of building such a weapon. This would lead to the establishment of the "Tube Alloys" project (another deliberately misleading code name), an industrial program involving dozens of scientists at various British universities, to research and develop the bomb.

On May 10, a month after the party in Hampstead, Peierls wrote to Fuchs inviting him to "take part in theoretical work involving mathematical problems of considerable complexity." He added: "I cannot disclose the nature or purpose of the work." The British government later justified the decision to recruit Fuchs into the atomic weapons project: "The very finest brains available were needed to assist in that research and such brains as Dr. Fuchs possesses are very rare indeed. He was known as, and has proved himself to be, one of the finest theoretical physicists living." Knowing that Fuchs had been "an active member of the Communist Party in Germany," MI5 debated the wisdom of granting him security clearance, but finally decided to "accept such risk as there might be." Fuchs guessed this secret new job was "in relation to atomic energy research," but it was only after he arrived in Birmingham and moved in with Peierls and his wife that he discovered the true nature of the assignment. Peierls had rightly surmised that Fuchs would "welcome an opportunity to participate in a project that was intended to forestall Hitler"; the use Fuchs would make of that participation was something Peierls never imagined. In June, Fuchs began working on the atom bomb. A few days later, Hitler invaded the Soviet Union.

On the surface an unworldly boffin, Fuchs remained a dedicated secret communist and a fierce anti-fascist. Like Ursula, he had recoiled from the Nazi-Soviet agreement, but "explained this away by reassuring himself that Russia had signed the pact simply to gain time." Britain was now rushing to develop the most powerful weapon the world had ever known, without informing Moscow. That struck Fuchs as unfair, a dereliction of the new Anglo-Soviet alliance. He later wrote: "I never saw myself as a spy. I just couldn't understand why the West was not prepared to share the atom bomb with Moscow. I was of the opinion that something with that immense destructive potential should be made available to the big powers equally." Fuchs had been taught to follow his conscience, and, in the monochrome moral universe he inhabited, informing Moscow about the new weapon was not an act of treachery to Britain but an expression of communist solidarity and an opportunity to contribute, personally, to the destruction of Nazism. The British authorities would later condemn Fuchs's actions as "the inward and convinced arrogance of a genuinely introspective mind," but Fuchs saw himself as a secret hero, as many spies do. "I had complete confidence in Russian policy [and] I therefore had no hesitation." The German attack on Russia galvanized him to work in secret for the Soviet Union: "I established contact through another member of the communist party."

The comrade in question was Jürgen Kuczynski.

In the summer of 1941, Fuchs visited Kuczynski in Hampstead and "informed him, with the most general expressions, about the type of my information." In his memoirs, Jürgen wrote: "Klaus naturally came to me as I was the political leader in England." Jürgen understood nothing about nuclear physics, but he knew how to seize an opportunity. He immediately contacted Ivan Mikhailovich Maisky, the Soviet ambassador to Britain and a personal friend. Maisky was embroiled in an office feud with Anatoli Gorski, the NKVD *rezident,* and so instead of alerting him, he passed the information to General Sklyarov, chief of Soviet military intelligence in London. Sklyarov cabled the Center, which "instructed him to recruit Fuchs," a task he delegated to his deputy, Colonel Semyon Kremer.

Kremer had served as commander of a Red Army tank corps before being seconded to military intelligence and sent to Britain in 1937 with the cover job of Soviet military attaché. MI5 put Kremer under surveillance; he was spotted "walking up and down the Charing Cross Road, buying the latest edition of *Jane's Fighting Ships* and every book on modern military tactics he could lay his hands on." But MI5 was not watching him on August 8, 1941, when Kremer entered "a private house to the south of Hyde Park." Fuchs arrived a few minutes later and knocked on the door, which was opened by Alexander Johnson, the man he had met at the party in Lawn Road four months earlier. Kremer gave the recognition code: "Greetings from Kuczynski."

By this time, Fuchs had been working with Peierls for two months, tackling problems of gaseous diffusion and designing a plant to produce enriched uranium, the critical component of a nuclear weapon. Fuchs handed Kremer six pages of notes summarizing what he knew about the building of the atom bomb, including the essence of the Frisch-Peierls memorandum and the uranium enrichment process. It was the first installment of an intelligence cornucopia.

"Why did you decide to transfer this information to the Soviet Union?" Kremer asked him.

"The USSR should also have its own bomb," Fuchs replied, adding that he wanted no payment and asked only that the intelligence be "placed on Stalin's desk."

Sklyarov dispatched the notes to Moscow in the diplomatic bag and sent a coded message to the Center marked "Urgent. Most important."

> BARCH conducted a meeting with the German physicist, Klaus Fuchs, who is in a special group in Birmingham University working on the theoretical aspects of creating a uranium bomb. Assuming that at least one per cent of the atomic energy of uranium explosive is released, a ten kilogram bomb will be equal to 1000 tons of dynamite. BRION.

Moscow responded immediately: "Take all measures for obtaining information about the uranium bomb." Fuchs was code-named "Otto."

Soviet military intelligence had recently acquired a new name, and a new boss. By order of Stalin, the Fourth Department was now known as the Main Intelligence Directorate, or the GRU. The new chief of military intelligence, General Aleksei Panfilov, offered his assessment of the material coming from Britain. If the new weapon worked, it "would put humanity on the road to hell."

Over the next six months, Fuchs handed over swaths of scientific secrets to Kremer, some two hundred pages of information from the heart of Britain's atomic weapons program. Usually they met during weekends at a busy bus stop, climbed on the same bus, and sat wordlessly on the top deck, side by side. Fuchs would alight first, leaving behind a package on the seat. Sometimes they caught a cab together and conducted business in the back. Fuchs had a slender understanding of spycraft. In complete violation of the principles of *konspiratsia,* he called Kremer several times on his office telephone, and according to a Russian source he once even appeared without warning at the Soviet embassy, carrying "forty pages of notes." Kremer's understanding of espionage protocol was not much better. He kept scanning behind them, looking for a tail—a sure way to arouse suspicion. "He irritated Fuchs by his insistence on taking long rides in London taxis, regularly doubling back in order to throw off anyone trying to tail them."

Kremer had little appreciation of the intelligence he was gathering; he would rather have been fighting in a tank than meeting this odd young scientist on the top of London buses. Much later, Fuchs referred to Jürgen Kuczynski's home as "my secret residence," suggesting he was a regular visitor to Lawn Road. The Soviet embassy was under surveillance and its telephones were bugged; the Kuczynskis were being watched; Kremer was a known Soviet intelligence officer. MI5 had numerous opportunities to spot what was going on and took none of them.

After one meeting with Fuchs, Kremer recalled: "He gave me a large notepad, of around 40cm by 20cm in size which was full of formulations and equations. He told me: 'Here is all that is necessary for your scientists to know how to organize production of nuclear weapons.' All the material was sent to Moscow and an instruction was received back not to lose contact with Fuchs. But, as usual, there wasn't anything said about how useful the material was."

The material was not just useful; it was priceless. In August 1941, another spy for the Soviet Union, the British civil servant John Cairncross, gave his handler a copy of the Maud Committee report outlining the aims of the nuclear weapons program. Fuchs provided the detailed reality of the bomb's development, step by experimental step: the designs for a diffusion plant, estimates of the critical mass for explosive U-235, the measurement of fission, and the increasing British cooperation with American nuclear scientists. At the end of 1941, Fuchs co-authored two important papers on the separation of the isotopes of U-235—and passed the findings to Kremer.

But in the summer of 1942, just as suddenly as Kremer had appeared in Fuchs's life, he disappeared from it, without warning or explanation. The Soviet officer abruptly returned to Moscow and then resumed command of a tank brigade on the Eastern Front, where he was wounded twice and eventually promoted to the rank of major general. Bizarrely, neither Kremer nor Moscow made any provision for maintaining contact with Klaus Fuchs. The reason for this mysterious hiatus has never been adequately explained. Kremer was itching to return to conventional warfare and getting on badly with his colleagues at the embassy. He may simply have quit in a fit of pique. But whatever the reason, Fuchs was left stranded without a handler at a crucial moment: he and Peierls had just made an important breakthrough in calculating the time required to produce enriched uranium and he wanted to tell Moscow about it. Once again, he turned to Jürgen Kuczynski, who this time decided to bypass the embassy. Instead, he informed his sister.

At a family gathering in Hampstead in July, Jürgen took Ursula aside and told her "a physicist by the name of F. had lost contact with a representative of the Soviet Embassy's military department, who called himself 'Johnson.'" That evening, back in Kidlington, she sent a message to Moscow requesting instructions. Possibly realizing that it had narrowly avoided a cock-up of historic proportions, the Center responded: "Make contact with Otto."

Ursula, as it happened, was already in the atomic secrets business, through a family friend.

Melita Norwood's espionage began in 1937. The daughter of a Latvian father and a British mother, Letty Sirnis was brought up in Bournemouth and joined the Communist Party at the age of twenty-five. Following her father's early death, the family moved to Hendon. Her sister had been a student of Robert Kuczynski's at the LSE, and her mother, Gertrude, helped the Kuczynski family find their first permanent British home in Lawn Road. In 1932, Letty became a secretary at the British Non-Ferrous Metals Research Association (BNFMRA), a semipublic company conducting metallurgical research. Five years later the NKVD recruited her as an informant. She married a communist mathematics teacher, Hilary Norwood, and moved to a semidetached house in Bexleyheath, where she raised a family, read pacifist literature, and made her own jam. After the purges left the KGB short-staffed, she was transferred to Soviet military intelligence. Melita Norwood, code-named "Hola," may have been the longest-serving Soviet agent on British soil, but she was also, for many years, the dullest. That changed in 1942 with the establishment of Britain's atomic weapons program. Much of the research into the properties of certain metals, including uranium, was carried out by BNFMRA, and suddenly Norwood, "the perfect secretary" in the estimation of her boss, had access to some very valuable secrets. In August 1941, Churchill became the first world leader to approve a nuclear weapons program, and within weeks Norwood made her first information drop to Soviet intelligence, a paper on the behavior of uranium at high temperatures. From then on, she supplied a steady stream of top secret information on the atomic project, supplementing, confirming, and in some cases expanding on the torrent of intelligence provided by Fuchs. Her motivation was remarkably similar to his—"I wanted Russia to be on an equal footing with the west"—as was her self-image, and self-delusion: "I never considered myself a spy." *The Times* later reported: "She would remove files on Tube Alloys from her superior's safe, photograph them with a miniature camera, then pass them on to her Soviet controller, whom she would meet *incognito* in the suburbs of southeast London." The controller was Ursula Beurton.

Since the Norwoods had long been friendly with the Kuczynskis, the two women always had a cover for meeting and could do so "even at each other's homes."

The Center was increasingly reliant on Agent Sonya, "our illegal station chief in England," whose high-grade intelligence came not just from individual informants like Norwood, but indirectly from the upper reaches of the British establishment. The Labour politician Sir Stafford Cripps was a close friend of Robert Kuczynski's and a trusted member of Churchill's War Cabinet. In 1942, recently returned from a two-year stint in Moscow as Britain's ambassador, he was particularly well informed about Anglo-Soviet relations and privy to important state secrets. With his academic German friend he was also extremely indiscreet. Kuczynski passed on to his daughter whatever he gleaned from Stafford Cripps and others, and she sent it all to Moscow.

In her other, parallel life, Ursula was fast becoming a British housewife. The children adapted effortlessly to their new environment. Michael attended the local primary school in Kidlington. In his short life he had learned German, Chinese, Polish, and French. Now, almost overnight, he learned English, with an Oxfordshire accent. When Ursula was away, Nina was cared for by neighbors. Villagers can be inquisitive and intrusive, but with so many strangers flooding into the countryside, including numerous refugees, no one paid much attention to the single mother living quietly on the Oxford Road. Her English was so good, and her accent so faint, that most people were unaware she was German and assumed her to be British or, at worst, French. The only problem, from the locals' perspective, was her name. "Beurton" looked suspiciously foreign, which, of course, it was. So they called her "Mrs. Burton" and refused to call her anything else. In a way, it was a mark of acceptance.

The two sides of Ursula's life, domesticity and espionage, the open and the secret, merged in a way that had never happened before. As Mrs. Burton from number 124 she had a settled home, contented children, friendly neighbors, and a supportive family; as Agent Sonya she had a camera for producing microdots, a network of subagents, a helpful and appreciative Soviet handler, and an illegal radio transmitter in her bedroom cupboard. She also got back her husband and fellow spy.

On July 30, 1942, the plane from Lisbon landed at Poole airport, and a tall, spare man with a British passport identifying him as John William Miller climbed down the steps onto the tarmac. True to his word, Victor Farrell of MI6 had provided Len Beurton with the means of escape; his journey from Geneva to Britain had proved, in the end, remarkably easy. The Swiss, French, Spanish, and Portuguese authorities waved Mr. Miller through without demur; the British did not. At Poole, his luggage was thoroughly searched and Len was subjected to an even more rigorous interrogation than the one Ursula had undergone.

Len Beurton blithely admitted the British passport was false, as was a second, Bolivian passport, found in his suitcase, in the name of Luis Carlos Bilboa. The rest of his statement was an elaborate tissue of lies. He claimed he had gone to Germany in 1939 "to try to sell certain property belonging to one Herr Rudolf [sic] Kuczynski, a refugee since the advent of Hitler to power, now professor of demography at London University"; he said he had left Switzerland because "things seemed to be blowing up a bit." When quizzed on how he had survived financially for three years without a job, Len "claimed to have inherited £20,000 from some French relatives" while working in Jersey before the war and had lived on the cash ever since.

The authorities smelled something fishy. Len made no mention of the tuberculosis that, according to Ursula, had prompted him to come to Switzerland in the first place; his father had been a penniless French waiter, so it seemed unlikely his relatives would amass £20,000, let alone leave it to a distant English cousin; he exhibited a distinctly "shifty manner in answering questions put to him." Quite how he had obtained his false passports required further investigation. "The interrogator admits himself quite incapable of forming a definite opinion about Beurton . . . he behaves somewhat suspiciously whenever confronted with any constituted authority (especially military) for which he seems to have an inherent antipathy and suspicion." Len was already on the security blacklist, and his answers suggested he should stay on it. He was released, but not before MI5 ensured he could not leave the country: "Would you ask the Passport Office not to grant an Exit Permit for Leon Beurton without reference to us?" Reflecting the ingrained sexism of the time, MI5 saw the male of the couple as the main potential threat, when the real focus of suspicion should have been his wife.

Ursula and Len had not seen each other since 1940. Their reunion was joyful and passionate. Len marveled at the way the children had grown in his absence, at Nina's grasp of toddler English and Michael's burgeoning interest in cricket. He had come to regard the children as his own. Family life resumed, almost as it had before, but with the dramatic alpine scenery exchanged for the verdant, rolling landscape of rural Oxfordshire. During long walks in the country around Kidlington, Ursula outlined her continuing espionage for the Soviet Union. She showed Len the radio hidden in their bedroom. She did not go into the details of her clandestine work, and Len did not ask. Even inside their marriage, Ursula operated on a need-to-know basis, and there was much that Len still did not need to know.

Three days after Len landed in Britain, a letter from the British government arrived demanding repayment for the cost of repatriating him from Spain in 1938. The bill sent a clear message. "It told us that the authorities had taken note of Len's return." Len wrote: "We started under a cloud, and so it remained."

On his arrival in Poole, Len stated that his purpose in coming to Britain was "to re-join his wife and report for [military] Service." With the first aim achieved, he now felt compelled to fulfill the second: Len volunteered to join the Royal Air Force.

While Len awaited his call-up papers, Michael studied the art of spin bowling, Nina learned to count, and Ursula, like every other housewife in Britain, made do on meager wartime rations (with some financial help from the Soviet Union), tended to her children, and chatted over the fence with the neighbors about the progress of the war. To all outward appearances, here was another ordinary family, happy to be reunited. Except that every few weeks, Ursula left her family, climbed on her bike, and secretly pedaled to a different part of the English countryside to walk arm in arm through the fields with another man.

CHAPTER 18

ATOMIC SPIES

I N THE LATE SUMMER OF 1942, A MAN AND A WOMAN, both refugees from Nazi Germany, sat in the café opposite Snow Hill railway station in Birmingham, deep in conversation. An eavesdropper would have heard nothing out of the ordinary. They chatted about books, films, and the war, initially in German, then switching to English, which both spoke fluently. They arranged to meet again in a month's time.

As they rose to leave, the man handed over a thick file, containing eighty-five pages of documents, the latest reports from the Tube Alloys project and the most dangerous secret in the world.

"It was pleasant just to have a conversation," Ursula wrote of this momentous first meeting with Klaus Fuchs. "I noticed, that very first time, how calm, thoughtful, tactful and cultured he was." In fact, Fuchs had arrived at the meeting in a state of acute anxiety, but was soothed by the "reassuring presence" of the woman who introduced herself as Sonya. Kremer had been aloof and businesslike, but here, he felt, was someone with whom he could "discuss his feelings."

Birmingham railway station was too public for a regular spy rendezvous. From the train window on the way home, Ursula spotted somewhere more appropriate.

The quiet market town of Banbury, midway between Oxford and Birmingham, was a place notable for being almost wholly unremarkable. An ancient nursery rhyme records the only event of significance to have taken place there.

> Ride a cock-horse to Banbury Cross,
> To see a fine lady upon a white horse;
> Rings on her fingers and bells on her toes,
> And she shall have music wherever she goes.

Over the ensuing eight centuries, little had happened to disturb the somnolence of this little town, which made it ideal for Ursula's purposes.

A month later, she met Fuchs near Banbury station and they strolled into the countryside, arms linked in accordance with "the old-established principle of illicit meetings," to outward appearances lovers on a secret tryst. The first task was to establish a dead-letter box, a secure hiding place to leave messages and arrange future meetings. A path led across empty meadows to some remote woodland out of sight of the road. Ursula had brought along a small trowel, and in the undergrowth, between the roots of a tree, she dug a hole. "Klaus stood beside me, and watched me through his spectacles." He made no offer to help, looking on with an expression of intense concentration, as if observing an experiment. "I thought this quite alright. I was more of an ordinary person and more practical than he. I looked up at him once and thought 'Oh, you dear, great professor.'"

For the next year, every few weeks, on a weekend morning, Ursula would catch a train to Banbury and leave a written message at the dead-letter box, stating when and where to meet that afternoon. Fuchs caught the afternoon train from Birmingham. Their meetings were always in the "country roads near Banbury," never in the same place twice, and each lasted less than half an hour. "It was more difficult to tail us in the open countryside," she wrote. And "it would arouse less suspicion if we took a little walk together." Besides, she enjoyed his company.

Fuchs knew nothing of Ursula's background and experiences, and she understood little about nuclear physics, but they shared a past, an ideology, and a secret. "No one who did not live in such isolation can guess how precious these meetings with a fellow German comrade were," she later wrote. "Our common involvement in trading in danger also added to our feeling of closeness." Fuchs seemed "sensitive and intelligent," but also unworldly, detached from reality, lonely in his duplicity. A bond formed swiftly.

Ursula claimed Fuchs was unaware that "the girl from Banbury" (as he later described her) was the sister of Comrade Jürgen Kuczynski. He was careful not to ask her real name, or where she lived. Jürgen had brought them together, but the siblings never discussed Fuchs. "Though my brother and I got on so well, I stuck strictly to the rules." Ursula did not yet realize the historic significance of the information she was passing on to the Center. But Moscow's response—enthusiastic, grateful, and increasingly demanding—left her in no doubt that she was playing the biggest fish of her career. Soviet military intelligence did not go in for flattery, but the responses to her messages were more effusive than anything she had received before: "Important"; "Very Valuable."

Fuchs's transfer of scientific secrets to the Soviet Union between 1941 and 1943 was one of the most concentrated spy hauls in history, some 570 pages of copied reports, calculations, drawings, formulae and diagrams, the designs for uranium enrichment, a step-by-step guide to the fast-moving development of the atomic weapon. Much of this material was too complex and technical to be coded and sent by radio, and so Ursula passed the documents to Sergei through a "brush contact," a surreptitious handover imperceptible to a casual observer. If Ursula needed to pass on urgent information, or bulky files, she alerted Aptekar by means of an agreed "signal site": "I had to travel to London and, at a certain time and in a certain place, drop a small piece of chalk and tread on it." Two days later she would cycle to the rendezvous site, a side road six miles beyond the junction of the A40 and A34 on the road from Oxford to Cheltenham; Aptekar would drive from London in the military attaché's car and arrive at the pickup site at an appointed time for a swift handover. At one of these meetings, the Soviet officer presented her with a new Minox camera for making microdots and copying documents, and a small but powerful transmitter measuring just six by eight inches, a sixth of the size of her homemade radio and easier to conceal. She dismantled her own equipment, but kept it in reserve "for emergency use."

Fuchs was privy to the innermost workings of the atomic project and he held nothing back. In the first year, he and Peierls wrote no fewer than eleven reports together, including seminal papers on isotope separation and calculating the destructive power of the bomb. According to his latest biographer, "it was via Fuchs and Sonya that Moscow received news of effectively all the scientific data produced by the Tube Alloys project for over a year." The GRU had been slow to appreciate Fuchs's value; with Sonya as his controller, the case moved into the highest gear, and the nuclear weapons project was awarded a Soviet code name that reflected the rising excitement in Moscow: "Enormos." Fuchs's request that his information should pass straight to Stalin's desk was fully realized. Fuchs and Sonya were now firmly on the Soviet leader's radar, which, as anyone close to that capricious murderer could attest, was not necessarily a comfortable place to be.

In April 1942, Molotov, the Soviet foreign minister, compiled a file of intelligence reports (the majority emanating from the United Kingdom) describing this new superweapon and handed it to the minister for the chemical industry with an order from Stalin to determine what action should be taken. The scientists advised that the Soviet Union commence its own atomic-bomb-building program as soon as possible. By the end of the year, the State Defense Committee had authorized the establishment of a laboratory to develop a uranium bomb under Igor Kurchatov, head of nuclear physics at the Leningrad Physicotechnical Institute. In February 1943, Soviet atomic bomb scientists set to work in earnest on a problem that had already been partly solved for them thanks to the flood of secret material flowing from Klaus Fuchs and Ursula Kuczynski.

Britain's discoveries in atomic science were also passing to the United States, more legally and formally, but no less secretly. Back in October 1941, President Roosevelt had sent a message to Winston Churchill suggesting they correspond on atomic research. America's entry into the war two months later gave fresh impetus to the collaboration. But it rapidly became clear that America was pulling ahead in the race to develop the bomb, and the center of gravity (and financial investment) in atomic weapons research was shifting across the Atlantic. America's Manhattan Project, with Britain and Canada as junior partners, would eventually swallow Tube Alloys, employ 130,000 people, and build the world's first nuclear weapon.

America and Britain were working on the bomb together, at astonishing scientific speed and in deepest secrecy. Neither was helping, or informing, its other main ally, the Soviet Union. But Moscow was secretly obtaining that help anyway, through its spies. Not only did Stalin know all about the bomb, but he knew that Britain and America did not know he knew (which is the gold dust of intelligence). And he demanded that his spies find out more.

In the autumn of 1942, Ursula, Len, and the children moved yet again, into a property belonging to one of Britain's most senior legal figures, a pillar of Anglo-Jewry and the very last person who might be suspected of housing a Soviet spy in his back garden. Judge Neville Laski, recently retired as president of the Board of Deputies of British Jews, lived in a large Regency mansion in Summertown, the leafy northern suburb of Oxford. Laski was a firm patriot. After Munich he had declared: "Above all, British Jews' primary obligation is their stern and unswerving allegiance to their citizenship." Laski's brother, Harold, was a left-wing political theorist, professor of politics at the LSE, and a friend of Robert Kuczynski's. When Neville Laski and his wife, Phina, known as Sissie, heard that Ursula's lease in Kidlington was about to expire, they offered to let her rent "Avenue Cottage," a charming four-room coach house behind the main building with a spiral staircase and its own entrance at 50a George Street (now Middle Way). "It was a funny little old house," wrote Ursula, "with a grassy patch for a back yard and a lot of old sheds."

The day she moved in, Ursula paid a late-morning visit to Mrs. Laski and found Sissie still lying in bed "in a lace-trimmed nightgown, taking breakfast from a silver tray, just like rich people in the films." Rather abashed by this spectacle, Ursula asked her new landlady for permission to "erect an aerial leading from our roof to one of her stables." Mrs. Laski graciously consented without the faintest suspicion that the aerial was anything other than "a normal one for any radio receiver." Ursula and Len hid the miniature transmitter in a cavity behind a moss-covered stone in the garden wall.

Klaus Fuchs was Ursula's most important source of secrets, but he was not the only one. In the course of a year, the Sonya network expanded to include at least a dozen spies, providing a wealth of intelligence: military, political, and scientific. Melita Norwood quietly copied every document of importance from the British Non-Ferrous Metals Research Association, which was playing a growing role in nuclear research; Jürgen and Robert Kuczynski tirelessly hoovered up information and gossip; Hans Kahle submitted reports at least once a month. In 1942, Ursula recruited a new British agent, an officer in the technical department of the RAF "willing to provide the USSR with constructive support against Hitler," by providing details of military aircraft development, including the trigger mechanism used to release the thousand-pound bombs carried by the Lancaster bomber. She code-named him "James." "He got hold of exact data for us, weights and dimensions, load-bearing capacity, special characteristics, and even contrived to let me have blueprints of machines that had not yet flown." A former welder and communist sympathizer, James declined payment, and "did not consider himself to be a 'spy,'" though that is indubitably what he was.

All of this intelligence had to be marshaled into reports, coded, and sent to Moscow. By the end of 1942, Ursula was transmitting two or three times a week. Little Michael wondered why his mother often slept in the afternoons: she was frequently exhausted from working through much of the night.

The Radio Security Service was set up at the start of the war to detect "illicit transmissions" within the United Kingdom. It was primarily aimed at uncovering Nazi agents sending radio messages to Germany, but by 1943 the "Secret Listeners" were also intercepting "considerable bundles of Russian traffic." The raw intercepted Morse code was sent to Bletchley Park for decoding. Unlike the Germans with their breakable Enigma code, Soviet intelligence used a system of "one-time pads" thought to be unbreakable. British intelligence might not be able to read Soviet radio traffic, but it was determined to stop it: whenever an illegal radio was detected, radio detection vans equipped with sophisticated direction-finding equipment were sent to comb the suspected area.

"We had to count on my transmitter being discovered at some

point," wrote Ursula. On Moscow's orders, Ursula and Len trained up a new radio operator, "Tom," a fitter at the Cowley car factory, who could take over in an emergency. Tom was a communist who believed he was directly helping the anti-fascist cause by aiding the Soviet Union, Britain's ally.

That attitude was not uncommon in wartime Britain, particularly among the informal networks of communist sympathizers. Len proved an effective spy recruiter. "My past as an International Brigader had positive aspects," he wrote. "It opened doors in progressive and liberal circles. The people's basic anti-fascist sentiments, strengthened by Goering's terror bombing and the enormous admiration earned by the Soviet Union in fighting alone, facilitated our task. In making contact a careful judgement of character was always essential." One of those he recruited was "an old acquaintance" who had fought alongside him in Spain. Ursula later tried to disguise this man's identity by describing him vaguely as a "chemist."

Len's recruit was probably the eccentric Marxist scientist J. B. S. Haldane, professor of biometry at University College, London, who had gone to Spain three times during the civil war to assist the Republican cause, where he befriended Len Beurton. In 1941, Haldane was in the Royal Navy's top-secret underwater-research establishment at Gosport. "Apart from information on tank-landing operations, he supplied us with an important instrument that was used in submarine radar," wrote Ursula. On receipt of this object, she hurried to London with a piece of chalk in her pocket. Two days later Sergei was waiting at the rendezvous site west of Oxford when Ursula arrived on her old bicycle with an important piece of experimental military hardware in her pannier. She wrote: "At that time radar was quite new and the Centre was very interested in it."

Returning from a trip to London, Ursula found Len beaming and the children still awake in a state of high excitement. They told her to close her eyes and then led her to the Morrison air-raid shelter in the garden: there, decorated with flags, was a brand-new bicycle. The old one, Len declared, was a "danger to life and limb," whereas the new bicycle would be useful for getting "to various illegal meeting places." Len was not a demonstrative man. Ursula was touched by a gift that was part love token, part espionage tool.

In the early spring of 1943, with war raging and her espionage network running at full tilt, Ursula discovered, to her delight, that she was pregnant again at the age of thirty-six. Len had taken some persuading that they should have a baby, pointing out that he could be called up for military service at any point and have to leave her to care for three young children and a burgeoning spy network alone. But Ursula was adamant. "I wanted a child from him [and] when, at the end of 1942, the encirclement of the German army began at Stalingrad, foreshadowing victory . . . I began to insist." What better way to celebrate Russian victory than a third child? Besides, "infants provided a good legalization." The more children she had, the less anyone would suspect her. As with all the major decisions of her life, the professional, the political, and the personal intertwined.

Ursula did not inform the Center that she was having another child. As a hard-driving, male-run bureaucracy employing few women, the GRU had no provision for maternity leave, and even if it had, Ursula would have turned it down. As the baby grew inside her, so did her workload.

Under pressure from Stalin, the Center was now sweating its prime asset in earnest. According to one GRU report, Fuchs was able to make plasticine impressions of various keys at the Birmingham research center, which were then passed, via Ursula, to Vladimir Barkovsky, head of scientific and technical intelligence in the London residency. "With the help of duplicate keys, made by Barkovsky personally, [Fuchs] was able to get a lot of secret documents, both from his safe and from his colleagues' safes." Barkovsky had taken over from Aptekar as the new "Sergei," liaising between Ursula and the "legal" spooks in the Soviet embassy: he reported to Moscow that Fuchs (now code-named "Rest," and later "Charles") "works for us with joy, but . . . rejects the slightest hint of a financial reward." Sometimes the flood of intelligence from Fuchs was almost too much for Ursula to cope with. At one of their meetings, he presented her with "a thick book of blueprints" more than one hundred pages long. "Forward it quickly," he told her, necessitating another dash to London, another chalk mark, and another rendezvous in a lonely country road.

In June 1943, Stalin passed Molotov a list of twelve questions about the atomic bomb project and demanded swift answers; the Russian foreign minister passed the list to the GRU's director, Lieutenant General Ivan Ilyichev, who immediately sent a telegram to the London residency, for the attention of Sonya. On June 28, Ursula met Fuchs in Banbury and passed on Stalin's "twelve urgent requirements." They were now spying to a shopping list drawn up by the Soviet leader himself. Fuchs duly compiled a complete account of all the intelligence he had furnished to date and everything he knew about the Tube Alloys project, a remarkable testament to his scientific prowess and, if it fell into British hands, the most damning evidence of his guilt.

SOME 3,500 MILES AWAY in Tehran, Rudolf Hamburger was pursuing the role of spy with just as much vigor as his ex-wife, and exactly none of her success. His incompetence might have been comical had it not ultimately proved tragic, with an impact on Ursula's life that neither could have predicted. Hamburger's mission in Iran had started well. Having obtained a job designing a new building for the Persian Finance Ministry, Rudi doggedly set about gathering information on the road and rail infrastructure built by British and Americans to keep the Soviet armies of the Eastern Front supplied. Ever suspicious of his allies, Stalin demanded that his spies find out if the accumulation of British and American forces so close to the Soviet border might presage more malign intentions. "My task," wrote Rudi, "was to monitor all these plans and movements, to establish the numbers of troops and the nature of the military forces which were being concentrated under the guise of 'transport deployments,' especially in the south of the country where the oil fields are." Moscow Center supplied him with a bulky radio transmitter in an aluminum case, which he hid, suspended by a rope, inside the disused chimney of his rented apartment. For more than a year, the architect-spy supplied a trickle of low-grade intelligence, much of it garnered from locals employed by the Allies. In the dry climate of Tehran, the bouts of malaria he had contracted in a Chinese prison recurred less frequently. He even saved some money, which he sent to Ursula via an American bank. A letter from Rudi arrived at Avenue Cottage just before Christmas 1942, after a tortuous journey through the wartime postal system. Eleven-year-old Michael was excited, imagining the day when his father would fulfill his promise to return. "I kept expecting him to appear, as he had before. I really loved him."

Rudi Hamburger's life in Tehran was lonely but exotic and, between architecture and espionage, extremely busy. His communism reflected the zeal of the convert. He was almost happy. Then, as usual, it all went wrong.

Ruhollah Karubian was an Armenian Iranian working as private secretary and translator for the American superintendent of the railways service. One afternoon, over tea, Hamburger bluntly asked Karubian to sell him secret information, declaring that "he was Russian and wanted to find out all he could about British troops and military installations." Rudi offered to "pay handsomely . . . for anything affecting American foreign policy in the Middle East." Karubian immediately relayed this startlingly unsubtle approach to his boss, who informed American military security. A microphone was installed in Karubian's sitting room, and the next time Hamburger came to tea a stenographer with earphones was hiding in the adjoining bedroom, taking notes. As instructed by American intelligence, Karubian feigned interest in Hamburger's offer and asked for details. "Hamburger persistently refused to disclose the names of the people for whom he was working." He did, however, offer a lecture on international politics: "Hitler must be beaten, but that shall never stop our work. You see, Karubian, today England, America and Russia are allies, but after the war is over they may be enemies again. My group wants every bit of information they can get. We want to make the new order complete after the war. We must know the answer to all the allies' motives." That was enough for the eavesdroppers. On April 19, Rudolf Hamburger was arrested by American military police. A search of his apartment uncovered $2,000 in traveler's checks and a false Honduran passport, but not the radio in the chimney. "Hamburger admitted he had been caught red-handed and was willing to accept the consequences, but he would not give his associates away." After a week in American detention, he was handed over to the British authorities in Iran.

Colonel Joe Spencer of the Defence Security Office knew he had a spy on his hands, but what sort of spy was unclear. Hamburger was clearly "very intelligent and easy to deal with," but the German architect "refused point blank to answer questions" and seemed "entirely unworried by threats and harsh questioning." Spencer left him to stew.

Rudi Hamburger was too honest a man, and too hopeless a spy, to retain his secrets for long. Deprived of reading matter and company, he grew depressed, then talkative. Spencer, in the time-honored manner of clever jailers, provided him with magazines, cigarettes, and congenial company. As the weeks passed, Rudi dropped ever-heavier hints. "He maintained that he was not working against the Allies but was merely collecting information for his 'Group,' the particulars of which he resolutely refused to disclose. He was quite confident that his 'Group' would ultimately intervene on his behalf. He hoped his Group would give him a good job as an architectural engineer, otherwise he would return to China."

Finally, in August, he admitted he was working for "an ally."

Spencer laughed: "There are twenty-five United Nations and you can't expect me to go around and ask them all."

"I'll give you a hint," said Hamburger. "What other ally beside the British and Americans is interested in transport in Persia?"

The next day, after four months in detention, Rudi came clean: "He admitted that he had for long been a professional agent of the Russians and would remain one. His task, he alleged, was to collect political information about allied intentions especially from army officers. He admitted he had bungled the interview with Karubian." Rudi suggested Spencer put in a phone call to the Soviet authorities to check out his story. "But promise not to say I made this suggestion, as my whole future depends on it."

Spencer contacted the Soviet military attaché, who confirmed, three days later, that "Hamburger was working for the Russians and asked for him to be handed over."

As far as Colonel Spencer was concerned, the affair was closed. "We handed him back to the Russians at dead of night on a lonely road surrounded by all the mystery of the most dramatic spy film. This was a simple case—the apprehension through ignorance of an Allied agent and his straightforward disposal." Rudi also believed the future would be straightforward. "Hamburger seemed quite confident that when he was handed over to the Russians they would do nothing to him. He said he would go on working as an agent, but probably elsewhere."

The British and Americans now had an extremely fat file on Rudi Hamburger, and proof that Ursula Kuczynski's first husband was a self-confessed Soviet spy. Ursula and Rudi might be divorced and thousands of miles apart, but their stories, and their fates, were still inextricably linked. As a spy, he posed little threat, except to his ex-wife.

Rudolf Hamburger was flown to Moscow at the end of August, convinced that he would receive, if not a hero's welcome, then at least a friendly, commiserating pat on the back and a new assignment. As before, when "the friends" had sprung him from a Chinese prison, the Center would probably send him on another comfortable rest cure, before redeploying him. After all, he "had demonstrated a remarkable degree of persistence, commitment and loyalty over the years." Rudi thought he might well be promoted.

He could not have been more mistaken.

Viewed through the lens of Soviet paranoia, Rudolf Hamburger was not just inept, but highly suspect.

Two days after arriving in Moscow, he was arrested, accused of working for American or British intelligence, and thrown into "investigatory detention," a euphemism for indefinite imprisonment and interrogation without trial. He had got away from the British too easily. "The circumstances of Hamburger's release from detention in Iran gave rise to the suspicion that he had been recruited by a foreign intelligence service." By the perverse logic of communist persecution, Rudi's protestations of innocence merely confirmed his guilt. "You were bought by our enemies and you came to work for them as a spy," the interrogator insisted. "Yes, you became a spy . . . come on, come on, you dirty spy, admit they bought you. You've become a spy. Confess." His request for a lawyer was ignored. "For twenty-four hours you are kept awake, through hunger and stress," he wrote. "If only you could think of nothing and sleep. The food is dire . . . hunger is a terrible torture." His health deteriorated rapidly. In a few months he lost forty-five pounds.

There was no formal trial, merely a verdict: Rudolf Hamburger was a "socially dangerous element" guilty of political crimes under Article 58 of the Penal Code and was sentenced to five years in prison. The Center did not intervene. His ex-wife's success as a Soviet intelligence officer counted for nothing. "My case as a foreigner is clear: enemy spy. They stamp me as their adversary, as a traitor, this is harder to bear than the prison cell, and the hunger." Like so many others, he was swallowed into the great maw of the Russian Gulag, another innocent enemy of the people. Rudolf Hamburger's descent into hell had begun.

AROUND THE TIME OF Rudi's arrest, Ursula Beurton was promoted to the rank of colonel, the only woman to rise so high in Soviet military intelligence. She was not informed of the promotion. The relationship between the spy and her spymasters, like all espionage relationships, operated on a "need to know" basis: Moscow decided that Sonya did not need to know what rank she had attained, nor that the father of her firstborn child was now a prisoner of the regime she served.

"Mrs. Burton" of Avenue Cottage, Summertown, spent the winter of 1942 cycling around Oxford on her new bike, collecting wartime rations, caring for her children and husband, following the progress of the war. She was polite, modest, and innocuous, another ordinary housewife, making do, digging for victory in the back garden vegetable patch. As she waited for her baby, she sewed a new seat cover for her bike, "daisies on a green background." She was on good terms with her neighbors and occasionally took tea with Sissie Laski in the main house. Nina attended nursery school in Summertown and joined the Girl Guides. Ursula's German accent eroded further. She was developing a genuine affinity for the British, admiring their stolid faith in the certainty of eventual victory. Like all ideologues, she saw the war through the prism of her own politics: "The British people were sympathetic to the Soviet Union."

Ursula's four sisters would each marry Englishmen and settle in Britain. Berta pined for her former life in Germany, but accepted that Britain was now their permanent home. Ursula's beloved Aunt

Alice, Robert's sister, and her husband, the gynecologist Georg Dor-palen, clung on in Berlin to the end. On September 22, 1942, Alice wrote to her beloved German housekeeper, Gertrud: "Now it is time to say goodbye and to thank you from the bottom of my heart for the friendship and helpfulness that you have shown us in difficult times. . . . My husband is wonderfully calm, and we are ready to face our grave fate. If only we survive it." Three days later the Dorpalens were rounded up and shipped to Theresienstadt concentration camp, where they were murdered. Ursula admired Uncle Georg's courage, but could not help wondering: "Was it also brave that when Hitler came to power he did not follow my father's advice, but remained in his German homeland, which he loved?"

Despite a growing patriotism for her adoptive country, Ursula spied on Britain without protest or doubt. Len, increasingly impatient for his call-up papers, was prepared to fight for Britain while spying for the Soviet Union. They saw no conflict of interest. The party and the revolution came first, and by defending communism Ursula believed she was helping Britain, regardless of whether Britain wished to be so helped. Years later she insisted: "We would have refuted any suggestion that we, or the [British] comrades working with us, were betraying Britain." She might not regard herself as a traitor to her adopted country, but that is how most Britons would have seen her; and there is something in her defensive tone that reflects her own discomfort. As always, she made friends easily. But she was deceiving every single one. Ursula believed it was possible to be both a Soviet spy and a British loyalist. MI5 did not agree.

Mrs. Burton of Avenue Cottage drank tea with the neighbors, joined in their complaints about the shortages, and agreed that the war must soon be over. Nina drew an enormous Union Jack and put it in the window. Michael and his friends staged mock battles, in which the British always "defeated the Hun." Ursula put a little money into the National Savings Movement to help fund the war effort.

Colonel Kuczynski of the Red Army, meanwhile, was running the largest network of spies in Britain: her sex, motherhood, pregnancy, and apparently humdrum domestic life together formed the perfect camouflage. Men simply did not believe a housewife making breakfast from powdered egg, packing her children off to school, and then cycling into the countryside could possibly be capable of important espionage. Ursula ruthlessly exploited the natural advantage of her gender.

Only a woman could have seen through Ursula's disguise. The counterintelligence section of MI5 contained only one woman.

And she was on Ursula's trail.

CHAPTER 19

MILICENT OF MI5

MISS MILICENT BAGOT WAS THE SORT OF ENGLISHWOMAN who strikes fear into the hearts of foreigners, children, and bank managers, and tends to be described as "formidable"—code for unmarried, humorless, and slightly terrifying. One of the few women in MI5, and the first to achieve senior rank, she was highly intelligent, dedicated, professional, and, when the occasion demanded, blisteringly rude. She wore austere spectacles and did not suffer fools gladly. Indeed, fools were seldom left in doubt about what they were. The daughter of a London solicitor, Bagot was educated by a French governess until the age of twelve, then at Putney High School before reading Classics at Lady Margaret Hall, Oxford. In 1929, at the age of twenty-two, she joined Scotland Yard Special Branch as a temporary clerk in the countersubversion section. When that division transferred to MI5 in 1931, Bagot went with it, beginning a lifelong career in the Security Service. She lived with her nanny in Putney. She wore a hat indoors. At 4:45 every Tuesday afternoon, whether or not there was a war on, she left the office to sing in the Bach Choir (she sang alto, and frequently fortissimo). "A stickler for procedure and a difficult colleague with robust opinions" was the verdict of one colleague. "She was exacting and demanding and did not dissemble when faced with those less intellectually gifted than herself." Around the office Bagot was known as "Millie," but never, ever within earshot. The renegade MI5 officer Peter Wright wrote: "She was slightly touched, but with an extraordinary memory for facts and files." Her colleagues might run for cover when Milicent was coming down the corridor in full voice, but none doubted her abilities. Even the FBI's director, J. Edgar Hoover, no admirer of either MI5 or women, wrote her a personal letter of appreciation. Though wholly different in character, she was Ursula's opposite and double: highly trained, devoted to her job, undaunted by men, and as firm in her anti-communist beliefs as Ursula was committed to communism. Bagot would eventually achieve literary immortality as the model for Connie Sachs, the eccentric and obsessive spinster in the novels of John le Carré.

No one in Britain knew more about the internal threat of communism than Milicent Bagot.

In 1941, MI5 formed "F Division" specifically to counter subversive activity. The anti-communist section, F2c, was theoretically run by a veteran officer, Hugh Shillito, but his was merely "a vague supervisory role because it was thought better to have a man nominally in charge." There was little question that Milicent wore the trousers in the communist-hunting unit. "Miss Bagot is a really outstanding character. She has been working on the Communist problem for over twenty years and has a positively encyclopaedic knowledge of the subject. . . . [She is] the most valuable member of the whole division." That glowing appraisal came from the overall chief of F Division and Bagot's immediate boss: Roger Hollis, the former tobacco company executive who had been knocking around communist circles in Shanghai at the same time as Ursula in the 1920s. The contrasting roles played by Milicent Bagot and Roger Hollis in the Sonya case would give rise to one of the longest and most damaging conspiracy theories in British history.

Milicent Bagot began tracking the Kuczynski family from the moment they arrived in Britain. She vigorously opposed Jürgen Kuczynski's release from internment. "We have a great deal of information about this man indicating that he is taking an active part in anti-British propaganda but we are finding some difficulty in convincing the Home Office," she wrote to MI6. The F Division files described Jürgen as "an extreme communist and fanatically pro-Stalin. One of Moscow's most brilliant and dangerous propagandists.

It is claimed that he is an illegal in contact with the Soviet Secret Service." When Ursula Kuczynski applied for a British passport, it was Bagot who pointed out there were existing files on both her and her father, and that the marriage to Len Beurton was almost certainly a scam to obtain British citizenship. She alerted the Oxford police when the Kuczynskis settled in Oxford in 1941 and reexamined the letters Ursula sent to her family from Switzerland between 1938 and 1941, which had been intercepted and photographed.

Milicent, it was said, "could smell a rat at twenty paces," and in the Kuczynskis she had picked up the scent of an entire nest. Bagot had Ursula Beurton firmly in her sights, but it was Len, as the male of the household and therefore by assumption the greater threat, who initially attracted more suspicion.

Just a few weeks after the Beurtons moved into Avenue Cottage, a policeman knocked on the door and politely invited Len to come to London on "any day that is convenient" for a meeting with "security officers." Len was unworried. Having assisted British intelligence in Geneva, he was expecting some sort of approach, and perhaps even a job offer. An MI5 officer, Desmond Vesey, and Arnold Baker of MI6 were waiting in Room 055 of the War Office (where MI5 held external meetings), when Len arrived on September 18, 1942. "There are several odd aspects to Beurton's story," MI5 noted: Ursula's assertion that her husband had been convalescing in Switzerland when he himself made no mention of ever having had tuberculosis; his claim to have inherited a large amount of money, in cash, from French relatives; his antipathy toward people in authority; and his "shifty manner." The two officers peppered him with questions, but after several hours Len was told he could return home. "On the whole Beurton made a good impression," wrote Vesey.

Milicent Bagot and her stalkers were not about to leave it there. The next day, a warrant was obtained to intercept the Beurtons' letters, on the grounds that "this man has recently returned from Switzerland where he is thought to have been in contact with agents of a foreign power," Hugh Shillito, Bagot's nominal boss and de facto deputy, wrote. "To my mind the story suggests many interesting possibilities. Beurton may have been engaged in espionage on behalf of the USSR against Germany from Switzerland. It is known that the Russians used the International Brigades as recruiting grounds for secret agents."

MI5 sent a memo to the Oxford security officer: "Please arrange for the police to make discreet inquiries . . . whether Beurton travels, when and where, what friends he has and how he is occupying his time." The police duly reported back that "the house is rather isolated and they appear to have little contact with neighbours . . . they appear to be living quite comfortably, paying 4 1/2 guineas a week in rent"—a considerable sum given that neither had jobs, or any other known source of income. Detective Inspector Arthur Rolf of the Thames Valley Police did, however, spot one conspicuous feature of Avenue Cottage: "They have rather a large wireless set and recently had a special pole erected for use for the aerial." That vital piece of information was passed to MI5 in January 1943, at a time when Ursula was running Klaus Fuchs at full tilt and transmitting to Moscow at least twice a week. Moreover, according to a senior officer of the Radio Security Service, the interceptors had identified an illegal radio transmitter operating somewhere in the Oxford area. A memo in the Beurtons' MI5 file baldly states: "The most interesting point appears to be [their] possession of a large wireless set, and you may think this is worthy of further inquiry."

But Roger Hollis, the head of F Section and Milicent Bagot's immediate superior, did not think the radio mast merited investigation. Nor did he follow up the other clues that life at Avenue Cottage was not what it seemed. Hollis similarly failed, or declined, to investigate Klaus Fuchs. Time after time, what now appear to be obvious leads that should have led straight to Ursula were left by Hollis to wither on the vine.

The theory that Roger Hollis was a Soviet spy, recruited in Shanghai by Richard Sorge and implanted inside British intelligence, first emerged publicly in 1981 and has been running ever since, refusing to die despite repeated official denials. After joining MI5 in 1938, Hollis was steadily promoted, eventually becoming director general in 1956, a post he held until his retirement nine years later. His accusers claim that Hollis's seniority enabled him to protect numerous Soviet spies in Britain, including Ursula, who deliberately fueled the conspiracy theory. In later life, she denied knowing Hollis from Shanghai but wondered: "Was it possible that there was someone at MI5 who was, at the same time, working for the Soviet Union and had protected us?" To this day, MI5 flatly rejects that possibility, its website insisting the allegations against Hollis "were investigated and found to be groundless."

But the pattern of Hollis's actions—or more accurately inaction—with respect to Ursula Beurton, Jürgen Kuczynski, and Klaus Fuchs is strange, to say the least. In 1940, when Milicent Bagot was campaigning to keep Jürgen interned, Hollis stated that he "didn't believe for a moment that Kuczynski is an OGPU [Soviet intelligence] agent," a view endorsed by the head of MI5 on the basis that Hollis "knows Kuczynski personally." (The nature of this personal connection has never been established.) According to the writer and journalist Chapman Pincher (Hollis's indefatigable accuser), when the American embassy asked MI5 to draw up a list of foreign communists in the United Kingdom, the Kuczynskis were omitted. Hollis was similarly unwilling to pursue Fuchs. "Miss Bagot seems to have highlighted the Fuchs case at once," writes Fuchs's latest biographer, but Hollis was "singularly relaxed" about the potential threat he posed. It may be no coincidence that Hollis was a friend of Neville Laski, in whose cottage Ursula was living with a large radio antenna over her head.

Paul Monk, heir to the late Chapman Pincher as chief prosecutor in the saga, writes that as head of F Section Hollis consistently stymied efforts by Bagot's section to investigate Ursula Beurton, her husband, family, and principal agent, Klaus Fuchs: "Bagot had been on SONIA's [sic] trail as far back as early 1940. . . . It was Hollis who squelched her suggestions that SONIA be treated with suspicion and kept under surveillance. . . . Bagot was suspicious of SONIA's movements, given her known background, but was waved aside by Hollis."

There are only two ways to interpret Hollis's behavior: he was either a traitor or a fool. To hide inside MI5 for nearly thirty years, while protecting a host of Soviet spies and covering his tracks, would have required a spy of rare intellectual agility. No one would have described Roger Hollis that way. He was a plodding, slightly droopy bureaucrat with the imaginative flair of an omelet. Lying is easy. Maintaining a panoply of lies, cover-ups, and diversions for years, and remembering them all, is exceptionally difficult. Even Kim Philby, with his preternatural talent for deception, left clues that exposed him in the end. Hollis simply was not equipped with those kinds of skills. The weight of evidence currently suggests that Hollis was not treacherous, but incompetent. He was really quite thick.

In Ursula's MI5 file is a note, written by Hollis in response to an FBI inquiry, which perfectly encapsulates his attitude: "Mrs. Burton appears to devote her time to her children and domestic affairs . . . she has not come to notice in any political connection." Like so many others, Hollis could not see Ursula for what she really was, because she was a woman.

IN CANADA ON AUGUST 19, 1943, Churchill and Roosevelt signed the Quebec Agreement, a secret arrangement to collaborate on building the atom bomb. The United States and Britain also agreed not to use the technology against each other or a third party without mutual agreement, and not to tell Stalin what they were doing. This vast industrial project would require the construction of nuclear reactors, diffusion plants, and a massive injection of American funds and expertise. British scientists would take part in the Manhattan Project, but as junior partners. To maintain security and keep the project beyond the reach of German bombers, the program would shift to the United States—and Klaus Fuchs would move with it. Central to the Anglo-American arrangement was a decision to keep all aspects of the atomic bomb project secret from the Soviet Union— further evidence that while the Allies might be on the same side, they were on very different historical paths.

Some claim that Moscow learned about the secret Quebec Agreement from Ursula, just sixteen days later. The Russian intelligence writer Vladimir Lota, citing sources "off limits to other researchers," writes: "On 4 September, U. Kuczynski reported to the Center information on the outcomes of the conference in Quebec."

The Quebec Agreement was a closely guarded secret, and how Ursula obtained it (if she did) remains a mystery. Fuchs almost certainly did not know about it. Perhaps this molten lump of weapons-grade intelligence came via Jürgen or Robert Kuczynski, through one of their British political contacts. But it is equally possible that the assertion Ursula passed on this information is false, concocted long after the event as propaganda to show her and the GRU in the best possible light. Ursula herself made no claim to have passed on the substance of the Quebec Agreement on September 4. But soon after that date, eight months pregnant, Ursula struggled to London in a rainstorm to meet Sergei (probably Barkovsky). "He brought a special message from the Director, praising me for a report I had sent," she wrote. "The Director had said: 'If we had five Sonyas in England, the war would be over sooner.'" It is possible that the praise (lavish by GRU standards) may have been in response to a report from Ursula informing Moscow that Britain and the United States were now formally working together to build the bomb, behind the back of the Soviet Union.

Ursula was buying groceries in Summertown when she went into labor. At 3:00 P.M. she gave birth to a boy, three weeks prematurely, in Oxford's Radcliffe Infirmary. By 5:00 P.M., she was sitting up in bed, writing to her mother: "At 12:45 I was still out shopping. And now the baby is already two hours old. So you can see what an easy time I had." Len was at another rendezvous with Soviet intelligence in London and arrived at the clinic late that evening. For several minutes he contemplated the tiny infant in Ursula's arms and then said: "I have never seen you so happy. You look like two Sonyas."

Peter Beurton was born on September 8, 1943. A few days earlier his mother may have passed a secret to the Soviet Union that started the Cold War; his father had spent the day at an illegal meeting with their Russian spy handler, and on seeing the mother of his child a few hours after the birth, he addressed her by her code name. Within hours, his mother was back at work, conducting espionage as usual.

In all other respects, Peter's birth was perfectly normal.

KLAUS FUCHS WAS AMONG the seventeen British-based scientists selected to join the Manhattan Project. He had been involved in Britain's atomic weapons research from the start, and Peierls insisted on taking along his gifted colleague. Before the scientists could leave for America, General Leslie Groves, director of the Manhattan Project, demanded "assurances that all have been properly cleared." A routine background check on Fuchs concluded he was "gentlemanly, inoffensive and a typical scholar . . . so absorbed in research work as to have little time for political matters." Hollis himself waved through the paperwork for Fuchs to become a British citizen in July 1942—"no objection is seen to this application." As a naturalized British citizen, Fuchs was now legally entitled to an exit permit and a nonimmigrant visa for the United States. The only objection was raised by the indefatigable Milicent Bagot, who wrote a terse note complaining that she had not been informed that Fuchs was now British: "We knew his naturalization was under consideration but [not that] it was a *fait accompli.*"

It fell to Ursula Beurton to ensure that in America Fuchs would be able to continue providing Moscow with a stream of atomic secrets, now from the heart of the Manhattan Project. Fuchs would initially be working at Columbia University in New York, and Ursula was instructed by the Center to identify a meeting point in the city and provide Fuchs with a set of signals, timings, and a password to facilitate contact with Soviet intelligence. Ursula reached back into the memories of her youth for a rendezvous spot: she chose the Henry Street Settlement, the immigrant hostel run by Lillian Wald where she had lived in 1928 as a twenty-one-year-old bookseller.

As the day of Fuchs's sailing approached, the Center sent a message: "Sonya. I have received your telegram about the departure of Otto to America. The locations and conditions of the meeting in New York are clear. Give Otto our thanks for helping us and give him £50 as a gift. Tell him that we think that his work with us in a new place will be as fruitful as in England."

Fuchs would continue spying with barely a pause: but in a different country, with a new handler, and for a different branch of Soviet intelligence.

Rivalry between Russia's civilian and military spies was, and remains, intense. The NKVD had evolved into the NKGB and would soon become the KGB, the largest and most feared intelligence bureaucracy in the world, part espionage-gathering machine, part security service, part secret police. In theory, military espionage was exclusively the responsibility of the GRU; in reality, the KGB under Vsevolod Merkulov, a member of Stalin's "Georgian mafia," recognized no limits to its power. Merkulov was one of the earliest Cold Warriors, with a particular antipathy for capitalist Britain. "Sooner or later there will be a clash between the Communist Bear and the Western Bulldog," he declared. "The time will come when we will water our Soviet horses in the Thames!"

The KGB was running an extensive spy network in the United Kingdom, and in 1943 it identified Fuchs as a potential target for recruitment, only to be informed that he had been a GRU agent for almost two years. The KGB did not like playing second fiddle to its military counterpart and in August 1943, four months after Merkulov was appointed, it launched a power grab. The "atom spies" working for the GRU were transferred, wholesale, to the KGB. Enormos, the operation to penetrate the Manhattan Project, was under Merkulov's control. Though he did not know it, Fuchs was now a KGB spy.

On February 5, 1944, Klaus Fuchs stood on the corner opposite the Henry Street Settlement on Manhattan's Lower East Side, holding a green book in one hand and a tennis ball in the other, exactly as Sonya had instructed. At 4:00 P.M. on the dot, a stocky man appeared, wearing a pair of gloves and holding a second pair in his left hand. After a minute he crossed the road, approached Fuchs, and asked: "Can you tell me the way to Chinatown?"

"I think Chinatown closes at 5 o'clock," Fuchs replied on cue.

The man introduced himself as "Raymond." His real name was Harry Gold, and he was a chemist, a communist, and a Soviet spy, Ursula's successor on the other side of the Atlantic. They walked to the subway and caught a train uptown, and then a cab to Manny Wolf's restaurant on Third Avenue. Gold later reported to the KGB: "He is about 5 foot 10 inches, thin, pale complexioned and at first was very reserved in manner . . . he obviously has worked with our people before, and he is fully aware of what he is doing." Ursula's choice of meeting place was "ideal," Gold wrote, and "beautifully deserted," a spot where "no one would think anything of two people walking towards one another and making conversation"—even if one was holding a tennis ball and the other had four gloves.

So began the next phase of Fuchs's espionage odyssey, during which he would witness the first atom bomb test in the New Mexico desert and pass the secret of its construction to Moscow. Before handing him over to the KGB, the Center made an assessment of the case: "During his time with the Red Army Intelligence Service, Fuchs transferred important materials containing theoretical calculations on the splitting of the uranium atom and the creation of an atomic bomb. . . . Total received from Fuchs for the period 1941–1943: more than 570 sheets of valuable materials."

Fuchs was out of Ursula's hands. But he was not out of her life. The German scientist had learned little about the "girl from Banbury" during their collaboration, but what he knew was enough to destroy her. The atom spy was Colonel Sonya's greatest triumph and potentially her nemesis, an unexploded bomb with a delayed fuse.

CHAPTER 20

OPERATION HAMMER

I N LATE JUNE 1944, URSULA RECEIVED A MESSAGE FROM
Jürgen, asking her to come to London urgently. As brother and
sister strolled across Hampstead Heath, Jürgen explained that he had
just received an unexpected visit from a young American intelligence
officer, who had asked for help recruiting spies to be parachuted into
Nazi Germany. The Americans were specifically looking for exiled
Germans living in London who were opposed to Hitler and might be
willing to carry out intelligence-gathering operations inside the
Third Reich on behalf of the Americans. "Do you know anyone like
that?" the earnest young American had asked. Jürgen certainly did
know several such people. And so did his sister. On her return to
Oxford, Ursula dashed off a message to the Center.

Lieutenant Joseph Gould of the U.S. Army was a publicist for the
motion picture industry, a union organizer, and a new recruit to
America's military intelligence service. A brash twenty-nine-year-
old New Yorker, he was enthusiastic, patriotic, and imaginative to a
fault, with a highly developed sense of the dramatic. Gould was a
director of his own unfolding spy movie. His intelligence reports
read like Hollywood film scripts.

When America joined the war, Gould enlisted in the U.S. Army's
intelligence branch and was dispatched to Britain immediately after
D-Day with a specific mission in mind.

The Office of Strategic Services (OSS), precursor to the CIA, had
been formed in 1942 to coordinate military espionage behind enemy

lines. Within the OSS was the Secret Intelligence Unit, and inside that was the Labor Branch, dedicated to using Europe's secret underground union organizations for intelligence gathering. Hitler had tried to smash the German labor movement, yet some organized labor groups had survived, a core of clandestine resistance to fascism. As the Allies closed in on the Third Reich from east and west, American intelligence was hungry for strategic information on the Reich's military and industrial production. Workers were in a unique position to provide it. "We can take advantage of the hatred of Hitler by members of the European labour movement," wrote Arthur Goldberg, the New York lawyer and future Supreme Court justice who headed the Labor Branch. Thousands of persecuted German trade unionists had fled abroad, and many had settled in Britain. If some of these anti-Nazi exiles could be smuggled back into Germany as spies, they could establish contact with the dissident labor groups, a readymade espionage network, and gain access to vital intelligence about German defenses, industrial and military production, politics, and civilian morale.

Thus was born the OSS plan code-named "Faust": a team of "good" Germans would be recruited and trained in the United Kingdom, equipped with the latest communications technology, and then parachuted into Germany, where they could blend in, link up with the workers' movements, and begin transmitting intelligence that would set the stage for the last act of the war. Finding people prepared to parachute blind into Hitler's Germany "without reception committees, safehouses, or friends" would not be easy, but, with his trade union expertise and bubbling energy, Joe Gould was the man to try.

Gould arrived in London on June 13, 1944, and set to work recruiting the cast for Faust. On an inspired hunch, he took himself off to a secondhand bookshop specializing in foreign books on New Bond Street, a known hangout for émigrés. The owner, Morris Abbey, "took an immediate liking" to the "round faced, bespectacled young army lieutenant" who entered his shop and declared—as if requesting a set of rare books—that he was collecting anti-Nazi Germans. The bookseller told Gould that one of his regular customers was a leader of the expatriate German community and a founding member of the Free German League of Culture, an offshoot of the anti-fascist Free Germany Movement—the loose affiliation of exiles united in opposition to Hitler. Abbey gave him the telephone number of Dr. Jürgen Kuczynski. A few days later Gould found himself taking tea in Hampstead with a "lean man in early middle age" and explaining that he was "looking for agents capable of undertaking delicate and highly hazardous missions inside Germany." As soon as the excitable young American left, Jürgen contacted his sister.

In German legend, Faust is a man prepared to give up his soul in his quest for earthly knowledge. Faust gets his wish, by making a pact with the devil.

Every spymaster's ambition is to infiltrate a spy into the enemy's intelligence service. The Soviets had successfully done this in MI6, with Kim Philby, and MI5, with Anthony Blunt. Here was Ursula's opportunity to plant not just one but several of her own agents inside the American intelligence service, on a top secret mission. On Moscow's instructions, she compiled a list of reliable German communists in Britain who might be prepared to work as spies for the Americans, but also willing to pass every scrap of information on to the Center. The Faust spies would be agents of American intelligence spying on Nazi Germany, but in reality double agents working for Ursula Kuczynski of the Red Army.

In spy jargon, a "cutout" is an intermediary who stands between a spy and his handler, ensuring that if an agent is apprehended he cannot identify his controller and compromise the whole network. Moscow warned Ursula to be "on her guard" and find someone to act as liaison between her and the Faust spies. She turned to an old acquaintance, Erich Henschke, the comrade who had helped her set up the Marxist Workers' Lending Library in 1929, selling communist literature from a Berlin basement fragrant with pigeon guano. Chased out of Germany by the Gestapo, Henschke had undergone military training in the Soviet Union and then volunteered to fight in the Spanish Civil War. Henschke was always a bruiser and a rigid party disciplinarian; along with his gun he carried a large megaphone, through which he exhorted his fellow communists into battle. In 1939, he was admitted to Britain with a false French identity card and an assumed name, "Karl Kastro." He was now working in the Wall's Ice Cream factory in Acton, and performing clerical work for the International Brigade Association. Ursula found Henschke "a slow thinker who found it difficult to reach decisions," but he was "conscientious and reliable" and knew everyone in the German community. Henschke was the ideal cutout.

Ursula instructed her brother to introduce Henschke to Gould. They got on famously, and the young New Yorker immediately offered Karl Kastro a job: a monthly salary of £5 in exchange for help in enrolling agents for Operation Faust.

Ursula handed Henschke a list of thirty potential recruits, mostly former German trade unionists who had fled to Britain via Czechoslovakia. She had already passed the names to Moscow for approval, along with biographies and photographs. "I did not take a single step without consulting the Centre," she wrote.

In August 1944, in a Hampstead pub, Gould held his first meeting with four Germans who would form the nucleus of the Faust operation. Paul Lindner was a thirty-three-year-old lathe operator from Berlin and an organizer of the German Metalworkers' Union, whose good looks were marred by a scarred face and a set of broken teeth, the legacy of a savage beating at Nazi hands. Lindner had escaped to Czechoslovakia with the Gestapo in pursuit and in 1939 made his way to Britain, where he met and married an Englishwoman and settled in London. Lindner's close friend was Anton "Toni" Ruh, a lithographer who had churned out anti-Nazi leaflets and fake passports for escaping Jews from his illegal Berlin printworks until he too was forced to flee and make his way to London via the Czech underground. Kurt Gruber was a coal miner from the Ruhr Valley; Adolph Buchholz, a metalworker from Spandau-Berlin. Each of these men had been active in the union movement and the anti-fascist resistance. They were all die-hard communists, handpicked by Ursula. Henschke had explained that while they would be working for the Americans, their ultimate masters were in Moscow. As Ursula put it: "The comrades knew that this had been approved by the Soviet Union."

The Germans, "uncomfortable in inexpensive suits and neckties," listened attentively as Gould explained that he was looking for men to parachute into different parts of Germany and send back information to American intelligence on conditions inside the Reich. "He inquired about their backgrounds, what cities they knew, where they might have contacts, who would shelter them." Under a formal employment contract from the U.S. government, each volunteer would receive $331 a month through an account at Chase National Bank. Their families would be paid compensation if they did not return. The Germans nodded keenly, finished their drinks, and asked for a little time "to think about these things and to talk with others of their group." A few days later Henschke told Gould the men were ready to volunteer; he did not say that the order to do so came directly from Ursula and the GRU. From the other candidates, Gould selected three more volunteers. The operation was split into five distinct missions, and, with the whimsy common in intelligence nomenclature, each was given a themed code name: "Hammer," "Chisel," "Pickaxe," "Mallet," and "Buzzsaw." These were dubbed, collectively, the "Tool" missions.

The new recruits did not reveal that they were all members of the KPD. How far Gould was aware of their politics remains unclear. He surely knew the men in his tool kit were left-wingers, but equally certainly he did not know they were secretly working for Moscow. Lindner later speculated that Gould might have been a communist sympathizer: "One could guess that he is an American comrade," he wrote. But Gould was not a communist. He was not interested in the politics of his recruits. These "Free Germans" clearly had the necessary pluck and union connections to play the parts allotted to them, and that was enough for Joe Gould.

Preparations for the Tool missions began at once. At Ringway Airfield near Manchester the Germans underwent intensive parachute training. At a secret spy school in Ruislip, they were issued with false names, identities, and cover stories, and put through rigorous physical training; they learned to shoot and how to kill soundlessly with a knife. Each recruit would be dropped as close as possible to his hometown, the better to blend in. Civilian clothing commandeered from newly arrived German refugees was stored in a warehouse on Brook Street; here the men selected their costumes for the forthcoming performance. "The common denominator was that all the goods—the suits, shirts, ties, hats, belt buckles, cufflinks, tiepins, shoelaces—had been manufactured in Germany." A single British label could mean death. German-made luggage, cigarettes, razors, toothpaste, and spectacles were bought in neutral Sweden and shipped to London in the State Department's diplomatic bag. The master forger of the OSS, Bob Work, a graduate of the Art Institute of Chicago, turned out a set of fake German passports, travel permits, and identity papers indistinguishable from the real things. The men had not seen Germany for years, so they were quietly inserted into German prisoner-of-war camps to learn about conditions inside the country and get a feel for living among their fellow countrymen again. What they learned there was disturbing: most of the German POWs clung tenaciously to the belief that Hitler would eventually triumph, though some thought he should have waited until victory before exterminating the Jews because the genocide had "brought the Jews of the USA and England into the frontline against us." The training at Ruislip followed a rigid schedule: "Tactics school on Mondays, how to deal with SS patrols Wednesdays, cartographical studies Fridays . . ."

The most important training involved the latest American breakthrough in communications technology: a handheld, portable, two-way radio transceiver that made ground-to-air communications possible for the first time. A predecessor of the mobile telephone, the equipment had been designed at the RCA electronics laboratories in New York before being refined and developed for the OSS by De Witt R. Goddard and Lieutenant Commander Stephen H. Simpson. The device would eventually become known as a "walkie-talkie," but at the time of its invention this pioneering gizmo went by a more cumbersome and quaint title: the "Joan-Eleanor system." "Joan" was the name for the handheld transmitter carried by the agent in the field, six inches long and weighing three pounds, with a collapsible antenna; "Eleanor" referred to the larger airborne transceiver carried on an aircraft flying overhead at a prearranged time. Goddard's wife was named Eleanor, and Joan, a major in the Women's Army Corps, was Simpson's girlfriend. The Joan-Eleanor (J-E) system operated at frequencies above 250 MHz, far higher than the Germans could monitor. This prototype VHF (very high frequency) radio enabled the users to communicate for up to twenty minutes in plain speech, cutting out the need for Morse code, encryption, and the sort of complex radio training Ursula had undergone. The words of the spy on the ground were picked up and taped on a wire recorder by an operator housed in a special oxygen-fed compartment in the fuselage of an adapted high-speed de Havilland Mosquito bomber flying at over twenty-five thousand feet, outside the range of German anti-aircraft artillery. An intelligence officer aboard the circling aircraft could communicate directly with the agent below. As a system of communication from behind enemy lines, the J-E was unprecedented, undetectable by the enemy, easy to use, and so secret that it would not be declassified until 1976. At the Ruislip training school the German volunteers learned to use Joan, while aircrews of the Twenty-five Bomber Group based at RAF Watton were instructed on handling Eleanor, under the code name "Redstocking." The call sign from Joan to Eleanor would be "Heinz"; the corresponding call sign from Eleanor to Joan would be "Vic." Special coded messages on the BBC, in numbers, would indicate to the agents inside Germany when to make transmissions and when and where to expect airdrops: the signal that there was about to be a broadcast of coded information relevant to the Tool missions was a burst of "Rustle of Spring," the popular solo piano piece written by Norwegian composer Christian Sinding.

On November 22, Simpson carried out the first operational test of the system by successfully recording transmissions from an OSS agent code-named "Bobbie" while circling at thirty thousand feet over Nazi-occupied Holland.

Washington was delighted with the way the mission was progressing. And so was Moscow.

At regular intervals, each of the German volunteers met Henschke in Hampstead. Paul Lindner described being "sworn in" as a GRU agent. "As of today," Henschke declared over a pint in the Wells Tavern, "you must remember you are working for our Soviet friends, and you must consider all questions as if you were under the command of the Red Army." Toni Ruh was enlisted with the same formality and passed on everything he learned "in the greatest detail" to the cutout: "We had to make reports to Comrade Henschke about all methods used in the school, also about the education in parachuting, about the task assignments, about our work in the prisoner-of-war camps and also about details from this [J-E] apparatus which we also did on an on-going basis." Henschke passed on the information to Ursula, who funneled it to Moscow. The Tool spies never met the woman sending those reports and pulling the strings, their secret spymistress.

Through Ursula, the Center knew almost as much about the Tool missions as the OSS, and much more than MI6: Moscow learned the false identities of the spies, their fake papers and clothing, their equipment, and the scheduled times of their transmissions. The Red Army knew where and when the spies would be landing, their contacts in the anti-Nazi resistance, and the real meanings of Redstocking, Hammer, and Buzzsaw; they even knew the numerical code system and the piano music that the BBC would broadcast to alert the agents on the ground to their instructions. With the Cold War looming, here was an inside track on how the Americans organized clandestine operations, OSS training methods, and personnel. But the most interesting aspect of the mission to Moscow was the Joan-Eleanor system. Russia had no such technology. Ursula's spies might drop it into the lap of the GRU.

"I reported all the details to the Centre, and the Director confirmed his interest," Ursula wrote. America was about to launch the last great intelligence operation of the war, and, unknown to anyone in the OSS, the Russians had a secret front-row seat.

Gould was impressed by the Tool recruits, and, like every spymaster, he felt a strong personal bond with his agents, particularly Paul Lindner and Toni Ruh, the two-man team on the Hammer mission destined to drop into Berlin, the heart of the Reich. Gould wondered if he was committing "the professional sin of growing too close to these men." He compiled detailed descriptions of both. Paul Lindner: "Face: Squarish; Complexion: usually pale. Subject notes that the fitter he feels, the more often he is asked if he is ill; will wrinkle brow when hunting for a word, may toss head occasionally; Distinguishing marks: red mark to right of nose bridge and under left eye, received from knuckle ring at hands of Nazis; also bayonet scar, upper right-hand buttock from SA handling in 1933." Then there was Toni Ruh, "a large man with greying hair and a quiet, reassuring solidity."

"This was a balanced team," wrote Gould. The two principal actors in the Hammer production were ideally cast in their respective roles, reflected Gould, who was entirely unaware they were following a very different script, and an invisible stage manager was directing everything from the wings. The Center instructed Ursula to focus on the Tool missions and do everything necessary to get the Joan-Eleanor system into Russian hands.

Within MI5, only Milicent Bagot picked up the scent of what was really going on, and then only the faintest whiff. The indefatigable sleuth of section F2c was not privy to the OSS missions, but she had been watching Erich Henschke, or Karl Kastro, for some time. In September 1943, she noted that although "undoubtedly a lifelong communist with strong Marxist convictions, this man has so far not given any trouble . . . he appears to live a quiet life." Her assessment was amended a year later, when an MI5 spy inside the Free Germany Movement reported that Kastro was not the innocent ice cream maker he appeared: "Kastro was connected to the Thälmann circle [and] received military training in the USSR and was part of the military apparat [unit] of the communist party [the Rotfrontkämpferbund, or Alliance of Red Front-Fighters]." She sent a note of warning to MI6: "Kastro is said to be an assumed name. . . . [He] has been described as a 'brutal and violent type.'" Milicent Bagot put Karl Kastro under surveillance. She did not trust Kastro and she had long suspected Ursula: if she caught them together, the game would be up.

While Gould saw no reason to question the loyalty of his recruits, the chill of the Cold War was already blowing through parts of the Allied wartime establishment. MI5 regarded the Free German League of Culture as a communist front. The OSS officer Bill Casey, the granite-minded lawyer in charge of the Secret Intelligence section who would go on to run the CIA, feared that some of those recruited for this highly sensitive mission might be communists. Casey's misgivings brought him into conflict with Arthur Goldberg of the Labor Branch, who pointed out that the OSS was specifically intended to recruit "irregular forces," including, presumably, people with irregular views. The dispute was referred upward to Major General William "Wild Bill" Donovan, founder and chief of the OSS.

Donovan was a man who relished battle: he had fought Pancho Villa in Mexico, the Germans in the First World War, J. Edgar Hoover at the FBI, and, as New York district attorney, the bootleggers during Prohibition. He had modeled his OSS directly on MI6. Donovan was a swashbuckler, more piratical than political. "Excitement made him snort like a racehorse," and the Tool missions chimed perfectly with his "brave, noble, headlong, gleeful, sometimes outrageous pursuit of action and skulduggery." Like Gould, he did not give a damn about the politics of the agents, observing that he would "put Stalin on the OSS payroll if it would help defeat Hitler." He had no idea, of course, that Stalin's agents already were on the Tool payroll. Donovan overruled Casey. The mission went ahead.

The same robust (or naïve) attitude influenced the American decision to employ one of the most prominent German communists in Britain on a top secret project of crucial importance. In November 1944, with the end in sight, the U.S. secretary of war ordered the creation of a new body to assess the economic damage being inflicted on Germany by Allied bombing, and to report on how far that campaign was eroding military, industrial, and agricultural production. The United States Strategic Bombing Survey (USSBS) did this in various ways: aerial surveillance, media reports, and even civilian nutrition offered clues to the effectiveness of the destruction; by carefully monitoring the serial numbers of destroyed tanks and planes, it could assess the level of arms production; freight train timetables were another index of economic health. There were some brilliant minds on the staff of the USSBS, including Richard Ruggles, a future economics professor at Harvard, and the celebrated liberal economist John Kenneth Galbraith. But what the survey team needed most was someone who understood the German economy firsthand and could provide a detailed, statistical insight into Hitler's arms industry and other key facets of Nazi production. There was only one such German in London.

Jürgen Kuczynski had just published the latest volume of his *History of Labour Conditions,* a detailed analysis of the German economy since 1933. In September, he received a letter inviting him to the American embassy, where he was offered a job on the USSBS, a substantial salary, a smart American uniform, and the rank of lieutenant colonel. He asked for "time to think it over." That time, of course, was used to alert Ursula, who immediately informed the Center: "The reply came quickly. They were interested." Brother and sister were now both colonels, in different armies.

The Tool agents were semisecret communists. Jürgen Kuczynski was an extremely public one. Even Roger Hollis, the head of MI5's antisubversion section who had consistently played down the threat posed by Kuczynski, felt moved to issue a warning that "those who make use of his services should be aware that his conclusions on economic conditions in Germany may be influenced by his political beliefs."

The USSBS would eventually compile 208 volumes of analysis, detailing the "decisive" impact of Allied strategic bombing. Only five members of the survey, including Jürgen, had access to the full reports, which were passed on to Roosevelt, Churchill, and Generals Eisenhower and Donovan. And Stalin. The Center gave Ursula a personal assurance that this intelligence haul, offering the clearest possible picture of Germany's economic disintegration, was going straight to "the Commander-in-Chief of the Soviet Army, J. V. Stalin."

As the war raced to its bloody finale, Ursula was swept up in an exhausting whirlwind of espionage, child-rearing, and housework: on any given day she might be coordinating intelligence gathered from her father, brother, Tom, the chemist, and others in her network, gathering intelligence from the Tool missions, while hanging out the washing, doing the dishes, and struggling to keep the domestic ship afloat at Avenue Cottage. Melita Norwood produced a steady flow of intelligence from the British Non-Ferrous Metals Research Association, which was now helping produce a plutonium reactor for the atomic bomb project. In a letter dictated to his personal assistant, Miss Norwood, G. L. Bailey reassured the government that his team would adhere to the "strictest secrecy [and] precautions will be taken to ensure that no unauthorized person obtains information." Letty also typed up minutes from the Tube Alloys meetings and made an extra carbon copy for Sonya.

Michael was an inquisitive and intelligent teenager. How long, Ursula wondered, could she go on concealing her "nocturnal transmissions" from him? With a heavy heart, she sent him to boarding school in Eastbourne, telling herself it was best for the boy. Michael still yearned for his father. "Gradually, as the years passed, I realized he wasn't coming back. I missed him terribly. My mother hardly ever talked about him." When she traveled to London to meet Sergei she had to find a babysitter for the younger children. Ursula's mother occasionally stepped in to help, but in September Berta came down with pneumonia. "Whatever happens, you should stay in hospital as long as the doctors think fit," Ursula wrote. On the nights she transmitted to Moscow she worked into the early hours, wondering if the radio interception vans were prowling nearby. Every scrap of paper used for coding and decoding she burned in the fireplace. To try to alleviate the load, she sent seven-year-old Nina to a boarding school near Epping Forest. After a few weeks, the child developed a burst appendix and was rushed to a hospital, close to death. For three days and nights Ursula sat at her bedside, tortured with guilt, and then brought her daughter home. "I swore I would never send her away again."

Len was not around to share the twin burdens of parenthood and spying, having finally been called up for RAF training. Whenever she could get away, Ursula cycled the twenty-five miles to visit Trainee Aircraftman Beurton in his barracks, but found him grumpy and bored. "Seeing each other twice a month is just not good enough," she wrote. He was rejected for both pilot training and, ironically enough, radio operations. His request to be transferred to a fighting unit was also turned down. Behind the scenes, MI5 quietly blocked his every application. Milicent Bagot and her team were not going to let Beurton out of the country. "Rather gloomy letters from Len," Ursula told her mother. Those morose letters were also being read by MI5. "I am arranging for him to be kept under observation," wrote Shillito, adding that the surveillance would be discreet. "I do not want any action taken that would indicate to Beurton that his case is not being dealt with in a normal manner."

In her optimistic moments, Ursula consoled herself that the Red Army was closing in on Berlin, the revolution would triumph, and a communist Germany would rise from the ruins. But in her darker hours, when the baby was crying and the mountain of radio work seemed insurmountable, she wondered if the war would ever end. Ursula was now a single mother, and a single spy. As always when her spirits were low, she turned in on herself, unwilling to let others glimpse the shadow of depression, the strain of her secret life. She confided in no one. Her habits of deception extended to her own feelings. In her darkest moments she lamented the impact the strange life she had chosen was having on her children, particularly Michael, who had spent his earliest years moving from country to country, language to language, with a succession of men who were not his father. "He should have had a different mother," she wrote. "He should have spent his whole childhood in one place, with a father coming home in the evening, and a mother always there for him."

Like every good communist, Ursula believed in anniversaries. On November 7, the date of the Bolshevik Revolution, she left the children with a neighbor and traveled to London to meet Sergei, who passed on anniversary greetings from the GRU director. She would have bought a red rose but there were none to be had in wartime Britain. Ursula returned to Avenue Cottage, cold and lonely. "I couldn't celebrate the day with anyone. My thoughts returned to the past."

It was almost two years since she had heard from Rudi Hamburger. She dared not ask Moscow what had become of him; and the Center would not have told her if she had. She feared he might be dead, but kept her fears from Michael and the other children. It was even longer since she had received word from Johann Patra. Agnes Smedley was back in America, living in a writers' colony in upstate New York and still propagandizing vigorously on behalf of Chinese communism. Ursula still had no idea of the fates of Shushin, Grisha, and Tumanyan. Alexander Foote and Sandor Radó must still be spying in Switzerland, if they had not yet been caught. All that remained to her of Richard Sorge was a single tattered photograph.

On the other side of the world, in the condemned cell of Tokyo's Sugamo Prison, Ursula's recruiter waited for the hangman.

Richard Sorge's spy network in Japan had achieved espionage miracles. Posing as an avid Nazi, whoring and boozing his way around Tokyo, Sorge penetrated both the German embassy and the cabinet of the Japanese prime minister, extracting the innermost secrets of both. In 1941, he had been able to reassure Moscow that Japan was unwilling and unable to invade Siberia, freeing up vital Soviet forces for the defense of Moscow. Two days before Operation Barbarossa, he had sent a message to the Center warning that "war between Germany and the USSR is inevitable." But Stalin, ungrateful and mistrustful, had dismissed Sorge's report of an imminent German attack as a false alarm.

When the Germans began to suspect Sorge might be batting for the other side, the vicious Gestapo colonel Josef Meisinger, a standout Nazi monster in a crowded field, was sent to investigate. Sorge quickly neutralized the threat by taking Meisinger on bibulous tours of Tokyo's nightlife.

The chance arrest of a minor agent in his network brought an end to Sorge's amazing run of luck. He was arrested, and tortured into a confession. The Japanese offered to swap him for one of their spies held by Russia, but Moscow disavowed him, denying he was a Soviet agent. It was said that Stalin did not want his rejection of Sorge's accurate warnings to get out. In Russia, Sorge's wife, Katya, was arrested on suspicion of being a German spy and sent to the Gulag, where she perished. His most important informant, the Japanese journalist Hotsumi Ozaki, was also arrested.

After two years in Sugamo, Sorge was finally convicted of espionage and sentenced to hang. The Japanese prosecutor who had argued for the death penalty declared: "I have never met anyone as great as he was."

Sorge was hanged on November 7, 1944. His last words, delivered in fluent Japanese with his hands and feet bound and the noose already around his neck, were "The Red Army!"—"The International Communist Party!"—"The Soviet Communist Party!"

During his long and brutal interrogation, Sorge had told the Japanese much that was true about his espionage career, and some that was not.

The great spy was repeatedly cross-examined about his Shanghai network in the 1920s, including its female spies. Sorge was unaware quite how successful Ursula had become, but he knew that if she was

Colonel Gaik Lazarevich Tumanyan, head of Soviet military intelligence in Asia and Ursula's boss from 1933–1938.

Ursula in about 1935: an unlikely looking Red Army officer.

General Yan Karlovich Berzin, the chief of the Fourth Department, executed during Stalin's purges.

Colonel Khadzi-Umar Mamsurov, known as "Comrade Hadshi," Ursula's Soviet spymaster from 1938.

Len Beurton in 1939. Ursula wrote: "He was twenty-five years old, with thick brown hair, eyebrows that met and clear hazel eyes."

Adolf Hitler in the Osteria Bavaria, his favorite Munich restaurant.

Alexander Allan Foote, Spanish Civil War veteran and opportunist spy.

Alexander "Sandor" Radó, the Jewish Hungarian cartographer and mastermind of the Rote Drei espionage network in Switzerland.

La Taupinière, the Molehill, Ursula's home in the Swiss mountains above Lake Geneva.

Olga Muth, known as "Ollo," the family nanny, seen here with Ursula's sisters Renate and Sabine.

Nina, Ursula's daughter by Johann Patra, age two. Ursula used the children's toys to smuggle radio parts.

Rudi Hamburger in 1939, soon after his recruitment by Soviet military intelligence.

Emily "Mickey" Hahn, the intrepid *New Yorker* correspondent, clad in male attire for a dinner party in Shanghai.

```
                                    Internee's No:..417.....
NAME: ....FUCHS...........................
        Given Names:...KLAUS.EMIL.JULIUS..   Hut 16
        ───────D E S C R I P T I O N───────
Age:...29.........Years
Height:...5....Ft. 10.....inches
Complexion:..dark.............
Colour of eyes:.brown.dark.....
Colour of hair:.brown.dark.....
Weight (approximate):....9 stone.
.....en or not:..clean.shaven
.....ited.....Nose:.xxxxx.straight
.....ild:..tall.............
....:...none.............
......wears glasses
.....3 false teeth in front.
```

Klaus Fuchs: internment card for the German-born physicist, who would become Ursula's spy inside the atomic weapons program.

Ursula dressed in her best suit before heading to London to meet her Soviet handler Nikolai Vladimirovitch Aptekar, alias "Sergei."

Erich Henschke, alias "Karl Kastro," the "cutout" between Ursula and her spies recruited by the OSS, America's military intelligence service.

Lieutenant Joe Gould, the American film publicist turned intelligence officer, who ran the Tool missions.

The "Joan-Eleanor system": a revolutionary new technology that enabled American intelligence to make direct radio contact from the air with spies inside Nazi Germany.

The Hammer spies Toni Ruh and Paul Lindner, who parachuted into Berlin on March 2, 1945.

The railway bridge over the road west of Great Rollright. The dead-drop site was in the hollow root of the fourth tree on the left after the crossroads beyond the bridge.

The Firs, Great Rollright. "Our first real home," wrote Ursula.

Ursula with her children in the garden of The Firs.

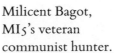

Milicent Bagot, MI5's veteran communist hunter.

William "Jim" Skardon, the legendary interrogator.

Roger Hollis, who joined MI5 in 1937 and rose to become its director general in 1956.

Melita Norwood, "Hola," the longest-serving Soviet spy on British soil.

Ursula with officers of the East German Ministry of State Security, beneath a portrait of Erich Honecker, the country's hard-line communist leader.

Russian and Chinese stamps commemorating three of the most important communist spies: Kim Philby, Agnes Smedley, and Richard Sorge.

still alive she would be spying against the Axis powers, and in danger. "Women are absolutely unfit for espionage work," he told his captors. "They have no understanding of political or other affairs and are a very poor source of information." This was, of course, the opposite of the truth. Sorge's network had included numerous women, Ursula foremost among them. He lied to the Japanese interrogators to divert attention from his protégée spy and fellow intelligence officer, in order to shield her.

Sorge, most faithless of lovers, was loyal to the end, in his way.

JOE GOULD SPENT CHRISTMAS DAY at Lindner's house with the other Tool spies. Everyone got drunk and sang German carols. Gould's son later described this as a moment of "mutual respect between a Jewish US Army officer and his seven German recruits who shared a common goal." Except that, as the Second World War merged into the Cold War, they were already on different sides.

A few weeks later, Gould asked Erich Henschke to accompany him on a trip to Paris. The liberated French capital was now home to the Free Germany Committee and Gould was keen, with Henschke's help, to gather "addresses of anti-fascists in Germany" that could be used as safe houses by the spies. Together they visited the Free Germany headquarters, as well as a group called Amicale des Volontaires de l'Espagne Républicaine (Friends of the Spanish Republican Volunteers). "He brought back all the addresses they needed," unaware that his list of reliable anti-Nazi contacts in Germany had been preapproved by the Center. Red Army intelligence was not just watching the Tool missions; it was running them at one remove, through Ursula and Henschke.

And Milicent Bagot was watching them.

Soon after Henschke returned to London, Bagot sent a memo to the head of Soviet operations at MI6, detailing her suspicions about Karl Kastro and asking for help in finding out more about the people this known communist had met in Paris, particularly the International Brigades veterans. "Have you any information about this French organization please?" Bagot wrote to Kim Philby.

By 1945, Philby had been a Soviet agent for ten years and an MI6 officer for five. Efficient and helpful, he had risen swiftly in British intelligence, while passing on reams of highly damaging information to his KGB handlers. He was exceptionally skilled at throwing a wrench, imperceptibly, into the works of any operation that might threaten communist or Soviet interests. Philby's response to Bagot's inquiry, on February 22, 1945, was perfectly unhelpful: "At present we have no information about the Amicale des Volontaires de l'Espagne Républicaine."

The last opportunity to uncover the Soviet penetration of the Tool missions had been missed.

A week later, Hammer was under way.

CHAPTER 21

RUSTLE OF
SPRING

HITHERTO URSULA HAD ALWAYS FOUGHT FASCISM ON FOR-
eign soil. The nearest she had come to an operation inside
Nazi Germany was the aborted assassination of Hitler. Now, as the
war entered its finale, her spies were heading into the heart of the
Reich.

At 9:00 P.M. on March 1, 1945, Joe Gould and the Hammer agents
arrived at RAF Watton in Norfolk. Paul Lindner and Toni Ruh carried knapsacks containing 14,000 Reichsmarks, ration stamps, food
concentrates, gas masks, invisible ink, and two diamonds, as well as
coffee and fourteen hundred American cigarettes for barter on the
black market. In their pockets were Bob Work's expertly forged papers identifying them as Ewald Engelke, of Frankfurt, and Anton
Vesely, a German-speaking Czech, both skilled defense workers excused from military service. In Lindner's wallet was a fake Nazi Party
membership card. Each man also carried a .32 pistol to defend himself against capture, and a poison capsule if that failed.

Unbeknownst to Gould, they also brought memorized instructions from Colonel Ursula Kuczynski: precise orders on how, where,
and when they could establish contact with Soviet intelligence in
Germany. The GRU was also planning to put penetration agents
into bomb-battered Berlin, and the war was moving so fast that Soviet forces might reach the capital within weeks. Through Henschke,
Ursula issued each of the agents with a special password, identifying

them as Soviet intelligence agents. Once contact was established with Soviet forces, they should "no longer follow any further commands from the OSS and instead only obey instructions received from the Red Army for the remainder of the Hammer Mission."

On the airfield stood an American A-26, a lightweight bomber with the bomb bay adapted to accommodate the two parachutists. Gould was nervous: "Only the most courageous and highly skilled hands could bring the Hammer Mission safely and accurately to its pinpoint, 47 kilometres away from Berlin, seven hundred feet over the ground." In the airfield hut, the two agents pulled canvas jumpsuits over their civilian clothes and strapped on parachutes. Gould handed them his flask of brandy; the Germans each took a long pull.

Gould was troubled "by the sensation that he was living through a movie scenario." Both men had wives and young children, and "the drama of the moment seemed to be at their expense." Even so, his account of the ensuing scene is cinematic in the extreme.

It was raining lightly, and through the dark ground-haze the only distinctly visible object was the high, huge, squarish tail of the A-26 fifty yards away. Paul and Toni smoked, the men talking to them quietly. Three minutes before midnight, Commander Simpson opened the door and gave the signal. In a moment we were standing in the propeller blast of the A-26, now poised and roaring on the runway. We saw the reddish light shining out of her bomb bay as we walked, leaning against the blast, to the plane. We moved to the doors and hoisted Paul and Toni to their seats. There was too much sound for talking, and it was not the time. We reached up from the runway to shake hands with them. Now the night was absolutely clear. Suddenly we saw the A-26 begin to move, and then she was racing down the runway. She was almost out of sight before we saw her rise, climb quickly, and bank off to the northeast.

The pilot, Lieutenant Robert Walker, came in low over Germany, at a steady speed of 300 mph. "He flew her on her side, twisted her, banked her through to confuse the enemy radar." At 2:05 A.M. the plane reached the drop point at Alt-Friesack, northwest of Berlin. The visibility was good, with patchy clouds and a bright moon. Walker opened the bomb bay, the dispatcher, Mishko Derr, tapped the two parachutists on the back, and Paul Lindner and Toni Ruh jumped into the darkness.

The two German spies landed in a field and buried their jump-suits, parachutes, weapons, and the Joan transceiver. Two decades earlier, Ursula had sat in a nearby hayloft with a group of young communists imagining what a communist-ruled Germany would be like. By 6:30 A.M. they were jolting along in a train to Berlin, just two more weary wartime commuters. Dawn was breaking when they reached the city. Freeda Lindner was still asleep when her son tapped gently on the front window of his childhood home in the suburb of Neukölln, southwest of the city center. She had not seen Paul since his escape from Germany in 1935 with the Gestapo in pursuit. "I knew you would come home to fight the Nazis one day," she said.

The next day, moving through the shattered city from one air-raid shelter to another, Ursula's spies began to collect information: bomb damage, defenses, ammunition storage depots, troop deployments, civilian morale, and, above all, Germany's capacity to maintain its industry, military and commercial, under the most ferocious bombardment the world had ever seen. Allied bombs had reduced great swaths of Berlin to ash and rubble. The Red Army was poised, thirty-five miles east of the city, for the final assault on Hitler's capital. And yet the city was still functioning, a dead man walking, devastated but dogged. In his bunker, Hitler continued to issue orders for the defense of Berlin, as the thousand-year Reich plunged to oblivion in a final orgy of blood. Goebbels's propagandists still daubed the walls: "Every German will defend his capital. We shall stop the Red hordes at the walls of our Berlin." Lindner and Ruh were amazed to discover that roughly two-thirds of Berlin's industry was still operative; the railway network was working; the electricity still flowed. The two spies drank it all in like undercover tourists. A week after landing, they returned to the drop point to retrieve their guns and communications equipment. Then they settled down in Frau Lindner's parlor to listen to the BBC and await the strains of Sinding's "Rustle of Spring."

———

BACK IN OXFORD, URSULA waited for word, her anxiety rising steadily. Like all spymasters, she felt a sense of almost parental responsibility for the men she had recruited, briefed through Henschke, and then dispatched into mortal danger. Sergei had promised to alert her if the spies established contact with the Red Army in Berlin. Every week, she called Henschke from the phone box in Summertown to ask if Gould had received any information on the fate of the men. There was no news. The BBC supplied only the most general information about the march on Berlin. To try to distract herself, Ursula wrote long letters to Len, describing the minutiae of their daily lives: Peter's expanding vocabulary and strong English accent; Nina's fascination with animals; Michael's academic progress at Eastbourne. She sewed a new dress for Nina. "One of the good things about sewing," she reflected, "is that you can think while you are doing it." Her thoughts constantly swirled back to an image of two men, floating down into the inferno of Berlin.

ON MARCH 11, HIGH ABOVE the German capital, radio operator Lieutenant Calhoun Ancrum of the U.S. air force prepared his Eleanor for her first conversation with Joan. Before climbing into the cramped compartment inside the Mosquito PR XVI bomber, Ancrum had enjoyed a nongaseous meal of steak, toast, sliced tomatoes, and grapefruit. At twenty-five thousand feet, an attack of wind could cause agonizing cramps. The Tool missions left nothing to chance— including the digestive systems of the flying crew. Demolition charges were strapped to the equipment. If the plane was forced to ditch inside Germany, the technology would be destroyed. Joan-Eleanor could not be allowed to fall into enemy hands. At 9:00 P.M. Ancrum switched on the transceiver.

"Is that you, Heinz?"

From six miles below, Paul Lindner's voice floated up from a wheat field outside Berlin.

"Is that you, Vic?"

"Can you hear me, Heinz?"

"I can't hear you, Vic . . ."

The exchange did not live up to the significance of the moment, but the crackling conversation over VHF radio represented a technological triumph: for the first time, the Western Allies could speak directly to their spies deep inside Nazi Germany. Over the next six weeks, at intervals dictated by the coded BBC messages, the Hammer agents described what they had seen and uncovered, much of it gleaned from the underground trade union resistance networks: Berlin's defenses, the road and rail systems, troop movements, and the location of still-functioning munitions plants, including a large tank factory—a shopping list of juicy bombing targets. On March 29 they reported that the huge Klingenberg power plant was still operational. In a nighttime reconnaissance of a rail yard on the outskirts, they counted twenty-six freight and eighteen passenger trains, sitting ducks for the Allied bombers.

Back at OSS headquarters in London, Bill Casey was jubilant. The Hammer team had made "a big breakthrough . . . including important air-target data on a still functioning power plant that kept key factories running, as well as detail on the importance of a Berlin transportation net and key spots where Allied bombs could disrupt it." The Soviet armies were advancing quickly, and the spies scrambled to furnish any information that might degrade Berlin's defenses ahead of the final assault. Lindner turned up at the rendezvous point appointed by Ursula, expecting to meet the promised GRU agent sent in advance of the approaching Soviet troops, but no one appeared.

MICHAEL CAME HOME FOR the Easter holidays. Ursula was Jewish, German, and atheist, but at her son's insistence she agreed to cook the children a traditional English Easter lunch, or as near as wartime rationing permitted: some scrag end of mutton scrounged from the butcher, potatoes and cabbage from the patch she had dug in the Laskis' back garden. With the meal cooking under Michael's vigilant eye, she walked into Summertown and, as she did every Sunday, put in a call to Erich Henschke. The tone of his voice revealed what had happened before he even uttered the code phrase she had been waiting for. The Hammer spies were in and had made contact. That meant the Joan-Eleanor system might soon be in Soviet hands. Her spies were safe, or as safe as they could be in a city under siege.

Easter lunch was a most joyful affair at Avenue Cottage that year. Michael ate six hot cross buns.

That same Easter Sunday, April 1, 1945, Lindner and Ruh made their way to a remote area northwest of Berlin, to collect a scheduled airdrop of food and other supplies. Around the city, German troops were digging in for a last-ditch defense: ragtag Wehrmacht units, Waffen-SS, but also old men and teenage boys of the Hitler Youth. Suddenly the spies found themselves in the midst of SS Panzer Division Hermann Goering, as it clanked northward for the final battle. A young lieutenant on a motorbike, officious and suspicious, demanded their papers. Lindner produced the forgeries identifying them as Ewald Engelke and Anton Vesely, and explained that they were returning to the city to join the loyal defenders. The skeptical officer told them to empty their rucksacks. The Joan transceiver was at the bottom of Ruh's bag, hidden beneath dirty clothes. Laboriously, as slowly as possible, he began to empty it, sock by sock, muttering in Czech. Paul shrugged, and made a remark about this "dumb Czech who didn't understand German." Inside his coat pocket, Lindner slipped the safety catch off his .32. Exasperated by the delay, the lieutenant waved them on—a decision that saved their lives and probably his own. "I would have gladly shot him," Paul Lindner later remarked.

On April 16, with the city encircled, the Soviets launched the final offensive. The forces of the Western Allies had dropped out of the race for Berlin. It had already been agreed that the city would be divided into four zones of occupation once the fighting was over, and General Eisenhower decided to leave the glory of capturing Hitler's capital to the Soviets. The Allied air bombardment ceased when Soviet troops entered the city and the Red Army artillery took over the shelling, pouring more explosive onto Berlin than the total tonnage of bombs already dropped by the Western Allies.

The Battle of Berlin was reaching a climax. On April 21, while attempting to make contact using the Joan-Eleanor equipment, the Hammer spies were almost overrun by Soviet forces sweeping in from the south, pushing the German defenders back, street by street. The following day, another message on the BBC instructed Lindner to cross into Soviet-held territory, while Ruh remained in Berlin. Thousands of Berliners were attempting to flee the city and being pushed back; Lindner was unable to break through the defensive perimeter.

The same afternoon saw one of the last battles of the Second World War, as the Germans attempted to defend Treptow in the southeast against a ferocious Soviet assault. Lindner, Ruh, and Lindner's father were caught up in the fighting and joined the attack on the German lines using abandoned weapons. Soviet troops, mistaking them for die-hard loyalists, opened fire on the trio, before realizing these were anti-Nazi partisans. Soviet troops were pouring into Berlin, and a vengeful campaign of rape, murder, and destruction was under way. The Hammer mission was over, at least in its American form.

That night, Lindner and Ruh made their way through the ravaged city to the Wartenberg district, and an address supplied by Henschke a month earlier. Walli Schmidt had been a member of the Young Communist League alongside Ursula and they had kept in touch over the years. Ursula knew her to be a committed party member. In February, Walli had received a message via the workers' underground network instructing her to stand by. It was 3:00 A.M. when Ruh (who had also known Schmidt in the 1920s) knocked gently on her door. Walli opened it a crack, and Ruh whispered the code word: "Sonya." On Walli's dark and deserted allotment behind the house, between a plum tree and the chicken coop, they carefully buried the Joan transceiver.

One of the final messages from the OSS instructed Lindner and Ruh to establish the "whereabouts of Hitler," with a view to killing the führer himself in a surgical bombing strike. There was no need. On April 22, after being told that his orders for a counterattack had not been fulfilled, Hitler suffered almost total nervous collapse. A week later, with Soviet forces just five hundred yards from the Führerbunker, he shot himself.

On the same day as Hitler's tearful breakdown, Lindner and Ruh approached a Red Army tank unit rolling into Neukölln, explained that they were Soviet military intelligence agents, and were brought before one Captain Martov.

Lindner and Ruh later described how Martov had refused to believe their story and, after finding OSS codebooks in their knapsacks, threatened to have them arrested and shot as enemy agents. When they were finally handed over to the U.S. Sixty-ninth Infantry Division near Leipzig, they claimed to have spent two months in Soviet captivity. This was certainly untrue. In Stalin's army only a madman would have failed to investigate their claim to be GRU agents, and a very swift inquiry would have established that Lindner and Ruh were telling the truth. Far more likely, having given the special GRU identifying password supplied by Ursula, they were taken to intelligence headquarters and fully debriefed on every aspect of their mission, notably the J-E system.

Within days of the Soviet occupation of Berlin, a Red Army officer appeared at Walli Schmidt's home in Wartenberg: together they exhumed Joan from the hole between the plum tree and chicken coop. With bureaucratic punctiliousness, the officer presented Walli with a receipt for one-half of a revolutionary new communications system. The Center sent a coded message to Agent Sonya in Britain indicating that the pickup had been completed.

On May 2, 1945, the commander of Berlin's defense force surrendered unconditionally to General Vasily Chuikov, the same soldier who, as Soviet defense attaché in Chungking in 1941, had helped to spring Rudi Hamburger from a Chinese prison. The war in Europe was over.

Lindner and Ruh were the lucky ones in the Tool story. The A-26 on the Chisel mission into the Ruhr Valley crashed on the night of March 19 near the town of Schwege, killing everyone on board. Werner Fischer (Buzzsaw) successfully landed near Leipzig on April 7, on a mission to report on German troop movements and conditions inside British POW camps, including Colditz. He was immediately surrounded by Red Army soldiers who had advanced deeper into southern Germany than the OSS realized. Fischer was carrying false papers identifying him as Ernst Lauterbach, a Gestapo special agent. He protested he was a German communist on an intelligence mission. The disbelieving soldiers shot him on the spot and threw his body in a ditch. Apart from Hammer, the only other mission to achieve its objectives was Pickaxe, whose two spies landed in Landshut, near Munich. According to Bill Casey, "the agents funnelled massive amounts of information about rail and road traffic, communications centres and troop movements, to waiting Mosquitoes during no fewer than nine Joan-Eleanor reports."

Lindner and Ruh, following GRU instructions, explained to the Americans that they were keen to return to Britain and continue working for American intelligence. An OSS officer, Henry Sutton, however, subjected them to a debriefing that was "pointed and not entirely amicable." Their "eagerness to return to Britain" struck him as "not quite right." These men were probably communists and had spent a considerable period in Soviet hands before being released. "How could Sutton be sure that they had not become double agents?" Gould might not be concerned about their politics, but Sutton most certainly was: "Because of the political background of these men there is serious doubt as to whether they could fit into our post-war German operations." As the Second World War ended and the Cold War began, tolerance of communism was turning to deep suspicion, expedient wartime alliance giving way to mounting postwar antagonism.

Even so, the Hammer agents were discharged in August 1945, with a paean of gratitude from the OSS "for the heroic and extremely valuable work that you did for us. During hostilities, you behaved coolly and efficiently and displayed remarkable ability in exploiting every means for fulfilling your difficult task. The successful completion of your mission was of very great value to the armed forces of the Allies and contributed greatly to the defeat of the enemy." The OSS also patted itself firmly on the back: "Contact with the agent teams by means of the J–E equipment was established and maintained successfully at a critical time in the assault on Germany. Vital information was obtained as to conditions in Berlin, the disposition of troops in the Berlin area and remaining targets for bombing . . . extremely valuable intelligence was obtained."

News of the fall of Berlin was greeted with unconstrained joy throughout Britain, and nowhere more than in Avenue Cottage, Oxford.

Ursula had been able to follow the progress of the Tool missions through the information passed on to Henschke by Gould. The Hammer spies had survived, though several of the other recruits had perished. She had made a vital contribution to the liberation of her home city from the curse of Nazism. And, most important of all, she had coordinated a mission to steer a brand-new item of American military technology into Soviet hands. She was helping Russia to build the bomb; she also helped them build the walkie-talkie. Even Len did not know what she had done. Hers was a secret, private celebration.

The Laskis organized a street party for VE (Victory in Europe) Day on May 8. "Tables stood end to end along the road," wrote Ursula. The residents pooled their meager rations to bake victory cakes. There were toasts with lemonade and beer, and the street was decked with homemade bunting. Ursula had never felt closer to her British neighbors, or more in tune with the national mood. She made a large Victoria sponge, which Nina decorated in red, white, and blue. "I shared everyone's joy."

And yet, as a Red Army officer, she was heading into a new battle. History was pivoting around her. Before the war, she had spied against fascists and anti-communists, Chinese, Japanese, and German; during the conflict, she had spied against both the Nazis and the Allies; after it, and henceforth, she would be spying against the West, the new enemies in a Cold War. A photograph of the Summertown neighborhood victory party includes a beaming Ursula, happily celebrating Hitler's downfall. One man is wearing an army uniform. Another raises two fingers in the V for Victory sign. But behind the image of shared relief, triumph, and optimism lay a hidden ideological divergence that would soon erupt in a new conflict. "Everyone hoped for a better world," she wrote. "But here our visions of the future differed."

TWO MONTHS LATER, in the remote deserts of New Mexico, scientists of the Manhattan Project detonated the first nuclear device, in a test code-named "Trinity," releasing a blast equivalent to twenty thousand tons of TNT. Among the scientists who watched the great mushroom cloud erupt into the dawn sky was Klaus Fuchs, one of the principal architects of the most powerful weapon yet devised by man. In August 1944, he had moved to the heart of the Manhattan Project in Los Alamos, described by one scientist as "the campus of a huge university whose faculty members were many of the most outstanding scientists in the western world, assembled to work out how to beat Hitler in the race to build an atomic bomb." In the Theoretical Physics Division, he worked under Hans Bethe, who considered Fuchs "one of the most valuable men in my division" and "one of the best theoretical physicists we had."

Through Harry Gold of the KGB, Fuchs had passed on every scrap of scientific intelligence to Moscow: they met in Queens, beside the Metropolitan Museum of Art in Manhattan, and in Cambridge, Massachusetts. Fuchs told Gold not only of the progress toward uranium and plutonium "atomic" bombs, but also of the accelerating research into the even more potent hydrogen bomb. In June 1945, Gold was waiting on a bench in downtown Santa Fe when Fuchs drove up in his "dilapidated old two-seater" and handed over a complete description of the plutonium bomb that would be tested in the desert a few weeks later. The Soviets were delighted to receive "the virtual blueprint for the Trinity device."

At the Potsdam Conference on July 24, President Truman informed Stalin that America had built "a new weapon of unusual destructive force." Stalin seemed unsurprised—which was itself unsurprising, because he already knew all about it.

Two weeks later, the U.S. air force dropped an atomic bomb on the Japanese city of Hiroshima, and then a second on Nagasaki. The war in the Pacific was over and the Cold War was starting in earnest.

For four years, Ursula's neighbors and friends in Britain had been her allies; across the rigid battle lines of the new conflict, they were now her enemies.

CHAPTER 22

GREAT ROLLRIGHT

G REAT ROLLRIGHT IS A PICTURESQUE RURAL HAMLET
surrounded by farmland in the heart of the north Oxfordshire
Cotswolds. In 1945, it had an eighteenth-century pub, the Unicorn,
a post office, a medieval church, and a population of 243 people,
mostly agricultural families who had lived there for generations. The
trains of the Banbury and Cheltenham line stopped at Rollright Halt
twice a day. Great Rollright is a grand name for a village that was
anything but: it was charming, remote, and exceedingly quiet. A
week after VE Day, Ursula and the children moved into "The Firs,"
a house of honey-colored Cotswold stone on the edge of the village
with four bedrooms, two sheds, and an outside privy. The house was
without electricity, telephone, or hot water. It was drafty in May
and frigid in December. But roses grew in profusion around the door
and "the gentle Cotswold hills" rolled away from the back door. Ursula loved it on sight.

Of all the places she had lived and spied, from China to Poland to
Switzerland, this house, "250 years old, with its thick wooden beams
and low ceilings, the yard and barn and wild garden," was the closest
to her heart. It was, she wrote, "our first real home." Avenue Cottage was too small for her growing children. Here there was ample
space, the rent was low, and a large locked cellar was ideal for concealing illegal radio equipment. The neighbors were friendly and in-
curious. Michael returned from Eastbourne during the holidays;

Nina, smart in her new school uniform, took the bus to the County Grammar School in Chipping Norton; Peter attended the village nursery school run by the vicar's wife. Ursula planted out a vegetable patch, built a hencoop in the garden, and eventually installed a young pig. A stray cat moved in and stayed. Nina christened her Penny.

As in many English villages, life in Great Rollright revolved around the pub, the twelfth-century church, the cricket club, local gossip, the harvest, and the annual fête. The family was welcomed without fanfare and swiftly absorbed. Befriended by a local farmer's wife, a Mrs. Malton, Ursula began to put down roots. She remained a staunch Marxist atheist, but the family seldom missed church. Eight-year-old Nina embraced Anglicanism with childish zeal. "During the sermon I sat at the front and listened carefully and believed every word." She decided to become a nun. Then changed her mind and decided to be a fighter pilot. The bell ringers at St. Andrew's frequently came for tea after Sunday service. Ursula's baked scones were really very good. As she had with Frau Füssli in Switzerland, Ursula spent long hours sitting by the kitchen fire discussing the minutiae of rural life with Mrs. Malton: the chickens, the weather, the children. She bought some secondhand furniture and hung the Chinese paintings she had brought from Shanghai. "It was strange how well the silk scrolls suited the old farmhouse." She took the children on a trip to Stratford-upon-Avon. "The children were each allowed four fizzy drinks, three ice creams, and two complete inspections of Woolworths." Ursula insisted they also visit the house where Shakespeare was born.

In the very heart of England, Ursula was becoming English, but without her English husband. Len's application to transfer from the RAF to the army was suddenly granted, and to his surprise Beurton was enlisted in the Coldstream Guards ("the most feudal of all British Regiments," Ursula wryly noted). He was posted to Germany and would not be discharged for another twenty-one months. MI5 warned Beurton's commanding officer to keep an eye on him: "His record is a strange one, and it is possible that he is, or has been, a Soviet agent. . . . [It is] undesirable that he should be employed as an interpreter in Germany or any location where he is likely to be in contact with Russians." Len had spent most of the previous year in RAF barracks. Now he was in a foreign country. "I was very much on my own," wrote Ursula. "But I had my work."

Melita Norwood's secrets from the British Non-Ferrous Metals Association flowed unchecked. Jürgen, demobilized from the Strategic Bombing Survey, was preparing to return to East Berlin, where communists would forge the German Democratic Republic (GDR) in East Germany under Soviet control. But he and his father remained usefully plugged into British political life. James, the RAF officer, supplied tidbits of technical information. The transmitter was in constant use. None of the villagers noticed the odd hours kept by Mrs. Burton, though her daughter did: "We children had to do daily chores in the house and in the garden. We came home from school each day at 4 p.m. Often at this time of day my mother was asleep. Other mothers didn't take a nap in the afternoons and I thought: *she* sends me into the garden to do some weeding while *she* takes a nap!" Toni Ruh, the former Hammer spy, found work with a defense contractor on his return to Britain. Early in 1946 he passed on, via Erich Henschke, a prototype aircraft part, "a special instrument for shooting in fighter planes." Ursula stashed the object in Peter's carriage, wheeled it to the woods near Great Rollright, and buried it. To her embarrassment, when she went to retrieve it, she could no longer recall the spot—her first mistake in twenty years of espionage. But in all other respects she was a model spy. Her radio was working well, as was the system for contacting and passing on information to the GRU; the payments from Red Army intelligence were regular and sufficient; Ursula's espionage network was running smoothly.

And then it abruptly stopped.

In the autumn of 1946, Ursula went to London for a routine rendezvous with the latest Sergei. The GRU officer did not turn up. Initially she was unconcerned. "We had a special arrangement to cope with loss of contact." A few miles west of Great Rollright, the Banbury and Cheltenham Direct Railway passed over the road running between Banbury and Oxford. Beyond the first crossroads after the crossing stood a line of trees; the fourth on the left had a hollow root. That was the dead-drop site where, if a rendezvous was missed, messages and money would be left for Ursula on a specific day of the month. A week after the missed rendezvous, Ursula cycled under the railway bridge, parked her bike, and, having checked no one was watching, reached into the hole. The dead-letter box was empty. It was bare the next month too. And the next. Had the network been compromised? Under the rules, if Moscow severed communication then she should not attempt to reestablish it by radio until instructed to do so. After two months without a word, Ursula was seriously worried, running low on money, and restless. "I had lived for this work for years, and now my days were empty." Every month, fearful that someone might spot the pattern of her movements, she cycled to an open stretch of road and felt inside an empty tree root. The Center had broken off contact completely. "There must have been a good reason," she told herself.

There was indeed a reason, but it was not a good one.

The GRU, the mighty military intelligence-gathering machine of the Soviet Union, had got the wrong tree.

Instead of leaving messages under the fourth plane tree after the *crossroads,* the GRU courier was depositing the cache in the fourth tree after the *underpass*—which, by unhappy coincidence, was also hollow at the root. In one of those human mistakes that are as common in espionage as every other profession, the GRU had cocked it up. But the Center was as baffled as Ursula. "For reasons unknown Sonya did not remove the money from the dead drop in the agreed upon period of time and we took the money back," a report noted. As far as the Center was concerned, it was Agent Sonya who had broken contact, which could mean only one thing: the British Security Service must be closing in on her. Which it was.

Ursula's past was returning to haunt her along three distinct routes, and through three different men—Rudi Hamburger, Alexander Foote, and Klaus Fuchs: her ex-husband, her former collaborator, and her best spy.

On March 25, 1946, the U.S. legal attaché and FBI representative in London, John Cimperman, sent a letter to Roger Hollis of MI5: "Please refer to previous correspondence on Rudolf Albert Hamburger, confessed Soviet Agent whose whereabouts has not been established since he left Iran on May 22, 1943. I would appreciate your making arrangements to interview Ursula Hamburger Beurton, the former wife of Hamburger, for the purposes of ascertaining Rudolf's present whereabouts." The FBI was actively investigating anyone with communist links. Rudi's brother Victor, now at the University of Chicago, was therefore a suspicious person.

The Americans were suddenly interested in the Soviet spy and his ex-wife.

Rudi Hamburger's present location was as far removed as it is possible to imagine from the gently undulating Cotswolds: he was in Karaganda Labor Camp, a huge Gulag covering fourteen thousand square miles of the Kazakhstan steppes. Here an army of inmates slaved in fifty coal mines, in a landscape so inhospitable that the camp barely needed its machine gun–toting guards. Anyone attempting to escape swiftly died in the frozen wilderness.

"Every morning, it seems inconceivable to me how I got here," Rudi wrote.

Hamburger's purgatory had started in Saratova Labor Camp on the Volga, five hundred miles south of Moscow, at the beginning of a five-year sentence for "political crimes."

"That's what I have become," he wrote. "A traitor, a terrorist, a public enemy." Saratova was a timber extraction camp, a penal colony powered by slave labor and the closest thing the Stalinist state could devise to a half-living hell. The inmates wore identical prison garb of jerkin and quilted black cotton cap, a uniform intended to enforce conformity and insufficient to keep out the biting cold. Their diet consisted of coarse black bread and watery soup: "Particles of carrot, fish skeletons, bones and disgusting fish heads that stare at you, with dead eyes." After six months of captivity, Rudi weighed under 110 pounds. When he dared to look in a mirror he saw a "greyshining skull, the pale, emaciated face of a prematurely aged man." There were no books, newspapers, or radio, and no communication with anyone on the outside. Rudi's fellow convicts included professional criminals running an internal tyranny of fear, violence, and extortion, but also political prisoners like himself, the "FiftyEighters," "socially dangerous elements" convicted under Article 58: students who had dared to demand freedom of expression, a couple who criticized the war that had taken their only son, a man who picked up and kept a Nazi propaganda leaflet dropped from a German plane.

"Keep calm and disciplined," Rudi told himself. "Watch your tongue. You live in the land of unlimited dictatorship. Keep silent." The boredom and hunger gnawed him to the soul: "Lying on the bare plank bed, you are like a tortured animal who dully awaits his bitter fate." He tried to forget his former existence and the things he had once loved. "It must be possible to renounce the luxury of feelings, not to remember aesthetic beauty which, embodied in art, architecture, music, was part of my life. . . . If you want to survive in the camp, you must not allow yourself to think."

A team of American military engineers visited Saratova to supervise the building of a chemicals factory as part of a wartime relief program. A kindly secretary offered Rudi an illustrated American magazine. "Finally, in a language familiar to me, I can read something to distract me from my desperate thoughts." A few weeks later the magazine was confiscated and he was accused of bringing anti-Soviet propaganda into the camp. A second trial began. "The judge has the sharp, cutting tone that I knew from my Prussian fatherland. His task is to inspire fear, to force the accused into the position of a guilty criminal from the outset, and stifle any attempt at resistance." Rudi's sentence was extended to eight more years and he was thrown into solitary confinement. "In the darkness of the cell, there is little difference between day and night. I am vegetating, a breeding ground for lice. . . . I use my wooden spoon to scratch floor-plans of buildings into the ice layer on the wall, of a house somewhere in dreamland. Mostly I lie in perfect lethargy."

News of the fall of Berlin reached the Gulag, and Rudi recorded the moment: " 'The war is over—the fascists are destroyed,' says a guard, laughing, and he throws his arms in the air with joy. A flush of happiness comes over me. The genocide is over, Hitler-fascism is defeated. Peace. Suddenly my own destiny seems small beside this tremendous event."

Rudi had lost everything, except his obstinacy. Starving, freezing, lice-infested, worked to the bone, falsely condemned by a callous communist regime, he clung to the ideology he had adopted at Ursula's urging. "The decade-long revolutionary shocks and the war have produced a generation of heroic men and women who are building a new society," he wrote. "The gulag cannot block the view of the stars with barbed wire."

In 1945, he was transferred to Karaganda to work on the design and construction of new barracks. "Despite life in the desolate steppe, this camp is easier to bear," he wrote. At least he could exercise his architectural skills, though building rows of identical wooden huts was a far cry from the Art Deco edifices he had crafted in Shanghai. He thought often of Ursula, and of Michael, the son he feared he would never see again. "Here, in a barren land devoid of life, the prospect of eight years of barbed wire crushes me to the ground. If I have not died by then, where will I go?"

MI5 was perplexed, and somewhat nettled, by the FBI's renewed interest in Ursula Beurton and her ex-husband, the Soviet spy who had been handed back to Moscow before vanishing. "The FBI are being singularly persistent about this case and I suspect they have some more recent information about Hamburger than we have," wrote John Marriott of MI5. The Americans had already been told, a year earlier, that Mrs. Beurton was above suspicion since she "appears to devote her time to her children and domestic affairs." But now Cimperman was back, demanding MI5 interview her and find out where her ex-husband was. "There seems no good reason for supposing the lady can answer his question," wrote Marriott. He told Cimperman: "This lady is known to be of communist sympathies and I should hesitate to interview her on a matter of this sort. Although our investigations into her present husband yielded no evidence to substantiate the suspicions which we entertained about him, nonetheless these suspicions still prevail and we are by no means satisfied that he is not a Soviet agent." Interviewing Ursula Beurton might tip off her husband, newly demobilized and now working in a plastics factory, that MI5 was suspicious of him. Once again, the exclusive focus on the man obscured the woman, and the more important spy.

Even so, Marriott dropped a note to Kim Philby at MI6. "You will recall that Rudolf Hamburger was a Soviet Agent who was detained in Iran in May 1943, first by the Americans and then by the British, and by the latter subsequently handed back to the Soviet authorities. The FBI have now asked us to question Ursula Beurton (who, as you will recall, was formerly the wife of Hamburger). For a variety of reasons I do not feel able to comply with this request. I am wondering whether you could let me have any information as to the present whereabouts of Rudolf Hamburger?"

Philby, the KGB's top spy in the United Kingdom, was fully apprised of the Ursula Beurton case. Whether he also knew she was a fellow spy for the Soviets, and deliberately shielded her, is unknown. Philby's response was exquisitely civil, and entirely obstructive. "With regret," he told MI5, MI6 had "no knowledge of the present whereabouts of Hamburger."

ON AUGUST 2, 1947, an Englishman walked into the legation in the British sector of Berlin and explained to the startled receptionist that he was a Soviet spy and wished to defect.

Alexander Foote had lived at least four different lives, under as many different names, since bidding farewell to Ursula in Switzerland in December 1940. A lynchpin of Sandor Radó's Rote Drei network, for two years he passed on a mass of military information to the Center, sometimes coding and decoding for twenty hours a day and living, as he put it, the "life of a monk." The Swiss authorities knew an illegal radio transmitter was being used somewhere in Lausanne. So did the German Abwehr. One or the other was bound to catch him eventually. Foote was taking down a message from Moscow at 1:15 A.M. on November 20, 1942, when he heard a "splintering crash" as an axe smashed through the front door of his apartment. He just had time to demolish his radio and burn his notes using lighter fuel and a brass ashtray kept on hand for that purpose, before the room filled with armed Swiss police. "I had been expecting some sort of action for weeks, and had destroyed all my records, cash accounts etc., and as a result there was nothing for the police save a heap of charred ashes and a damaged transmitter." Foote was arrested and taken to Bois-Mermet Prison. His interrogation was remarkably civilized. "It is useless for you to deny your activities, Foote," Inspector Pasche of the Swiss security service explained, as they shared a bottle of Scotch in Foote's cell. "There is no suggestion that you have acted against Swiss interests, and I am personally inclined in your favour as you have been working against Germany, the only country in the world which threatens Swiss independence. It is now only necessary for you to make a complete confession and you will be released immediately." Foote, equally well-mannered, said he would not confess to anything, and that if Pasche was correct and he was released, the Soviets would assume he had betrayed them and kill him. "I demanded that I remained locked up." Foote enjoyed being in prison. "For the first time in years I was able to relax completely, and I was left in peace to work my way gradually through the prison library."

On his release in September 1944, Foote made his way to Paris, contacted the Soviet military mission, and sent a message to the Center. A few weeks later, he was issued with a false Soviet passport under the name Alfred Fedorovich Lapidus and ordered to board the first Soviet plane leaving liberated Paris, bound for Moscow. One of his fellow passengers was Sandor Radó, the rotund mastermind of the Rote Drei who had escaped capture in Switzerland and made his way to Paris. Another was Gavril Ilyich Myasnikov, a veteran Bolshevik who had taken part in the murder of Grand Duke Michael Alexandrovich of Russia, the first of the Romanovs to be assassinated. After falling afoul of Lenin, Myasnikov had gone into exile in France, but was now returning at the invitation of the Soviet embassy. Foote found him "a likeable old ruffian" and was impressed by his claim to be "going to Russia to put Stalin in his place."

As the plane took off at 9:00 A.M. on January 6, 1945, Foote was reflective and apprehensive. His commitment to communism had never been more than skin-deep. "For a long time I had been disillusioned and unhappy about the attitude of the Centre," but he still felt a residual duty. "Deliberately to desert the work would have been in my eyes equivalent to desertion in the face of the enemy." Besides, his spymasters owed him a debt for all his hard work. If they believed him.

During a stopover in Cairo, Foote and Radó shared a room at the Luna Park Hotel. The Hungarian cartographer seemed more than usually gloomy. "The first night he hardly said a word and declined to come out with me into Cairo for a last fling." During the night

Radó vanished, leaving behind his hat, coat, and luggage: "Mute evidence," Foote remarked, "of a spy who had lost his nerve." One of the greatest wartime communist spies did not trust Stalin to reciprocate his loyalty, and with good reason.

The plane landed in Moscow on January 14. Myasnikov boasted that Molotov, the Soviet foreign minister, would send an official limousine to collect him. Sure enough, a car was waiting, but "the grim faces of the escort" suggested to Foote that the welcome was not going to be quite as warm as the old Bolshevik was expecting. Myasnikov was arrested on the spot. Eight months later, he was murdered.

Foote's reception committee was much more attractive: Major Vera Poliakova of the Red Army, the English-speaking officer who had run the Swiss networks from Moscow throughout the war. With her dark hair and slim figure, Poliakova was "quite a beauty," Foote reflected. He was taken to a modern block of flats, shown into a two-room apartment, and introduced to a burly man named Ivan: "Interpreter, escort, guard, all in one." The questioning started next morning, and it was not friendly. "It was obvious from the tone of the questions that the Centre regarded me as an *agent provocateur* planted on them by the British." For days, and then weeks, Poliakova peppered him with questions, sometimes in person, sometimes written, detailed and overlapping, a mesh of confusing and contradictory interrogation designed to trip him up. Sandor Radó, she told him, was "a criminal who had embezzled funds in Switzerland." The GRU would bring him back. Sure enough, after being refused political asylum by the British embassy in Cairo, Radó tried and failed to commit suicide. In August 1945 he was extradited to Russia and sentenced to ten years in prison for espionage.

"It will not be long before Russia can collect people from anywhere in the world if they are wanted," Poliakova told Foote, a warning of "the fate I might expect if I deserted." So, far from flirting with him, Poliakova was offering to drag Foote back and kill him if he tried to defect.

Foote was given a new alias as Alexander Alexandrovitch Dimoff and told he could explore the city, so long as Ivan accompanied him. On one of these excursions they were stopped by a militiaman and told to produce papers. Ivan told the man to contact his superior. Moments later a KGB officer, five feet tall and sporting a livid black eye, arrived and began shouting. Poliakova had told them not to answer questions, so when the little man angrily demanded that he identify himself, Foote looked down on the ranting blob of officialdom and told him, slowly and precisely, to "Fuck off." The little KGB man scribbled in his notebook. The contretemps was sorted out by means of a single phone call and Foote and his minder returned to the flat, but the incident left a permanent misunderstanding: whenever Foote went out for a walk the militiamen cordially greeted him as "Comrade Fuckof."

After six weeks of daily interrogations, Major Poliakova appeared once more, now accompanied by a senior officer who spoke perfect English and sported an incongruously gaudy tie. "In his early forties, he was intelligent and intellectual, and a first class interrogator." This was none other than the director of the GRU himself, come to grill Foote in person. The interrogation lasted until the small hours, and started again the next day. "I felt I was on trial for my life," wrote Foote. Finally, the general rose and slapped Foote on the back. "He stated there was nothing with which I could be reproached and I was entirely exonerated and he thanked me for my efforts in Switzerland." When, Foote asked, could he go back to work for the greater glory of the Soviet Union? The director was cagey. "It would be necessary to let things calm down for a period before I could be used abroad again." The ordeal had been shattering, but Foote felt the danger had lifted. "We parted, with him convinced, I think, of my flaming enthusiasm for the cause in general and Soviet espionage in particular. That was the impression I wished to convey."

That impression was false. What little zeal Foote once had for communism was evaporating amid the harsh realities of life in Soviet Russia. "I was determined to get out and return to a world where freedom was more than a propaganda phrase. The only way that I could get out alive was to feign enthusiasm for any espionage plan put up, and then get out of the clutches of the Centre as fast as possible." It would be another year before the opportunity arose. In the spring of 1947, the GRU ordered Foote to travel to Berlin posing as "Albert Müller," a German soldier with an English mother (hence his accent) who had been captured by the Russians near Stalingrad and now sought repatriation to Germany. Once he had obtained German identity papers, he was to travel to Argentina. There, posing as an unreconstructed fascist, he should infiltrate the circle of high-ranking escaped Nazis and then use South America as a springboard to establish a new spy network inside the United States. "The Centre's network in the States was in a bad way" after the exposure of several agents, Major Poliakova explained, and the Red Army was "determined to build it up again from the bottom." Foote would be the architect.

In late February, traveling under the alias "Granatoff," Foote flew to Berlin. "Unless I bungled things at the last moment," he wrote, "there seemed every chance that shortly I would be able to cut myself loose from the Centre forever." On a sunny summer afternoon in 1947, Albert Müller showed his papers to the guards at the crossing between the Soviet and British zones of Berlin, and walked straight into the arms of British intelligence. Two days later, with an MI6 escort, he was back in London.

Alexander Foote told MI6 almost everything. He described how, as a young fighter returning from Spain, he had been recruited in London and sent to Switzerland; he explained how Ursula Kuczynski, Agent Sonya, had trained him and Len Beurton in wireless operations and bomb making; he revealed their aborted plots to kill Hitler and blow up the *Graf Zeppelin,* and described how Ursula's nanny had almost destroyed the network. He detailed the workings of Sandor Radó's network, his own arrest and release by the Swiss authorities, and the events that had led him from Lausanne to Paris to Moscow to Berlin, and finally to London. Holed up in a safe house at 19 Rugby Mansions, the spy offered up chapter and verse, furnishing MI6 with its first detailed description of wartime Soviet intelligence in Switzerland. Foote displayed a "complete lack of nerves" and boundless self-confidence. "He considers himself to be a first class operative," MI6 noted. When asked why he had switched sides, Foote explained that he was disillusioned by the "lack of freedom" in Russia and had turned against his former masters "because he felt they were going to make war." The interrogator was dubious: "I doubt whether Foote has any real political principles whatever."

Foote hinted that he would like a job in British intelligence, perhaps as a double agent. "The Russians have every confidence in me, they know I can do almost anything, and so I can." MI6 was impressed. "Foote has not lost his nerve and is certainly not on the run," but he was too unpredictable to use as a double agent. "There is a possibility that a man of Foote's character and position might turn to crime . . . it might be best to leave him to his own devices."

Alexander Foote had told MI6 the truth, but not all of it. Ursula Kuczynski, he insisted, had retired from the spy business long ago.

He described how upset Ursula had been by the Nazi-Soviet pact and Stalin's invasion of Finland, which was true, and claimed that as a result she had severed all links with Moscow, which was false. Her departure for England, he said, had brought her espionage career to an end. He spoke vaguely of some "continuing connections with Russia," but insisted that from 1941 onward she had been inactive. "She was thankful to sink back into respectable obscurity," Foote claimed. "Moscow was equally thankful to let her go. I do not think since that time she has had any connection with a Russian spy net." Foote knew this was a flat-out lie. He was willing to tell MI6 all about Soviet espionage, but he was not prepared to betray his old friend. And his efforts to protect her did not end there.

The German communist Fred Uhlman had played a role in Foote's recruitment back in 1938, when he put Ursula in touch with his former comrades in arms from the Spanish Civil War. Nine years later, he answered the door of his Hampstead home. "In front of him stood an agitated individual he did not immediately recognize and took for a beggar or a sick man." It was his old comrade, Footie. "He refused to come in, trembled and stammered incoherently: 'Len and Sonya, great danger, not to work, destroy everything.' Then he ran away." Uhlman passed an urgent message to Ursula describing this strange visit.

Foote's frantic words meant little to Uhlman, but to Ursula they spelled calamity. Her former collaborator must have gone over to the other side. Doubtless he had spilled the beans about their work in Switzerland, but out of residual loyalty and a "British sense of fair play" he had "risked a secret warning before the security officials could visit our house." He had not betrayed her. Ursula's agents never did. But he had brought the British spy hunters almost to her door.

Inside the GRU, Foote's disappearance sparked consternation and recrimination. Major Poliakova was sacked instantly, and then disappeared. All Foote's intelligence contacts, most important Ursula, were now compromised. The Center had already severed contact with her accidentally. Now the disconnection was intentional. Sonya was on her own.

Ursula waited for MI5 to turn up. She did not have to wait long.

Milicent Bagot's long-held suspicions were confirmed: Ursula Beurton was, or had been, a Soviet spy. She went back over the letters Ursula had sent to her family from Switzerland. One, written to her sister-in-law Marguerite in 1940, looked, on closer examination, distinctly dubious. "Except knitting (which is not my strong side) one is not allowed to do much here," Ursula had written. "But reading an appeal for getting ready for blood transmission, I replied. They examined me and found that I have very useful blood, and it can serve all different blood groups." Bagot suspected the letter contained a secret message: "blood transmission" was code for "radio transmissions," and the reference to "different groups" was interpreted as a hidden clue that Ursula was training others as radio operators. MI5 concluded: "Cryptic passages appear to refer to secret political activities."

A subject of hitherto tepid interest to Bagot's bosses was suddenly white-hot. The case was taken out of Milicent's hands, and Sir Percy Sillitoe, the new director general of MI5 and a former police chief, took over. Letters to and from The Firs were intercepted and closely scrutinized; the telephones of Ursula's siblings were tapped; Ursula's bank statements were combed for evidence of suspicious money movements. Len was now working as a machine fitter at the Northern Aluminium Company in Banbury, where MI5 had an informant, a former policeman named Richard Kerley. When Len was at his workstation, Kerley opened Len's briefcase in the staff cloakroom and reported that it contained "various kinds of books and leaflets of communist propaganda." Discreet local inquiries revealed nothing out of the ordinary in her behavior, and some in MI5 wondered how Ursula could possibly have time to spy since "her hands are fairly full with domestic duties."

It was impossible to put The Firs under direct surveillance, since any stranger turning up in a remote village like Great Rollright would have been spotted at once. The local policeman was told to keep a special watch on the Beurtons, and the chief constable of the Oxfordshire County Constabulary, Lieutenant Colonel Herman Rutherford, was secretly briefed on the case: "We hope through the medium of your observation and our investigation to find out some more about their activities so that we can determine whether or not they are engaged in espionage at the present time." Colonel Rutherford "expressed great interest" in the case. This was an understatement. Rutherford was wildly overexcited. The prospect of digging a communist spy out of Great Rollright was simply thrilling, and the chief constable wanted to arrest her in person.

There was no time to waste. "Ursula, if not already regarded by the Russians as 'blown,' will undoubtedly be so when Foote's defection to the British is known," MI5 warned. "The possibility cannot be excluded that she came here with a mission." She should be questioned at once, "preferably before the Russians have had time to inform her of Foote's fate."

The best person for the job was Milicent Bagot. Instead, the case was handed over to William "Jim" Skardon, former police inspector, head of the surveillance squad known as the "Watchers," and the country's "foremost exponent" of cross-examination. Skardon read Ursula's file with relish: soon MI5's grand inquisitor would be bending his steps to Great Rollright to break her.

CHAPTER 23

A VERY
TOUGH NUT

I N THE SUMMER OF 1947, URSULA'S PARENTS CAME TO STAY
at The Firs. She did not tell them of her fears. Berta was pale and
weak. One night, at 2:00 A.M., Ursula heard groans coming from
their bedroom. "Mother was having a heart attack." Through the
thin walls Ursula heard her cry out: "Oh my little boy." "She was
thinking of Jürgen, her eldest, whom she had loved most of all her
children." Great Rollright's only public telephone, on the village
green, was out of order. Ursula pedaled fast through the darkness to
Chipping Norton and woke the doctor, who drove her back in his
car. "It was too late." Ursula's relationship with her mother had always been confrontational, but her death was a profound blow. Berta
was buried in the churchyard at Great Rollright. After forty-five
years of marriage, in good times and bad, Robert Kuczynski was
devastated. Ursula persuaded him to remain at The Firs.

A few weeks later a letter arrived from Victor Hamburger. "I
have a bit of good news: Rudi is alive." Victor had received a postcard from one Maria Jablonska, a Polish woman from Danzig recently released from the Gulag. "I have returned home from Russia
and I am happy to be able to tell you that your brother Rudolf is
alive. He is very homesick after his family and mostly after Misha
please write by return of postcard and I will give you more details."
Victor's letter continued: "You can imagine how happy we all are . . .
of course we must give up almost all hope of seeing him again in the

next few years." Ursula debated whether to tell Michael that his father was a prisoner in Russia. "She told me in a very roundabout way, but said he was 'in exile,'" Michael remembered. "She did not say where."

MI5 read the letter with interest and passed word to John Cimperman of the FBI that Hamburger was alive and incarcerated in a Russian labor camp. Colonel Joe Spencer, the British security officer who had interrogated Rudi in Tehran before handing him over to the Soviets, was also informed: "It appears the kind Russian reception which he told you he expected was not forthcoming, and he still has five years to serve in his concentration camp."

Ursula was comforted by the news, but it brought fresh uncertainties: What cruelties had poor Rudi suffered? How much longer would he remain a prisoner of the Soviet Union? Would he ever see their son again?

As summer waned, Ursula mourned her mother, feared for Rudi, yearned for some supportive signal from the Center, pondered Foote's secret message, and waited for the knock on the door that would herald the arrival of MI5's bloodhounds.

It came at exactly 1:20 on the afternoon of Saturday, September 13, 1947.

Ursula opened the door to find a policeman on the doorstep flanked by two men in civilian clothes. The policeman removed his helmet and announced himself as "Detective Constable Herbert of Chipping Norton police station." His companions were introduced as "Mr. Saville" (Michael Serpell of MI5) and "Mr. Sneddon"—in reality Jim Skardon, MI5's fabled interrogator.

"These gentlemen would like to talk to you, Mrs. Burton. May we come in?"

Robert Kuczynski was reading a magazine in the sitting room. He rose and "gracefully bowed himself out." After showing Ursula his police badge, Detective Herbert also departed. The two men perched awkwardly on the settee. Ursula took in her uninvited guests.

Serpell, an "expert in communist subversion," was acutely embarrassed to be interrogating a housewife in her apron. Skardon, however, might have been dressed for the part of spycatcher in chief: he wore a gray mackintosh and trilby, along with a thin, unpersuasive moustache and a faintly sardonic expression—disguise for the fact that he had very little idea what he was doing. "A dapper, pipe-smoking former policeman, Skardon had a high opinion of his own abilities," according to one colleague, which he strongly encouraged others to share. He did not like women and refused to allow female officers to take part in surveillance operations since this might expose their male colleagues to "extramarital temptations." He was ponderous, punctilious, polite, and, as chief watcher, startlingly unobservant. "He epitomized, in his manner, the world of sensible middle-class values—tea in the afternoons and lace curtains," a cast of mind that was to prove highly ineffective against hard-boiled Soviet spies. He would interview Kim Philby ten times, and declared himself more convinced of his innocence at the end than he had been at the start. He interviewed Anthony Blunt on eleven occasions over a thirteen-year period and cleared him every time, fooled by Blunt's "upper class bluster." He also exonerated John Cairncross, another of the Cambridge Five, and Edith Tudor-Hart, who had first recommended Philby to the KGB. For a celebrated spycatcher, he was remarkably bad at catching spies.

Skardon's first mistake was to underestimate his quarry. "Mrs. Beurton is a somewhat unimpressive type with frowsy unkempt hair, perceptibly greying, and of rather untidy appearance." His second error was to reveal his hand. "You were a Russian agent for a long time, until the Finnish war disillusioned you," Skardon declared. "Without pausing for breath," he went on: "We know that you haven't been active in England and we haven't come to arrest you."

At a stroke, Skardon had exposed the weakness of MI5's position. Ursula's espionage in Switzerland had been aimed at Germany; she could only be held to account if she had spied in Britain, against Britain or her allies, and Skardon had just revealed he had not a scrap of evidence she had done so.

"This 'psychological' attempt to take me by surprise was so funny and inept, and so far from throwing me off balance, that I almost burst out laughing."

"Would you like a cup of tea?" she asked. "Shall I fetch my husband?"

Ursula called Len in from the garden and put the kettle on, knowing she already had the upper hand. If she simply stonewalled, then Mr. Sneddon would have nothing to go on; and nothing was exactly what she intended to give him.

Len entered the sitting room. "Beurton looks uncommonly young even for his 33 years," Skardon wrote. "But he was completely overshadowed by his wife who quite dominates the household."

Once tea was served, Skardon resumed. "I went straight into the attack and told Mrs. Beurton we had a vast amount of information in our possession and we required her cooperation to help clear up ambiguities." The evidence, he hinted darkly, came from a "leakage from the Russian Intelligence Service."

Ursula smiled sweetly. "I do not think I can cooperate. I do not intend to tell lies, and therefore prefer not to answer questions."

Skardon had never come across a woman like this before. He liked them tidy and meek. "It is fair to say right away by the stand that she took she tacitly admitted that she had worked for the Soviet Intelligence in the past. The manner in which she did so was a credit to her earlier training, for every possible piece of cajolery, artifice and guile that could be was employed, without any success whatsoever."

Skardon pressed on. "We know you became disillusioned with communism after the invasion of Finland by the Soviet Union. We know you are a loyal British subject and would not engage in any blameworthy enterprise here. You have nothing to fear. We know you have not been guilty of anything in this country. Since you have recognized the real worth of communism, why not cooperate and tell us about your time in Switzerland?"

Again, Ursula deflected him.

"I confirmed my loyalty, but said that did not oblige me to talk about my life before I became a British citizen. I replied that while I had experienced disappointments, I could not describe myself as anti-communist. Besides, I was of the opinion that there was no contradiction between being a loyal British citizen and holding left-wing views."

Skardon was frustrated. It is impossible to demonstrate that you are a champion interrogator if someone refuses to answer your questions. "She made no denial whatever, repeatedly sheltering behind the rock of 'non-cooperation.'"

Skardon turned his attention, "somewhat sourly," to Len: "We know about your close acquaintance with Allan [*sic*] Foote."

"Footie?" said Len, as if half recalling a name from the distant past. "Oh yes. What is he doing these days?"

Skardon's thinly genial manner was evaporating fast. Ursula offered more tea, and asked if she might be excused for a few minutes as she was baking a cake for a children's party to celebrate Peter's fourth birthday.

Left alone with what they perceived to be "the weaker vessel," Skardon and Serpell went to work on Len. "We broke into Beurton's taciturnity, but in spite of every inducement we did no more than elicit from him that he met Mrs. Beurton in Brighton in 1936." Len claimed he had bumped into her again "quite by chance" in Switzerland, "as one meets people in the Prix-Unis [*sic*]."

Skardon was now properly peeved. "After a longish interval Mrs. Beurton returned, still in an uncooperative frame of mind. We used every conceivable argument with her [but] she said that even to explain why she was not cooperative would be to deal with the past, and she preferred to say nothing rather than to mislead."

Skardon told Ursula that her "loyalty to her former employers" would not be reciprocated; she replied that "her loyalties were to ideals rather than people." He warned that some of her family might "come under suspicion" if she did not come clean; she "preserved a Slav-like indifference."

After nearly three hours of fruitless jousting over the teacups, Skardon rose and stiffly announced that they would return the next day "in the hope that upon consideration she would change her attitude."

She did not.

"Once more, all the advantages of cooperation and, by inference, the dangers of reticence, were detailed to her, but she remained adamant."

Only once did her guard slip. Foote had candidly admitted to committing perjury in the Swiss courts, by falsely testifying that

Rudi Hamburger had committed adultery with Brigitte in a London hotel in order to secure Ursula's divorce. Skardon wrote: "Mr. Serpell very skilfully worried Mrs. Beurton by using the word 'divorce' repeatedly." Ursula and Len exchanged surreptitious glances. "There is no doubt that this dissolution of her marriage is a weak chink in her armour, but the papers appear to be in order, and there seems little justification for an all-out attempt to invalidate the Beurton–Hamburger marriage and throw her back to German nationality."

The second day of interrogation ended like the first, in stalemate. As they left, Serpell attempted some small talk, admiring Ursula's roses blooming over the front door. "It is beautiful here. I shouldn't mind living like this."

Ursula grinned. "That could be arranged. I am letting rooms."

Skardon wrote up an irritable report of the interrogation.

We got little positive information. There is reason to believe that Mrs. Beurton gave up her agency for the Russians on ideological grounds when they behaved so badly, from an anti-fascist point of view, at the beginning of the war. She is quite clearly fanatically anti-fascist and agreed to some extent that she was disappointed with the Russian policy of 1939/40, commenting that many people lose faith in Governments, but retain their political beliefs. There is one gleam of light in this rather abject failure to make Mrs. Beurton talk. She agreed that if for any reason she changed her mind she would communicate with us through Detective Herbert at Chipping Norton. There is just a chance, though remote, that she may take this opportunity. The good the interview can have done may be to strengthen the desire of the Beurtons to have nothing more to do with intelligence work. We are reasonably satisfied that they are not at present engaged in espionage, and there is no reason to suppose that they have been for some time.

Sir Percy Sillitoe wrote to Colonel Rutherford of the Oxfordshire police, dashing his hopes of a dramatic arrest. "The interrogation was disappointing, no fresh light being thrown on the lives of these people . . . there is no reason to suspect them of present or even recent espionage activities, although both are communists."

MI5 believed the fiction that Ursula had given up spying back in 1940. To catch her, Skardon would need hard evidence that she had spied in Britain, and he did not have any. Yet.

Ursula was more rattled by the encounter with MI5 than she showed. Robert Kuczynski was also deeply worried, and suffering from the cancer that would kill him within a few months; he rushed back to London to tell Brigitte what had happened. News that Ursula had been interrogated flew round the family. Jürgen had already moved back to Berlin, and he now wrote urging Ursula to come and join him in building the new communist state of East Germany. "Try as soon as possible to come and visit us. You must see the situation for yourself and then decide about everything and make your plans accordingly."

Ursula was tempted by Jürgen's suggestion. The unpleasant Mr. Sneddon had been seen off, but for how long? Len was miserable, bored by his job at the aluminum factory and hardly sleeping. The artillery fire he had been exposed to in Spain had left him with raging headaches. "His depressions became more frequent. He withdrew into silence for days on end." Though she continued to check the dead-drop site, there seemed no hope of the GRU reestablishing contact. "My life had run aground."

But at precisely the moment when she began to imagine a new existence, Ursula's past reappeared in the distinctive shape of the woman who had first brought her into the world of espionage. By chance she discovered that Agnes Smedley was in Britain, living just a few miles away in Oxford.

Smedley's restless and angry campaign on behalf of international communism was coming to an end. In 1941, she had returned to the United States and taken up residence in the Yaddo writers' colony in upstate New York to write a biography of the Chinese Red Army general Zhu De, while continuing to work, in the words of the *Chicago Tribune,* as "the principal apologist for communist China." The FBI was watching. She was forced out of Yaddo in 1948. A few months later a U.S. Army intelligence report identified her as a key figure in Richard Sorge's spy ring, unleashing a slew of front-page headlines around the country: "Army Says Soviet Spies Got Tokyo War Secrets; Accuses Woman Writer." She threatened to sue—a dangerous tactic, given that she was guilty. The McCarthyite communist hunters were in full cry. She embraced her own martyrdom: "The reptile press burned another witch at the stake." Agnes's health had been undermined by her years in the Chinese war zones, and while her heart was ready for another fight, her mind and body were not. She booked a one-way passage to England and took refuge in the Oxford home of her friend Margaret Sloss.

Ursula longed to see Agnes again, but feared doing so might lead MI5 to her old friend. "An irresponsible visit from me might have jeopardized her politically. In any case, I did not know how she might have changed over the years. How should I approach her?" They might both be under MI5 surveillance. If she was spotted making contact with an accused Soviet spy, that would only reinforce their suspicions. Should she take the risk of linking up with Agnes, with all that this might entail, or avoid contact with her oldest friend, her first mentor? Once again, her heart pulled Ursula one way, and her spycraft another. Back in China, at the moment their relationship ruptured, Smedley had accused Ursula of putting personal issues ahead of her commitment to the cause. Her decision now proved that the reverse was true: she decided she must not, and would not, try to reestablish contact with the woman who had recruited her. Agnes Smedley had ceased spying years earlier, but Ursula had not: that gulf was unbridgeable.

Other voices floated back from her past, impossibly distant now. From Shanghai, Johann Patra sent beseeching letters in fractured English, urging Ursula to write to the German emigrant relief organization in China supporting his claim to be a refugee from Nazism who should be repatriated to Germany. The GRU had severed contact with him too, and the rule against contact between spies no longer applied. He was working as a mechanic, earning barely enough to avoid starvation.

"Foreigners are leaving China for various countries: North and

South America, Australia, Russia, Europe etc. The UNRRA [United Nations Relief and Rehabilitation Administration] would finance my trip to another country if I wish to go. What do you think of this? After all, your advice is important! If I were to go to another country, to South or Central America say, I might possibly earn more money, and I should be able to help you. I have also learned to think in practical terms. You are really more tied to Europe than I am." Patra explained that he had married a German woman named Luisa and they had adopted a child. "Can you think of it that I have a wife and child? You could never understand that. You thought that I am more of stone. I like him just as if he would be mine. . . . I gave him the name Peter. The economic and political situation here is very bad, and the time for drastic changes will have to come. I should very much like to see you. I am so proud of you. You are happy in important matters." She wrote to the emigrant organization as Patra requested, but heard nothing back.

Robert Kuczynski died on November 25, 1947, and was buried alongside Berta in Great Rollright. The obituaries lauded a pioneering statistician. There was no mention anywhere of his secret work, through his daughter, for the USSR. Ursula was plunged into deep mourning. "We had known what to expect for some time, but all the same his death has been a great shock," she wrote to Jürgen. "Father was marvellous, right to the end." Ursula had adored and revered her father, proved herself a political force in his eyes, and recruited him into the secret world. His death severed yet another link with Britain. The appeal of a new life back in her homeland was growing. She was still only forty years old, young enough to start again. Jürgen, now living in the Soviet sector of Berlin, was pressing: "Come and visit us. . . . Once and for all give up the empty life you are living and you will easily have your choice of political work over here." Jürgen knew his letters would be read by MI5: "political work" was a euphemism for spying. She replied: "Apart from making a home for my husband and children, my life seems fairly useless. . . . Writing? How much I would love to do that. . . . I must make Len's evening meal. He is just coming off the late shift."

East Germany, occupied and administered by Soviet forces, was being fashioned into the German Democratic Republic, surrounding but not including West Berlin. A state run by German communists, and a slavish satellite of Moscow, the GDR would become a place of strict ideological conformity enforced by an all-seeing secret police force, the Stasi. But in 1948 it represented a beacon of hope for German communists. In the eyes of people like Jürgen, the "Socialist Workers' and Peasants' state" would be a Marxist-Leninist paradise, and he intended to be part of it. He urged Ursula to come too: there would be plenty of opportunities in the new Germany for faithful communist spies.

Still she hesitated. Len spoke poor German. The children were now completely English. "They loved Great Rollright." That summer, she and Len took the children to Butlin's holiday camp on the south coast. Nina described this quintessentially British postwar holiday as the "loveliest experience" she had known in her short life. "During the whole day there were loudspeaker announcements, every evening there were dances, there were roundabouts and swings. The highpoint was the beauty contest. Lovely legs and a pretty face—that was all you needed. After this visit I had a new dream—I wanted to marry Mr. Butlin, become rich and be able to take my holiday every year in such a camp." Peter made his older sister cry by telling her, "You'll be lucky to marry a rag-and-bone man." Nina was an ardent royalist, collecting every newspaper cutting about the royal family and pasting them into a large scrapbook. She particularly admired Princess Elizabeth. "When I was told to fetch a large cabbage from the garden, I screamed: 'The princess doesn't have to do such work in the garden.'" Little Peter collected Dinky toys, the miniature vehicles made from zinc alloy. Michael had won a scholarship to read philosophy at Aberdeen University. Could Ursula really remove her British children from the place they saw as home? How would they all adapt to life under communism? She had not been lying to Skardon when she spoke of her "disappointments" with communism. Tearing herself away from Britain to a land she had last seen twenty years before seemed like madness. Great Rollright soothed her. "If I felt low, I would just wander to a favourite spot nearby where I had a view across the fields and hills."

In 1948, she applied for a temporary visa to enter Berlin, but was told visas were still available only to visitors on official business. Jürgen came up with an alternative plan: he would be traveling to Czechoslovakia early the next year on academic business and suggested they meet there instead. The orphaned Ursula felt an urgent need to see her older brother, lay out her troubles, and get some "good advice." She flew to Prague on January 18, 1949. MI5 alerted the MI6 station chief in the city that she was on her way: "Ursula Beurton was an active espionage character in Switzerland during the war . . . let me know if she comes to your notice in Czechoslovakia." The reunion was a disappointment. Jürgen was busy with self-important meetings and could spare her just an hour of his time. He was all business. "Jürgen never had any time for soul-baring or displays of emotion." Ursula should return to Berlin, he insisted, but obtain Moscow's approval first. "It would be very difficult for you to stay in Germany without the Centre's agreement." Jürgen never broke the habit of telling his sisters what to do. Against espionage rules, she wrote a letter to the director of the GRU, noting that she had not heard from the Center for two years, describing the dead-drop site beyond the first crossroads after the railway crossing near Great Rollright, and requesting permission to come to Germany. She signed the letter "Sonya," sealed it inside an envelope addressed to the military attaché, and then, having ensured she was not being followed, delivered it by hand to the Soviet embassy in Prague. Then she returned to England and waited.

The Cold War battle lines were redrawn with grim clarity on August 29, 1949, when the Soviet Union conducted its first secret nuclear weapons test in Kazakhstan. U.S. weather reconnaissance aircraft picked up the radioactive debris, and, on September 23, President Truman announced: "We have evidence that within recent weeks an atomic explosion occurred in the USSR." Soviet atomic scientists had achieved remarkable results thanks to their spies inside the Manhattan Project, chief among them Klaus Fuchs. Ursula read of the bomb test and felt a surge of pride. The Soviet bomb was virtually a copy of the American one. In the United States the successful test was code-named "Joe-1" in jocular reference to Stalin, but the intelligence community was shocked by the swift progress of the Soviet atomic weapons program. The CIA had estimated the Russians would not develop the bomb before 1953 at the earliest; MI6's estimate was even longer. Overnight, America's assumed nuclear monopoly had evaporated. Pressure to develop the hydrogen bomb increased. Hawks in the U.S. administration, including General Curtis "Old Iron Pants" LeMay of the U.S. Air Force, had urged hitting the Soviets with atomic bombs before they built their own, to ensure American global hegemony. Now any attack would invite an equally devastating response: the fragile, terrifying era of mutually assured destruction was under way. Spies like Ursula Beurton and Klaus Fuchs claimed to be safeguarding military equilibrium by stealing nuclear secrets from one side to give to the other. They believed they were making the world safer, while making communism stronger.

Inside MI5, the Ursula Beurton case remained open. Every few months, a desultory discussion took place about whether to send investigators back to The Firs. "Ursula Beurton should be re-interrogated," wrote Colonel James Robertson of the counterespionage branch. "I believe individuals of this type ought to be interrogated repeatedly until it is established beyond doubt that nothing more can be extracted from them." But Skardon was disinclined to bother: "I have given considerable thought to the possibility of re-interrogating Ursula Beurton . . . nothing has arisen recently to make such an effort likely to be more productive, and as it is impossible to assume a successful outcome, I do not feel disposed to reopen the matter." It was agreed that the best thing to do about Mrs. Beurton was nothing at all: "She has been once interrogated with no result and is a very tough nut."

The winter of 1949 was bitterly cold. Len skidded off his motorbike and badly broke an arm and a leg. The doctor said he would be off work for at least eight months. The aluminum factory took the opportunity to sack him. Her small legacy from her father was running out. Len sunk deeper into depression. Nina's pet mouse froze to death on the windowsill of The Firs. The water pipes burst. Bored, baffled by the GRU's continued silence, uncertain of the future, Ursula found her espionage career was in deep freeze.

One morning in late January, more out of habit than hope, Ursula cycled yet again to the dead-drop site. The road was icy and treacherous as she followed the familiar route, under the railway and past the crossroads. She leaned her bike against the fourth tree and reached into the root. Her hand closed around a small package. With freezing fingers she tore it open: cash and a letter from the Center granting permission for her to go to Germany. After three years, Sonya had come in from the cold.

Ursula was keen to see her homeland again, but not certain she wished to live there. Michael, now nearly nineteen years old, was in his second year of university in Scotland. Even if Len agreed to leave, he could not travel with his leg in a cast. She made unhurried preparations for a holiday in Berlin. Visa restrictions had now been relaxed and she was told there would be little problem obtaining the necessary permit. There was no hurry. She had evaded the Chinese and Japanese secret police, the Swiss security service, and the Gestapo. There was little to fear from the plodding Mr. Sneddon and his sad moustache. MI5 clearly knew nothing of her recent espionage.

On February 3, 1950, Ursula picked up the newspaper from the doorstep of The Firs and felt a lurch of "shock and sorrow" as she read the front-page headline: "German Atomic Scientist Arrested." Klaus Fuchs, the scientist who gave Russia the bomb, had been caught.

Four years earlier, Fuchs had returned from the United States to take up a post as head of theoretical physics at the Atomic Energy Research Establishment at Harwell in Oxfordshire, where scientists were designing a nuclear reactor to produce energy for civilian use. A second, secret agenda was the production of plutonium for making atomic weapons independently of the United States. Fuchs was a pivotal member of the team.

As a GRU officer, Ursula was unaware of his return, for Fuchs was now a KGB asset. For a time he eschewed spying, but after a year back in Britain he received instructions to meet a KGB contact, Alexander Feklisov, in the Nag's Head pub in Wood Green, North London, carrying a copy of the *Tribune*. The contact, holding a red book, would bring over a beer and say: "Stout is not so good, I prefer lager." To which Fuchs should reply: "I think Guinness is best."

From then on, every few months, Fuchs met Feklisov at various

London pubs. Over Guinness and lager, he handed over a fresh trove of secret scientific intelligence: Britain's atomic bomb planning, the construction of experimental reactors, pages of notes on plutonium production, and precise calculations of the nuclear tests that would enable Soviet scientists to assess the Western nuclear stockpile. He also described key features of the hydrogen bomb being developed in the United States—information that prompted the Soviet Union to work on its own "super-bomb."

Fuchs's KGB handlers went overboard with the spycraft. If he needed an emergency rendezvous, for example, he was required to throw a copy of the soft porn magazine *Men Only* over a garden wall in Kew on the corner of Stanmore and Kew Roads, between the third and fourth trees, and write a message on the tenth page, then place a chalk mark on the fence on the north side of Holmesdale Road opposite a tree at the eastern end of the road, which would indicate to the occupier of the house on Stanmore Road that there was something for him in the garden. It would have been easier to memorize the formulae for plutonium production.

Fuchs had been scrupulous in following the rules. He made no mistakes. Another routine MI5 review of his record uncovered nothing incriminating.

Fuchs was brought down because a breakthrough by American cryptographers allowed the decoding, at least partially, of thousands of wartime messages sent by the KGB and GRU. The spy hunters could peer back into the past. The historical wireless traffic, code-named "Venona," revealed that the Soviets had deployed a senior mole inside the Manhattan Project, and by July 1949, the month before the first Soviet bomb test, British and American investigators had concluded that the spy must be Klaus Fuchs. The Venona traffic was too secret to be revealed in court. Tapping Fuchs's phone, intercepting his letters, and intense surveillance produced nothing. The only way to get a conviction would be to extract a confession. MI5 sent in Jim Skardon.

By this time Fuchs had been a spy for eight years, and the strain was telling. He had come to admire Britain greatly. At exactly the moment MI5 picked up the scent, he broke off contact with his Soviet handler.

On December 21, 1949, Skardon confronted Fuchs in his office at Harwell. He used the same blunt approach he had attempted with Ursula. "I am in possession of precise information which shows you have been guilty of espionage on behalf of the Soviet Union." Fuchs thought for a moment and replied ambiguously: "I don't think so . . . perhaps you will tell me what the evidence is?" Since the MI5 sleuth was not privy to Venona, Skardon could not. After four hours, the interrogator had got nowhere, and was uncertain of Fuchs's guilt. After a second interview, he decided he was innocent. A third was inconclusive. Skardon was maintaining his unfailing capacity to miss the spy under his very nose.

But on January 23, 1950, Fuchs asked Mr. Sneddon to come to his home in Harwell.

"He was obviously under considerable mental stress," Skardon wrote. "I suggested that he should unburden his mind and clear his conscience by telling me the full story." Fuchs demurred, and instead of pressing home his advantage Skardon suggested they break off and have lunch in a pub. "During the meal he seemed to be resolving the matter and to be considerably abstracted." By the time they got back to the house, Fuchs had made up his mind. "He said that he had decided it would be in his best interests to answer my questions." This breakthrough would later be cited as evidence of Skardon's genius as an interrogator. In fact, Fuchs simply decided to tell all with no further prompting. Indeed, Skardon was astonished when Fuchs confessed that he had spent the previous eight years spying for the Soviet Union, "passing information relating to atomic energy at irregular but frequent meetings."

Three days later, Fuchs signed a ten-page confession in Room 055 of the War Office. Like Fuchs's espionage, his decision to confess was framed as an act of principle, with an echo from his father's pulpit: "There are certain standards of moral behaviour which are in you and that you cannot disregard. . . . I still believe in communism. But not as it is practised in Russia today."

Fuchs naïvely believed that, having got the truth off his chest, he would be allowed to continue working at Harwell. He was shocked to be taken into custody.

The arrest of Klaus Fuchs made the front pages of every newspaper in Britain, including Ursula's *Oxford Times*. She felt a chill of pure fear as she continued reading: the German scientist had passed atomic secrets to Moscow by "meeting a foreign woman with black hair in Banbury." Even the inept Mr. Sneddon, surely, could not miss so obvious a clue.

Ursula was now in greater danger than at any time since Olga Muth's betrayal. In urgent conclave with Len, she discussed the implications of Fuchs's arrest. Since Detective Constable Herbert of Chipping Norton had not yet turned up with an arrest warrant, Fuchs had probably not revealed her name. Perhaps he did not know it. "I had never been in his home nor he in mine," she wrote. "I had never spent the night in Birmingham where he worked, so that no hotel registration could be found." Fuchs may not have betrayed her yet, but he had plainly divulged some details of their meetings, and under oath in a courtroom he would surely reveal more. In the meantime, MI5 would be assembling clues. "I expected my arrest any day." The Fuchs trial was due to open on February 28. Mr. Sneddon would be coming for her very soon. But getting out of Britain would not be easy.

Obtaining a German visa would take at least ten days if MI5 did not block it. She told the two younger children they were going on holiday. In Aberdeen, Michael was unaware that his mother was preparing to defect to East Germany. Len would have to stay behind and join them when his leg healed, if he was not in prison.

A year earlier, to bring in some extra cash, Ursula had started letting the spare room to a young couple, Geoffrey and Madeleine Greathead. Geoffrey was a farmworker, while Madeleine worked as a cleaner in the home of the local squire. Mrs. Greathead was a cheerful presence in the house, but extremely inquisitive. That February, she noticed Ursula seemed particularly "harassed" and had burned a large pile of papers in the yard. "We were never allowed into the cellar. She would ask me if I minded looking after the children when she went to London, which she did quite often." Madeleine loved to gossip. "We began to feel suspicious. We would talk about our suspicions, but folk would look at you as if it was all made up." Madeleine liked Ursula—"she showed me how to make ice cream and sponge cakes"—but she sensed there was something strange afoot and decided to keep an eye on her landlady and find out what she was up to. Ursula had spent the previous twenty years on the alert for signs of surveillance; she immediately realized that Madeleine's questions were more than idle curiosity. Once again, she was living with a spy under her own roof.

She bought three air tickets to Hamburg. In four large American kit bags, she packed clothes and supplies for herself and the children. Her arrangements recalled the moment, twenty years earlier, when she had assembled an escape kit for herself and baby Michael in Shanghai, and awaited a signal from Richard Sorge to flee for the communist-held Chinese interior. Her nerves stretched to the snapping point, she scanned the fields of Great Rollright for signs of MI5's watchers.

Skardon, meanwhile, was slowly and methodically grilling Fuchs in his cell in Brixton Prison. The extent of his espionage in both the United Kingdom and the United States shocked intelligence chiefs on both sides of the Atlantic. Fuchs did not deny giving the Soviet Union the atomic bomb. But, like Foote before him, he did not tell MI5 everything. On February 8, two days before Fuchs was formally arraigned on charges of violating the Official Secrets Act, Skardon laid out dozens of photographs of "individuals who had been known to have been or suspected of being engaged in intelligence activities" in the United Kingdom, and asked Fuchs if he could identify any of them. One was a photo of Ursula Beurton. Fuchs put several pictures to one side, murmuring that "the face seemed familiar." But he skipped over the photo of Ursula. As he did over those of Jürgen Kuczynski and Hans Kahle. Six days later, Skardon was back, pressing Fuchs for more details of his Soviet handlers. "The second contact," Skardon duly recorded, "was a woman whom FUCHS met in a country lane near Banbury, Oxfordshire. . . . This woman was in his opinion an alien, although she spoke good English, this being the language in which his espionage transactions were carried out. He has described her as a short, unprepossessing woman in her middle 30s. Although Fuchs has been shown a large number of possible photographs, he has been unable to identify any of them as that of the woman in question."

MI5's failure to make the obvious connection to Ursula Beurton was, with hindsight, a counterintelligence blunder of historic proportions. Fuchs had admitted meeting a foreign, female Soviet spy in Banbury; a few months earlier, Jim Skardon had interrogated a foreign, female Soviet spy just ten miles away in Great Rollright. Indeed, there was only one foreign, female Soviet spy on MI5's radar. And yet it concluded: "Without further information it seems improbable that this contact will be identified."

On February 18, Ursula's application for a permit to "visit friends" in Germany was returned by the Home Office stamped "No Objection." The first major hurdle had been cleared. But her name was on the MI5 watch list. Sooner or later, a very loud alarm bell would sound inside the Security Service, a notice would be sent to all airports, and the door would slam shut. How long that might take was a matter of guesswork. The wheels of British bureaucracy tend to turn slowly, or at least unpredictably. Village gossip, by contrast, can travel with almost magical speed. The children were talking openly about the "holiday" they were taking—in the middle of school term. What kind of housewife goes abroad leaving her husband to fend for himself with a broken leg? Four big kit bags seemed a lot of luggage for a woman and two small children going on a short vacation. Word of the strange goings-on at The Firs might already have reached the lounge bar of The Unicorn. From there it could travel, almost instantly, to the ears of Detective Constable Herbert.

Madeleine Greathead was taking a close interest in Ursula's travel plans and asking a lot of questions. Ursula resolved to divert the lodger's attention and use her to spread some disinformation. "One day Ursula asked me if I could help her with some pressing as she was returning to Germany the next day to claim her father's estate." With the nosy lodger out of the way attending to a mountain of washing and ironing, Ursula made her final preparations. She extracted the transmitter from the cellar, wrapped it in sacking, and buried it in the undergrowth. Today, somewhere in Great Rollright woods, lies a rusting homemade shortwave radio, a spy's buried legacy. Then she carefully packed up the few mementos she would take with her: the Chinese prints from Shanghai, a postcard from Switzerland, and a framed photograph of Richard Sorge. Finally she climbed on her bicycle and rode toward Banbury, performing the usual countersurveillance routine, doubling back twice to ensure she was not being followed. At the hollow tree root beyond the crossing, she inserted a message for the GRU, explaining that she was quitting her post and slipping away to Berlin. Then Agent Sonya cycled home for the last time.

The following afternoon, Len loaded the kit bags into the boot of the Chipping Norton taxi. Ursula embraced him tightly, wondering, once more, if she would ever see him again. "Farewell or goodbye—we did not know which it would be." Nina and Peter were fizzing with excitement at the prospect of riding on an airplane. They hugged Mrs. Greathead and Penny the cat, climbed into the backseat, and waved to Len through the back window until he disappeared from view.

As she waited on the hard benches in the departure lounge of London airport (now Heathrow), the children happily playing poker dice at her feet, Ursula stared rigidly at the doors, a bubble of anxiety steadily rising in her stomach. At any moment the police must surely burst in and arrest her. The trial of Klaus Fuchs would begin the next day, and he had probably already identified the "girl from Banbury." Even now Detective Constable Herbert, alerted by the suspicious Mrs. Greathead, might be picking up the telephone to MI5. Britain had adopted her, and now she was fleeing the land she had come to love. The next few minutes would decide whether she disappeared to a country she no longer knew or spent the next decade or more in a British prison, condemned as a notorious communist spy. She resolved to say nothing if she was arrested, admit nothing. She would maintain the discipline of a trained Soviet intelligence officer. Colonel Kuczynski would not crack. But what would Michael do when his mother's face was splashed across every newspaper? If she and Len were convicted, what would become of the children?

She scanned the crowd for a man in a trilby, flanked by policemen, approaching with a smile of triumph beneath his weak moustache.

But Mr. Sneddon never appeared.

The air hostess welcomed them aboard, more concerned with a group of inebriated Italian football fans than the innocuous woman holding tight to the hands of her two chattering children. From the window seat, Ursula gazed out on the rain-spattered runway, where a military plane was taxiing for takeoff. Instinctively, she memorized its markings. Then the door closed on England for the last time.

On February 27, 1950, Ursula and her children flew to Germany. She would not return for another forty years.

CHAPTER 24

RUTH WERNER

O N MARCH 1, 1950, AFTER A TRIAL LASTING NINETY minutes, Klaus Fuchs was found guilty of "communicating information to a potential enemy" and given the maximum sentence of fourteen years. Jim Skardon visited him in HM Prison Stafford a few months later and handed over a photograph of a woman with "a very untidy mop of hair." (Ursula's unladylike scruffiness never ceased to irk him.) "In placing the photograph of Ursula Beurton before Fuchs I said to him: 'This is a photograph which I have already shown to you earlier.' And he immediately said: 'That is the woman at Banbury.' He has no doubt that she is the contact but is unable to say why he failed to identify her when the photograph was placed before him on the previous occasion." Ursula was beyond Mr. Sneddon's grasp.

The spy hunters refused to believe she had gone. MI5 chief Sir Percy Sillitoe wrote to Colonel Rutherford of the Oxford Police: "I am anxious to establish the present whereabouts of Ursula Beurton. . . . She intended to visit friends in Berlin, and it is of course possible that she has not returned." Detective Herbert of Chipping Norton reported that The Firs now stood empty, all the furniture had been sold, and Len Beurton had disappeared. To add to MI5's discomfort, confirmation of Ursula's escape came from the FBI. John Cimperman wrote an angry note to John Marriott: "Some time ago you were asked to have her interviewed [but] it was not deemed desirable. Information has now been received to the effect that Ursula

Beurton has left England to return to Germany." Far too late, MI5 instructed border control to intercept Ursula if she entered or left Britain. "Subject is an active communist and is connected with persons engaged in espionage on behalf of a foreign power; black hair, brown eyes; last known location: Berlin; Occupation: Housewife."

Embarrassed by its failure to seize Ursula in time, MI5 later propagated a myth that she had "bolted back to Germany in 1947." Dick White, the head of MI5, told his biographer that she had fled two days after the interview with Skardon (knowing full well she had remained in the United Kingdom for another two and a half years).

The East Berlin that Ursula returned to in February 1950 was a city mutilated by war, with piles of rubble in the streets and the blackened hulks of burned-out buildings. There were no hotel rooms available. After just a few days, the children were asking to return to Great Rollright and wondering where Len was. Nina missed Penny the cat. Peter wanted his Dinky toys. Jürgen had informed the Soviet authorities of Ursula's arrival; he told her to be patient. She moved into a cold one-room apartment with her children and waited for the Center to make contact. "I lived in isolation." She enrolled the children in the nearest school. Speaking little German, they were teased mercilessly. During the long days, she wandered the city and pondered all that had happened to her. After the intense drama of the escape from Britain, it was as if she had arrived in a gray half-world, populated by people who had managed to survive, and nothing more. Jürgen was far too busy to help her settle in. There was little to eat and nothing to do. Yet for the first time in two decades she did not feel stalked. She had no radio transmitter to hide, no agents to contact, no need to conceal her politics. Ursula experienced a sensation she had never known before, and at first did not recognize: she felt a sort of peace.

Finally, in May, word came via Jürgen that the Center was sending an emissary. A GRU officer she did not know arrived at her door in civilian clothes and announced, rather stiffly, that he was taking her out for a "festive meal." The officer was friendly, but formal. He congratulated her on her work in China, Poland, Switzerland, and Britain, and apologized for the confusion over the dead-drop site in

Oxfordshire that had interrupted contact for so long. The world was changing fast, he explained. Comrade Stalin had warned that the capitalist West was building nuclear weapons for an attack on the Soviet Union. War was looming on the Korean peninsula. The GRU would play a vital role in the coming conflict, and there was important work to be done. When would Ursula be ready to resume her work for Soviet military intelligence?

Ursula pushed away her plate, took a deep breath, and explained that she no longer wished to be a spy.

The man from Moscow was speechless.

Looking back, Ursula could not pinpoint the moment she decided to renounce espionage. Perhaps it was Fuchs's arrest, or during the long months when the Center had left her adrift. Or perhaps it was the moment she fled Britain. Over the last four months in Berlin, lonely but unafraid, she had tasted tranquility, the calm that comes from laying down arms, an armistice of the soul. The GRU officer tried to change her mind, but she was adamant. "I wanted to live as a citizen. I told him that nothing had altered in my commitment to the Soviet Union and the work I had done, but that my nerves and powers of concentration were no longer as good as they had been. I felt that twenty years were enough."

The profession of Soviet spy is not an easy one to resign from. The GRU was a difficult club to join, and an even harder one to leave. Intelligence officers tended to depart the service when they were old, disgraced, or dead. Early retirement was not in the contract, and anyone attempting to quit was considered a potential traitor. Twenty years earlier, Sorge had darkly warned Ursula what would happen to her if she ever tried to back out. She had taken many risks for the Red Army, but the bravest of all was her determination to quit it.

Ursula had made up her mind. "I stood by my decision."

And the Center let her go. Just as she had survived the purges unscathed, so the GRU allowed her to leave its ranks in a way that no other officer would have been permitted to do. Stalin's power was founded on abject obedience, but Ursula, as in so much else, was an exception to the rule. It was a mark of her prestige that she walked away from the spying business without recrimination, reprisal, or regret.

Ursula was given a job putting out propaganda for the Press Department of the East German government. She wrote daily press releases and edited the fortnightly *Bulletin against American Imperialism*. Her boss was Gerhart Eisler, the ideological enforcer who had spied on her during her initial recruitment in Shanghai and insisted she should wear a hat.

Once again, the children adapted to a wholly new life. Nina abandoned her obsession with the British royal family and joined the Free German Youth. Peter swiftly exchanged his rural-accented English for Berlin slang. As soon as his leg healed, Len Beurton flew to Berlin, arriving in June 1950. MI5 did not try to stop him. He was employed by the East German state news service. After leaving Aberdeen a year later, Michael, an idealistic young socialist, also settled in communist East Germany. The family was reunited.

East Germany was a surveillance state, where citizens were encouraged, bribed, or forced to spy on one another. The Ministry of State Security, or Stasi, was one of the most efficient and repressive secret police forces in history, with a vast network of informers. Everyone was spied upon, and Ursula was no exception.

The initial Stasi reports on Ursula were positive, noting that she had "spent twenty years abroad carrying out confidential work for the Party." Her character was described as "modest and self-effacing . . . she is open, honest and reliable." But like everyone returning from the West, particularly Jews and anyone implicated in intelligence, an odor of suspicion hung over her. "Everyone who had been in exile in a capitalist country was deemed untrustworthy," she wrote. The Stasi demanded to know about her interrogation by MI5, the recruitment of Alexander Foote, and, oddly, Marie Ginsberg, the secretary at the League of Nations in Geneva who had helped her obtain a fake passport. Ginsberg was suspected of links to a "US–Zionist espionage organization." The Stasi noted disapprovingly that Ursula "comes from a bourgeois family background." She was summoned to testify before the Central Party Control Commission. A confidential Stasi report described her as too independent-minded:

"She has still not overcome all her petit-bourgeois tendencies, among which an individualist attitude is revealed." Ursula had made a career out of evading surveillance, and she chafed at the unremitting scrutiny of the state. She even wrote to Erich Mielke, the fearsome Stasi chief, protesting that her neighbors were being quizzed about her political reliability. "At one of the houses, the parents were not at home, so they asked the 18-year-old daughter to pass judgment on my trustworthiness and behaviour." She told Mielke: "Tell your officers to refrain from such snooping." She received an apology. But the surveillance continued.

In December 1950, MI6 contemplated "abducting the Beurtons from the eastern part of the city with the help of the CIA." The tentative plan passed through the hands of Kim Philby, who once again alerted Moscow, enabling the Soviets to "initiate appropriate defensive measures." With anti-Semitic spy hysteria rising in East Germany, British intelligence spotted another opportunity. If the regime carried out a purge of Jewish communists, then Ursula Beurton and Jürgen Kuczynski would be targets. MI5 came up with a plan to try to recruit them, or at least persuade both to redefect to the United Kingdom. On January 23, 1953, Colonel Robertson sent a note to MI6 suggesting that Ursula and Jürgen be offered a deal: safe haven in Britain and immunity from prosecution in exchange for their cooperation. "These persons are likely to possess valuable information about Russian espionage, and it is worth going to considerable lengths to get them, and with them their information. . . . We recognize that however alarmed these people may be by the uncertainty of their future under communist regimes this might be outweighed by fear of legal or other punitive action on the part of the British authorities . . . do whatever possible to let it become known to them that they have no fears on that particular score." It is unclear whether this offer was made, or how Ursula and Jürgen responded to it, since MI6 files remain closed.

In late 1953, Ursula was officially reprimanded for leaving confidential documents on her desk instead of locking them in a safe. For someone who had hidden world-changing secrets for decades, there was rich irony in being told she had committed a "gross breach of trust" by leaving out an innocuous press release. She resigned, moved briefly to a post in the Foreign Ministry, and then stopped working for the state altogether.

But Ursula's life had one more surprising chapter. In 1956, she became a full-time writer, adopting yet another name, a new vocation, and a fresh identity. Henceforth she would be Ruth Werner, novelist.

Ursula had written from earliest childhood, channeling a vivid imagination into her stories of romance and adventure. Spies and novelists are not so very different: each conjures up an imagined world and attempts to lure others into it. Some of the greatest writers of the twentieth century were also spies, including Graham Greene, Somerset Maugham, Ian Fleming, and John le Carré. In many ways Ursula's life had been a fiction, presenting one sort of person to the world, while being someone else in reality. As Ruth Werner she became, once again, another person.

Ursula went on to write fourteen books, mostly stories for children and young adults. These were labeled as fiction, but they were richly autobiographical, depicting her experiences as a young communist in Berlin, her love affairs, her life in China and Switzerland. The books were partly a ruse to circumvent the East German censors and write about her secret life, but they also fed an inner compulsion. She had always seen herself as the central character in her own rolling drama; she was a natural thriller writer, in life and on paper. Ursula was careful to disguise identities, but these tales were, in essence, true, beautifully written, and closely observed descriptions of an adventurous, incident-packed life. They sold extremely well; several were bestsellers. Ursula became far more famous as Ruth Werner, a pseudonym picked at random, than she would ever be under her own name.

In 1956, three years after Stalin's death, he was denounced by his successor, Nikita Khrushchev, and the truth about the full horror of the purges began to emerge. Ursula was appalled, and furious, to learn about Stalin's crimes and the extent of the criminal butchery. "I lost so many friends," she wrote. Back in 1937, in Moscow, she had known that innocent men and women were being murdered, including many of those closest to her, but she had not protested. To have done so would have been suicidal. Like millions of others, she had looked away and got on with her job. She suffered survivor's guilt. "Why I was left unscathed? I don't know, perhaps because the choice of so-called guilty ones was a matter of chance."

The year that Ursula switched careers and changed her name, Rudolf Hamburger finally emerged from the Gulag.

For ten years, Rudi took notes and drew sketches, recording his hunger, exhaustion, cold, boredom, and love as one of 1.5 million prisoners in the Soviet labor system. In Karaganda Labor Camp on the Kazakh steppes, Rudi met Fatima, an Iranian woman imprisoned after an unauthorized Muslim meeting in her home. She worked in the kitchens. They made love in the stores hut. "In the hasty pleasure of love we can forget the inhumanity of our long exile," he wrote. Fatima got pregnant and aborted the child. Soon after, Rudi was moved again. "She cries and her black, wet eyes accompany me until the gate is far behind me. . . . Is there still happiness, peace, humanity somewhere in the world?" he wondered. Transferred to a lumber camp in the foothills of the Urals but too weak for forestry work, the once-promising architect performed routine building maintenance. "It all appalls me," he wrote. "The insignificant tasks I am set, the barracks and barbed wire to prevent me from forgetting where I am, the hunger and the bugs. What do I have to look forward to, if I do survive through to freedom, starved, bitten by beasts, grey-haired, a creature alienated from life and work? But Fatima was right—do not give up. To give up is death." A fellow inmate received four kilos of sugar from home, sat on his bed, consumed it in a single sitting, and immediately died: suicide by sugar. In 1951, Rudi was transferred to yet another camp, whose inmates were constructing the world's largest hydroelectric power plant, and then back to the "dreaded Urals."

In 1953, Rudolf Hamburger was formally released, into an alternative captivity. He could not leave the Soviet Union. "Where do you want to go?" he was asked. He had no passport, and only his discharge papers to identify himself. "What do I know of this country after nine and a half years of hermetic seclusion? I am like a blind man asked if he wants his room painted red or blue." He wound up in the small Ukrainian city of Millerovo, managing a construction site. By now, Ursula and others knew of his whereabouts and were lobbying for his return to Germany, but Rudi did not fit into the defined bureaucratic categories, being neither a prisoner of war nor a refugee from Nazi Germany. It would take another two years before the paperwork was completed.

Finally, in July 1955, Rudi Hamburger returned to Berlin. Ursula had told her children he was "coming back after a long stay in the Soviet Union." Michael had last seen his father sixteen years earlier. Ursula also took this opportunity to explain to her daughter that her father was not Rudi, as she always believed, but a Lithuanian sailor she knew nothing about. Fifteen-year-old Nina responded primly: "Mummy, I am not at all happy that you had so many men."

Rudi had been damaged by a decade of captivity, but not destroyed. "It was not a broken man that I met, but he had changed from the picture I had of him," Ursula wrote. "Greying, slightly bowed, a brittle voice, and dazed, like a man emerging from a cellar into the light, a semi-stranger with a smile that hid a touch of melancholy." His politics unchanged, Hamburger joined the communist-dominated ruling Socialist Unity Party. "Perhaps we will develop in the future a completely new, unprecedented type of human being, a man born of the new economic system," he wrote. He settled in Dresden, where he was employed as an architect by the city council. Rudi never spoke of his experience in the camps, remarking only (and, in a way, accurately) that he had "worked on Soviet construction sites." Michael did not discover his father had been in the Gulag until the 1970s.

In 1958, Rudi Hamburger was recruited as a Stasi informant, with the code name "Karl Winkler." His task, as one of the Stasi's 170,000 snoopers, was to report on his colleagues. He refused to collect and pass on compromising material, but his work for the Stasi was rated "good." Rudolf Hamburger had been brutally mistreated by the communist espionage system, and he ended up working for it.

Rudi and Ursula's son, Michael Hamburger, became one of Germany's leading Shakespeare scholars. For thirty years, he worked as dramaturge and director at the Deutsches Theater in Berlin. Nina Hamburger was a teacher. Peter Beurton, the youngest, became a distinguished biologist-philosopher at the Academy of Sciences in

East Berlin. Ursula's children idolized her, did not entirely trust her, and wondered how well they really knew her. "I do not think my mother had us children as cover for her spy work," said Nina in later life; it was more a question than a statement. Looking back, Peter reflected on the dual, competing drives in his mother's life: "There were two important things to her, her children and the communist cause. I don't know what she would have done if she had had to choose between them." Ursula's younger son resented the way his mother had seemed to dig out her children's secrets. "She always asked two questions too many. She always wanted to know a little more than I wanted to tell. There was always a tension. My sister told her everything. My brother told her nothing, and kept his secrets hidden."

For Michael, in particular, an extraordinary childhood left deep scars. The father he adored had disappeared, inexplicably, for most of his youth. His mother was not the person she had seemed. The knowledge that she had risked her children for her cause haunted him. "She did what she did out of conviction, for the liberation of mankind, and I am proud of her for that. But if she had been caught in Poland, I would have been packed off to an orphanage, or worse. That thought still gives me tremors." By the age of ten he had lived in six different countries and more than a dozen homes. The family life Michael remembered with such poignancy had been riddled with secrets. "I have been married and divorced three times," Michael Hamburger said at the age of eighty-eight. "Perhaps I never really learned to trust anyone." He died in January 2020, soon after reading the manuscript of this book.

In 1966, another of Ursula's lovers lurched back into her life. Johann Patra was now living in Brazil with his wife and son, working as an electrical engineer, and growing vegetables on a small farm. "As you know, I've never been interested in material wealth," he wrote to her. He spoke of emigrating to East Germany. Ursula invited him to visit, but warned that he might find it hard to adapt. The following January, a gaunt, trembling figure she hardly recognized appeared at the door. "He was close to a breakdown. He could not speak. Nor, for that matter, could I."

When Johann had recovered his composure, he described his life.

The Center had never reestablished contact with him in China, but he had maintained links with the communists and discovered the fate of the Mukden network. "Shushin was killed; she didn't betray anyone; her husband was arrested a little later, I don't know what they did to him, but he lost his mind and is supposed to have confessed." No one knew what had become of their children. In 1949, with the final defeat of Chiang Kai-shek's Nationalists and the founding of the People's Republic, all foreigners had been forced to leave China. He felt homesick for Europe. They talked for hours, but Ursula sensed an unbridgeable gulf. "We were strangers to each other." Patra remained an inflexible Marxist. "He was not prepared to consider other opinions. It was like talking to a brick wall. But all his good qualities were still there: his will-power, his self-sacrifice, his compassion." It struck her again that their relationship would never have worked; he left without ever meeting his daughter, Nina. From São Paulo, Patra wrote a letter explaining that he had changed his mind about coming to Germany, having concluded the revolution would never happen in Europe. "In the GDR, too, middle-class values prevail."

In 1977, eleven years later, a package for Ursula arrived from Brazil, a cloth parcel stitched with care. "I weighed it in my hand. The parcel was not heavy. While I was cutting the seams with the scissors, I saw Johann in front of me, sewing it slowly and carefully with a thick needle and coarse thread. The memory brought sadness and pain. A narrow cardboard box, lined with wood shavings and a Brazilian newspaper. What had he sent me?" She removed the last wrappings of tissue paper, and the circular china disk lay in the palm of her hand: the porcelain seller's gong.

A month later, she learned that Johann Patra was dead.

Ursula outlived all her lovers. Len Beurton was never fully comfortable living in East Germany and was prone to bouts of depression. Ursula had recruited him into intelligence, trained him, and married him. He had always been the junior partner, providing solidity and care, but little of the excitement or romance of her earlier loves. Len sometimes talked of returning to the United Kingdom, but he never did. The orphan from Barking never stopped loving the girl he had met, holding a bag of oranges, outside a Swiss supermarket. Len died in 1997 at the age of eighty-three. Rudolf Hamburger died in Dresden in 1980. Ten years later he was posthumously rehabilitated by Moscow. His memoir of the Gulag, *Ten Years in the Camps,* was published in 2013 and has been described by one critic as "uplifting in its irrepressible hope for humanity."

She had loved Rudi for his kindness, Patra for his revolutionary strength, and Len for his long, sweet comradeship. But she had found the love of her life in 1931, screeching through Shanghai on the back of a fast motorbike. The framed photograph of Richard Sorge hung on Ursula's study wall for the rest of her life. "She was in love with Sorge," said her son Michael. "She was always in love with him."

The communists showered Ursula with honors and acclaim. In 1969, a second Order of the Red Banner followed the first, received in the Kremlin in 1937. She was awarded the National Prize of East Germany, the Order of Karl Marx, the Patriotic Order of Merit, and the Jubilee Medal.

In 1977, she published an autobiography, *Sonya's Report,* revealing that the famous writer had been a prolific spy. Her children were astonished to discover their mother's past. It was an instant bestseller. The book was written under Stasi control; the prudish state censors told her to remove the parts relating to her unconventional love life. She refused: "I have no reason to feel ashamed on moral or ethical grounds. Shame on you for demanding such an omission." Even so, the final book was partly a work of communist propaganda. The original, unexpurgated version, including what the state did not want her to reveal, is in the Stasi archives. At the age of eighty-four, she was permitted to travel to Britain to publicize her memoirs. Some MPs called for her arrest, but the attorney general ruled against prosecution. An embarrassing trial was the last thing MI5 wanted.

Ursula's communist convictions mellowed, adjusted, and gently dissipated, but it never evaporated. Her faith was profoundly shaken by discovering the truth about Stalin's Great Purge, but she defended her past: "I had not worked those twenty years with Stalin in mind." Her enemy, she insisted, was always fascism. "For that reason I hold my head up high." Yet she was too much of a realist to pretend that Soviet communism truly reflected the ideals she had espoused as a teenager. The crushing of the Hungarian revolt against Moscow in

1956; the building of the Berlin Wall in 1961, ostensibly to keep fascists out of East Germany but in reality to prevent its citizens from escaping; the crushing of the Prague Spring in 1968, when Soviet tanks rolled into Czechoslovakia to destroy the fledgling reform movement: Ursula witnessed these events with mounting anxiety. By the 1970s, she had come to the realization, in her words, "that what we thought was socialism was fatally flawed."

Looking back over her life, she accepted she had been naïve. In old age she condemned "the dogmatism within the party which increased with the years, the exaggeration of our achievements and the covering up of our faults, the isolation of the politburo from the people." She felt "bitterness against the party leaders who could manipulate me and mislead me" and wondered if she should have distanced herself from the decaying East German regime. She admitted she had "knuckled under to what I knew was wrong" and taken advantage of the opportunities offered by the state. "I fought the ills that were known to me, but only to the extent that would permit me to keep my party membership and to write further books."

But even as communism crumbled in the late 1980s, her core left-wing values remained unchanged. "I still believed that a better socialism could be achieved . . . with *glasnost* and *perestroika,* with more democracy instead of dictatorship and absolute power, with realistic economic measures."

The fall of the Berlin Wall in 1989 came as both a shock and a relief. "You cannot divide a nation forever by a wall," she wrote.

On October 18, 1989, as the old leadership of the GDR was swept away, eighty-two-year-old Ursula addressed a huge rally in Berlin's Lustgarten and predicted a new era of reformed communism. "My speech is about loss of trust in the party," she said, her words interrupted by bursts of applause. "I have to say to you, after the changes that are now happening, go and become part of the Party, work in it, change the future, work as clean socialists! I have courage, I am optimistic because I know it will happen." It didn't, leaving Ursula disillusioned for the first time in her life. In a last interview, she was asked how she felt about German reunification and the collapse of communism. "It does not change my own view of how the world should be," she said. "But it does create in me a certain hopelessness, which I never had before."

Ursula Kuczynski was not a feminist. She had no interest in the role or rights of women in the wider world. Like other independent-minded women of her time, she had entered a male-dominated profession and excelled at it, using every possible advantage that her gender gave her. She was impelled by ideology, certainly, but hers was not the sort of communism adopted over sherry in warm Cambridge common rooms by faddish middle-class English undergraduates in the 1930s. Hers was a faith born of painful personal experience: the savage inequalities of Weimar, the horrors of Nazism and a world that left dead babies lying in the streets. She was ambitious, romantic, risk-addicted, occasionally selfish, huge-hearted, and tough as only someone who had lived through the worst of twentieth-century history could be. She was never betrayed. Dozens of people—in Germany, China, Poland, Switzerland, and the United Kingdom—had ample opportunity to expose Ursula, and bring her life and espionage to a swift and unpleasant end. None, save Ollo, ever did. For a die-hard communist, she was exceptionally good fun, stylish, and warm. She had a gift for friendship, an ability to inspire enduring loyalty, and a willingness to listen and support people whose opinions were radically different from her own. As a revolutionary, she was surprisingly open-minded. She knew how to love and how to be loved. Like all great survivors, she was fantastically lucky.

Ursula Kuczynski died on July 7, 2000, at the age of ninety-three.

A few weeks later, at a ceremony marking the fifty-fifth anniversary of victory in the Second World War, Russia's president, Vladimir Putin, signed a decree proclaiming Ursula a "super-agent of military intelligence" and awarding her the Order of Friendship.

Ursula Kuczynski lived long, as the porcelain mender had predicted. She was ten years old when the Bolshevik Revolution took place and eighty-two when the Berlin Wall came down. Her life spanned the whole of communism, from its tumultuous beginnings to its cataclysmic downfall. She embraced that ideology with the unqualified fervor of youth, and saw it die from the disappointed perspective of extreme old age. She spent her adult life fighting for something she believed to be right, and died knowing that much of it had been wrong. But she still looked back with satisfaction: she had fought Nazism, loved well, raised a family, written a small library of good books, and helped the Soviet Union keep nuclear pace with the West, ensuring a fragile peace. She lived several whole lives in one very long one, a woman of multiple names, numerous roles, and many disguises.

But even in oldest age, her unconscious reminded her that she was still, and always had been, a spy: "A nightmare haunts my sleep: the enemy is at my heels and I have no time to destroy the information."

AFTERWORD
THE LIVES
OF OTHERS

KLAUS FUCHS WAS RELEASED AFTER NINE YEARS IN prison and flew directly to East Germany. Grete Keilson, a Communist Party official and an old acquaintance, greeted him at the airport; they married three months later. Fuchs was feted by the GDR, awarded the Patriotic Order of Merit, the Order of Karl Marx, and the National Prize. Fuchs missed living in the West, but never expressed any regret. He died in 1988. The East German spymaster Markus Wolf wrote that Fuchs had "made the single greatest contribution to Moscow's ability to build an atom bomb [and] changed the world's balance of power by breaking America's nuclear monopoly." **Harry Gold,** Fuchs's KGB handler in the United States, was sentenced to thirty years in prison. He was released after serving half his sentence and spent the rest of his life working as a clinical chemist in the pathology department of John F. Kennedy Hospital in Philadelphia.

Jim Skardon went on not to catch a succession of spies. He was perplexed that he had "never been given any sort of promotion to senior officer before his retirement in 1961." Two years later **Kim Philby** escaped to Moscow and later wrote a memoir mocking Skardon's "scrupulously courteous" interrogation methods—by which he meant entirely ineffectual. **Milicent Bagot** remained a pillar of MI5, unsettling her male colleagues by the force of her personality and the depth of her knowledge about communist subversion. She wrote a detailed account of the Comintern's international machinations and was one of the first officers to raise doubts about Philby's loyalty. Long after Bagot's retirement in 1967, MI5 continued to seek her help in rooting out communist spies. She never missed a choir rehearsal and died in 2006. **Roger Hollis** became director general of MI5 in 1956 and remained in that post until his retirement in 1965. The investigation into whether he had been a GRU mole was ongoing at the time of his death in 1973, and the theory that he was a traitor rumbles on, refusing to die. One good reason to doubt it is Vladimir Putin. Russia's president, a former KGB colonel, is proud of his country's espionage history. If Hollis had been a top-level Soviet spy from 1932 until 1965, the GRU files would contain a mass of evidence. None has ever come to light, even though "authorized" Russian historians have, from time to time, been granted access to those archives. Proof that Russia ran a British traitor inside MI5 who was never caught would be a publicity coup of immense value to Moscow. This, then, is the main objection to the theory that Hollis protected Ursula: if the head of MI5 *had* been a Soviet supermole, Putin would be unable to resist boasting about it.

Three months after Ursula left Britain, **Agnes Smedley** died in Oxford after surgery for an ulcer. The Danish writer Karin Michaëlis described her as "a lonely bird of tremendous wingspread, a bird that will never build a nest [who] renounced everything, fame, personal happiness, comfort, safety, for one thing: complete dedication to a great cause." Her ashes were buried at the Babaoshan Revolutionary Cemetery in Peking in 1951. The full extent of Smedley's espionage was not revealed until 2005.

The body of **Richard Sorge** was exhumed after the war by his Japanese lover, Hanako Ishii, cremated, and reinterred in Tokyo's Tama Cemetery. He was finally acknowledged by Moscow in 1964, declared a Hero of the Soviet Union, and elevated to cult status by KGB propagandists. In 2016, a Moscow railway station was named after him. **Chen Hansheng,** Sorge's closest Chinese collaborator, is regarded as a pioneer of social science in China. His research underpinned Maoist theories on the strength of the "peasant masses," but he fell afoul of the communist regime and was accused of being a Nationalist spy. Denied medical treatment for glaucoma during the Cultural Revolution, he lost his sight. Chen died in 2004 at the age of 107. The novelist **Ding Ling,** Ursula's friend in Shanghai, wrote some three hundred books and suffered the full gamut of persecution under Chinese communism: Mao's initial approval, then condemnation for criticizing the party's male chauvinism, enforced public self-confession, censorship, imprisonment for five years during the Cultural Revolution, forced labor for twelve more, and finally rehabilitation in 1978. **Patrick T. Givens,** the cheerful Shanghai spy hunter, left the Municipal Police in 1936 and retired to the three-hundred-year-old Bansha Castle in Tipperary. **Hadshi Mamsurov,** Ursula's boss at the GRU, survived the purges, the lethal infighting inside Soviet intelligence, and the war; he formed the "Spetznaz" special forces, liberated two concentration camps, and retired to his native Ossetia with the rank of general. The intrepid American journalist **Emily Hahn** continued to write for *The New Yorker* well into her eighties.

Alexander Foote published his memoirs, *Handbook for Spies,* disguising Ursula as "Maria Schultz." MI5 collaborated on the publication, regarding the book as "a successful exercise in anti-Soviet propaganda." A baseless theory has since emerged that Foote was a double agent, working for MI6 all along. He was given a job in the Ministry of Agriculture and Fisheries, and became a friend of the writer and broadcaster Malcolm Muggeridge. In a rare moment of understatement, Foote described his clerical work as "very tedious" compared to life as a spy. He died in 1956. **Sandor Radó** was released from a Soviet prison in November 1954, after the death of Stalin, and returned to Hungary. Two years later, he was officially rehabilitated and appointed head of the Hungarian cartographic service, and then professor of cartography at Budapest's University of Economic Sciences. In 1958, **Melita Norwood** was secretly awarded the Soviet Red Banner of Labor, the civilian counterpart to Ursula's military medal. She was identified by MI5 as a security risk in 1965, but not publicly exposed until 1999, when the KGB archivist Vasili Mitrokhin defected with six trunkloads of files: these described Agent Hola as "a committed, reliable and disciplined agent [who] handed over a very large number of documents of a scientific and technical nature." When the story broke, she was photographed by the press outside her suburban home laden with shopping and thus memorably dubbed "The Spy Who Came in from the Co-op." At eighty-seven, she was too elderly to face prosecution. Soon after her exposure, Norwood received a signed copy of Ursula's autobiography, with a handwritten message from her former handler: "To Letty, Sonya salutes you!"

Joe Gould resumed his career in the film industry after the war, becoming advertising manager for United Artists Corporation and then Paramount, where he organized publicity for the Hitchcock film *Psycho*. His last job was as director of public affairs for the Center for Defense Information in Washington, D.C. In 2009, he was posthumously awarded the Bronze Star for his wartime work.

The survivors of the Tool missions settled in East Germany after the war. **Erich Henschke** became editor of the *Berliner Zeitung*, then a Berlin city councillor, and finally a correspondent for East German state television. **Paul Lindner** was made editor in chief of Radio Berlin International. **Toni Ruh** was appointed director of customs for the GDR and then East Germany's ambassador to Romania, where he killed himself, for reasons unknown, in 1964. Lindner died of natural causes five years later. The Hammer spies were each awarded the Silver Star at a ceremony in 2006 and commended for "gallantry in keeping with the highest traditions of the military service." Lindner and Ruh were the first German nationals, and the only Soviet spies, to receive American medals for wartime bravery.

In October 1950, **Olga Muth** turned up at the British embassy in West Berlin and offered to spill the beans on Ursula Beurton. The former nanny told MI6 that she had worked for the Kuczynskis since 1911. "Ursula started to use the greeting 'Heil Moscow!' when she was about 20 years old," said Ollo, as she launched into a rehearsed denunciation. Muth went on to describe Ursula's espionage in Poland, Danzig, and Switzerland, her radio equipment, and the secret meetings in the Molehill. She related how her employer had told her "to turn a blind eye to these activities, and to forget all that went on." Triumphantly, Ollo reached her summation: "Ursula was nothing more or less than a Russian spy." None of this was news to MI6, and anyway Ursula was out of reach in East Berlin. British intelligence suspected Ollo's sudden appearance was a plot orchestrated by Mrs. Beurton herself: "The possibility cannot be excluded that Ur-

sula has sent her to us to discover our present interest in the family."
Olga Muth was politely ushered out of the building. Once again,
British officialdom had declined to hear Ollo's condemnation: the
first time, in Switzerland, because she was incomprehensible; and the
second because it was suspected she might be Ursula's spy.

The four younger Kuczynski sisters, **Brigitte, Barbara, Sabine,**
and **Renate,** remained in Britain, at first monitored closely by MI5,
then tolerated, and finally forgotten by the Security Service. **Jürgen
Kuczynski** renounced British citizenship and settled permanently in
East Germany. Appointed a professor at Humboldt University, he
founded the Institute for Economic History, sat in the East German
Parliament, and ran the Society for the Study of Soviet Culture, instructing its members: "He who hates and despises human progress
as it is manifested in the Soviet Union is himself odious and con-
temptible." He was an unreconstructed Stalinist who criticized
Stalinism in his 1973 memoirs and earned a rebuke from the party; he
described himself as a "true party-line dissident." Jürgen was regarded as a loose cannon by party officials and was even briefly suspected of being an "imperialist agent," yet he prospered in the new
communist state. In 1971, he was appointed adviser on external economic affairs to Erich Honecker, the GDR's hard-line leader. And he
continued to write, compulsively, more than four thousand works in
all, including his monumental, forty-volume *History of Labour Conditions.* He estimated his own output at "roughly 100 books," proving
that his numeracy was no match for his literacy. The vast Kuczynski
library, seventy thousand volumes collected by three generations,
now occupies one hundred meters of shelving in the Berlin Central
Library.

Jürgen died in 1997 at the age of ninety-two.

Jürgen and Ursula bickered, competed, resented, and adored each
other until the end of their days. After a particularly explosive row,
the cause of which is lost to history, he wrote: "Do you really feel
that you can seriously jeopardize our relationship! You suggest that I
would desert you in a world in which so much dirt is being thrown,
or that I could change my relationship to you, something that forms
a firm basis in my life. . . . On this matter you won't be able to change
things because the past has too strong a pull."

ACKNOWLEDGMENTS

THIS BOOK WOULD HAVE BEEN IMPOSSIBLE TO WRITE without the help of Ursula's family and in particular her sons, Peter Beurton and the late Michael Hamburger. Both responded to my inquiries and repeated visits with boundless patience and hospitality. Following Michael's death in January 2020, his son and daughter, Max and Hannah, kindly took over the complex and time-consuming task of assembling, collating, and copying the family's large photographic archive.

John Green, historian and author of the definitive biography of the Kuczynski family, has been unstintingly generous in sharing his expertise, conducting additional research in the German archives, and following up numerous leads. Galina Green of Trend Translations did a superb job of translating Ursula's books into English. I am also grateful to the staff of the National Archives in Kew and the Bundesarchiv and Stasi archives in Berlin. Robert Hands did another masterful copyedit on the first draft, as he has for each of my last six books, while Cecilia Mackay's photographic research has been immaculate. I have been fortunate to have access to the work of a number of scholars and academics working in German, including Thomas Kampen, Bernd-Rainer Barth, and Matthew Stibbe. Mikhail Bogdanov and Tom Parfitt were exceptionally helpful in Russia. Andrew Marshall first alerted me to the story of the Tool missions. Several friends and experts (some of whom have asked to not be named) read the manuscript, improving it greatly and saving me from numerous errors; they include Rosie Goldsmith, Jon Halliday, Natascha McElhone, Sandra Pearce, Roland Philipps, and Anne Robinson.

The publishing teams at Viking and Crown have done another superlative job, in difficult coronavirus times, with great professionalism and enthusiasm. Jonny Geller, my agent, has been a rock of support and wisdom.

Yet again, my children have accompanied their father on another book marathon with endless good humor and tolerance. I spent much of the lockdown in 1920s Berlin and 1930s Shanghai; my thanks to my beloved Barney, Finn, and Molly for their excellent company throughout the journey. And finally, to Juliet, my love.

NOTES

U RSULA KUCZYNSKI WROTE EXTENSIVELY ABOUT HER
life, in both fiction and nonfiction. Her memoir, *Sonjas Rapport*, was published in German in 1977, with an English-language version in 1991 (*Sonya's Report*) and a fuller edition in German in 2006. The original unexpurgated manuscript, complete with cuts and comments made by the Stasi censor (and her acerbic handwritten responses), is in the Stasi archives in Berlin. In addition, as Ruth Werner, she wrote thirteen works of fiction (see bibliography for a selection), three of which are essentially autobiographical: *Ein ungewöhnliches Mädchen* (*An Unusual Girl*), *Der Gong des Porzellanhändlers* (*The Porcelain Mender's Gong*), and *Muhme Mehle* (a nickname for Olga Muth). She also wrote hundreds of letters (extensively extracted in Panitz, *Geheimtreff Banbury*) and a childhood diary. I am grateful to her sons, Peter Beurton and the late Michael Hamburger, for permission to translate and quote from these. Rudolf Hamburger's memoir *Zehn Jahre Lager* (*Ten Years in the Camps*) was published in 2013, more than three decades after his death, with an introduction by Michael Hamburger. Additional material is derived from Nina Blankenfeld's book *Die Tochter bin ich* (*I Am the Daughter*), Peter Beurton's unpublished recollections, Michael Hamburger's unfinished memoir, interviews with Ursula's sons and other family members, and the various radio and television interviews she gave in later life.

The MI5 files on the Kuczynski family in the National Archives (TNA) are Ursula and Len Beurton: KV 6/41–45; Jürgen and Marguerite: KV 2/1871–1880 and HO 405/30996; Robert: HO 396/50/28; Berta: HO 396/50/25; Renate: KV 2/2889–2893 and HO 396/50/27; Barbara: KV2/2936–2937; Bridget: KV 2/1569; Sabine: KV 2/2931–2933; Rudolf Hamburger: KV 2/1610.

Ursula's files in the Bundesarchiv (the Ruth Werner legacy papers) are filed under NY 4502. The Kuczynski/Werner files in the Stasi archives (Der Bundesbeauftragte für die Unterlagen des Staatssicherheitsdienstes der ehemaligen Deutschen Demokratischen Republik) can be found under Bfs HA IX/11 FV 98/66 (eighteen thousand pages in total, comprising some ninety individual files).

Selected significant quotations are cited below, along with a guide to the principal sources for each chapter.

1. WHIRL

5 **"Everything shimmering brown and gold"**: See Werner, *Ein ungewöhnliches Mädchen*. The other key sources on Ursula's early life are Werner, *Sonya's Report*, letters and diaries cited in Panitz, *Geheimtreff Banbury*, and the recollections of Peter Beurton and the late Michael Hamburger.

6 **"Kuczynski always forms"**: Quoted in Green, *A Political Family*.

19 **"I have no country"**: Smedley, *Daughter of Earth*.

19 **"the mother of women's literary radicalism"**: Cited in Price, *The Lives of Agnes Smedley*.

19 **"Go tell Mike Gold"**: Baker, *Ernest Hemingway*.

2. WHORE OF THE ORIENT

22 **"An accordion sounded"**: Werner, *Sonya's Report*.

24 **"anything was possible"**: Ballard, *Miracles of Life*.

26 **"She spent her afternoons"**: Hahn, *China to Me*.

27 **"an Art Deco masterpiece"**: Austin Williams, *The Architectural Review*, October 22, 2018.

Hamburger's early life and architecture are described in Kögel, *Zwei Poelzigschüler;* see also Hamburger, *Zehn Jahre Lager*.

Descriptions of Ursula's life in Shanghai are from Werner, *Ein ungewöhnliches Mädchen* and *Sonya's Report,* and letters cited in Panitz, *Geheimtreff Banbury*.

Principal sources on the life of Agnes Smedley are Price, *The Lives of Agnes Smedley,* and MacKinnon, *Agnes Smedley: The Life and Times of an American Radical*. Smedley's MI5 files are TNA KV 2/2207–2208; the Agnes Smedley archive, comprising forty-six boxes of material, is held by Arizona State University: http://

www.azarchivesonline.org/xtf/view?docId=ead/asu/smedley.xml;query=agnes
%20smedley;brand=default.

3. AGENT RAMSAY

For the life of Richard Sorge, see Matthews, *An Impeccable Spy;* Whymant, *Stalin's Spy;* and Willoughby, *Shanghai Conspiracy.*

43 **"purging the party of spies"**: "The Man from Moscow," *Time,* Feb. 17, 1947.

45 **"I realize how rotten"**: Werner, *Ein ungewöhnliches Mädchen.*

46 **"miserable, drinking heavily"**: Barlow, *I Myself Am a Woman.*

47 **"the tiger's bench"**: Wakeman, *Policing Shanghai.* For Tom Givens, see also Hergé's *The Blue Lotus.*

For 1920s Shanghai, see Sergeant, *Shanghai,* and Snow, *Random Notes on China.*

4. WHEN SONYA IS DANCING

52 **"The White Terror is ghastly"**: Quoted in Price, *The Lives of Agnes Smedley.*

Descriptions of Sorge's spy network are in Werner, *Sonya's Report;* Matthews, *An Impeccable Spy;* Whymant, *Stalin's Spy.*

56 **"a recruiting station for the 4th Bureau"**: Willoughby, *Shanghai Conspiracy.*

58 **"whose stock phrase was 'my Prince, ples' "**: Quoted in Wakeman, *Policing Shanghai.*

58 **"When Sonya is dancing"**: See Stasi file NY/4502/sig 14393.

59 **"When word of the affair reached"**: Matthews, *An Impeccable Spy.*

For the Noulens case, see Wakeman, *Policing Shanghai,* and Litten, "The Noulens Affair"; Noulens's MI5 files, TNA KV 2/2562.

63 **"having no parallel in history"**: Harold Isaacs, quoted in Wakeman, *Policing Shanghai.*

5. THE SPIES WHO LOVED HER

67 **"one of the guests"**: Matthews, *An Impeccable Spy.*

Sources on the Hollis affair may be divided into two camps. His most notable accusers are Wright, *Spycatcher;* Pincher, *Treachery: Betrayals, Blunders and Cover-ups;* and Paul Monk, https://quadrant.org.au/magazine/2010/04/christopher

-andrew-and-the-strange-case-of-roger-hollis/. His defenders include Andrew, *Defence of the Realm,* and MI5, https://www.mi5.gov.uk/sir-roger-hollis.

The subject is explored extensively by Antony Percy at www.coldspur.com. See also Tyrer, "The Unresolved Mystery of ELLI."

76 **"We now have a longing"**: For this and other letters, see Panitz, *Geheimtreff Banbury.*

77 **"nobody would dare touch"**: Statement of the steering committee of the Central Jewish German organization (Centralverein deutscher Staatsbürger jüdischen Glaubens).

77 **"an almost blind loyalty"**: See Green, *A Political Family.*

6. SPARROW

79 **"cold-bloodedness of the Centre"**: See Foote, *Handbook for Spies.*

For Ursula's experiences in Moscow, see Werner, *Ein ungewöhnliches Mädchen* and *Sonya's Report.*

85 **"Candidates were accepted"**: Cited in Price, *The Lives of Agnes Smedley.*

88 **"You are soon going to be sent away"**: The period in Mukden is described in Werner, *Der Gong des Porzellanhändlers.*

The careers of Soviet intelligence officers, including Tumanyan, Patra, and Mamsurov, are described in detail in Bochkarev and Kolpakidi, *Superfrau iz GRU.* Unreliable in parts, this source nonetheless benefits from access to GRU files.

7. ABOARD THE *CONTE VERDE*

The voyage aboard the SS *Conte Verde* is described in Werner, *Der Gong des Porzellanhändlers* and *Sonya's Report,* letters cited in Panitz, *Geheimtreff Banbury,* unfinished manuscript by Michael Hamburger, and intercepted correspondence in MI5 files.

8. OUR WOMAN IN MANCHURIA

Ursula's intelligence operations in Mukden and her relationship with Patra are described in Werner, *Der Gong des Porzellanhändlers.*

9. VAGABOND LIFE

115 **"Last month anti-Japanese groups"**: These and subsequent letters are quoted in Panitz, *Geheimtreff Banbury;* "Hans von Schlewitz," "Shushin," "Wang," and "Chu" (Werner, *Der Gong des Porzellanhändlers*) are probably pseudonyms.

116 **"*Ich kann nicht mehr*"**: For the life and death of Elisabeth Naef, see Price, *The Lives of Agnes Smedley,* and Fuechtner, Haynes, and Jones, *A Global History of Sexual Science.*

120 **"the last Victorian Communist"**: See Green, *A Political Family.*

10. FROM PEKING TO POLAND

For the life and career of Rudolf Hamburger, see his MI5 file, TNA KV 2/1610, and the Stasi file on Hamburger, MfS HA IX/II. FV 98/66. See also Kögel, *Zwei Poelzigschüler,* and Hamburger, *Zehn Jahre Lager.*

The career of Nikola Zidarov is described in Bochkarev and Kolpakidi, *Superfrau iz GRU.*

The Hoffman network is described in Werner, *Sonya's Report.*

11. IN FOR A PENNY

139 **"Who is going to remember this riffraff"**: For Stalin's purges, see Conquest, *The Great Terror,* and Kuromiya, *The Voices of the Dead.*

140 **"The whole Fourth Directorate"**: See Matthews, *An Impeccable Spy.*

144 **under the name "Eriki Noki"**: Franz Obermanns's MI5 file, TNA KV 6/48.

147 **"I understand that should I overstay"**: See Ursula's MI5 files, TNA KV 6/41–45.

149 **"restless sales manager"**: See Foote, *Handbook for Spies;* Foote's MI5 files, TNA KV 2/1611–1616.

12. THE MOLEHILL

152 **"Before us the meadows"**: For the GRU network in Switzerland, see Werner, *Sonya's Report,* and Foote, *Handbook for Spies.*

153 **"The British Prime Minister"**: http://news.bbc.co.uk/onthisday/hi/dates/stories/september/30/newsid_3115000/3115476.stm.

154 **"He should be beaten"**: The life of Olga Muth is described in Werner, *Muhme Mehle.*

154 **"No foreign propagandist"**: *The Times,* November 11, 1938.

156 **"It is possible that F[oote] had a flirtation"**: Foote's MI6 files, TNA KV 2/1611–1616.

157 **Lillian Jakobi** and **Frau Füssli**: See Werner, *Muhme Mehle;* they are probably pseudonyms.

159 **"Eggs and mayonnaise"**: For Osteria Bavaria, see TNA KV 2/1611–1616; notes in Stasi file Bfs HA IX/11 FV 98/66 Bd 19; Foote, *Handbook for Spies;* and the Mitford Society: https://themitfordsociety.wordpress.com/tag/osteria-bavaria/.

162 **"I was twenty-five"**: Unpublished account written by Len Beurton, courtesy of Peter Beurton; see also Beurton's MI5 files, TNA KV 6/41–45. For

Beurton's service in Spain, see Baxell, *British Volunteers in the Spanish Civil War* and *Unlikely Warriors*.

13. A MARRIAGE OF CONVENIENCE

For the Molotov-Ribbentrop Pact, see Moorhouse, *The Devils' Alliance*.

180 **"Style, elegance, restraint"**: Len Beurton, unpublished address, courtesy of Peter Beurton, private archive.
181 **"spreading defeatism"**: Home Office file, TNA HO 396/50/28.
181 **"Everyone knows"**: The battle over Jürgen's internment is described in Green, *A Political Family,* and Kuczynski's MI5 files, TNA KV 2/1871–1880.
182 **"at all times, whatever happens"**: Quoted in Leitz, *Nazi Germany and Neutral Europe.*
182 **"misbegotten branch of our Volk"**: Quoted in Bormann, *Hitler's Table Talk.*

14. THE BABY SNATCHER

184 **"It was just like the movies"**: Hahn, *China to Me.*
185 **"one of the few places"**: See Kögel, *Zwei Poelzigschüler,* and Hamburger, *Zehn Jahre Lager.*

For the Rote Drei, see https://www.cia.gov/library/center-for-the-study-of -intelligence/kent-csi/vol13no3/html/v13i3a05p_0001.htm; Tarrant, *The Red Orchestra;* Read and Fisher, *Operation Lucy;* Nelson, *Red Orchestra.* See also Hamel's MI5 file, TNA KV 2/1615.

188 **"thickset, verging on the plump"**: Werner, *Sonya's Report;* Sandor Radó's MI5 files, TNA KV 2/1647–1649.
188 **"a tall, slender, almost fragile-looking woman"**: Radó, *Codename Dora.*
190 **"If anyone says something nice"**: Werner, *Muhme Mehle.*
193 **"Her ravings in broken English"**: Foote, *Handbook for Spies.*

15. THE HAPPY TIME

201 **"Wake Arms. Epping 1 & 15"**: See TNA KV 6/43. For MI5 tracking of the Beurtons, see TNA KV 6/41–45.
204 **"H's Bruder als Späher"**: Hamburger, *Zehn Jahre Lager.*
205 **"She staggered like a stumbling horse"**: Prysor, *Citizen Sailors.*

16. BARBAROSSA

207   "**They unpack their supper**": Werner, *Sonya's Report.*
208   "**Jürgen was angry about Sonia's**": Foote, *Handbook for Spies.*
209   "**a tough looking man**": Haslam, *Near and Distant Neighbours.*
210   "**We only have to kick the door in**": Quoted in Hardesty and Ginberg, *Red Phoenix Rising.*
212   "**I unhesitatingly recommend Jürgen Kuczynski**": For this and other messages to and from the Center decoded by Venona, see Vassiliev, *Yellow Notebooks,* https://www.wilsoncenter.org/sites/default/files/Vassiliev -Notebooks-and-Venona-Index-Concordance_update-2014-11-01.pdf. See also Haynes, Klehr, and Vassiliev, *Spies,* and West, *Venona.*
215   "**Inactive, missing his wife**": Ashdown, *Nein!*

17. THE ROAD TO HELL

The most detailed and recent analysis of the Fuchs case is in Close, *Trinity.* Other biographical treatments include Williams, *Klaus Fuchs;* Rossiter, *The Spy Who Changed the World;* Moss, *Klaus Fuchs;* Moorehead, *The Traitors;* and Montgomery Hyde, *The Atom Bomb Spies.* Fuchs's MI5 files are TNA KV 2/1245–1270.
    Frisch-Peierls memo: http://www.atomicarchive.com/Docs/Begin/Frisch Peierls.shtml.

222   "**Klaus naturally came to me**": Kuczynski, *Memoiren.*
223   "**would put humanity on the road to hell**": Quoted in Close, *Trinity.*

Melita Norwood's life and career are described in Burke, *The Spy Who Came in from the Co-op.*

226   "**She would remove files**": https://www.thetimes.co.uk/article/melita -norwood-x2lrfkj7vm5.
226   "**our illegal station chief**": Vassiliev, *Yellow Notebooks.*

Len Beurton interview and investigation TNA KV 6/41–45.

18. ATOMIC SPIES

230   "**It was pleasant**": Werner, *Sonya's Report.*
230   "**discuss his feelings**": Obituary of Ruth Werner, *The Economist,* July 13, 2000.
233   "**it was via Fuchs and Sonya**": Close, *Trinity.*
234   "**Above all, British Jews' primary obligation**": https://link.springer .com/chapter/10.1057%2F9780230598416_2.
235   "**considerable bundles of Russian traffic**": Pincher, *Treachery.*

236 **"My past as an International Brigader"**: Len Beurton, unpublished address, courtesy of Peter Beurton, private archive.

Hans Kahle's MI5 files, TNA KV 2/1561–1566.

237 **"With the help of duplicate keys"**: Bochkarev and Kolpakidi, *Superfrau iz GRU.*

238 **"My task"**: Hamburger, *Zehn Jahre Lager.*

239 **"he was Russian"**: Hamburger's MI5 file, TNA KV 2/1610.

19. MILICENT OF MI5

245 **"She was slightly touched"**: Wright, *Spycatcher.*

246 **"a vague supervisory role"**: Cited in Smith, *The Secret Agent's Bedside Reader.*

246 **"We have a great deal of information"**: Jürgen Kuczynski's MI5 files, TNA KV 2/1871–1880.

247 **"could smell a rat at twenty paces"**: Close, *Trinity.*

247 **"any day that is convenient"**: See the Beurtons' MI5 files, TNA KV 6/41–45.

249 **"Miss Bagot seems to have highlighted"**: Close, *Trinity.*

249 **"Bagot had been on SONIA's [sic] trail"**: Paul Monk: https://quadrant .org.au/magazine/2010/04/christopher-andrew-and-the-strange-case-of -roger-hollis/.

250 **"On 4 September, U. Kuczynski"**: For the Quebec Agreement debate, see ibid.; Pincher, *Treachery;* Lota, *GRU i atomnaia bomba;* Antony Percy at www.coldspur.com.

253 **"Sooner or later there will be"**: Tolstoy, *Victims of Yalta.*

253 **"He is about 5 foot 10 inches"**: Hornblum, *The Invisible Harry Gold.*

20. OPERATION HAMMER

The best account of the Tool missions is Gould, *German Anti-Nazi Espionage in the Second World War.* See also Persico, *Piercing the Reich;* and CIA Library, https:// www.cia.gov/library/center-for-the-study-of-intelligence/csi-publications/csi -studies/studies/vol46no1/article03.html.

American intelligence records of the missions are retained by the U.S. National Archives (USNA): OSS Record Group 226. See also OSS War Diary, vol. 6, 421–56.

Interviews with Hammer agents in 1953 by GDR investigative commission are in the Archives of the Political Parties and Mass Organizations of the GDR [SAPMO]: DY 30/IV 2/4/123, BL 123–282.

258 **"uncomfortable in inexpensive suits and neckties"**: Persico, *Piercing the Reich.*

263 "undoubtedly a lifelong communist": Karl Kastro's (Erich Henschke) MI5 file, TNA KV 2/3908.

264 "Excitement made him snort": Dunlop, *Donovan*.

265 "those who make use": Kuczynski's MI5 files, TNA KV 2/1871–1880.

For United States Strategic Bombing Survey records, see http://www.ibiblio .org/hyperwar/AAF/USSBS/.

268 "I have never met anyone": Matthews, *An Impeccable Spy*.

21. RUSTLE OF SPRING

272 "no longer follow": See SAPMO archives, DY 30/IV 2/4/123, BL 123–282.

272 "Only the most courageous": USNA, OSS Record Group 226.

274 "One of the good things": Werner, *Ein ungewöhnliches Mädchen*.

281 "the campus of a huge university": Close, *Trinity*.

281 "a new weapon": Putz, "What If the United States Had Told the Soviet Union about the Bomb?"

22. GREAT ROLLRIGHT

Descriptions of life in Great Rollright are from Werner, *Sonya's Report;* Blankenfeld, *Die Tochter bin ich;* and interviews with Michael Hamburger and Peter Beurton.

286 "That's what I have become": Hamburger, *Zehn Jahre Lager*.

288 "The FBI are being singularly persistent": See the Beurtons' MI5 files, TNA KV 6/41–45.

289 "splintering crash": Foote, *Handbook for Spies*.

293 "complete lack of nerves": Foote's MI5 files, TNA KV 2/1611–1616.

294 "In front of him stood": Werner, *Sonya's Report*.

295 "Except knitting": For MI5's pursuit of Ursula and the Kuczynskis, see Brinson and Dove, *A Matter of Intelligence*.

23. A VERY TOUGH NUT

297 "Oh my little boy": Werner, *Sonya's Report*.

297 "I have a bit of good news": Hamburger's MI5 files, TNA KV 2/1610.

298 "gracefully bowed himself out": The Skardon interview is in the Beurtons' MI5 files, TNA KV 6/41–45.

299 "A dapper, pipe-smoking former policeman": Wright, *Spycatcher*.

299 "upper class bluster": Close, *Trinity*.

303 "the principal apologist for communist China": Price, *The Lives of Agnes Smedley*.

304 "Foreigners are leaving China": Intercepted letter in the Beurtons' MI5 files, TNA KV 6/41–45.

306 **"During the whole day"**: Blankenfeld, *Die Tochter bin ich.*

306 **"If I felt low"**: Werner, *Sonya's Report.*

307 **"We have evidence"**: Raymond H. Geselbracht, ed., "The Truman Administration during 1949: A Chronology," Harry S. Truman Library.

309 **"Stout is not so good"**: Close, *Trinity;* see also Fuchs's MI5 files, TNA KV 2/1245–1270.

312 **"We were never allowed"**: http://www.greathead.org/greathead2-0/Sonia.htm.

24. RUTH WERNER

Ursula's Stasi files are Bfs HA IX/11 FV 98/66 Bd 19.

318 **"bolted back to Germany in 1947"**: Pincher, *Treachery.*

319 **"I wanted to live as a citizen"**: Werner, *Sonya's Report.*

320 **"spent twenty years abroad"**: Bfs HA IX/11 FV 98/66 Bd 19.

321 **"These persons are likely to possess"**: For MI6's efforts to recruit the Kuczynskis, see Stibbe, "Jürgen Kuczynski and the Search for a (Non-existent) Western Spy Ring in the East German Communist Party in 1953."

322 **"I lost so many friends"**: Werner, *Sonya's Report.*

323 **"In the hasty pleasure of love"**: Hamburger, *Zehn Jahre Lager.*

324 **was rated "good"**: Hamburger's Stasi files, MfS HA IX/II. FV 98/66.

325 **"There were two important things"**: Reflections of Ursula's children are from author interviews; see also "Codename Sonya," BBC Radio 4, 2002, https://genome.ch.bbc.co.uk/59623532dbb240c3aa1c2bd002b932f5.

326 **"I weighed it in my hand"**: Werner, *Der Gong des Porzellanhändlers.*

330 **"A nightmare haunts my sleep"**: Werner, *Sonya's Report.*

AFTERWORD: THE LIVES OF OTHERS

331 **"made the single greatest contribution"**: Close, *Trinity.*

331 **"scrupulously courteous"**: Philby, *My Silent War.*

332 **"a lonely bird of tremendous wingspread"**: Price, *The Lives of Agnes Smedley.*

333 **"a successful exercise in anti-Soviet propaganda"**: Pincher, *Treachery.*

333 **"a committed, reliable and disciplined agent"**: Andrew and Mitrokhin, *The Mitrokhin Archive.*

334 **"The Spy Who Came in from the Co-op"**: *The Times,* September 11, 1999.

334 **"To Letty, Sonya salutes you!"**: Pincher, *Treachery.*

334 **"gallantry in keeping"**: See Gould, *German Anti-Nazi Espionage in the Second World War.*

334 **"Ursula started to use the greeting"**: See the Beurtons' MI5 files, TNA KV 6/41–45.

335 **"He who hates and despises"**: For Jürgen Kuczynski's later years, see Green, *A Political Family*.

335 **"Do you really feel"**: Undated letter, courtesy of Peter Beurton.

SELECT BIBLIOGRAPHY

Aaronovitch, David. *Party Animals: My Family and Other Communists.* London, 2016.

Andrew, Christopher. *The Defence of the Realm: The Authorized History of MI5.* London, 2009.

Andrew, Christopher, and Vasili Mitrokhin. *The Mitrokhin Archive.* London, 1999.

Ashdown, Paddy. *Nein! Standing Up to Hitler, 1935–1944.* London, 2018.

Baker, Carlos. *Ernest Hemingway: A Life Story.* New York, 1969.

Ballard, J. G. *Miracles of Life: Shanghai to Shepperton; an Autobiography.* New York, 2008.

Barlow, Tani E. *I Myself Am a Woman: Selected Writings of Ding Ling.* Boston, 1989.

Baxell, Richard. *British Volunteers in the Spanish Civil War.* London, 2004.

———. *Unlikely Warriors: The Extraordinary Story of the Britons Who Fought for Spain.* London, 2012.

Blankenfeld, Janina. *Die Tochter bin ich.* Berlin, 1985.

Bochkarev, Viktor, and Aleksandr Kolpakidi. *Superfrau iz GRU.* Moscow, 2002.

Bormann, Martin, ed. *Hitler's Table Talk, 1941–1944.* Translated by Norman Cameron. London, 2000.

Bower, Tom. *The Perfect English Spy: Sir Dick White and the Secret War, 1935–90.* London, 1995.

Brinson, Charmian. "The Free German Movement in Britain, 1943–1945." *Yearbook of the Research Centre for German and Austrian Exile Studies,* vol. 15, 2014.

Brinson, Charmian, and Richard Dove. *A Matter of Intelligence: MI5 and the Surveillance of Anti-Nazi Refugees, 1933–1950.* Manchester, 2014.

Burke, David. *The Lawn Road Flats: Spies, Writers and Artists.* Martlesham, 2014.

———. *The Spy Who Came in from the Co-op: Melita Norwood and the Ending of Cold War Espionage.* Martlesham, 2008.

Casey, William. *The Secret War against Hitler.* Washington, D.C., 1988.

Close, Frank. *Trinity: The Treachery and Pursuit of the Most Dangerous Spy in History.* London, 2019.

Conquest, Robert. *The Great Terror: Stalin's Purge of the Thirties,* rev. ed. London, 1990.

Dunlop, Richard. *Donovan: America's Master Spy.* New York, 1982.

Figes, Orlando. *The Whisperers: Private Life in Stalin's Russia.* London, 2007.

Fischer, Benjamin B. "Farewell to Sonia, the Spy Who Haunted Britain." *International Journal of Intelligence and Counterintelligence,* vol. 15, issue 1, 2002.

Foote, Alexander. *Handbook for Spies.* London, 2011.

Fuechtner, Veronika, Douglas E. Haynes, and Ryan M. Jones, eds., *A Global History of Sexual Science, 1880–1960.* Berkeley, Calif., 2017.

Glees, Anthony. *The Secrets of the Service.* London, 1987.

Gold, Michael. *Jews without Money.* New York, 1930.

Gould, Jonathan S. *German Anti-Nazi Espionage in the Second World War: The OSS and the Men of the TOOL Missions.* New York, 2018.

———. "Strange Bedfellows: The OSS and the London Free Germans." CIA Library, https://www.cia.gov/library/center-for-the-study-of-intelligence/csi-publications/csi-studies/studies/vol46no1/article03.html.

Green, John. *A Political Family: The Kuczynskis, Fascism, Espionage and the Cold War.* Abingdon, 2017.

Guha, Ramachandra. *India after Gandhi: The History of the World's Largest Democracy.* London, 2007.

Hahn, Emily. *China to Me: A Partial Autobiography.* New York, 1944.

Hamburger, Rudolf. *Zehn Jahre Lager.* Munich, 2013.

Hardesty, Von, and Ilya Ginberg. *Red Phoenix Rising: The Soviet Air Force in World War II.* Lawrence, Kans., 2012.

Hartland, Michael. *The Third Betrayal.* London, 1986.

Haslam, Jonathan. *Near and Distant Neighbours: A New History of Soviet Intelligence.* Oxford, 2015.

Haynes, John Earl, Harvey Klehr, and Alexander Vassiliev. *Spies: The Rise and Fall of the KGB in America.* New Haven, Conn., 2010.

Hennessy, Peter. *The Secret State: Whitehall and the Cold War.* London, 2002.

Holloway, David. *Stalin and the Bomb.* London, 1994.

Hornblum, Allen M. *The Invisible Harry Gold: The Man Who Gave the Soviets the Atom Bomb.* New Haven, Conn., 2010.

Hyde, H. Montgomery. *The Atom Bomb Spies.* London, 1980.

Kögel, Eduard. *Zwei Poelzigschüler in der Emigration,* dissertation. Weimar, 2007.

Krivitsky, Walter. *I Was Stalin's Agent.* London, 1940.

Kuczynski, Jürgen. *Memoiren,* 4 vols. Berlin, 1981–99.

Kuczynski, Rita. *Wall Flower: A Life on the German Border.* Toronto, 2015.

Kuromiya, Hiroaki. *The Voices of the Dead: Stalin's Great Terror in the 1930s.* New Haven, Conn., 2007.

Lamphere, Robert J., and Tom Shachtman. *The FBI–KGB War: A Special Agent's Story.* New York, 1986.

Leitz, Christian. *Nazi Germany and Neutral Europe during the Second World War*, Manchester, 2001.

Litten, Frederick S. "The Noulens Affair." *The China Quarterly*, vol. 138, June 1994.

Lota, Vladimir. *GRU i atomnaia bomba*. Moscow, 2002.

MacKinnon, J. R., and S. R. MacKinnon. *Agnes Smedley: The Life and Times of an American Radical*. Berkeley, Calif., 1988.

Matthews, Owen. *An Impeccable Spy: Richard Sorge, Stalin's Master Agent*. London, 2019.

Moorehead, Alan. *The Traitors: The Double Life of Fuchs, Pontecorvo and Nunn May*. London, 1952.

Moorhouse, Roger. *The Devils' Alliance: Hitler's Pact with Stalin, 1939–41*. London, 2014.

Moss, Norman. *Klaus Fuchs: The Man Who Stole the Atom Bomb*. London, 1987.

Nelson, Anne. *Red Orchestra*. New York, 2009.

Panitz, Eberhard. *Geheimtreff Banbury: Wie die Atombombe zu den Russen kam*. Berlin, 2003.

Persico, Joseph E. *Piercing the Reich*. New York, 1979.

———. *Roosevelt's Secret War: FDR and World War II Espionage*. New York, 2001.

Philby, Kim. *My Silent War*. London, 1968.

Pincher, Chapman. *Treachery: Betrayals, Blunders and Cover-ups; Six Decades of Espionage*. London, 2012.

Price, Ruth. *The Lives of Agnes Smedley*. Oxford, 2005.

Prysor, Glyn. *Citizen Sailors: The Royal Navy in the Second World War*. London, 2012.

Putz, Catherine. "What If the United States Had Told the Soviet Union about the Bomb?" *The Diplomat*, May 18, 2016.

Radó, Sandor. *Codename Dora*. New York, 1990.

Read, Anthony, and David Fisher. *Operation Lucy: Most Secret Spy Ring of the Second World War*. London, 1980.

Rossiter, Mike. *The Spy Who Changed the World*. London, 2014.

Sebag Montefiore, Simon. *Stalin: The Court of the Red Tsar*. London, 2003.

Sergeant, Harriet. *Shanghai: Collision Point of Cultures, 1918–1939*. New York, 1990.

Smedley, Agnes. *Daughter of Earth*. New York, 1987.

Smith, Michael, ed. *The Secret Agent's Bedside Reader: A Compendium of Spy Writing*. London, 2014.

Snow, Edgar. *Random Notes on China*. Cambridge, Mass., 1957.

Stibbe, Matthew. "Jürgen Kuczynski and the Search for a (Non-existent) Western Spy Ring in the East German Communist Party in 1953." *Contemporary European History*, vol. 20, issue 1, 2011.

Tarrant, V. E. *The Red Orchestra: The Soviet Spy Network inside Nazi Europe*. London, 1995.

Tolstoy, Nikolai. *Victims of Yalta*. London, 1979.

Tyrer, William A. "The Unresolved Mystery of ELLI." *International Journal of Intelligence and CounterIntelligence,* vol. 29, no. 4, 2016, 785–808.

Vassiliev, Alexander. *Yellow Notebooks.* 1995. https://digitalarchive.wilsoncenter.org/collection/86/vassiliev-notebooks.

Wakeman, Frederic, Jr. *Policing Shanghai, 1927–1937.* Berkeley, Calif., 1995.

Watson, Peter. *Fallout: Conspiracy, Cover-Up, and the Deceitful Case for the Atom Bomb.* London, 2018.

Werner, Ruth. *Ein ungewöhnliches Mädchen.* Berlin, 1959.

———. *Der Gong des Porzellanhändlers.* Berlin, 1976.

———. *Muhme Mehle.* Berlin, 2002.

———. *Olga Benario: Die Geschichte eines tapferen Lebens.* Berlin, 1961.

———. *Sonjas Rapport.* Berlin, 1977; rev. ed., 2006.

———. *Sonya's Report.* London, 1991.

West, Nigel. *Venona: The Greatest Secret of the Cold War.* London, 1999.

———. *Mortal Crimes: The Greatest Theft in History; The Soviet Penetration of the Manhattan Project.* New York, 2004.

Whymant, Robert. *Stalin's Spy: Richard Sorge and the Tokyo Espionage Ring.* New York, 1996.

Williams, Robert Chadwell. *Klaus Fuchs, Atom Spy.* Cambridge, Mass., 1987.

Willoughby, Charles. *Shanghai Conspiracy: The Sorge Spy Ring.* Boston, 1952.

Wolf, Markus. *In eigenem Auftrag.* Schneekluth, 1991.

Wright, Peter. *Spycatcher: The Candid Autobiography of a Senior Intelligence Officer.* London, 1987.

PHOTO CREDITS

FIRST PHOTO INSERT

PAGE 1: ullstein bild/Getty Images (top); Kuczynski family archive (right); courtesy of Peter Beurton (bottom)

PAGE 2: Courtesy of Peter Beurton (top and middle); courtesy of Ann Simpson (bottom)

PAGE 3: BArch, Bild 102-01355 (top); BStU, MfS, HA IX/11, FV 98/66, Bd. 40, S. 125 (middle); collection of the Hamburger family (bottom)

PAGE 4: CPA Media/Alamy (top); collection of the Hamburger family (middle); Agnes Smedley Photographs, University Archives, Arizona State University Library (bottom)

PAGE 5: Whereabouts of original photo unknown, from Ruth Werner, *Sonjas Rapport,* Berlin: Neues Leben, 1977 (top); BStU, MfS, HA IX/11, FV 98/66, Bd. 20, S. 98 (middle); collection of the Hamburger family (bottom)

PAGE 6: Sputnik/TopFoto (top); whereabouts of original photo unknown, from Ruth Werner, *Sonya's Report,* London: Chatto & Windus, 1991 (middle); collection of the Hamburger family (bottom)

PAGE 7: Collection of the Hamburger family (top left, top right); BStU, MfS, HA IX/11, FV 98/66, Bd. 39, S. 142 (middle); collection of the Hamburger family (bottom)

PAGE 8: BArch, Bild 10-2167-04 (top); Wellcome Library, London under

CC-BY 4.0 (middle); photograph by Helen Foster Snow, courtesy L. Tom Perry Special Collections, Brigham Young University (bottom)

SECOND PHOTO INSERT

PAGE 1: Courtesy of Peter Beurton (top left); BStU, MfS, HA IX/11, FV 98/66, Bd. 39, S. 139 (top right); source unknown (bottom left, bottom right)

PAGE 2: Collection of the Hamburger family (top left); NACP, RG 242.28: National Archives Collection of Foreign Records Seized (top right); BStU, MfS, HA IX/11, FV 98/66, Bd. 39, S. 145 (bottom left); courtesy of András Trom (bottom right)

PAGE 3: BStU, MfS, HA IX/11, FV 98/66, Bd. 40, S. 7 (top); courtesy of Ann Simpson (middle); collection of the Hamburger family (bottom)

PAGE 4: Collection of the Hamburger family (top left); photograph by Sybill Clay and Stella Caffyn, estate of Emily Hahn (top right); National Archives, Kew, KV2/1253 (middle); courtesy of Peter Beurton (bottom)

PAGE 5: National Archives, Kew, KV2/3908 (top left); private collection, from Jonathan S. Gould, *German Anti-Nazi Espionage in the Second World War: The OSS and the Men of the TOOL Missions,* Abingdon, Oxon; New York, NY: Routledge, 2019 (top right); NACP, RG 226: Records of the Office of Strategic Services (middle, bottom left, bottom right)

PAGE 6: Courtesy of Peter Beurton

PAGE 7: Reproduced by permission of the Principal of Lady Margaret Hall, University of Oxford (top left); AP/Shutterstock (top right); Keystone/Alamy (middle); © Martin Pope/Camera Press, London (bottom)

PAGE 8: BArch, Bild 10-2167-11 (top)

INDEX

AGENT SONYA

BEN MACINTYRE

Random House
Book Club

Because
Stories Are
Better Shared

™

QUESTIONS AND TOPICS FOR DISCUSSION

IN ORDER TO PROVIDE READING GROUPS WITH THE MOST informed and thought-provoking questions possible, it is necessary to reveal certain aspects of the story line of this book. If you have not finished reading *Agent Sonya,* we respectfully suggest that you do so before reviewing this guide.

1. Before reading *Agent Sonya,* how much did you know about Ursula Kuczynski, communism, and the Cold War era? Which historical aspects of the book surprised you the most? Did you learn new details about this period in history?

2. Why do you think Ursula was drawn to and became a champion of the communist cause?

3. How does this story reflect the great ideological clash of the twentieth century—between communism, fascism, and Western democracy?

4. Why do you think Ursula became and stayed a spy for so many years, despite all the risks and challenges? What was she attracted to most? Can you imagine ever doing what she did?

5. What is Ursula's most commendable quality? Her least? Is she someone you would want to have known?

6. There were many important supporting characters (and spies) in this book—who will you remember most, and why?

7. What did you think about Ursula's husbands and lovers? How did they each support her? What did you think about their own life decisions?

8. What role did sexism play in potentially enabling Ursula to operate undetected throughout her career?

9. Is there a scene (or scenes) in *Agent Sonya* that will stay with you? What will you remember most about this book? Do you plan to read more about the Cold War?

10. What role do the different settings play? Do you think similar events or espionage could have occurred in any other era?

11. What were your impressions of the author's voice and style? What specific themes did Ben Macintyre emphasize most throughout the book?

12. What did you like or dislike about the book that hasn't been discussed already?

13. If this book were to be made into a movie, whom would you cast for the main roles?

14. What other books by Ben Macintyre have you read? Which did you enjoy most?

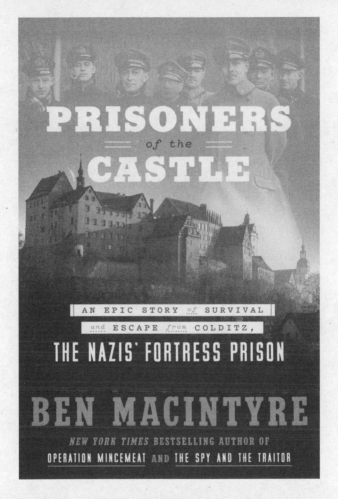

Franz Josef

Every evening, Sergeant Major Gustav Rothenberger carried out an inspection of the castle perimeter, checking that the sentries were alert at their posts and hoping to catch one napping. Rothenberger was a stickler for routine, and the last stop on his rounds was always the east side of the building, where a narrow walkway, with a sheer drop on one side and the mighty castle wall rising on the other, led to a barbed wire gate. Beyond that lay the park and the woods. Guards with machine guns were posted at intervals of thirty feet along the length of the terrace. Two more sentries guarded the gate itself, one patrolling a raised metal catwalk with a clear line of fire down the terrace.

Shortly before midnight on a warm September night in 1943, the Sergeant Major (or Stabsfeldwebel in German) appeared on the terrace as usual, accompanied by two soldiers with slung rifles. The prisoners had been locked into their quarters two hours earlier. Colditz was quiet. Powerful floodlights threw the guards' distorted silhouettes against the granite face of the castle.

Rothenberger cut an unmistakable figure. A native of Saxony, he had won the Iron Cross during the First World War and was said to wear his campaign medals in bed. He was feared and admired by the men under his command in Number 3 platoon of the guard company. The prisoners took every opportunity to mock their captors, but treated this bristling martinet with cautious respect, as a soldier from an earlier age: battle-scarred, disciplined, and extravagantly hairy. The most distinctive thing about Rothenberger was his facial plumage, a spectacular mustache and mutton-chop combination. The old soldier was immensely proud of his huge gingery whiskers, brushing, clipping, and waxing them to points, as if grooming an exotic pet. The British POWs called him "Franz Josef" [sic], after the Austro-Hungarian emperor with the handlebar mustache, but never, ever to his face.

Rothenberger marched up smartly to the first guard on the terrace and barked: "There is an attempted escape on the west side. Report to the guardhouse immediately." The startled sentry saluted, clicked his heels, and took off; the officer dismissed the second guard, and then the third. The two sentries manning the gate were surprised to see Rothenberger rounding the corner of the terrace with two replacement guards in tow. They were not due to go off duty for another two hours. "You're relieved early," snapped the mustachioed sergeant major. "Give me the key." Rothenberger appeared to be particularly irritable tonight; but appearances can be deceptive.

A close inspection of Rothenberger's facial hair would have revealed that it was made from dismantled shaving brushes, colored ginger-gray with watercolor paints from the prison shop and attached with glue; his uniform, like those of his escorts, was stitched with precision out of prison blankets, and dyed the correct shade of German field gray; the Iron Cross on his breast was made from zinc stripped off the castle roof and molded into shape with a hot kitchen knife; his headgear had been fashioned out of a peaked RAF cap using felt and string; his pistol holster was cardboard, shined up with brown boot polish, from which poked a piece of wood painted to look like the butt of a 9mm Walther P38 pistol; the two soldiers in greatcoats carried dummy rifles with wooden barrels polished with pencil lead, bolts fashioned from bits of steel bedstead, and tin triggers formed from metal cutlery.

The sergeant major was a replica Rothenberger, a fake Franz Josef. His name was Michael Sinclair, a twenty-five-year-old British lieutenant who had already escaped twice from Colditz before being caught and brought back. Sinclair was fluent in German, a talented amateur actor, and an obsessive. He thought only of escaping, and talked about nothing else. "I'm getting out of here," he insisted, repeatedly. This was not an expression of hope, but a statement of belief. Some of the other prisoners found his single-mindedness off-putting: There was something desperate in Sinclair's determination. For four months, he had studied Rothenberger's gait, posture, and accent, his routine, his mannerisms, and the way he swore when angry, which was often.

High above the terrace, thirty-five more British officers waited in the darkness. The bars on the windows of the sixth floor had already been sawn through. The men wore handmade civilian clothes. Each carried a counterfeit travel pass, forged using a typewriter of wood and wire, a photograph taken with a camera made from a cigar box and spectacles, and authorized with the official German eagle stamp carved out of a shoe heel using a razor blade. "It's going to work," someone whispered, as the first guard hurried off. "It's really going to work."

The plan was simple: with the sentries out of the way, a first group of twenty would climb down the outside of the building on ropes made from knotted bedsheets, Sinclair would unlock the gate to the park, and they would all scramble down the slope into the nearby woods. If they got away, the rest would follow a few minutes later. Once in the trees, they would split into pairs and spread out into the countryside, before making for Germany's borders by a variety of prearranged routes. The "Franz Josef plan" depended on ingrained German habits of military obedience, preparation, timing, luck, and the credibility of Sinclair's false whiskers. The escapers calculated it would take four and a half minutes before the dismissed guards reached the guardhouse and found the real Rothenberger. At which point all hell would break loose. Many of the prisoners crouching in the dark had been captives for almost three years. During that time numerous escapes had been attempted with only a small handful of successes. In the escalating internal war between the guarded and the guards, a major victory beckoned. If it worked, this would be the first mass breakout in Colditz history.

The *Kommandant* of Colditz had recently issued orders that everyone, without exception, entering or leaving the castle must produce a pass, with a different color for each day. The sentry at the gate was sticking to the rules. Later, he would claim that the mustache before him "did not quite curl properly"; in truth he was merely obeying orders, even though Rothenberger had issued those orders and was now apparently telling him to disobey them. The sentry's voice floated up to the windows above: "Nein, Herr Stabsfeldwebel. *Nein!*" Sinclair cursed him for his insolence. "Are you daft? Don't you know your own sergeant?" But finally, he reached into his pocket and handed over an exit pass, or *Ausweis,* dated, signed, and stamped.

This was a copy of a real pass obtained from a bribed German guard. It was a perfect duplicate in every respect. Except it was the wrong color. The fake pass was gray. It was supposed to be yellow.

The sentry stared at it for a moment, and back at "Franz Josef" Rothenberger. Then he slowly raised his rifle.

Read on for an excerpt from

BEN MACINTYRE'S

New York Times bestseller

The Spy and the Traitor

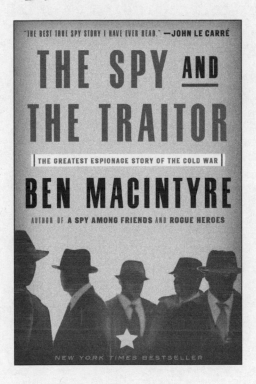

"The best truc spy story I have ever read."
—**John le Carré**

CROWN
Available wherever books are sold

INTRODUCTION

F OR THE KGB'S COUNTERINTELLIGENCE SECTION, Directorate K, this was a routine bugging job.

It took less than a minute to spring the locks on the front door of the flat on the eighth floor of 103 Leninsky Prospekt, a Moscow tower block occupied by KGB officers and their families. While two men in gloves and overalls set about methodically searching the apartment, two technicians wired the place, swiftly and invisibly, implanting eavesdropping devices behind the wallpaper and baseboards, inserting a live microphone into the telephone mouthpiece and video cameras in the light fixtures in the sitting room, bedroom, and kitchen. By the time they had finished, an hour later, there was barely a corner in the flat where the KGB did not have eyes and ears. Finally, they put on face masks and sprinkled radioactive dust on the clothes and shoes in the closet, sufficiently low in concentration to avoid poisoning, but enough to enable the KGB's Geiger counters to track the wearer's movements. Then they left, and carefully locked the front door behind them.

A few hours later, a senior Russian intelligence officer landed at Moscow's Sheremetyevo airport on the Aeroflot flight from London.

Colonel Oleg Antonyevich Gordievsky of the KGB was at the pinnacle of his career. A prodigy of the Soviet intelligence service, he had diligently risen through the ranks, serving in Scandinavia, Moscow, and Britain with hardly a blemish on his record. And now, at the age of forty-six, he had been promoted to chief of the KGB station in London, a plum posting, and invited to return to Moscow to be formally anointed by the head of the KGB. A career spy, Gordievsky was tipped to ascend to the uppermost ranks of that vast and ruthless

security and intelligence network that controlled the Soviet Union.

A stocky, athletic figure, Gordievsky strode confidently through the airport crowds. Inside him, though, a low terror bubbled. For Oleg Gordievsky, KGB veteran, faithful secret servant of the Soviet Union, was a British spy.

Recruited a dozen years earlier by MI6, Britain's foreign-intelligence service, the agent code-named NOCTON had proven to be one of the most valuable spies in history. The immense amount of information he fed back to his British handlers had changed the course of the Cold War, cracking open Soviet spy networks, helping to avert nuclear war, and furnishing the West with a unique insight into the Kremlin's thinking during a critically dangerous period in world affairs. Both Ronald Reagan and Margaret Thatcher had been briefed on the extraordinary trove of secrets provided by the Russian spy, though neither the American president nor the British prime minister knew his real identity. Even Gordievsky's young wife was entirely unaware of his double life.

Gordievsky's appointment as KGB *rezident* (the Russian term for a KGB head of station, known as a *rezidentura*) had prompted rejoicing among the tiny circle of MI6 officers privy to the case. As the most senior Soviet intelligence operative in Britain, Gordievsky would henceforth have access to the innermost secrets of Russian espionage: he would be able to inform the West about what the KGB was planning to do, before it did it; the KGB in Britain would be neutered. And yet the abrupt summons back to Moscow had unsettled the NOCTON team. Some sensed a trap. At a hastily convened meeting in a London safe house with his MI6 handlers, Gordievsky had been offered the option to defect and remain in Britain with his family. Everyone at the meeting understood the stakes: if he returned as official KGB *rezident* then MI6, the CIA, and their Western allies would hit the intelligence jackpot, but if Gordievsky was walking into a trap he would lose everything, including his life. He had thought long and hard before making up his mind: "I will go back."

Once again, the MI6 officers went over Gordievsky's emergency escape plan, code-named PIMLICO, that had been drawn up seven years earlier in the hope that it would never have to be activated. MI6 had never exfiltrated anyone from the USSR before, let alone a KGB officer. Elaborate and hazardous, the escape plan could be triggered only as a last resort.

Gordievsky had been trained to spot danger. As he walked through the airport, his nerves ragged with internal stress, he saw signs of peril everywhere. The passport officer seemed to study his papers for an inordinate length of time before waving him through. Where was the official who was supposed to be meeting him, a minimal courtesy for a KGB colonel arriving back from overseas? The airport was always stiff with surveillance, but today the nondescript men and women standing around apparently idly seemed even more numerous than normal. Gordievsky climbed into a taxi, telling himself that if the KGB knew the truth, he would have been arrested the moment he set foot on Russian soil and already on his way to the KGB cells to face interrogation and torture, followed by execution.

As far as he could tell, no one followed him as he entered the familiar apartment block on Leninsky Prospekt and took the elevator to the eighth floor. He had not been inside the family flat since January.

The first lock on the front door opened easily, and then the second. But the door would not budge. The third lock on the door, an old-fashioned dead bolt dating back to the construction of the apartment block, had been locked.

But Gordievsky never used the third lock. Indeed, he had never had the key. That must mean that someone with a skeleton key had been inside, and on leaving had mistakenly triple-locked the door. That someone must have been the KGB.

The fears of the previous week crystallized in a freezing rush, with the chilling, paralyzing recognition that his apartment had been entered, searched, and probably bugged. He was under suspicion. Someone had betrayed him. The KGB was watching him. The spy was being spied upon by his fellow spies.

Chapter 1

THE KGB

O LEG GORDIEVSKY WAS BORN INTO THE KGB: SHAPED BY it, loved by it, twisted, damaged, and very nearly destroyed by it. The Soviet spy service was in his heart and in his blood. His father worked for the intelligence service all his life, and wore his KGB uniform every day, including weekends. The Gordievskys lived amid the spy fraternity in a designated apartment block, ate special food reserved for officers, and spent their free time socializing with other spy families. Gordievsky was a child of the KGB.

The KGB—the *Komitet Gosudarstvennoy Bezopasnosti,* or Committee for State Security—was the most complex and far-reaching intelligence agency ever created. The direct successor of Stalin's spy network, it combined the roles of foreign- and domestic-intelligence gathering, internal security enforcement, and state police. Oppressive, mysterious, and ubiquitous, the KGB penetrated and controlled every aspect of Soviet life. It rooted out internal dissent, guarded the Communist leadership, mounted espionage and counterintelligence operations against enemy powers, and cowed the peoples of the USSR into abject obedience. It recruited agents and planted spies worldwide, gathering, buying, and stealing military, political, and scientific secrets from anywhere and everywhere. At the height of its power, with more than one million officers, agents, and informants, the KGB shaped Soviet society more profoundly than any other institution.

To the West, the initials were a byword for internal terror and external aggression and subversion, shorthand for all the cruelty of a totalitarian regime run by a faceless official mafia. But the KGB was not regarded that way by those who lived under its stern rule. Certainly it inspired fear and obedience, but the KGB was also admired as a Praetorian guard, a bulwark against Western imperialist and capitalist aggression, and the guardian of Communism. Membership in this elite and privileged force was a source of admiration and pride. Those who joined the service did so for life. "There is no such thing as a former KGB man," the former KGB officer Vladimir Putin once said. This was an exclusive club to join—and an impossible one to leave. Entering the ranks of the KGB was an honor and a duty to those with sufficient talent and ambition to do so.

Oleg Gordievsky never seriously contemplated doing anything else.

His father, Anton Lavrentyevich Gordievsky, the son of a railway worker, had been a teacher before the revolution of 1917 transformed him into a dedicated, unquestioning Communist, a rigid enforcer of ideological orthodoxy. "The Party was God," his son later wrote, and the older Gordievsky never wavered in his devotion, even when his faith demanded that he take part in unspeakable crimes. In 1932, he helped enforce the "Sovietization" of Kazakhstan, organizing the expropriation of food from peasants to feed the Soviet armies and cities. Around 1.5 million people perished in the resulting famine. Anton saw state-induced starvation at close quarters. That year, he joined the office of state security, and then the NKVD, the People's Commissariat for Internal Affairs, Stalin's secret police and the precursor of the KGB. An officer in the political directorate, he was responsible for political discipline and indoctrination. Anton married Olga Nikolayevna Gornova, a twenty-four-year-old statistician, and the couple moved into a Moscow apartment block reserved for the intelligence elite. A first child, Vasili, was born in 1932. The Gordievskys thrived under Stalin.

When Comrade Stalin announced that the revolution was facing a lethal threat from within, Anton Gordievsky stood ready to help remove the traitors. The Great Purge of 1936 to 1938 saw the wholesale liquidation of "enemies of the state": suspected fifth columnists and hidden Trotskyists, terrorists and saboteurs, counterrevolutionary spies, Party and government officials, peasants, Jews, teachers, generals, members of the intelligentsia, Poles, Red Army soldiers, and many more. Most were entirely innocent. In Stalin's paranoid police state, the safest way to ensure survival was to denounce someone else. "Better that ten innocent people should suffer than one spy get away," said Nikolai Yezhov, chief of the NKVD. "When you chop wood, chips fly." The informers whispered, the torturers and executioners set to work, and the Siberian gulags swelled to bursting. But as in every revolution, the enforcers themselves inevitably became suspect. The NKVD began to investigate and purge itself. At the height of the bloodletting, the Gordievskys' apartment block was raided more than a dozen times in a six-month period. The arrests came at night: the man of the family was led away first, and then the rest.

It seems probable that some of these enemies of the state were identified by Anton Gordievsky. "The NKVD is always right," he said: a conclusion both wholly sensible and entirely wrong.

A second son, Oleg Antonyevich Gordievsky, was born on October 10, 1938, just as the Great Terror was winding down and war was looming. To friends and neighbors, the Gordievskys appeared to be ideal Soviet citizens, ideologically pure, loyal to Party and state, and now the parents to two strapping boys. A daughter, Marina, was born seven years after Oleg. The Gordievskys were well fed, privileged, and secure.

But on closer examination there were fissures in the family façade, and layers of deception beneath the surface. Anton Gordievsky never spoke about what he had done during the famines, the purges, and the terror. The elder Gordievsky was a prime example of the species *Homo Sovieticus*, an obedient state servant forged by Communist repression. But underneath he was fearful, horrified, and perhaps gnawed by guilt. Oleg later came to see his father as "a frightened man."

Olga Gordievsky, Oleg's mother, was made of less tractable material. She never joined the Party, and she did not believe that the NKVD was infallible. Her father had been dispossessed of his water mill by the Communists; her brother sent to the eastern Siberian gulag for criticizing collective agriculture; she had seen many friends dragged from their homes and marched away in the night. With a peasant's ingrained common sense, she understood the caprice and vindictiveness of state terror, but kept her mouth shut.

Oleg and Vasili, separated in age by six years, grew up in wartime. One of Gordievsky's earliest memories was of watching lines of bedraggled German prisoners being paraded through the streets of Moscow, "trapped, guarded, and led like animals." Anton was frequently absent for long periods, lecturing the troops on Party ideology.

Oleg Gordievsky dutifully learned the tenets of Communist orthodoxy: he attended School 130, where he showed an early aptitude for history and languages; he learned about the heroes of Communism, at home and abroad. Despite the thick veil of disinformation surrounding the West, foreign countries fascinated him. At the age of six, he began reading *British Ally*, a propaganda sheet put out in Russian by the British embassy to encourage Anglo-Russian understanding. He studied German. As expected of all teenagers, he joined the Komsomol, the Communist Youth League.

His father brought home three official newspapers and spouted the Communist propaganda they contained. The NKVD morphed into the KGB, and Anton Gordievsky obediently followed. Oleg's mother exuded a quiet resistance that only occasionally revealed itself in waspish, half-whispered asides. Religious worship was illegal under Communism, and the boys were raised as atheists, but their maternal grandmother had Vasili secretly baptized into the Russian Orthodox Church, and would have christened Oleg, too, had their horrified father not found out and intervened.

Oleg Gordievsky grew up in a tight-knit, loving family suffused with duplicity. Anton Gordievsky venerated the Party and proclaimed himself a fearless upholder of Communism, but inside was a small and terrified man who had witnessed terrible events. Olga Gordievsky, the ideal KGB wife, nursed a secret disdain for the system. Oleg's grandmother secretly worshipped an illegal, outlawed God. None of the adults in the family revealed what they really felt—to one another, or anyone else. Amid the stifling conformity of Stalin's Russia, it was possible to believe differently in secret but far too dangerous for honesty, even with members of your own family. From boyhood, Oleg saw that it was possible to live a double life, to love those around you while concealing your true inner self, to appear to be one person to the external world and quite another inside.

Oleg Gordievsky emerged from school with a silver medal, head of the local Komsomol, a competent, intelligent, athletic, unquestioning, and unremarkable product of the Soviet system. But he had also learned to compartmentalize. In different ways, his father, mother, and grandmother were all people in disguise. The young Gordievsky grew up around secrets.

Stalin died in 1953. Three years later he was denounced, at the 20th Party Congress, by his successor, Nikita Khrushchev. Anton Gordievsky was staggered. The official condemnation of Stalin, his son believed, "went a long way towards destroying the ideological and philosophical foundations of his life." He did not like the way Russia was changing. But his son did.

The "Khrushchev Thaw" was brief and restricted, but it was a period of genuine liberalization that saw the relaxation of censorship and the release of thousands of political prisoners. These were heady times to be young, Russian, and hopeful.

At the age of seventeen, Oleg enrolled at the prestigious Moscow State Institute of International Relations. There, exhilarated by the new atmosphere, he engaged in earnest discussions with his peers about how to bring about "socialism with a human face." He went too far. Some of his mother's nonconformity had seeped into him. One day, he wrote a speech, naive in its defense of freedom and democracy, concepts he barely understood. He recorded it in the language laboratory and played it to some fellow students. They were appalled. "You must destroy this at once, Oleg, and never mention these things again." Suddenly fearful, he wondered if one of his classmates had informed the authorities of his "radical" opinions. The KGB had spies inside the institute.

The limits of Khrushchev's reformism were brutally demonstrated in 1956 when the Soviet tanks rolled into Hungary to put down a nationwide uprising against Soviet rule. Despite the all-embracing Soviet censorship and propaganda, news of the crushed rebellion filtered back to Russia. "All warmth disappeared," Oleg recalled of the ensuing clampdown. "An icy wind set in."

The Institute of International Relations was the Soviet Union's most elite university, described by Henry Kissinger as "the Russian Harvard." Run by the Ministry of Foreign Affairs, it was the premier training ground for diplomats, scientists, economists, politicians—and spies. Gordievsky studied history, geography, economics, and international relations, all through the warping prism of Communist ideology. The institute provided instruction in fifty-six languages, more than any other university in the world. Language skills offered one clear pathway into the KGB and the foreign travel that he craved. Already fluent in German, he applied to study English, but the courses were overenrolled. "Learn Swedish," suggested his older brother, who had already joined the KGB. "It is the doorway to the rest of Scandinavia." Gordievsky took his advice.

The institute library stocked some foreign newspapers and periodicals that, though heavily redacted, offered a glimpse of the wider world. These he began to read, discreetly, for showing overt interest in the West was itself grounds for suspicion. Sometimes at night he would secretly listen to the BBC World Service or the Voice of America, despite the radio-jamming system imposed by Soviet censors, and picked up "the first faint scent of truth."

Like all human beings, in later life Gordievsky tended to see his past through the lens of experience, to imagine that he had always secretly harbored the seeds of insubordination, to believe his fate was somehow hardwired into his character. It was not. As a student, he was a keen Communist, eager to serve the Soviet state in the KGB, like his father and brother. The Hungarian Uprising had caught his youthful imagination, but he was no revolutionary. "I was still within the system but my feelings of disillusionment were growing." In this he was no different from many of his student contemporaries.

At the age of nineteen, Gordievsky took up cross-country running. Something about the solitary nature of the sport appealed to him, the rhythm of intense exertion over a long period, in private competition with himself, testing his own limits. Oleg could be gregarious, attractive to women, and flirtatious. His looks were bluntly handsome, with hair swept back from his forehead and open, rather soft features. In repose, his expression seemed stern, but when his eyes flashed with dark humor, his face lit up. In company he was often convivial and comradely, but there was something hard and hidden inside. He was not lonely, or a loner, but he was comfortable in his own company. He seldom revealed his feelings. Typically hungry for self-improvement, Oleg believed that cross-country running was "character building." For hours he would run, through Moscow's streets and parks, alone with his thoughts.

One of the few students he grew close to was Stanislaw Kaplan, a fellow runner on the university track team. "Standa" Kaplan was Czechoslovakian and had already obtained a degree from Charles University in Prague by the time he arrived at the institute as one of several hundred gifted students from the Soviet bloc. Like others from countries only recently subjugated to Communism, Kaplan's "individuality had not been stifled," Gordievsky wrote years later. A year older, he was studying to be a military translator. The two young men found they shared compatible ambitions and similar ideas. "He was liberal-minded and held strongly sceptical views about communism," wrote Gordievsky, who found Kaplan's forthright opinions exciting, and slightly alarming. With his dark good looks, Standa was a magnet to women. The two students became firm friends, running together, chasing girls, and eating in a Czech restaurant off Gorky Park.

An equally important influence was his idolized older brother,

Vasili, who was now training to become an "illegal," one of the Soviet Union's vast global army of deep undercover agents.

The KGB ran two distinct species of spy in foreign countries. The first worked under formal cover, as a member of the Soviet diplomatic or consular staff, a cultural or military attaché, accredited journalist or trade representative. Diplomatic protection meant that these "legal" spies could not be prosecuted for espionage if their activities were uncovered, but only declared persona non grata and expelled from the country. By contrast, an "illegal" spy (*nelegal*, in Russian) had no official status, usually traveled under a false name with fake papers, and simply blended invisibly into whatever country he or she was posted to. (In the West such spies are known as NOCs, standing for non-official cover.) The KGB planted illegals all over the world, who posed as ordinary citizens, submerged and subversive. Like legal spies, they gathered information, recruited agents, and conducted various forms of espionage. Sometimes, as "sleepers," they might remain hidden for long periods before being activated. These were also potential fifth columnists, poised to go into battle should war erupt between East and West. Illegals operated beneath the official radar and therefore could not be financed in ways that might be traced or communicate through secure diplomatic channels. But unlike spies accredited to an embassy, they left few traces for counterintelligence investigators to follow. Every Soviet embassy contained a permanent KGB station, or *rezidentura*, with a number of KGB officers in various official guises, all under the command of a *rezident* (head of station in MI6 parlance, or station chief to the CIA). One task facing Western counterintelligence was working out which Soviet officials were genuine diplomats and which were really spies. Tracking down the illegals was far harder.

The First Chief Directorate (FCD) was the KGB department responsible for foreign intelligence. Within this, Directorate S (standing for "special") trained, deployed, and managed the illegals. Vasili Gordievsky was formally recruited into Directorate S in 1960.

The KGB maintained an office inside the Institute of International Relations, staffed by two officers on the lookout for potential recruits. Vasili mentioned to his bosses in Directorate S that his younger brother, proficient in languages, might be interested in the same line of work.

Early in 1961, Oleg Gordievsky was invited in for a chat, and then told to go to a building near the KGB headquarters in Dzerzhinsky Square, where he was politely interviewed, in German, by a middle-aged woman, who complimented him on his grasp of the language. From that instant, he was part of the system. Gordievsky did not seek to join the KGB; this was not a club you applied to. It chose you.

BEN MACINTYRE is a writer-at-large for *The Times* (U.K.) and the bestselling author of *The Spy and the Traitor, A Spy Among Friends, Double Cross, Operation Mincemeat, Agent Zigzag,* and *Rogue Heroes,* among other books. Macintyre has also written and presented BBC documentaries of his work.

ABOUT THE TYPE

This book was set in Bembo, a typeface based on an old-style
Roman face that was used for Cardinal Pietro Bembo's tract
De Aetna in 1495. Bembo was cut by Francesco Griffo
(1450–1518) in the early sixteenth century for Italian
Renaissance printer and publisher Aldus Manutius (1449–1515).
The Lanston Monotype Company of Philadelphia brought
the well-proportioned letterforms of Bembo to the
United States in the 1930s.

RANDOM HOUSE BOOK CLUB

Because Stories Are Better Shared

Discover
Exciting new books that spark conversation every week.

Connect
With authors on tour—or in your living room. (Request an Author Chat for your book club!)

Discuss
Stories that move you with fellow book lovers on Facebook, on Goodreads, or at in-person meet-ups.

Enhance
Your reading experience with discussion prompts, digital book club kits, and more, available on our website.

Join our online book club community!
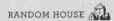 randomhousebookclub.com

Random House Book Club™

Because Stories Are Better Shared

RANDOM HOUSE

Half
Magic

E D W A R D   E A G E R

Illustrated by N. M. Bodecker

An Odyssey Classic
Harcourt Brace Jovanovich, Publishers
San Diego   New York   London

Library of Congress Cataloging-in-Publication Data

Eager, Edward.
Half magic.
"An Odyssey classic."
Reprint. Originally published: New York: Harcourt Brace, c1954.
Summary: Four children spending their summer in a city apartment enjoy a series
of fantastic adventures by double-wishing on an ancient coin.
1. Children's stories, American. [1. Fantasy]
I. Bodecker, N. M., ill. II. Title.
PZ7.E115Hal 1985 [Fic] 84-19816
ISBN 0-15-233081-X (pbk.)

Printed in the United States of America

A B C D E

CONTENTS

Half Magic

1

How It Began

It began one day in summer about thirty years ago, and it happened to four children.

Jane was the oldest and Mark was the only boy, and between them they ran everything.

Katharine was the middle girl, of docile disposition and a comfort to her mother. She knew she was a comfort, and docile, because she'd heard her mother say so. And the others knew she was, too, by now, because ever since that day Katharine *would* keep boasting about what a comfort she was, and how docile, until Jane declared she would utter a piercing shriek and fall over dead if she heard another word about it. This will give you some idea of what Jane and Katharine were like.

Martha was the youngest, and very difficult.

The children never went to the country or a lake in the summer, the way their friends did, because their father was dead and their mother worked very hard on the other newspaper, the one almost nobody on the block took. A woman named Miss Bick came in every day to care for the children, but she couldn't seem to care for them very much, nor they for her. And she wouldn't take them to the country or a lake; she said it was too much to expect and the sound of waves affected her heart.

"Clear Lake isn't the ocean; you can hardly hear it," Jane told her.

"It would attract lightning," Miss Bick said, which Jane thought cowardly, besides being unfair arguing. If you're going to argue, and Jane usually was, you want people to line up all their objections at a time; then you can knock them all down at once. But Miss Bick was always sly.

Still, even without the country or a lake, the summer was a fine thing, particularly when you were at the beginning of it, looking ahead into it. There would be months of beautifully long, empty days, and each other to play with, and the books from the library.

In the summer you could take out ten books at a time, instead of three, and keep them a month, instead of two weeks. Of course you could take only four of the fiction books, which were the best, but Jane liked plays and they were nonfiction, and Katharine liked poetry and that was nonfiction, and Martha was still the age for picture books, and they didn't count as fiction but were often nearly as good.

Mark hadn't found out yet what kind of nonfiction he liked, but he was still trying. Each month he would carry home his ten books and read the four good fiction ones in the first four days, and then read one page each from the other six, and then give up. Next month he would take them back and try again. The nonfiction books he tried were mostly called things like "When I was a Boy in Greece," or "Happy Days on the Prairie"—things that made them sound like stories, only they weren't. They made Mark furious.

"It's being made to learn things not on purpose. It's unfair," he said. "It's sly." Unfairness and slyness the four children hated above all.

The library was two miles away, and walking there with a lot of heavy, already-read books was dull, but coming home was splendid—walking slowly, stopping from time to time on different strange front steps, dipping into the different books. One day Katharine, the poetry-lover, tried to read *Evangeline* out loud on the way home, and Martha sat right down on the sidewalk after seven blocks of it, and refused to go a step farther if she had to hear another word of it. That will tell you about Martha.

After that Jane and Mark made a rule that nobody could read bits out loud and bother the others. But this summer the rule was changed. This summer the children had found some books by a writer named

4

E. Nesbit, surely the most wonderful books in the world. They read every one that the library had, right away, except a book called *The Enchanted Castle*, which had been out.

And now yesterday *The Enchanted Castle* had come in, and they took it out, and Jane, because she could read fastest and loudest, read it out loud all the way home, and when they got home she went on reading, and when their mother came home they hardly said a word to her, and when dinner was served they didn't notice a thing they ate. Bedtime came at the moment when the magic ring in the book changed from a ring of invisibility to a wishing ring. It was a terrible place to stop, but their mother had one of her strict moments; so stop they did.

And so naturally they all woke up even earlier than usual this morning, and Jane started right in reading out loud and didn't stop till she got to the end of the last page.

There was a contented silence when she closed the book, and then, after a little, it began to get discontented.

Martha broke it, saying what they were all thinking.

"Why don't things like that ever happen to *us*?"

"Magic never happens, not really," said Mark, who was old enough to be sure about this.

5

"How do you know?" asked Katharine, who was nearly as old as Mark, but not nearly so sure about anything.

"Only in fairy stories."

"It *wasn't* a fairy story. There weren't any dragons or witches or poor woodcutters, just real children like us!"

They were all talking at once now.

"They *aren't* like us. We're never in the country for the summer, and walk down strange roads and find castles!"

"We never go to the seashore and meet mermaids and sand fairies!"

"Or go to our uncle's, and there's a magic garden!"

"If the Nesbit children do stay in the city it's London, and *that*'s interesting, and then they find phoenixes and magic carpets! Nothing like that ever happens here!"

"There's Mrs. Hudson's house," Jane said. "That's a *little* like a castle."

"There's the Miss Kings' garden."

"We could *pretend* . . ."

It was Martha who said this, and the others turned on her.

"Beast!"

"Spoilsport!"

Because of course the only way pretending is any good is if you never say right out that that's what you're doing. Martha knew this perfectly well, but in her youth she sometimes forgot. So now Mark threw a pillow at her, and so did Jane and Katharine, and in the excitement that followed their mother woke up, and Miss Bick arrived and started giving orders, and "all was flotsam and jetsam," in the poetic words of Katharine.

Two hours later, with breakfast eaten, Mother gone to work and the dishes done, the four children escaped at last, and came out into the sun. It was fine weather, warm and blue-skied and full of possibilities, and the day began well, with a glint of something metal in a crack in the sidewalk.

"Dibs on the nickel," Jane said, and scooped it into her pocket with the rest of her allowance, still jingling there unspent. She would get round to thinking about spending it after the adventures of the morning.

The adventures of the morning began with promise. Mrs. Hudson's house looked *quite* like an Enchanted Castle, with its stone wall around and iron dog on the lawn. But when Mark crawled into the peony bed and Jane stood on his shoulders and held Martha up to the kitchen window, all Martha saw was Mrs. Hudson mixing something in a bowl.

"Eye of newt and toe of frog, probably," Katharine thought, but Martha said it looked more like simple one-egg cake.

And then when one of the black ants that live in all peony beds bit Mark, and he dropped Jane and Martha with a crash, nothing happened except Mrs. Hudson's coming out and chasing them with a broom the way she always did, and saying she'd tell their mother. This didn't worry them much, because their mother always said it was Mrs. Hudson's own fault, that people who had trouble with children brought it on themselves, but it was boring.

So then the children went farther down the street and looked at the Miss Kings' garden. Bees were humming pleasantly round the columbines, and there were Canterbury bells and purple foxgloves looking satisfactorily old-fashioned, and for a moment it seemed as though anything might happen.

But then Miss Mamie King came out and told them that a dear little fairy lived in the biggest purple foxglove, and this wasn't the kind of talk the children wanted to hear at all. They stayed only long enough to be polite, before trooping dispiritedly back to sit on their own front steps.

They sat there and couldn't think of anything exciting to do, and nothing went on happening, and it was then that Jane was so disgusted that she said right out loud she wished there'd be a fire!

The other three looked shocked at hearing such wickedness, and then they looked more shocked at what they heard next.

What they heard next was a fire siren!

Fire trucks started tearing past—the engine, puffing out smoke the way it used to do in those days, the Chief's car, the hook and ladder, the Chemicals!

Mark and Katharine and Martha looked at Jane, and Jane looked back at them with wild wonder in her eyes. Then they started running.

The fire was eight blocks away, and it took them a long time to get there, because Martha wasn't allowed to cross streets by herself, and couldn't run fast yet, like the others; so they had to keep waiting for her to catch up, at all the corners.

And when they finally reached the house where the trucks had stopped, it wasn't the house that was on fire. It was a playhouse in the backyard, the fanciest playhouse the children had ever seen, two stories high and with dormer windows.

You all know what watching a fire is like, the glory of the flames streaming out through the windows, and the wonderful moment when the roof falls in, or even better if there's a tower and it falls through the roof. This playhouse *did* have a tower, and it fell through the roof most beautifully, with a crash and a shower of sparks.

And the fact that it *was* a playhouse, and small like the children, made it seem even more like a special fire that was planned just for them. And the little girl the playhouse belonged to turned out to be an unmistakably spoiled and unpleasant type named Genevieve, with long golden curls that had probably never been cut; so *that* was all right. And furthermore, the children overheard her father say he'd buy her a new playhouse with the insurance money.

So altogether there was no reason for any but feelings of the deepest satisfaction in the breasts of the four children, as they stood breathing heavily and watching the firemen deal with the flames, which they did with that heroic calm typical of fire departments the world over.

And it wasn't until the last flame was drowned, and the playhouse stood there a wet and smoking mess of ashes and charred boards that guilt rose up in Jane and turned her joy to ashes, too.

"Oh, what you did," Martha whispered at her.

"I don't want to talk about it," Jane said. But

she went over to a woman who seemed to be the nurse of the golden-haired Genevieve, and asked her how it started.

"All of a piece it went up, like the Fourth of July as ever was," said the nurse. "And it's my opinion," she added, looking at Jane very suspiciously, "that it was *set*! What are *you* doing here, little girl?"

Jane turned right around and walked out of the yard, holding herself as straight as possible and trying to keep from running. The other three went after her.

"Is Jane magic?" Martha whispered to Katharine.

"I don't know. I think so," Katharine whispered back.

Jane glared at them. They went for two blocks in silence.

"Are we magic, too?"

"I don't know. I'm scared to find out."

Jane glared. Once more silence fell.

But this time Martha couldn't hold herself in for more than half a block.

"Will we be burnt as *witches*?"

Jane whirled on them furiously.

"I wish," she started to say.

1 1

"Don't!" Katharine almost screamed, and Jane turned white, shut her lips tight, and started walking faster.

Mark made the others run to catch up.

"This won't do any good. We've got to talk it over," he told Jane.

"Yes, talk it over," said Martha, looking less worried. She had great respect for Mark, who was a boy and knew everything.

"The thing is," Mark went on, "was it just an accident, or did we want so much to be magic we *got* that way, somehow? The thing is, each of us ought to make a wish. That'll prove it one way or the other."

But Martha balked at this. You could never tell with Martha. Sometimes she would act just as grown-up as the others, and then suddenly she would be a baby. Now she was a baby. Her lip trembled, and she said she didn't want to make a wish and she *wouldn't* make a wish and she wished they'd never started to play this game in the first place.

After consultation, Mark and Katharine decided this could count as Martha's wish, but it didn't seem to have come true, because if it had they wouldn't remember any of the morning, and yet they remembered it all too clearly. But just as a test Mark turned to Jane.

"What have we been doing?" he asked.

"Watching a fire," Jane said bitterly, and at that moment the fire trucks went by on their way home to the station, to prove it.

So then Mark rather depressedly wished his shoes were seven-league boots, but when he tried to jump seven leagues it turned out they weren't.

Katharine wished Shakespeare would come up and talk to her. She forgot to say exactly *when* she wanted this to happen, but after they waited a minute and he didn't appear, they decided he probably wasn't coming.

So it seemed that if there was any magic among them, Jane had it all.

But try as they might, they couldn't persuade Jane to make another wish, even a little safe one. She just kept shaking her head at all their arguments, and when argument descended to insult she didn't say a word, which was most unlike Jane.

When they got home she said she had a headache, and went out on the sleeping porch, and shut the door. She wouldn't even come downstairs for lunch, but stayed out there alone all the afternoon, moodily eating a whole box of Social Tea biscuits and talking to Carrie, the cat. Miss Bick despaired of her.

When their mother came home she knew some-

1 3

thing was wrong. But being an understanding parent she didn't ask questions.

At dinner she announced that she was going out for the evening. Jane didn't look up from her brooding silence, but the others were interested. The children always hoped their mother was going on exciting adventures, though she seldom was. Tonight she was going to see Aunt Grace and Uncle Edwin.

"Why?" Mark wanted to know.

"They were very kind to me after your father died. They have been very kind to *you*."

"Useful presents!" Mark was scornful.

"Will Aunt Grace say 'Just a little chocolate cake, best you ever tasted, I made it myself?'" Katharine wanted to know.

"You shouldn't laugh at your Aunt Grace. I don't know what your father would say."

"Father laughed at her, too."

"It isn't the same thing."

"Why?"

This kind of conversation was always very interesting to the children, and could have gone on forever so far as they were concerned, but somehow no grown-ups ever seemed to feel that way about conversations. Their mother put a stop to this one by leaving for Aunt Grace's.

When she had gone things got strange again.

Jane kept hovering in and out of the room where the others were playing a halfhearted game of Flinch, until everyone was driven wild.

Finally Mark burst out.

"Why don't you tell us?"

Jane shook her head.

"I can't. You wouldn't understand."

Naturally this made everyone furious.

"Just because she's magic she thinks she's smarter!" Martha said.

"*I* don't think she's magic at all!" This was Katharine. "Only she's afraid to make a wish and find out!"

"I'm not! I *am!*" Jane cried, not very clearly. "Only I don't know why, or how much! It's like having one foot almost asleep, but not quite—you can't use it and you can't enjoy it! I'm afraid to even *think* a wish! I'm afraid to think at *all!*"

If you have ever had magic powers descend on you suddenly out of the blue, you'll know how Jane felt.

When you have magic powers and know it, it can be a fine feeling, like a pleasant tingling inside. But in order to enjoy that tingling, you have to know just how much magic you have and what the rules are for using it. And Jane didn't have any idea how much she had or how to use it, and this made her unhappy and the others couldn't see why, and said so, and Jane answered back, and by the time they went to bed no one was speaking to anyone else.

What bothered Jane most was a feeling that she'd forgotten something, and that if she could remember it she'd know the reason for everything that had happened. It was as if the reason were there in her mind somewhere, if only she could reach it. She leaned into her mind, reaching, reaching . . .

The next thing she knew, she was sitting straight up in bed and the clock was striking eleven, and she had remembered. It was as though she'd gone on thinking in her sleep. Sometimes this happens.

She got up and felt her way to the dresser where she'd put her money, without looking at it, when she came home from the fire. First she felt the top of the dresser. Then she lit the lamp and looked.

The nickel she'd found in the crack in the sidewalk was gone.

And then Jane began thinking really hard.

2

What Happened to Their Mother

At Aunt Grace and Uncle Edwin's the air was hot and stuffy and the furniture was hot and stuffy and Aunt Grace and Uncle Edwin were stuffy.

"Poor things, they're so kind, really," the children's mother thought to herself.

But she had to remind herself of this very hard when Aunt Grace got out the snapshot albums.

"Now I know you'll be interested in these pictures of our trip to Yellowstone Park, Alison." Aunt Grace settled herself among the cushions of the davenport as though she expected to stay there a long time.

"I think you showed them to me last time, Aunt Grace."

"No, no, dear, that was *Glacier* Park. Edwin, move the floor lamp so Alison can see. This is the Old Faithful geyser. It comes up faithfully every hour, you see. That woman standing there isn't anyone we know. It's some woman from Ohio who kept trying to get in the picture. Edwin had to speak to her. Turn over the page."

The next page of the snapshot album showed Old Faithful from a different angle. The woman from Ohio had got only halfway into the picture; otherwise it looked just the same as the first one.

The children's mother patted back a yawn.

"I really must be going, Aunt Grace."

"Nonsense, dear. You must stay for cake and coffee. Just a little chocolate cake, best you ever tasted, I made it myself."

The children's mother suppressed a smile. Katharine had said Aunt Grace would say that—she always did.

The clock struck eleven.

"Oh, dear," their mother said to herself. "And that long bus ride home, too! I wish I were home right now!"

Next moment all the lights in the room seemed to have gone out, only there seemed to be a moon and some stars shining in through the roof.

Their mother looked for Aunt Grace's stuffy, kind face, but Aunt Grace wasn't there. Instead, a clump of rather gangling milkweeds stared back at her. The hot, stuffy chair seemed suddenly to have grown cold and prickly. She looked down and around.

She was sitting on a weedy hummock by the side of a road. There were no houses in sight, nor any light but the far-off moon and stars.

What had happened? Had she suddenly gone mad? Or could she have said good-bye to Aunt Grace and Uncle Edwin, started to walk home instead of taking the bus, and then fainted?

But why couldn't she remember saying good-bye? Such a thing had never happened to her before in her life!

She thought she recognized the stretch of road before her. Aunt Grace and Uncle Edwin lived in a suburb, with half a mile of open country between them and the town. Half a mile with only one bus stop, the children's mother remembered. She must be somewhere in that half-mile, but would the bus stop be ahead or behind her?

The sky ahead showed a glow from the lights of town, and she started walking toward it.

The moon was a thin new one and didn't shed much light, and the woodsy thickets on either side of the road were dark and spooky. Things moved in the branches of trees. The children's mother didn't like it at all.

What was she, a successful newspaperwoman and the mother of four children, doing, wandering the roads by night like this?

When she was set upon and murdered by highwaymen and her body was found next morning, what would the children think? What would anyone think? It must be a bad dream. Soon she would wake up. Now she would keep walking.

She kept walking.

Behind her an engine throbbed and lights shone. She turned, holding up her hand, hoping it was the bus.

It wasn't the bus, just someone's car. But the car stopped by her, and rather a small gentleman looked out.

"Would you like a ride?"

"Well, no, not really," the children's mother said, which was not true at all; she would like one very much. But she had always told the children particularly not to go riding with strangers.

"Did your car break down?"

"Well, no, not exactly."

"Just taking a walk?"

"Well, no."

The rather small gentleman had opened the door of the car now.

"Get in," he said.

To her surprise, the children's mother got in.

They rode along for a bit in silence. The children's mother tried to study the gentleman's face out of the corner of her eye, and was displeased to see that he wore a beard. Beards always seemed to her rather sinister. Why would anyone wear one, unless he had something to hide?

But this beard was only a small, pointed one, and the rest of the gentleman's face, or as much of it as she could see in the dark car, seemed pleasant. She found herself wanting to tell him of her strange adventure. Of course she couldn't. It would sound too silly.

The gentleman broke the silence.

"Lonely out this way after dark," he said. "Rather dangerous for walking, I should say."

"I should say so, too," said the children's mother. "I can't think what can have happened. There I was, talking to Aunt Grace, and suddenly *there* I was, by the side of the road!"

And, in spite of having decided not to, she began telling the small gentleman all about it.

"There's only one explanation," she said, at the end of it. "I must have lost my memory, just for a minute."

"Oh, there's never only *one* explanation," said the rather small gentleman. "It depends on which one you want to believe! *I* believe in believing six impossible things before breakfast, myself. Not that I usually get the chance. The trouble with life is that not enough impossible things happen for us to believe in, don't you agree? Where did you say you live?"

"I didn't," said the children's mother. Really, this night was growing odder and odder. She wasn't used to meeting people who talked exactly like the White Queen, or to giving her address to perfect strangers, either—still, if she wanted to get home there didn't seem to be anything else to do.

She gave him her address, and a moment later they were driving up before the house.

She thanked the small gentleman for his trouble. He bowed, hesitated as though he meant to say something further, then seemed to think better of it, and drove away.

It wasn't until he was gone that the children's mother realized that she didn't even know his name, nor he hers. Still, they would probably never see each other again.

She turned and started up the walk, then stopped in horror.

All the lights in the living room were ablaze!

Thinking of every terrible thing that could possibly have happened, she ran up the walk, turned her key in the lock, and hurried inside.

Huddled on a corner of the sofa sat Jane, wrapped in a blanket and looking small and white and forlorn.

Her mother was by her side and had her arms round her in a second. All thoughts of her own strange evening, and of the rather small gentleman, vanished from her head.

"What is it, tummy-ache or bad dreams?" she cried. "You should have telephoned me!"

"It isn't either one," Jane said. "Mother, did you borrow a nickel that was on my dresser?"

"*What?*" cried her mother. "Did you wait up all this time to ask me *that?*"

And immediately she began to scold, as is the habit of parents when they've been worried about their children and find that they needn't have been.

"Really, Jane, you must *not* be so money-grubbing!" she said. "Yes, I borrowed a nickel for carfare. I only had one nickel and a five-dollar bill, and they're always so mean about making change . . ."

"Did you *spend* it?" Jane interrupted, her voice horrified.

"I spent a nickel, going. What does it matter? I'll pay you back tomorrow."

"Did you spend the other nickel, coming home?"

Her mother looked confused, for a moment.

"Well, no, as a matter of fact I didn't. Someone gave me a lift."

"Do you know which one you spent, the one you had or the one you borrowed?"

"Oh, for Heaven's sake! No, I don't!"

"Could I have the one you didn't spend? Now, please?"

"Jane, what *is* all this? Anyone would think you were a starving Little Match Girl, or something!" Then her mother relented. "Oh well, if it'll make you happy!"

She dug in her purse.

"Here. Now go to bed."

Jane took one quick look at the thing her mother had given her, then folded her hand tightly around it. She had guessed right. It wasn't a nickel.

She lingered in the doorway.

"Mother."

"What is it now?"

"Well, did you . . . did anything . . . anything sort of *unusual* happen tonight?"

"What do you mean? Of course not! Why?"

"Oh, nothing!"

Jane searched in her mind for an excuse. She couldn't tell her mother the truth; she'd never believe it. It would only upset her.

"It's just that I . . . I had this *dream* about you, and I got worried. I dreamed you *wished* for something!"

"You did? That's strange." Her mother looked interested suddenly. She went on, almost to herself, as though she were remembering. "As a matter of fact, I *did* wish something. I wished I were at home. And it was just then that . . ."

"That *what*?" Jane was excited.

Her mother put on her "drop the subject" expression.

"Nothing. I came home. Someone gave me a ride. A . . . a friend of Uncle Edwin's."

She didn't look at Jane. It was awful to be lying like this, to her own child. But she couldn't tell Jane the truth; she'd never believe it. It would only upset her.

"I see." But Jane didn't leave. She stood tracing a pattern in the hall carpet with one foot. She went on carefully, not looking at her mother.

"In my dream, when you wished you were home, I'm not sure what came next. I don't think you *were* home, exactly . . ."

"Ha! I certainly wasn't!"

"But you were *somewhere*!"

"Somewhere in a weed patch, halfway out Bancroft Street, most likely!"

Now Jane looked up, and straight at her.

"We're just talking about my dream, aren't we? It didn't really happen?"

"Of course not."

It was her mother who was looking away now. But now Jane knew.

Clutching the thing in her hand tighter, she ran up the stairs and into her room.

Her mother stood thinking. How strange that Jane should have guessed! No stranger, though, than everything else about this strange evening. Probably none of it had really happened at all. Probably she was ill and imagining things—coming down with flu or something. She had better get some rest. She turned out the living room lights and went upstairs.

Jane stood in her own room, looking at the thing in her hand. It was the size of a nickel and the shape of a nickel and the color of a nickel, but it wasn't a nickel.

It was worn thin—probably by centuries of time, Jane told herself. And instead of a buffalo or a Liberty head, it bore strange signs. Jane held it closer to the light to study the signs.

There was a rap at the door.

"Lights out!" called her mother's voice.

Jane put out the light.

But she knew that she held in her hand the talisman that was going to turn this summer into a time of wild adventure and delight for all of them.

She must hide it in a safe place till morning.

Feeling her way across the room in the dark, she opened the closet door. There was a shoebag on the inside of the door, one of those flowered cotton affairs with many compartments for shoes, though Jane seldom remembered to put hers away in it.

She dropped the magic thing into one of the compartments in the shoebag. No one would disturb it there.

Then she got into bed.

Her last thought was that she must wake up early in the morning, by dawn at *least*, and call the others.

They must hold a Conference, and decide just how they were going to use this wonderful gift that had descended upon them out of the blue.

It was going to be an Enchanted Summer!

And Jane fell asleep.

3

What Happened to Mark

Of course it didn't work out that way at all.

In the morning Jane was so tired from her midnight vigil that she slept right through breakfast. Their mother (who was tired, too) thought Jane needed the rest, and told Miss Bick not to call her.

Miss Bick looked disapproving as usual, but did as she was told. The children's mother went off to work, and Katharine and Martha (under protest) washed and dried the breakfast dishes without the usual charming companionship of their elder sister. Katharine was the washer and Martha the drier.

"I'd like to know what's going on around here," Katharine complained, over the cereal bowls. "Lights on at all hours and Mother and Jane holding secret midnight conspiracies in the living room. I heard them! And now Mother letting Jane stay in bed half the morning—I don't know what this house is coming to!"

"It's that magic. It's mysterious. I don't like it," Martha said.

Katharine had reached the awful pans that needed scouring now, and Martha went away and left her with them, as is the traitorous habit of all dishdriers.

She went into Jane's room. Drawn shades and a huddled form in the bed greeted her.

"Wake up," she said to the form, in a half-hearted way.

"Go away," said Jane, from under a sheet and blanket.

Martha felt depressed.

Carrie the cat had followed her into the room. Carrie's full name was Carrie Chapman Cat. Katharine had named her after a famous lady whose name she had seen in the newspaper. Carrie was a fat, not very interesting cat, kept mainly for mousing purposes, and the children ordinarily paid very little attention to her, or she to them.

But this morning everything was so gloomy and strange that Martha felt the need of comfort. She sat down on the floor, leaned her head back against the open door of Jane's closet, took Carrie in her lap, and stroked her.

There was a silence, except for the heavy breathing of Jane.

Martha felt a wish for companionship.

"Oh dear, if you could only talk," she said to Carrie.

"Purrxx," said Carrie the cat. "Wah oo merglitz. Fitzahhh!"

"What?" said Martha, startled.

"Wah oo merglitz," said Carrie. "Widl. Wifi uzz."

"Oh!" said Martha. "Oh!"

She got up, dropping Carrie rather heavily to the floor, and backed away, white with horror.

"Foo!" said Carrie resentfully. "Idgwit! At urt!"

Mark appeared in the doorway.

"Are my roller skates in here?" he demanded. "Jane borrowed them last week when her strap broke."

Martha ran to him and clutched him.

"It's that magic! I've got it now!" she cried. "I wished Carrie could talk, and now listen to her!"

Carrie chose this moment to put on an offended silence.

"Bushwah," Mark said gruffly. He had found his roller skates in Jane's shoebag and was putting them on. "That old cat. She always was crazy, anyway!"

"Azy ooselfitz!" said Carrie suddenly.

Mark looked surprised. Then he shook his head in disbelief.

"That's not talking," he said. "Probably just having a fit or something."

"But I wished she could talk, and then it began. Like Jane yesterday!"

"Just a coincidence," said Mark. "Yesterday, too. I don't believe in that old magic. Just Jane being smart. Just a lot of crazy girls."

He banged away through the house and out the front door, on his skates. Miss Bick could be heard, following in his wake and lamenting the fate of the floor polish.

Martha gave up. There was no sense in appealing to Mark in this mood. Sometimes he got tired of being the only boy in a family of girls, and when that happened there was no comfort in him. But she refused to be left here alone with the sleeping Jane and the gibbering Carrie.

Or could Mark have been right? Was it just a coincidence? She looked at Carrie doubtfully.

"Did you say something?" she inquired politely.

"Idlwidl baxbix!" said Carrie. "Wah. Oom. Pow-itzer grompaw."

Martha fled the room, calling for Katharine.

Katharine met her in the hall.

"Don't talk to *me*!" she said. "Pan-shirker!"

"Oh, Kathie, don't be cross!" Martha entreated. "Something terrible's happened! *I*'ve got it now, only it comes all wrong!"

And she told Katharine of the behavior of Carrie.

The two sisters, clutched in each other's arms, cautiously approached the door of Jane's room and looked in.

Carrie was still there, pacing the floor, lashing her tail and muttering a horrid monologue.

"Idlwidl bixbax," she was saying. "Grompaw. Fooz! Idjwitz! Oo fitzwanna talkwitz inna fitzplace annahoo?"

She seemed to be trying desperately to express herself. It was agony to watch and still worse to hear.

"This can't go on," said Katharine.

She strode courageously into the room, making a wide circle around the still muttering Carrie, approached the huddled figure in the bed, and shook it.

"Fitzachoo!" said Jane.

"Now *she's* doing it!" Martha wailed, from the doorway.

Katharine looked shaken.

"I *think* it's just sleep-talk," she said. "The time has come for desperate measures."

"Let *me*," said Martha, glad to get away from the doorway even for a second.

She ran to the bathroom and fetched a wet sponge. Avoiding the sputtering Carrie, she ran back to the bed and trickled the sponge upon Jane.

Jane sat up in bed and struck her sister full in the face.

In the tears and apologies and mopping-up that followed, Jane awoke sufficiently to be engaged in sensible conversation and to notice the gurglings and spittings of Carrie.

"What did somebody do—wish she could talk?" she asked.

"Yes, *I* did. How did you know?" Martha stared in amazement.

"How did you happen to find the charm? Who told you you could go through my things?"

"I didn't! I don't know what you mean!"

"Wait a minute. Where were you standing when you wished it?"

"I wasn't. I was sitting down." And Martha showed her where.

"You must have leaned back and touched it."

"Touched *what*?" said Martha.

"*What* charm?" said Katharine.

"The charm in the shoebag," said Jane. "Wait till I tell you."

She told them.

"I don't see how you're so sure," said Martha, when she had finished. "About Mother last night, I mean."

"She just as good as said so," said Jane, "and I Sherlock Holmsed the rest. Don't you see? She wished she were home and ended up *halfway* home! I wished there'd be a fire and got a *little* fire! A *child's-size* fire! Martha wished Carrie could talk and she can *half* talk!"

"Wah. Oom. Fitzbattleaxe," remarked Carrie.

"Exactly," said Jane. "It's that nickel I found, only it isn't a nickel! It's a magic charm and it does things by halves! So far we've each got *half* of what we wished for—all we have to do from now on is ask it for twice as much as we really want! You see?"

"I haven't had fractions yet," said Martha.

Jane explained further. Martha became weary of the explanation.

"What would twice as much as never having to learn fractions be?" she wanted to know, at last.

"Don't be silly—you don't want to ask it things like *that*!" Katharine cried in scorn.

"Nobody's going to ask for anything till we talk it over and decide," Jane announced firmly. "We don't want to waste any more wishes—we can't tell how soon we might wear it out! We'll make plans, and then take turns. My turn yesterday doesn't count, 'cause I didn't know. I get to go first, 'cause I'm the oldest."

"What would twice as much as not being the youngest anymore be?" was the bitter question of Martha, who was tired of always coming last.

But the others paid her no heed.

"*I* mean to ask for all kinds of really wonderful, exciting, important things!" Katharine was saying. "Only I'm not sure just what yet."

"Idjwitz! Selfitz! Fitz*me*fitz!" said Carrie, suddenly.

They looked at her in remorse. Now that they knew the reason for them, her outcries weren't so alarming anymore—they'd even almost forgotten about her. But, in spite of the fact that she seemed to be learning to express herself a little more clearly, she was plainly so enraged by her half-talking state that something had to be done.

"Poor Carrie, I'll fix you up first of all," Jane promised. "The charm's right in here."

She put her hand into the shoebag. But it wasn't.

She put her hand into another compartment. The charm wasn't there, either!

She began wildly searching through all the different sections, taking out pairs of shoes and shaking them. The magic thing wasn't in any of them. Jane began to get in one of her rages.

"Really, what a house!" she cried. "Nothing ever stays where you put it! Has Miss Bick been cleaning my room again?"

"No, she said it needed it but it was beyond her!"

"Mark!" was the next thought of Jane. "I *wondered* where he was! Has anyone seen him?"

"I did," reported Martha. "He came in here and got his roller skates, just a few minutes ago."

"Roller skates!" Jane's voice was a wail. "They were in the shoebag! He must have found the charm and taken it! A person might as well be living in a den of thieves around here!"

"I don't think he did," Martha said. "He said the whole thing was just a coincidence."

"He probably never noticed the magic charm at all," Katharine pointed out reasonably. "He probably just put the skates on with it *in* one of them, where you probably put it in the dark last night, without realizing. It probably got stuck down there in the tightening part. It's probably still there, only he probably doesn't know. He'll probably make a wish pretty soon, and then suddenly . . ."

"*Stop!*" Jane could bear no more. "We've got to find him! Before he wishes for some awful thing and gets half of it! Where do you suppose he could have gone?"

Jane was rushing into her clothes now.

"Wah! *Me*fitz! *Me*fitz!" said Carrie, crossly.

"All right. We'll take you along." Martha, who was beginning to understand Carrie's half-language, hoisted her up under one arm.

They met Miss Bick in the hall.

"Where are you taking that cat?" she wanted to know.

"Idjwit! Foo! Fitzouta thewayfitz!" said Carrie savagely.

Miss Bick backed away, turning pale.

"That cat is *ill*!" she cried.

"I know. We're taking her to the vet's," Katharine called back over her shoulder.

Like everything else lately, the lie was only *half* an untruth. They *were* taking Carrie to be cured, if the charm could cure her.

The children emerged from the house, and stood looking around. Fortunately they lived on a corner lot, and could look down streets running in all four directions.

But no welcome sound of whirring skate wheels, no welcome sight of an eleven-year-old boy rewarded them. Finally they started hurrying south on Maplewood Avenue, not because south looked any more promising than east or north or west, but because they had to start somewhere. Martha tried to muffle the sounds Carrie kept making by holding her close to her, but the few passers-by they met kept turning to stare after them.

"Wah! Oom! Fitzpatrix!" Carrie screamed at the passers-by. She almost seemed to be enjoying herself.

"Hush. Hush," Martha told her. She was having hard work running fast enough to keep up with her sisters. "It won't be long now. At least, oh, I hope it won't!"

Meanwhile Mark had been skating around the neighborhood for some time. It was a dark, gloomy day and he wished the sun would come out. A minute later it did sort of half peep through the clouds.

Now that he was older, roller skating didn't seem quite the thing of whirlwind speed that it used to be, back in the days when it was new to him. He wished the skates would go faster. Pretty soon it seemed as though they did, a little.

But just skating around by himself wasn't very much fun. He wished all the guys were back from their vacations. He wished that when he came to the vacant lot up ahead, he'd see them there, playing baseball as usual.

And for a second, as he whizzed past the vacant lot, he did seem to sort of half-see a ghostly game in progress.

He rounded the corner and came down his own block on Maplewood. As he passed Mrs. Hudson's house he wished, as he'd often wished before, that just for once the iron dog in the yard would be alive, instead of only iron.

Then he looked back. For a minute he thought he heard a faint muffled bark, and it seemed as though the iron tail had tried to wag. Mark guessed he must have a pretty vivid imagination, all right, the way Miss Amrhein, his last year's teacher, had always said.

Thinking of Miss Amrhein reminded him of school. Maybe somebody'd be hanging around the playground, somebody else who hadn't gone away for vacation. He turned at the corner, and skated down Monroe Street toward the school building.

———

It was just after Mark turned the corner that Jane and Katharine and Martha came out of the house and started hurrying down the street.

As they passed Mrs. Hudson's yard, Carrie the cat struggled out of Martha's arms and ran up to the iron dog.

"Yah!" she cried, hissing and spitting at him. "Fitzbully! Fitzmutt! Curfitz!"

A strangled growl came from within the iron dog, and he strained forward, trembling, as though trying to lunge at Carrie.

Jane gave a cry of triumph.

"Look!" she cried. "It's half-alive! Mark must have been here! He must have wished! Hurry up— we're on the right track!"

Martha dragged Carrie away from the iron dog and rushed on after the others. At the corner they hesitated, then turned and ran down Monroe Street, toward the school.

Mark stood looking around the playground. It was deserted, as he might have known it would be. Disappointed, he hauled himself up on the trapeze bar, hung by his knees, and swung head downward. He almost—but not quite—wished it were time for school to begin again; so all the kids would be back. A person might as well be on a desert island as in this empty town!

The thought of desert islands reminded him that he hadn't reread *Robinson Crusoe* yet this year. He was still thinking about *Robinson Crusoe* when his sisters came running into the playground.

"Thank goodness we found you in time to warn you!" Jane cried. "What have you been doing?"

Mark, still hanging head downwards, looked up at her.

"I was just wishing we were all on a desert island," he said.

Next moment the trapeze seemed to give way and he fell heavily to the ground. But instead of landing on the scratchy gravel of the playground, he fell on hot sand.

He rolled over and looked around him. His sisters sat nearby, looking only a trifle less surprised than he felt. Above, a flaming-hot sun blazed in a cloudless sky. Otherwise there didn't seem to be anything anywhere but sand.

"What happened? Where are we?" he cried dazedly.

Jane sighed grimly.

"You just got half a wish," she told him. "Desert, yes. Island, no."

Mark looked around again. It was all too true. Desert there certainly was, but no welcome sight of distant waves graced the horizon—only more sand, mile on monotonous mile of it.

"It's all right," Jane went on, a bit wearily. "I just *do* wish everybody wouldn't keep wasting wishes, though! Take off your skates and I'll get us home again."

To make Mark understand even a part of the situation was the work of several moments. They told him about the half-fire, about Mother, about Carrie. At last he began to believe.

He took off one of the skates and shook it. Nothing happened. He took off the other skate and shook it.

Something metal shot through the air in a bright arc, glittering in the pitiless light of the desert sun, then fell into the sand.

Each of the children would have sworn that he knew just where the magic thing had fallen, and four pairs of hands set to work with a will, burrowing in the sandy hotness. One pair of paws set to work also, Carrie the cat having decided to be helpful for once. There was a good bit of getting in each other's way and arguing.

Five minutes later the magic charm had still not been found. The sand was beginning to feel hotter.

Fingers were getting sorer and tempers shorter.

"Don't crawl where I'm digging," said Katharine to Martha.

"Don't dig where I'm crawling," said Martha to Katharine.

"The way that charm keeps not staying put," said Jane, "you'd think it *wanted* everything to work out wrong!"

Ten more minutes passed.

"I for one," said Martha, sitting back exhausted, "will never play in a sandbox again."

"All the perfumes of Arabia would not sweeten this old sand," agreed the poetical Katharine, also sitting back.

"But we have to find it!" Jane cried, still digging desperately. "Otherwise we'll never get home! We'll die of thirst and some Arab will find our bleached bones months later and never know who we were!"

"I'm thirsty now," said Martha. "I'm hungry, too," she added.

"How do we know this really *is* Arabia?" asked Mark. "Maybe it's just Death Valley."

"Either way," said Jane, "is small comfort. Keep digging. Though it *is* like looking for a camel in a needle's eye," she admitted.

It was then that the caravan appeared.

It was a rather shopworn-looking caravan, only

three mangy camels with one ragged Arab driving them, and some very meager, empty-looking packs on the camels' backs, but it served to make plain to the four children that they were, in fact, in that fabled wasteland they had read of so much in fact and fiction.

"Lost in the Sahara!" cried Katharine dramatically.

Mark was more practical.

"Caravan ahoy!" he shouted. "S O S! Help! Lend a hand!"

The three mangy camels and the ragged Arab altered their course and came toward them.

As they drew nearer, the four children began to wish they wouldn't. The ragged Arab's expression was crafty, and definitely unattractive. As he came to a stop before them he smiled, which made him look more unpleasant than ever.

"Bismillah!" he said.

"How!" said Martha.

"What do you think he is, an Indian?" hissed Mark, under his breath. He addressed the Arab. "Allee samee show humble servant nearest oasis chop-chop?"

"He won't understand that either—that's Chinese!" said Jane.

But the Arab seemed to comprehend.

"Western children follow Achmed," he said.

Jane refused to go.

"We can't leave the charm!" she cried. "It's our only chance to get home!"

"We might get to a place where there's Western Union. We could cable Mother collect. She might send for us," said Katharine doubtfully.

"It would cost untold millions and take *ages*!" cried Jane. "I won't budge from this spot! We'll find the magic thing if we keep looking!"

But the Arab, Achmed, seized her by the arm and propelled her, none too gently, toward the nearest camel.

"Do what he says," Mark whispered to Jane. "We have to get some water, anyway. We can always find this spot again if we leave the roller skates to mark it."

He didn't add that his fear was that the wind might bury the skates in sand before they could return. He didn't mention some other fears that were bothering him, either.

Jane allowed the Arab to help her up onto the nearest camel. Mark helped Katharine climb onto the second one, and the Arab lifted Martha onto the third. With Mark and the Arab on foot, they started away over the desert.

After a bit, Jane began to enjoy the new sensation of riding camel-back, and forgot the charm for the moment. Katharine too seemed almost happy, but the up-and-down motion made Martha seasick and she begged to be taken down.

Mark helped her off the camel and she walked along with him. But her short legs soon tired, and her feet grew sore from the hot sand burning through the thin soles of her shoes. Mark had to half-carry her and the going was slow. They lagged a bit behind the others.

What worried Mark was that he didn't trust Achmed the Arab. Achmed had been all too eager to take the children with him, and Mark didn't like his smile.

Presently Mark's fears were confirmed. Carrie the cat seemed to be making friends with the third camel, the one Martha had been riding. She frisked along by the camel's side. The camel leaned his head down to hers. It almost looked as though they were conversing together, the way animals undoubtedly do.

A moment later Carrie ran back to Mark and Martha. Her fur was standing on end with anger and excitement.

"Foo! Idjwitz!" she hissed at Mark. "Fitzachmed fitzwicked! Fitzkidnap! Ransomowitz!"

"I was afraid of that," said Mark. "Who told you?"

"Fitzcamel!"

Martha began to cry.

"Don't worry," Mark told her. "We'll escape somehow."

But he wished he knew how. Fortunately just then the oasis came into sight, which distracted Martha's attention.

It wasn't a very big oasis—no Western Union— but there were two or three date palms and a spring of water. Everyone stopped for a welcome drink. The dates were delicious. Martha took off her shoes to cool her feet with water from the spring. There was a good deal of sand in her shoes, and as she shook it out it was Mark who first saw the round, shining, silvery thing that fell out with it.

Though he'd never had a real look at it before,

he didn't need to be told what it was. His hand shot out and he caught the charm in mid-air before it could be lost again.

Katharine had seen it a second after Mark.

"I *told* you not to crawl where I was digging!" she told Martha.

Jane had seen it a second after Katharine.

"It's the charm!" she cried. "Wish us home! Here, let me!"

But the Arab, Achmed, was standing nearby, and had seen the shining thing, too. He strode forward, seized Mark by the wrist, and brought the silver charm close to his eyes, close enough to see the mystic marks on it.

The expression of his face changed. No longer did he look like a kidnapper who was planning and plotting wickedness. He looked like a righteous man who has caught a thief in his house, or even worse, in the temple of his gods. His voice was stern.

"Western child steal sacred charm," he cried. "Sacred charm lost many years. Give back!"

His hand closed on the charm but Mark's hand had closed on it first. Mark said the only thing that came into his mind.

"I wish you were half a mile away!"

And immediately, of course, Achmed the Arab was *half* of half a mile, or a *quarter* of a mile, away.

The children could just see him, like a tiny dot far off on the desert sands. But the dot was coming nearer, as Achmed ran toward them again.

"Quick! Let me—I'll get us home! You don't know how!" Jane cried to Mark, but Mark waved her away. He was thinking.

"After all, maybe the charm *did* belong to his race," he said.

"It belongs to us now!" said Jane.

"Losers weepers finders keepers!" said Katharine.

"But maybe it *was* stolen. From a temple or somewhere," said Mark, slowly. "You know how people used to be unjust to natives in the olden days. It doesn't seem fair."

The others had to agree that it didn't. All except Carrie, who was seldom troubled by noble motives.

"Fitzachmed fitzwicked!" she reminded Mark.

"After all, he *was* going to kidnap us!" agreed Martha.

"He *was*?" cried Jane and Katharine, in surprise and excitement.

"Yes, he was, but let's not go into that now," said Mark. "I'll tell you later. After all, maybe he wouldn't have if he weren't poor and downtrodden. And we're supposed to be kind to our enemies, aren't we?"

Achmed the Arab was coming nearer now. Mark waited till he was close enough for them to see his face. Then he spoke aloud a wish he had thought out very carefully.

"I wish that Achmed the Arab may have twice as much as he deserves of whatever it is that he would wish for with this charm!" Mark said.

And of course the charm, to which arithmetic was as nothing, cut the wish neatly in half and in that moment the Arab Achmed received as much as he deserved of happiness.

Suddenly there were five camels in the caravan instead of three. The camels were young and healthy instead of old and mangy. The harnesses were new and trim instead of old and worn through. The meager, empty-looking packs bulged with rich stuffs for trading.

A plump Arab lady appeared suddenly at Achmed's side, leading six plump Arab children by the hand. She smiled coyly at Achmed.

Achmed stopped short and looked at the caravan, at the lady, at the Arab children. He gave a great cry of happiness. On his face a look of peace replaced the old crafty shiftiness. He turned toward the East and fell on his face on the sand. His voice lifted in what sounded like a prayer of thanksgiving.

And it was then that Mark, still waving away

the proffered help of Jane, spoke aloud the second wish he had carefully thought out.

"I wish that the four of us, and Carrie the cat, may travel in the direction of home, only twice as far."

Next thing they knew, they were all sitting on their own front steps.

The first thing they did was walk down the street to Mrs. Hudson's house. The iron dog still trembled in half-life on the lawn.

At that moment Mrs. Hudson came out of the house, her market basket on her arm. She took one look at the shaking dog.

"Earthquake! Earthquake!" she cried, and ran back inside the house.

Mark, who was getting quite good at it, made a third wish.

"I wish that this dog," he said, "may be twice as alive or twice as un-alive as it wishes to be."

Immediately the dog stopped trembling and stood still and cold as iron (which it was again).

"Wouldn't you think it'd rather have been real?" said Katharine in wonder.

"I guess iron things are happier *being* iron," said Mark, who had learned a lot in one day.

The four children now turned to the case of Carrie the cat.

"Wouldn't you like to go on talking, only plainer?" asked Martha, who had grown to enjoy her conversations with her pet.

"Notonna fitztintype," said Carrie. "Fitzsilence fitzgolden!"

The others then decided that Mark had had enough wishes for one day and they would take on this problem.

"I wish that Carrie the cat couldn't talk any of the time!" said Martha, not stopping to think it out.

"Well, you certainly messed that up," said Carrie the cat. "Now of course I can't talk half the time but the rest of the time I can talk perfectly plainly, not that I want to, of course, but here I go, talk, talk, talk, and here I *will* go for the next thirty seconds, and then thirty seconds of silence I suppose, and then talk, talk, talk again, just as though I had anything to say, which I don't, being always one for quiet meditation myself; still, duty calls; so speak the words trippingly on the tongue, only three more seconds to go now, the rest is silence, Shakespeare!"

She broke off suddenly, but only for thirty seconds. Then she began again. The children held their ears till the next silent period. Then Katharine made a hurried suggestion.

"The thing is, we want her to just mew, the way

she used to," she said. "The thing is to think of a word that has 'mew' for half of it."

"*I* know!" said Jane. And she made a wish. "I wish that Carrie the cat may in future say nothing but the word 'music.' "

"Sick!" said Carrie the cat. "Sick sick sick sick sick sick sick sick sick sick sick sick sick."

She *looked* sick.

"Better let me," said Mark. "I've had practice." He took the charm in his hand. "I wish that Carrie the cat may be exactly twice as silent as she wishes to be."

"Mew," said Carrie the cat. "Purr."

And without so much as a look of gratitude at Mark for restoring her to normalcy, she hurried off after a passing robin.

Tired but happy, the children trooped homeward. It had been a long, full day, but everything had worked out beautifully in the end.

Miss Bick met them with reproaches for having stayed out all day and missed their lunch.

"Just wait till I tell your mother!" she said.

And the children did.

Their mother looked very grave that night, when Miss Bick had told her.

"I don't want you children wandering away from the house like that again," she said to them at din-

ner. "As a matter of fact, you may as well know—
something rather frightening has been happening.
There seems to be an epidemic of kidnapping, or
at least lost children. We kept getting reports at the
paper all day, from different lakes and camps and
places. A lot of little boys have disappeared. Mostly
friends of yours, Mark, I'm afraid. Freddy Fox and
Richey Gould and Michael Robinson, only there's
a report he turned up halfway home and doesn't
know how he got there. . . ."

Mark choked suddenly on his milk, and turned
bright red.

He signaled the others in a private way the four
children had. They finished dinner as soon as they
could, and gathered in Mark's room.

"It's awful!" Mark cried, as soon as the door
was safely shut. "I just remembered! This morning
I wished all the guys were home. Now there they
all are, halfway home and wandering the countryside! I've got to fix them up!"

He took the charm from his pocket, where he'd
put it after the last wish of the afternoon.

"I wish all the guys I wished home to be back
twice as far as they were before I wished!" he said.

The others agreed that that ought to do it. But
Mark was still worried.

"We have to be careful from now on," he said.

"We don't want any more mistakes. That could have been bad."

"We'll hide it in a safe place," said Jane, "until tomorrow."

"I know where," said Katharine.

She led the others to the room she shared with Martha. There was a loose board in the floor with a space under it that the children had used to hide things in, back in the days when they were young.

The children hid the charm in this secret place.

"A mouse might find it and make a wish," Martha objected.

But the others felt that half the wish of a mouse could do little to upset their plans.

They had many plans to make.

"We'll spend the night thinking up wishes," said Jane. "It'll be better from now on, because now we all *know*. We'll make sensible wishes from now on. Tomorrow the real fun will begin."

And, in a way, it did.

4

What Happened to Katharine

Next morning there were no secret meetings before breakfast.

Jane stayed in her room and Mark stayed in his room, and in the room they shared Katharine and Martha hardly conversed at all.

Each of the children was too busy making private plans and deciding on favorite wishes.

Breakfast was eaten in silence, but not without the exchange of some excited looks. The children's mother was aware that something was in the air, and wondered what new trial lay in store for her.

When their mother had gone to work and the

dishes and other loathly tasks were done, the four children gathered in Katharine and Martha's room. Katharine had already checked to see that the charm still lay in its cubbyhole, unharmed by wish of mouse or termite.

Jane had drawn up some rules.

"The wishes are to go by turns," she said. "Nobody's to make any main wish that doesn't include all the rest of us. If there have to be any smaller wishes later on in the same adventure, the person who wished the main wish gets to make them, except in case of emergency. Like if he loses the charm and one of the other ones finds it. I get to go first."

Katharine had something to say about that.

"I don't see why," she said. "You always get dibs on first 'cause you're the oldest, and grownups always pick Martha 'cause she's the baby, and Mark has a wonderful double life with all this and being a boy, too! Middle ones never get any privileges at all! Besides, who hasn't had a wish of her own yet? Think back!"

It was true. Jane had had the half-fire, and Martha had made Carrie half-talk, and Mark had taken them to half of a desert island.

Jane had to agree that Katharine deserved a chance. But she couldn't keep from giving advice.

"We don't want any old visits with Henry Wadsworth Longfellow," she said. "Make it something that's fun for everybody."

"I'm going to," said Katharine. "But I can't decide between wishing we could all fly like birds and wishing we had all the money in the world."

"Those aren't any good," said Jane. "People always wish those in stories, and it never works out at *all*! They either fly too near the sun and get burned, or end up crushed under all the money!"

"We could make it *paper* money," suggested Katharine.

A discussion followed as to how many million dollars in large bills it would take to crush a person to death. By the time the four children got back to the subject of the magic charm seventeen valuable minutes had been wasted.

But now Mark had an idea.

"We've found out the charm can take us through space," he said. "What about time?"

"You mean travel around in the past?" Jane's eyes were glowing. "See Captain Kidd and Nero?"

"I've always wanted to live back in the olden romantic days," said Katharine, getting excited, too. "In days of old when knights were bold!"

The others were joining in by now. For once the four children were all in complete agreement.

"Put in about tournaments," said Mark.

"And quests," said Jane.

"Put in a good deed, too," said Martha. "Just to be on the safe side."

"Don't forget to say two times everything," said all three. They clustered eagerly around Katharine as she took hold of the charm.

"I wish," said Katharine, "that we may go back twice as far as to the days of King Arthur, and see two tournaments and go on two quests and do two good deeds."

The next thing the four children knew, they were standing in the midst of a crowded highway. Four queens were just passing, riding under a silken canopy. The next moment seven merry milkmaids skipped past, going a-Maying. In the distance a gallant knight was chasing a grimly giant with puissant valor, and in the other direction a grimly giant was chasing a gallant knight for all he was worth. Some pilgrims stopped and asked the four children the way to Canterbury. The four children didn't know.

But by now they were tired of the crowded traffic conditions on the King's Highway, and crossed into a field, where the grass seemed greener and fresher than any they had ever seen in their own time. A tall figure lay on the ground nearby, under an apple tree. It was a knight in full armor, and he was sound asleep.

The four children knew he was asleep, because Martha lifted the visor of his helmet and peeked inside. A gentle snore issued forth.

The knight's sword lay on the ground beside him, and Mark reached to pick it up.

Immediately the sleeping knight awoke, and sat up.

"Who steals my purse steals trash," he said, "but who steals my sword steals honor itself, and him will I harry by wood and by water till I cleave him from his brainpan to his thighbone!"

"I beg your pardon, sir," said Mark.

"We didn't mean anything," said Jane.

"We're sorry," said Katharine.

The knight rubbed his eyes with his mailed fist. Instead of the miscreant thief he had expected to see, he saw Mark and Jane and Katharine and Martha.

"Who be you?" he said. "Hath some grimly foe murdered me in my sleep? Am I in Heaven? Be ye cherubim or seraphim?"

"We be neither," said Katharine. "And this isn't Heaven. We are four children."

"Pish," said the knight. "Ye be like no children these eyes have ever beheld. Your garb is outlandish."

"People who live in tin armor shouldn't make remarks," said Katharine.

At this moment there was an interruption. A lady came riding up on a milk-white palfrey. She seemed considerably excited.

"Hist, gallant knight!" she cried.

The knight rose to his feet, and bowed politely. The lady began batting her eyes, and looking at him in a way that made the children feel ashamed for her.

"Thank Heaven I found you," she went on. "You alone of all the world can help me, if your name be Sir Launcelot, as I am let to know it is!"

The children stared at the knight, open-mouthed with awe.

"Are you really Sir Launcelot?" Mark asked him.

"That is my name," said the knight.

The four children stared at him harder.

Now that he wasn't looking so sleepy they could see that it was true. No other in all the world could wear so manly a bearing, so noble a face. They were in the presence of Sir Launcelot du Lake, the greatest knight in all the Age of Chivalry!

"How is Elaine?" Katharine wanted to know right away, "and little Galahad?"

"I know not the folk you mention," said Sir Launcelot.

"Oh, yes, you do, sooner or later," said Katharine. "You probably just haven't come to them yet."

"Be ye a prophetess?" cried Sir Launcelot, becoming interested. "Can ye read the future? Tell me more!"

But the lady on the milk-white palfrey was growing impatient.

"Away, poppets!" she said, getting between the four children and Sir Launcelot. "Gallant knight, I crave your assistance. In a dolorous tower nearby a dread ogre is distressing some gentlewomen. I am Preceptress of the Distressed Gentlewoman Society. We need your help."

"Naturally," said Sir Launcelot. He whistled, and his trusty horse appeared from behind the apple tree, where it had been cropping apples. Sir Launcelot started to mount the horse.

The four children looked at each other. They did not like what they had seen of the lady at all, and they liked the way she had spoken to them even less.

Katharine stepped forward.

"I wouldn't go if I were you," she said. "It's probably a trap."

The lady gave her an evil look.

"Even so," said Sir Launcelot, "needs must when duty calls." He adjusted his reins.

Katharine drew herself up to her full four feet four.

"As you noticed before, I be a mighty prophetess!" she cried. "And I say unto you, go not where this lady bids. She will bring you nothing but disaster!"

"I shall go where I please," said Sir Launcelot.

"So there!" said the lady.

"You'll be sorry!" said Katharine.

"Enough of parley," said Sir Launcelot. "Never yet did Launcelot turn from a worthy quest. I know who ye be now. Ye be four false wizards come to me in the guise of children to tempt me from my course. 'Tis vain. Out of the way. Flee, churls. Avaunt and quit my sight, thy bones are marrowless. Giddy-up."

Sir Launcelot chirruped to his horse, and the lady chirruped to hers, and away they went, galloping down the King's Highway. The four children had to scatter to both sides to avoid the flying hooves.

Of course it was but the work of a moment and a simple problem in fractions for Katharine to wish they all had horses and could follow.

Immediately they had, and they did.

Sir Launcelot turned, and saw the four children close at his heels, mounted now on four dashing chargers.

"Away, fiends!" he said.

"Shan't!" said Katharine.

They went on.

The four children had never ridden horseback before, but they found that it came to them quite easily, though Martha's horse was a bit big for her, and she had trouble posting.

And it was particularly interesting when, every time the lady started casting loving looks at Sir Launcelot, the children would ride up close behind and make jeering noises, and Sir Launcelot would turn in his saddle and shout, "Begone, demons!" at them. This happened every few minutes. Sir Launcelot seemed to get a little bit angrier each time.

When they had ridden a goodly pace they came to a dark wood, stretching along both sides of the highway. Just at the edge of the wood, the lady cried out that her horse had cast a shoe. Sir Launcelot reined in to go to her aid. The four children stopped at a safe distance.

Then, just as Sir Launcelot was dismounting, three knights rode out of the wood. One was dressed all in red, one in green and one in black. Before the children could cry out, the knights rushed at Sir Launcelot from behind.

It was three against one and most unfair. But

even so, Sir Launcelot's strength would have been as the strength of at least nine if he hadn't been taken by surprise. As it was, he had no time even to touch his hand to his sword before the three knights had seized and disarmed him, bound him hand and foot, flung him across the saddle of his own horse, and galloped off into the wood with him, a hapless prisoner.

The lady turned on the four children.

"Ha ha!" she cried. "Now they will take him to my castle, where he will lie in a deep dungeon and be beaten every day with thorns! And so we shall serve all knights of the Round Table who happen this way! Death to King Arthur!"

"Why, you false thing, you!" said Jane.

"I told him so!" said Katharine.

"Let's go home!" said Martha.

"No, we have to rescue him!" said Mark.

"Ho ho!" said the lady. "Just you try it! Your magic is a mere nothing compared with mine, elf-spawn! Know that I am the great enchantress, Morgan le Fay!"

"You *would* be!" said Katharine, who didn't like being called "elfspawn," as who would? "I remember you in the books, always making trouble. I wish you'd go jump in the lake!"

Katharine wasn't thinking of the charm when she wished this, or she might have worded it differently. But that didn't stop the charm.

"Good old charm!" said Mark, as he watched what happened.

Morgan le Fay didn't go jump in the lake; she merely fell in a pool. Luckily there was a pool handy. She slid backwards off her horse and landed in it in a sitting position. And luckier still, the pool had a muddy bottom, and Morgan le Fay stuck there long enough for Katharine to make another, calmer wish, which was that she would *stay* stuck, and unable to use any of her magic, for twice as long as would be necessary.

This done, the four children turned their horses into the wood, and set about following the wicked knights. Morgan le Fay hurled a few curses after them from among the water weeds, but these soon died away in the distance.

There was no path to follow through the wood. The branches of trees hung low and thick, and the earth beneath them was damp and dark and dank, and no birds sang.

"This," said Katharine, "is what I would call a tulgey wood."

"Don't!" cried Martha. "Suppose something came whiffling through it!"

The four children pressed on. Suddenly they came to a clearing, and there amidst a tangle of lambkill and henbane and deadly nightshade they saw the witch's castle rising just ahead of them. Poison ivy mantled its walls. There were snakes in the moat and bats in the belfry. The four children did not like the look of it at all.

"What do we do now?" said Jane.

"Wish him free, of course," said Mark.

"Just stand out here and wish? That's too easy!" said Katharine.

"I'm not going inside that castle!" said Martha.

"Nay," said Katharine, who did not seem to be so docile today as she used to be. "Ye forget that I be a mighty prophetess. Trust ye unto my clever strategy!"

"Bushwah," said Mark. "Less talk and more action."

Katharine put her hand on the charm. "I wish that two doors of this castle may stand open for us," she said.

So then the children had to look for the one door that did. They found it at last, a little back door with a small drawbridge of its own, over the moat. The drawbridge was down and the door was ajar. The children went over the drawbridge.

"Beware!" croaked the magic talking frogs in the moat.

They went in through the doorway. A long dark passage lay beyond.

"Beware!" squeaked the magic talking mice in the walls.

The children went along the passage. It wound and twisted a good deal. The magic cobwebs hanging from the ceiling brushed at their faces and caught at their clothing, trying to hold them back, but they broke away and pushed on.

At last the passage ended at a heavy doorway. From beyond it came the sound of loud voices raised in something that was probably intended to be music. The children eased the door open a crack and peeked through, into a large hall.

The red knight and the green knight and the black knight were enjoying a hearty meal, and washing down each mouthful with a draught of nut-brown ale. They were singing at the table, which was rude of them, and the words of their song were ruder still.

"Speak roughly to our Launcelot
  And beat him with a brier!
And kick him in the pants a lot—
  Of this we never tire!
We've put him in a dungeon cell
And there we'll beat him very well!
  Clink, canikin, clink!"

The four children looked at each other indignantly; then they peeked through again.

Some varlets had appeared in the hall. They cleared away the dishes, left the dessert platter on the table, and departed.

The dessert was a number of round plum puddings, all aflame with blazing blue brandy. The black knight stood up to serve them.

At that moment Katharine remembered a story she had once read. She decided to have some fun with the three knights.

"I wish two of those puddings were stuck to the end of your nose!" she cried, putting her hand on the charm and staring straight at the black knight, through the crack of the doorway. And immediately one of them was.

But this pudding, unlike the one in the story, was still burning blue with brandy-fire; so that not only was it humiliating to the black knight, but hurt a good deal as well. And furthermore, his long black whiskers, of which he was inordinately proud, began to singe badly. He gave a wild howl, and his face turned nearly as black as his garments, with rage.

"Ods blood, who hath played this scurvy trick upon me?" he cried, beating at his nose and whiskers with his hands, and then yelling with pain as the flames scorched his fingers.

"Tee hee hee," tittered the green knight. "You look very funny!"

The black knight whirled on him.

"Be it *you*, then, who hath played this scurvy trick?" he cried.

"No, it be not I," said the green knight, "but you look very funny, just the same!"

"Oh, I do, do I?" shouted the black knight, in

a passion. And he whipped his sword out of its scabbard, and swapped off the green knight's head.

The red knight jumped to his feet.

"I say, Albemarle, that was going a bit too far!" he cried.

"Oh, I don't know," said the black knight. "He was exceedingly provoking! Come and help me get this great pudding thing off my nose!"

"Well," said the red knight, looking at him rather dubiously, "I don't know if I can, but I'll *try*!"

And he whipped *his* sword out of *its* scabbard, and swapped off the pudding from the black knight's nose. Unfortunately (for him) he swapped off a good bit of the nose, too.

The black knight gave a wild bellow and hurled himself at the red knight, sword in hand. The red knight parried his thrust. A moment later they were joined in deadly combat, leaping about the hall, smashing furniture, and hacking off parts of each other with the greatest abandon.

Behind the door, the four children shut their eyes, held their ears, and cowered trembling in each other's arms.

The combat did not last long. Two sword blades flashed in the air, and a second later two heads fell on the floor, followed, more slowly, by two bodies.

There was a silence. Katharine hadn't meant her wish to end in such a gory and final way. But she reminded herself to be bloody, bold and resolute, and crept through the door into the hall, followed by the three others. All four averted their eyes from what they would have seen if they had looked at the floor.

"I do think you might have managed it neater," said Jane. "How can we get through to the dungeon with all these different pieces of knight lying around underfoot?"

"The point is that I managed it at all," said Katharine, more cheerfully than she felt. "And we don't have to walk; we can wish ourselves there."

She put her hand on the charm and wished that they were twice as far as the dungeon door and that she had two keys to the dungeon in her hand.

After that, of course, it was but a matter of turning the key, and out walked Sir Launcelot, followed by several dozen other knights who had also been prisoners of the enchantress and her friends, and who looked somewhat the worse for their daily beatings.

The other captive knights fell on their knees, kissing the children's hands and hailing them as their deliverers. Sir Launcelot also thanked the children quite politely, but somehow he didn't seem so happy to be free as the children had expected he would.

A moment later, when the other captive knights had left to resume their interrupted quests, the children found out why.

"You saved me by magical means?" Sir Launcelot asked.

"That's right," said Katharine, proudly. "I did it with my little charm."

"That mislikes me much," said Sir Launcelot. "I would it were otherwise."

"Well, really!" said Katharine. "I suppose you'd rather have stayed in there being beaten?"

"Sooner that," said Sir Launcelot, "than bring shame to my honor by taking unfair magical advantage of a foe, however deadly!"

"Well, if you're all that particular," said Katharine, annoyed, "I can easily put them back together again." And she led him into the great hall, and showed him the different pieces of the three knights.

"Please do so," said Sir Launcelot.

"Shall I lock you up in the dungeon again?" asked Katharine, sarcastically. "Doesn't it hurt your conscience that I set you free?"

"That much advantage," said Sir Launcelot, "I think I can take. Some fair jailer's daughter would probably have let me out sooner or later, anyway."

"Oh, is that so?" said Katharine. "I'm sorry I troubled, I'm sure! Is there anything else?"

"Well, yes," said Sir Launcelot. "You might just fetch me my sword and armor, which these cowardly knaves have taken from me."

Thoroughly cross with him by now, Katharine wished the sword and armor back on him; then, working out the fractions carefully, she spoke the wish that was to bring the red knight, the green knight, and the black knight back to life.

It was very interesting watching the different pieces of the different-colored knights reassembling themselves on the hall floor, and the four children were sorry when it was over.

But by then something even more interesting was going on. Because by then Sir Launcelot was fighting the three knights singlehanded, and that was a sight worth coming back many centuries to see.

Sir Launcelot did not seem to appreciate the four children's interest, however.

"Go away. Thank you very much. Good-bye," he called, pinning the green knight against the wall with a table, and holding the red and black ones at bay with his sword.

"Can't we help?" Mark wanted to know.

"No. Go away," said Sir Launcelot, cracking the

red knight on the pate, thwacking the black knight in the chest with his backhand swing, and leaping over the table to take a whack at the green one.

"Can't we even *watch*?" Jane wailed.

"No. It makes me nervous. I want to be alone," said Sir Launcelot, ducking under the table to send the red knight sprawling, then turning to face the black and green ones again.

Katharine sighed, and made a wish.

Next moment the four children were on their horses once more, riding along the King's Highway.

"We might at least have waited in the yard," complained Martha. "Now we'll never know how it ended!"

"He'll come out on top; trust *him*!" said Katharine. "I *do* get tired of people who are always right, all the time! Anyway, we'll be seeing him again, I imagine. At the tournament."

"Gee, yes, the tournament. I was forgetting," said Mark. "When do you suppose it'll be?"

"Not for weeks, maybe, by the time here," said Katharine. "But for us, a mere wish on the charm . . ."

And she merely wished.

"I can't get used to this being rushed around," complained Martha a second later, as she found herself somewhere else for the third time in three minutes. "Where are we now, and when is it?"

"Camelot, I should think," said Katharine, "in tournament time! Look!"

Jane and Mark and Martha looked. Camelot and the field of tournament looked exactly as you all would expect them to look, from the descriptions in *The Boy's King Arthur* and the wonderful books of Mr. T. H. White. Trumpets were blowing clarion calls, and pennons fluttered on the blue air, and armor flashed in the bright light, and gallant knights and trusty squires and faithful pages and ladies fair and lowly varlets were crowding into the stands in hundreds, to watch the chivalrous sport.

The four children had front-row grandstand seats, for Katharine had made that a part of her wish. She had forgotten to say anything in her wish about getting rid of the four horses, and at first these made some trouble by wanting to sit in the grandstand, too, much to the annoyance of the people sitting behind. But Katharine wished them twice as far as away, and they disappeared.

At this, the people behind got up and left in a hurry, looking back at the four children and muttering about witchcraft and sorcery.

The children paid small heed. They were too busy looking around them and drinking in the sights.

King Arthur sat enthroned on a high platform at one end of the field. The children could see him clearly, with his kind, simple, understanding face, like the warm sun come to shine on merry England. Queen Guinevere was seated at his right, and Merlin, the magician, thin and wise and gray-bearded, at his left.

And now the trumpets blew an extra long fanfare, and the tournament began.

Sir Launcelot was among the first to ride out on the field. The children recognized him by his armor.

"I told you he'd come out all right," said Katharine, a bit bitterly.

But when Sir Launcelot got going in that tournament, even Katharine had to admire him.

He smote down five knights with his first spear, and four knights with his second spear, and unhorsed three more with his sword, until all the people sitting round on the benches began crying out, "Oh, Gramercy, what marvelous deeds that knight doth do in that there field!"

Jane sighed a satisfied sigh. "Kind of glorious, isn't it?" she murmured.

"It's the most wonderful age in human history," said Mark, solemnly. "If only it didn't have to end!"

"Why did it?" asked Martha, who hadn't read *The Boy's King Arthur* yet.

"Partly 'cause some of the other knights got tired of being knocked down all the time and having Launcelot always win," Mark told her.

"Yes," said Katharine, in rather a peculiar voice, "it would really be a good deed, in a way, if somebody knocked *him* down for a change, wouldn't it?"

Mark gave her a sharp look, but just then Sir Launcelot started knocking down more knights, and he had to watch the field. When he looked again, Katharine wasn't there.

Mark nudged Jane hard, as a horrible thought came into his mind.

Jane turned and saw the empty spot where Katharine had been, and Mark could tell that she was having the same thought, too.

Just then there was an interruption in the tournament. A strange knight rode out on the field of combat, and straight up to King Arthur's platform.

"I crave your Majesty's permission to challenge Sir Launcelot to single combat!" cried the strange knight in a voice loud enough for the children to hear clearly from where they sat.

The hearts of Jane and Mark sank.

Even Martha now guessed the horrid truth. "How dare she?" she whispered.

"I don't know," said Mark. "She's been getting

too full of herself ever since we started this wish!"

"Wait till I get her home!" said Jane grimly.

"How call they you, strange sir?" King Arthur was saying, meanwhile, "and whence do you hail?"

"They call me Sir Kath," said the strange knight, "and I hail from Toledo, Ohio."

"I know not this Toledo," said King Arthur, "but fight if you will. Let the combat begin."

The trumpets sounded another clarion call, the strange knight faced Sir Launcelot, and there began the strangest combat, it is safe to say, ever witnessed by the knights of the Round, or any other, Table.

The intrepid Katharine thought herself very clever at this moment. She had wished she were wearing two suits of armor and riding two horses, and she had wished she were two and a half times as tall and strong as Sir Launcelot, and she had wished that she would defeat him twice. And immediately here she was, wearing one suit of armor and riding one horse, and she was one and a quarter times as tall and strong, and she couldn't wait to defeat him once.

But in her cleverness she had forgotten one thing. She had forgotten to wish that she knew the rules of jousting. And here she was, facing the greatest knight in the world, and she didn't know how to start. She knew she'd win in the end, because she'd wished it that way, but what was she to do in the beginning and middle?

Before she could work out another wish to take care of this, Sir Launcelot rode at her, struck her with his lance, and knocked her back onto her horse's tail. Then he rode at her from the opposite direction, and knocked her forward onto her horse's neck.

The crowd roared with laughter.

The feelings of Jane, Mark and Martha may well be imagined.

As for the feelings of Katharine, they knew no bounds. She still held the magic charm clutched in one hot hand, and she wasn't bothering about correct arithmetic now.

"I wish I could fight ten times as well as you, you bully! Yah!" were the words that the valiant Sir Kath spoke, upon the field. It was a cry of pure temper.

And immediately she could fight five times as well as Sir Launcelot, and everyone knows how good *he* was.

What followed would have to be seen to be believed.

Katharine came down like several wolves on the fold. She seemed to spring from all sides at once. Her sword flashed like a living thunderbolt. Her lance whipped about, now here, now there, like a snake gone mad.

"Zounds!" cried the people, and "Lackaday" and "Wurra wurra!"

Jane, Mark and Martha watched with clasped hands.

If Sir Launcelot had not been the greatest knight in the world he would never have lived to tell the tale. Even as it was, the end was swift. In something less than a trice he was unseated from his horse, fell to the ground with a crash, and did not rise again.

Katharine galloped round and round the field, bowing graciously to the applause of the crowd.

But she soon noticed that the crowd wasn't applauding very loudly. And it was only the traitorous knights like Sir Mordred and Sir Agravaine, the ones who were jealous of Launcelot, who were applauding at all.

The rest of the crowd was strangely silent. For Launcelot, the flower of knighthood, the darling of the people's hearts, the greatest champion of the Round Table, had been defeated!

Queen Guinevere looked furious. King Arthur looked sad. The attendant knights, except for the traitorous ones, looked absolutely wretched. Merlin looked as if he didn't believe it.

Jane and Mark and Martha looked as though they believed it, but didn't want to.

And it was then that the full knowledge of what she had done swept over Katharine.

She had succeeded and she had failed. She, a mere girl, had defeated the greatest knight in history. But she had pretended to herself that she was doing it for a good deed and really it had been just because she was annoyed with Launcelot for not appreciating her help enough, back in Morgan le Fay's castle.

Her cheeks flamed and she felt miserable. It was hot inside her helmet suddenly, and she dragged it off. Then she remembered too late that she'd forgotten something else, when she made her wish. She had wished to be in armor, and to be on horseback, and to be tall and strong, and to win. But she had forgotten to say anything about not being Katharine any longer.

Now, as the helmet came away, her long brown hair streamed down onto her shoulders, and her nine-year-old, little-girl face blinked at the astonished crowd.

Those sitting nearest the ringside saw. Sir Mordred tittered. Sir Agravaine sneered. The mean knights who were jealous of Sir Launcelot began to laugh, and mingled with the laughter were the cruel words, "Beaten by a girl!"

Some horrid little urchins took up the cry, and made a rude song of it:

> "Launcelot's a chur-ul,"
> Beaten by a gir-ul!"

Sir Launcelot came to, and sat up. He heard the laughter, and he heard the song. He looked at Katharine. Katharine looked away, but not before he had recognized her. He got to his feet. There was silence all round the field; even the mean knights stopped laughing.

Sir Launcelot came over to Katharine. "Why have you done this to me?" he said.

"I didn't mean to," said Katharine. She began to cry.

With flushed cheeks but with head held high, Sir Launcelot strode to King Arthur's platform and knelt in the dust before it. In a low voice he asked leave to go on a far quest, a year's journey away at least, that he might hide his shame till by a hundred deeds of valor he would win back his lost honor and expunge the dread words, "Beaten by a girl," forever.

King Arthur did not trust himself to speak. He nodded his consent.

Queen Guinevere did not even look at Sir Launcelot, as he walked away from the field of tournament.

Katharine went on crying.

Merlin spoke a word in King Arthur's ear. King Arthur nodded. He rose, offered an arm to Guinevere, and led her from the stand. Merlin spoke another word, this time to the attendant knights. They began clearing the people from the field.

Most of the people went quietly, but three children in the front row of the grandstand put up quite a fuss, saying that they had to find their sister Katharine, who'd done something terrible, but a sister was a sister and they'd stick up for her, anyway. The knights cleared them away with the rest.

Presently, after what seemed like at least a year, Katharine found herself alone before Merlin. She was still crying.

Merlin looked at her sternly.

"Fie on your weeping," he said. "I wot well that ye be a false enchantress, come here in this guise to defeat our champion and discredit our Table Round!"

"I'm not! I didn't!" said Katharine.

"Ye be, too!" said Merlin, "and you certainly have! After today our name is mud in Camelot!"

"Oh, oh," wept Katharine.

"Silence, sorceress," said Merlin. He waved his wand at her. "I command that you appear before me in your true form!"

Immediately Katharine wasn't tall, or strong, or in armor any more, but just Katharine.

Merlin looked surprised.

"These fiends begin early!" he said. "However, doubtless ye be but the instrument of a greater power." He waved his wand again. "I command that your allies, cohorts, aids, accomplices and companions be brought hither to stand at your side!"

Jane and Mark and Martha appeared beside Katharine, looking nearly as unhappy and uncomfortable as she.

Merlin looked really quite startled. Then he shook his head sadly.

"So young," he said, "and yet so wicked!"

"We're not!" said Martha, making a rude face. The behavior of the others was more seemly.

"You see, sir," began Mark.

"We didn't mean to," began Jane.

"Let me," said Katharine. "I started it."

And in a rush of words and tears she told Merlin

everything, beginning with the charm, and her wish to travel back in time, and going on to what she had hoped to do, and what she'd done and where she'd gone wrong.

"I wanted to do a good deed," she said, "and I *did* one, when I rescued Launcelot from that old dungeon. But then he wasn't properly grateful at all, and made me undo it, so he could rescue himself, all for the sake of his old honor! And that made me cross! And just now I pretended I was defeating him so the other knights wouldn't be so jealous of him, but really I was just trying to get back at him for being so stuck-up! And I always wanted to fight in a real tournament, anyway!"

"Well, now you have," said Merlin, "and what good did you do by it? Just made everybody thoroughly unhappy!"

"I know," said Katharine.

"That's what comes of meddling," said Merlin. "There is a pattern to history, and when you try to change that pattern, no good may follow."

Katharine hung her head.

"However," went on Merlin, and to the surprise of the four children he was smiling now, "all is not lost. I have a few magic tricks of my own, you know. Let me see, how shall I handle this? I *could* turn time back, I suppose, and make it as though this day had never happened, but it would take a lot out of me."

"Really?" said Katharine in surprise. "It would be a mere nothing to *us*!"

Merlin looked at her a bit grimly.

"Oh, it would, would it?" he said.

"Oh, yes," went on Katharine happily. "I could wish Launcelot were twice as near as here again, and then I could wish that he'd defeat me twice, and then I could wish that the people would honor him twice as much as they ever did, and then I could wish . . ."

"Hold!" cried Merlin, in alarm. "A truce to your wishes, before you get us in worse trouble! I think I had best see this wonderful charm of yours." He made a pass at Katharine with his wand. "If there be any magic among you, let it appear now or forever hold its peace."

Katharine's hot hand, which for so long had clutched the charm, opened in spite of itself, and the charm lay in plain sight, on her palm.

Merlin looked at it. His eyes widened. He swept his tall hat from his head, and bowed low before the charm, three times. Then he turned to the children.

"This is a very old and powerful magic," he said. "Older and more powerful than my own. It is, in fact, too powerful and too dangerous for four children, no matter how well they may intend, to have in their keeping. I am afraid I must ask you to surrender it."

He made another pass with his wand. The charm leaped gracefully from Katharine's hand to his own.

Mark spoke.

"But it came to us in our own time," he said, "and that's a part of history, too, just as much as this is. Maybe we were *meant* to find it. Maybe there's some good thing we're supposed to do with it. There is a pattern to history, and when you try to change that pattern, no good may follow."

Merlin looked at him.

"You are a wise child," he said.

"Just average," said Mark, modestly.

"Dear me," said Merlin. "If that be so, if all children be as sensible as you in this far future time you dwell in . . ." He broke off. "What century did you say you come from?"

"We didn't," said Mark, "but it's the twentieth."

"The twentieth century," mused Merlin. "What a happy age it must be—truly the Golden Age that we are told is to come."

He stood thinking a moment. Then he smiled.

"Very well. Go back to your twentieth century," he said, "and take your magic with you, and do your best with it. But first, I have something to say."

He held the charm at arm's length, rather as though he feared it might bite him, and addressed it with great respect.

"I wish," he said, "that in six minutes it may be as though these children had never appeared here. Except that they—and I—will remember. And I further wish that our tournament may begin all over again and proceed as originally planned by history. Only twice as much so," he added, to be on the safe side.

"Now may I have it back, please?" Katharine asked, when he had done.

"In a minute," said Merlin. "By the way, have you been making a lot of wishes lately? It feels rather worn out to me. It won't last forever, you know."

"Oh dear, we were afraid of that," said Jane. "How many more do we get?"

"That would be telling," said Merlin. "But you'd best not waste too many. It might be later than you think."

"Oh!" cried Martha. "Maybe we'll never get home!"

"Don't worry," said Merlin, smiling at her. "There are still a few wishes left for you. And one more for me." Again he held the charm out before him.

"And I thirdly wish," he said, "for the future protection of the world from the terrible good intentions of these children, and for their protection against their own folly, that this charm may, for twice the length of time that it shall be in their hands, grant no further wishes carrying said children out of their own century and country, but that they may find whatsoever boon the magic may have in store for them in their own time and place." He put the charm into Katharine's hands. "And now you'd best be going. Because in less than a minute by my wish, it will be as though you'd never appeared here. And if you aren't home when that happens, goodness knows where you *will* be!"

"But what about the good deed I wished?" said Katharine. "None of the ones I tried worked out!"

"My child," said Merlin, and his smile was very kind now, "you have done your good deed. You have brought me word that for as far into time as the twentieth century, the memory of Arthur, and of the Round Table, which I helped him to create, will be living yet. And that in that far age people will still care for the ideal I began, enough to come back through time and space to try to be of service to it. You have brought me that word, and now I can finish my work in peace, and know that I have done well. And if that's not a good deed, I should like to know what is. Now good-bye. Wish quickly. You have exactly seventeen seconds."

Katharine wished.

And because their mother and Miss Bick had been worried yesterday by their being so long away, she put in that when they got home, they should only have been gone two minutes, by real time.

This was really quite thoughtful of Katharine. Perhaps she, too, like Mark the day before, had learned something during her day of adventure.

The next thing the four children knew, they were sitting together in Katharine and Martha's room, and it was still that morning, and they had only been away from home a minute. Yet that minute was packed with memories.

"Did we dream it?" Katharine asked.

"I don't think so, or we wouldn't all remember it," said Mark.

"And we all do, don't we?" said Jane.

And they all did.

"What did that last mean, that Merlin wished on the charm?" Martha wanted to know.

"It means we have to keep our wishes close to home from now on," Mark told her.

"No more travels to foreign climes," said Jane, "and I was all set to take us on a pirate ship next!"

"No more olden times," said Mark, "and I've always wanted to see the Battle of Troy!"

"You might not have liked it, once you got there," said Katharine, from the depths of her experience. "Traveling in olden times is *hard*."

"I don't care," said Martha. "I don't care if I never travel at all. I'm glad to be home. Aren't you?"

And they all were.

5

What Happened to Martha

As a matter of fact, the four children were all so glad to be home that they stayed around the house all the rest of that day.

And that one minute of the morning had been so crowded with adventure that somehow they didn't feel as though they wanted any more excitement for some time.

They put the charm away in its safe place under the flooring, and spent the morning and afternoon playing the most ordinary games they knew, even the tame childish ones that Martha liked and seldom got to play, like Statuary and Old Witch.

At dinner that night, when their mother asked them what they'd been doing all day, they said, "Oh, nothing," and seemed more interested in talking about what *she*'d been doing, at the office.

After dinner there weren't any secret conferences. Instead, the four children prevailed on their mother to join them in a game of Parcheesi.

And when she tired of Parcheesi, as mothers soon will, and offered to read them *A Connecticut Yankee in King Arthur's Court* until bedtime instead, Katharine said quickly that she'd rather hear a good, solid, down-to-normal, everyday book like *Five Little Peppers and How They Grew.*

All this was most unlike the four children.

When they'd finally gone to bed, their mother stole into their various rooms, and felt their foreheads and ears. But none of them had a fever.

The trouble was that the adventure with Sir Launcelot had seemed to point a moral.

And if you have ever had a moral pointed at you, you will know that it is not a completely pleasant feeling. You are grateful for being improved, and you hope you will remember and do better next time, but you do not want to think about it very much just now.

And, as Mark put it next morning, it was a moot question what to do with the charm next. Even wishing to do good deeds with it did not seem to be proof against the occurrence of that hot water in which the four children so often found themselves.

"Of course it has to be just nowadays and in our own country after this," Mark said, "but still! What if we messed up the President and Congress next time, the way we did King Arthur? We could cause a national emergency!"

"I know!" said Jane. "We must proceed with Utter Caution. I've been thinking about it all night, and I'm going to make my next wish really serious. I decided the two things I want most in the world are no more wars and that I knew everything!"

Katharine shook her head doubtfully.

"That's *too* serious," she said. "That's kind of like interfering with God. That might be even worse than trying to change history."

"Is there anything that's serious and fun at the same time?" Martha wondered.

It didn't seem very likely that there was.

And what with this problem, and the horrid thought that with each wish the charm's power was waning away, and that any day the next wasted wish might be its last, the four children decided to wait until tomorrow before getting on with the serious wishing.

Maybe by tomorrow Jane would have an inspiration. It was her turn next.

Meanwhile today they would have a good old-fashioned day out, the kind of day that had seemed the height of excitement to them, back in the time before the charm had crossed their path. They would put all their allowances together, go downtown on the street car and spend the day, have lunch and see a movie.

To phone their mother and persuade her to tell Miss Bick to let them go was a mere matter of five minutes' wheedling.

Miss Bick made her usual remarks of gloomy foreboding, but the children turned deaf ears, and assembled in Katharine and Martha's room.

"Shall we take it with us or leave it?" Katharine wanted to know.

No one needed to be told what "it" was.

"If we leave it Miss Bick'll be sure to find it," Mark pointed out, "no matter how carefully concealed."

"Think if she made a wish and got half of it!" cried Martha. "What do you suppose it would be?"

"I'd rather not," said Jane. "Some depths are better left unplumbed."

So Jane brought the charm along, wrapped in a special package of old Christmas paper, in her handbag. All the children tied strings around the little finger of each hand, to remind them not to wish for anything, no matter what happened. Then they emerged, and stood waiting at the corner, where they had so often beguiled the summer days by putting pieces of watermelon on the car tracks and waiting for them to squish.

The ride downtown on the street car was uneventful—only the usual trouble between the people who wanted the windows left closed, and the four children, who wanted them open.

Downtown, the children looked in shop windows for a while, then entered that lovely place, the five-and-ten. They bought and ate some saltwater taffy, listened to a young lady play "I Wish I Could Shimmy Like My Sister Kate" on the piano, and bought and ate some parched corn.

It was then time for lunch.

The four children always lunched at the best soda fountain in town. Today Jane ordered a banana split with chocolate ice cream and raspberry sauce, and Katharine enjoyed a Moonbeam Sundae, thick with pineapple syrup and three kinds of sherbet. Martha always had the same thing, a soda she'd invented, marshmallow with vanilla ice cream, which made the others gag.

There were two things listed on the menu which had intrigued Mark for years. One was called celery soda and the other was called malt marrow, and

Mark wondered very much what they could be. Each time he came he promised himself he'd order them next time, but next time his courage always failed. Today he thought of it, thought better of it, and had a double hot fudge dope.

After lunch it was time to choose what movie to see.

The children did this by first making a tour of all the movie theaters in town and looking at the pictures on the outside. A time of argument followed. Mark liked Westerns and thrilling escapes, but Martha wouldn't go inside any theater that had pictures of fighting.

Jane and Katharine liked ladies with long hair and big eyes and tragic stories. They wanted to see a movie called Barbara LaMarr in *Sandra*. Mark finally agreed, because there were a lot of pictures outside of a man who wore a mustache, and that meant he was the villain, and that meant that somebody would hit him sooner or later. Martha agreed because all the other theaters had either pictures with fighting or Charlie Chaplin.

All of the four children hated Charlie Chaplin, because he was the only thing grown-ups would ever take them to.

When they came into the theater Barbara LaMarr

in *Sandra* had already reached its middle, and the children couldn't figure out exactly what was happening. But then neither could the rest of the audience.

"But, George, I do not seem to grasp it all!" the woman behind the four children kept saying to her husband.

The four children did not grasp any of it, but Barbara LaMarr had lots of hair and great big eyes, and when strong men wanted to kiss her and she pushed them away and made suffering faces at the audience with her eyebrows, Jane and Katharine thought it was thrilling, and probably quite like the way life was, when you were grown-up.

Mark didn't think much of the love blah, but he watched the villain getting more villainous, and the hero getting more heroic, and patiently waited for them to slug it out.

Martha hated it.

That was always the way with Martha. She wanted to go to the movies like anything until she got there, and then she hated it. Now she kept pestering the others to read her the words and tell her what was happening (for in those days movies did not talk). And when the others wouldn't, she began to whine.

"Be quiet," said Jane.

"I want to go home," said Martha.

"You can't!" said Jane.

"Shush!" said all the other people in the theater.

"I want to, anyway," said Martha.

Jane finally had to put her under the seat. This usually happened in the end.

"Let me out!" said Martha, rising up from below.

But Jane pushed down heavily on the seat, and Martha collapsed under it.

It was dark and gloomy down there, with nothing to look at but dust and old gum other people had got tired of. Martha thought of crying, but she had tried this once in the past, and Jane had kicked her. She decided she might as well go to sleep.

Meanwhile, on the screen above, the hero was finally having his fight with the villain, and Jane and Mark and Katharine forgot all about Martha in their excitement. Jane also forgot to keep hold of her handbag, and it slipped from her lap and fell to the floor.

The wretched Martha, thankful for small favors, took the handbag and put it under her head, though it made rather a lumpy pillow.

I hope it is not necessary to remind you of what was in the handbag.

Jane remembered suddenly, and felt for it, in a

panic. It wasn't on her lap. She reached down to feel for it on the floor. At that moment she heard Martha speak.

"Ho hum. I wish I weren't here!" Martha said sleepily.

"Darn!" was the first thought of Jane. "Another wish wasted. Now she'll be only *half* here, I suppose."

Then, as the idea of this sank in, her blood froze. She didn't dare to look. Would just a severed head and shoulders meet her gaze, or would there be only a pair of gruesome legs running around down there?

At last she made herself lean over and see.

The charm hadn't worked it out that way at all. Martha was half there, to be sure, but it was *all* of her that was half there! Her outline was clear, but her features and everything that came between were sort of foggy and transparent. It was as though it were the ghost of Martha that stared up at Jane.

She stared up at Jane and saw her horrified expression; then she stared down at herself. And then Martha—or the half of her that was still there—lost her head completely. Uttering a low wail, she struggled to her feet, scrambled out through the row of seats, and ran up the aisle.

It is not often that one is watching a movie, and suddenly a wailing ghostly figure rises from the floor and scrambles past one.

Most of the ladies Martha scrambled past merely fainted.

The woman who had not grasped it all, before, now gave a shriek, and grasped her husband.

"Oh!" cried Jane, in a rage, catching up her handbag. "I wish I'd never even *heard* of that charm!"

And immediately she had only *half* heard of it. It was like a story she had read somewhere and half forgotten. And so naturally she didn't think of using the charm to bring Martha back to normal again. Instead, she ran up the aisle after her. Mark and Katharine ran after Jane.

An usher, running down the aisle to see what the commotion was, ran into them. He saw the handbag, heard the woman screaming, and decided Jane had stolen the bag. This slowed the children up a little, though no one was seriously hurt. The scratch the usher received was a mere scratch.

Meanwhile the ghostly Martha had run on up the aisle. In the darkness of the theater, not many people noticed her, but in the brightly lit lobby it was another story. The ticket-taker squealed, and threw her tickets in the air. The manager came running out of his office. He saw Martha, and turned pale.

"Oh, what next?" he cried, tearing his hair. "As if business weren't bad enough already, now the theater is *haunted*!" He aimed a blow at her with his cashbox. "Get along with you, you pesky thing!" he cried. "Why don't you go back where you came from?"

The hapless Martha moaned, and flitted on through the lobby, and into the street.

The appearance of her ghostly form upon the sidewalk caused quite a stir among the city's crowd of shoppers.

"It's an advertising stunt!" said a stout woman. "What they won't think of to sell these here moom pitchers next!"

"It's a sign!" said a thin woman. "It's the end of the world, and me in this old dress!"

"Tell it to go away!" groaned a well-dressed gentleman. "And I'll give back every cent I stole!"

"It's an outrage!" muttered an elderly person. "I shall complain to my Congressman!"

"It's a little girl, only she's only half there," said a child, but of course nobody paid any attention to *her*!

Some people who were afraid of ghosts started running, to get away from the horrible sight.

Martha started running in the opposite direction, to get away from the people.

Other people saw them running, and began to run, too, without knowing why. In no time at all a panic began to spread, as it will when people start behaving in this way, without thinking.

"What's the matter?" said a man to another man who was running by him. "You look as if you'd seen a ghost!"

"I just did!" cried the man. "Look!" And he pointed at the fleeing Martha.

"Don't be silly. There's no such thing," said the first man, who happened to be a learned professor. He glanced at the misty Martha. "Marsh gas," he said. "Very interesting."

"Martians? Did you say Martians?" said a third man, who happened to be passing. "The Martians are invading us!" he cried, without waiting for an answer. He began to run and everyone who heard him began running, too.

By the time Jane and Mark and Katharine had dealt with the usher and emerged from the movie theater, pandemonium reigned in the street. Someone had called the fire department and turned in a general alarm. Someone else had telephoned the police and asked them to send the riot squad. The wails of approaching fire sirens and the screeches of police whistles added confusion to the scene.

A crowd of people rushed past the theater.

"The Martians have landed!" they cried, pointing back in the opposite direction. "We saw one of them, all transparent and horrible!"

Jane and Mark and Katharine looked up the street in the direction the people were pointing in. Far in the distance they could just make out the dim figure of Martha, running along all by herself. They ran after her.

By this time no one was paying any attention to Martha at all. Everyone was too busy worrying about imaginary men from Mars.

But somehow, once she had started running, Martha found that she couldn't stop. And the more she ran, the more frightened she felt. This often happens.

She came to a corner, and turned it. The noise of the shouting and the sirens died away behind her. She was in a quiet street she had never seen before, a street of little shops. The street was deserted. Martha chose the middle shop and went in.

A few seconds later Jane and Mark and Katharine came round the corner and stood looking at the little shops. There was no sign of any part of Martha.

"Use the charm!" Mark cried. "Wish!"

"Oh, that old story!" said Jane. "Who ever believed that?"

Mark and Katharine stared at her with open mouths.

"What did you say?" said Mark.

Jane didn't answer. Quickly making up her mind, she chose a shop at one end of the row, and started in. Mark and Katharine, wondering what in the world had happened to Jane, followed. Then the three children stopped in the doorway, horrified.

The shop was a jeweler's, and costly diamonds and rich rings glittered on its counters. In the shop were a man and a woman. The man had a cap pulled low over his eyes. The woman wore a black-and-white skirt and a red blouse.

"Come on," the man was saying. "Now's de chance to loot de joint while everybody's away watchin' de riot!"

The man and woman started loading their pockets with pieces of jewelry from the counter. Katharine chose this moment to sneeze. The man and woman turned, and saw the three children standing in the doorway.

The man with the cap advanced toward Jane in a menacing fashion.

"O.K.," he said. "Hand over de bag."

Jane clutched her handbag to her. She seemed to half remember that there was a particular reason why she shouldn't lose it, but she couldn't think what the reason was. She didn't know what to do.

But Mark knew. He put his hand on the bag Jane was holding, and wished he and Jane and Katharine were where Martha was, only twice as far.

The next moment the man in the cap and the woman in the red blouse were alone, looking at the spot where the three children had been.

"Jeepers creepers!" said the man in the cap. "Dey've flew de coop!"

When Martha ran into the middle shop, at first she didn't see anybody, only books.

There were books in shelves on all the walls, and books on tables in all the corners. There was a large desk in the middle of the shop, piled high with books, and at first that seemed to be all. Then a face peered at Martha from over the pile of books on the desk, and a second later a rather small gentleman emerged from behind it. The gentleman wore a small pointed beard, and he held an open book in one hand.

He looked at Martha.

Martha looked back at him, waiting for him to

scream, or faint, or run away, the way everyone else had.

But the rather small gentleman did none of these things. He smiled, and bowed politely.

"Good afternoon," he said. "I presume this is a ghostly visitation? I am honored. Did you come out of one of the books? You might be Little Nell, I suppose, or Amy March, though the clothes don't look right."

"No, I'm Martha," said Martha. "And I didn't come out of a book; I came by magic charm."

And although she was old enough by now to know that no grown-up ever will credit any story that has magic in it, she proceeded to tell the small gentleman all about the charm, starting from the beginning. The small gentleman seemed particularly interested in the part about the children's mother.

"This didn't happen out on West Bancroft Street, by any chance, did it?" he interrupted her to ask. "About three nights ago?"

"Why, yes! How did you know?" said Martha, amazed.

"Never mind," said the small gentleman. "Do go on. Tell me more."

So Martha told him all about the movies, and Jane's putting her under the seat, and the wish she had made, and all that had happened afterwards.

"And so here I am," she ended, "only I'm only half here."

"So I see," said the small gentleman.

"It's kind of an interesting feeling, now I'm not scared anymore," said Martha. "Only I'm about ready for it to stop now. Mother'll be expecting us by dinnertime, and I'm afraid she might not like it if I came home like this. She isn't good with magic, the way you are. It upsets her."

"Yes, I know it does," said the small gentleman, absently.

"Oh, do you know Mother?" said Martha.

"Well, not exactly," said the small gentleman.

"Then how do you know about her? Are you magic, too? Are you a wizard or something? I thought you might be, when I saw that beard. Do you know any tricks to put me back together again?"

"I'm afraid not," said the small gentleman.

"Of course if Mark and Jane and Katharine were here," Martha went on, "they've got the charm, and they could wish me back. Don't you have any spells to sort of summon people?"

The small gentleman shook his head. "No spells. And I'm not a wizard, I'm sorry to say. This is the first magic thing that ever happened to me, though I always hoped something would. But maybe we can find them by regular means. What did they do when you ran out of the theater? Did they run after you?"

Martha looked startled. "Why!" she said. "I never even thought to look back!"

"They probably did," said the small gentleman. "They've probably been following you all the time. They're probably outside the shop right now, looking for you!"

"I'll go see," said Martha, starting for the door.

And it was at that exact moment that Mark, in the jewelry store down the street, made the wish that was to take him and Jane and Katharine to Martha's side. Immediately they were there.

"I did it!" said Martha. "I found them!"

"No, you didn't. Mark wished on the charm," said Katharine.

"I don't see why you all keep talking like that," said Jane. "There's no such thing as charms."

"Oh?" said the small gentleman. "That's not what your sister's been telling me."

"Who are you?" said Jane, rudely.

"Quiet," said Mark. "This is no time for mere bickering. We've got to fix up what we did. We've got to stop that awful panic. It's terrible—we were going to be so careful, and look what happened! You'd think that charm would have better sense!"

"There is no charm," said Jane.

"Stop saying that," said Mark. "Listen!"

The distant sound of fire sirens and police whistles and a cry of people could be heard.

"Now that you mention it," said the small gentleman, "I *did* think I noticed some slight disturbance, earlier."

"Slight," said Mark, "is not the word. Compared with the events of today, the Johnstown Flood will go down in history as a mere trifle!"

"I know it's my fault for wishing that wish," said Martha, "but I think it's everybody else's fault, too. Why did they all have to get so excited and start running?"

"One of the last admirable things about people," said the small gentleman, "is the way they are afraid of whatever they don't understand."

"And by now thousands are probably killed or homeless," went on Mark, drearily, "and burglars on every hand looting the deserted city! And Mother knows we're downtown!" he added, as a new thought struck him. "She'll be worried, and out looking for us!"

"If I may make a suggestion," said the small gentleman, "now if ever is a time for a really good wish."

"I'd be ashamed," said Jane. "Misleading these innocent children, pretending you believe in it!"

"Oh, what's the matter with her? Stop her, somebody!" said Katharine.

"Let me," said Martha. "I got us into this. I ought to get us out."

She tried to take the handbag from Mark. But of course the handbag just fell through her misty hand onto the floor. So then Mark held the bag, and Martha draped herself against it, in a clinging, clammy sort of way, like fog against a windowpane, as Katharine afterwards put it, and wished that Jane might be twice cured of whatever it was that ailed her. And right away Jane remembered about the charm.

The next wish was that their mother might find them safe and sound in four minutes' time.

"That gives me two minutes," said Martha, "to put myself back together in." For the third time she draped herself against the bag. "I wish," she began.

But there was an interruption.

Some people had appeared in the doorway of the shop. It was the man in the cap and the woman in the red blouse. Their pockets were bulging, probably with ill-gotten loot. The man looked round at the walls of bookshelves.

"Dis joint ain't no good, Mae," he said. "Dey ain't got nothin' but books."

"May I help you?" asked the small gentleman, stepping forward.

"How could you help me, if you ain't got nothin' but books?" said the man. Then he broke off, as he saw the four children. "Well, if it ain't de vanishin' marvels!" he said. "Kids, you got some disappearin' act! You carry it in dat bag?"

"What bag?" said Mark, putting the handbag behind him.

The man had seen Martha now.

"What's de matter wid *her*?" he said. "She get stuck half disappeared?" Then he smiled grimly. "O.K.," he said. "Tricks like dem I can use. Hand over de bag."

"I won't," Mark started to say, bravely. But before he could say it, the man snatched the bag from his hands and turned to run.

For the second time that afternoon Mark made a wish in the very nick, in the words of Katharine. He dove at the man in a flying tackle, and as the two of them went down together, he touched the bag and wished that he might capture the thieves singlehanded.

Of course one-half as good as singlehanded is double-handed; so it took him both hands to do it.

But thirty seconds later, when the two minutes were up and the children's mother walked into the bookshop, a startling scene met her gaze.

A male and a female thief lay bound and gagged on the floor, while Mark stood over them victoriously, his hands dripping diamonds and rubies.

Watching him in admiration were Jane and Katharine and Martha, only Martha seemed to be completely transparent.

And perhaps oddest of all, there stood the rather small gentleman with the beard who had given her a lift on the night she visited Uncle Edwin and Aunt Grace and had the strange adventure.

The combination of all these surprises, after the worry she had had during the panic in the streets, proved too much for her. She stood swaying in the doorway for a moment, a prey to conflicting emotions. Then she tottered to a chair and collapsed. Like many another in that unfortunate city, during the half hour since Martha made her first wish, she had fainted.

The small gentleman bent over her and chafed her wrists.

"She'll be all right, won't she?" Martha asked, anxiously.

"I think so. I'm sure so," said the small gentleman.

"Good. To work, then," said Martha. And she draped herself against the handbag and wished that

1 1 7

she might be twice as much there as she ever was.

"That's better," she said, a moment later, looking down at her old, solid self with satisfaction. Then she took the handbag firmly in her own substantial hand, and wished that the man in the cap and the woman in the red blouse might become twice as reformed in their characters as any two thieves had ever yet become.

Mark and Katharine unbound and ungagged the two thieves.

"Oh, what a wicked one I went and been," said the man in the cap. "Now I'm sorry."

"I been twice as wicked as you was," said the woman in the red blouse. "I'm twice as sorry, too!"

"You ain't," said the man in the cap. "You ain't capable."

Tiring of this, Martha wished them twice as far as where they belonged, and they went away, probably to join the Salvation Army.

The next thing was to wish the stolen jewelry all back where it belonged, too, and this was a simple problem. Then came a harder one.

"I wish," said Martha, "that anybody who's been hurt or upset, or anything that's been broken, or gone wrong because I wished that wish, may be twice as good as it was before. And I wish that everything that has happened because I made that wish should go right out of everybody's mind, and be as though it were a dream. Only twice as much so."

"Except me, please," said the small gentleman. He was standing looking down at their mother in rather an odd way. "I should hate not to remember every bit of this afternoon."

"Except," Martha began. Then she broke off. "What's your name?"

"Smith," said the small gentleman.

"Except Mr. Smith," said Martha. "And us, too, of course," she added.

They stood listening.

In the distance the sound of the fire sirens and the police whistles and the crowd broke off suddenly. There was a silence. Then faintly, the normal roar of city traffic, usually so ugly, but for this one time so beautiful to hear, fell on their charmed ears.

Martha relaxed with a sigh.

"I was afraid it might wear out before it got through that one," she said.

"It was a pretty big wish," Mark agreed. "It must have been quite a strain on it. Maybe that'll be the last wish we get."

"Let's wait a while before we find out," said Katharine.

Their mother stirred, and opened her eyes. She looked around her.

"Where am I?" she said, just like fainted people in books. Then she saw the four children, and held out her arms.

The three girls ran to her. So, even though he was a boy, did Mark.

"I had such a terrible dream," their mother said. "I dreamed there was an awful panic in the city, and I was out in it, looking for you, and then——"

"And then you came into my shop and found them," said Mr. Smith.

Their mother looked at him.

"It really is you," she said.

"Yes," he said.

"But I thought——" their mother began.

"I could have sworn——" she began again.

She passed her hand over her forehead, and smiled rather palely at Mr. Smith. "Every time we meet I seem to think something strange has just happened!"

She got to her feet and looked round the room again.

"There really weren't any thieves or diamond necklaces, were there?" she said.

"What?" said Mark.

"You must have dreamed it," said Martha.

"I think I'd better go home and lie down," said their mother. "I feel very peculiar."

"Ahem," said Mr. Smith, clearing his throat nervously. "I have a better idea. Couldn't you all come out to dinner with me? We could go to a movie or something afterwards."

"We really couldn't," said their mother. "And yet I think I'd like to," she added suddenly, in rather a surprised voice.

"Only no movies, please," said Martha.

"Well, then," said their mother, rather shyly, "perhaps we could all go out to our house after dinner." She looked at Mr. Smith, and laughed. "We seem to be fated to know each other better!" she said.

And perhaps they were.

Because that's what they did.

What Happened to Jane

The dinner with Mr. Smith and the evening that followed were an almost complete success. And the biggest success of the evening, for Mark and Katharine and Martha, was Mr. Smith himself.

The four children generally divided all grownups into four classes. There were the ones like Miss Bick and Uncle Edwin and Aunt Grace and Mrs. Hudson who—frankly, and cruel as it might be to say it—just weren't good with children at all. There was nothing to do about these, the four children felt, except be as polite as possible and hope they would go away soon.

Then there were the ones like Miss Mamie King, who—when they were with children—always seemed to want to pretend *they* were children, too. This was no doubt kindly meant, but often ended with the four children's feeling embarrassed for them.

Somewhat better were the opposite ones who went around treating children as though the children were as grown-up as they were, themselves. This was flattering, but sometimes a strain to live up to. Many of the four children's school teachers fell into this class.

Last and best and rarest of all were the ones who seemed to feel that children were children and grown-ups were grown-ups and that was that, and yet at the same time there wasn't any reason why they couldn't get along perfectly well and naturally together, and even occasionally communicate, without changing that fact.

Mr. Smith turned out to be one of these.

He allowed, and even urged, the four children to choose anything they wanted from the menu at dinner, at the same time frankly advising Mark that he thought he would enjoy rare steak and fried onions more than he would codfish tongues.

Jane said she wasn't very hungry, and would her mother order something for her, please? And no, she didn't think she cared for any dessert, thank you. The other three stared at her in disbelief.

After dinner came the ride home, and that was exciting, for everyone did not own a motor car in those days, and the four children were among the ones who didn't. Mr. Smith showed them the way to shift from high into second without stopping, and Mark thought this almost as magical as anything the charm had done for them so far.

Jane said she had seen it before. The other three thought this rude of her.

When they arrived at home Mr. Smith proved an adept player of Fan Tan and I Doubt It, and when card-playing palled was enthralling in his description of his travels in Darkest Australia.

Jane said she was tired and didn't feel like playing games or talking, and she guessed she'd go to bed and finish *Hildegarde's Harvest* instead. The other three looked at each other, and decided they had better have a word with Jane later on.

But when at last, very late, they were sent to bed, and stopped to peek into her room, she was asleep, or pretending to be.

And the next morning they didn't get a chance to ask her what had been the matter, because the next morning was Saturday and Saturday mornings in that house were always a thing of frenzy.

On Saturdays the children's mother came home from work early, and Miss Bick stayed only a half day, and those were two good things about Saturday.

But on Saturdays Miss Bick always seemed bent on cramming a whole day's fussing and nagging into one morning, and today the four children were kept so busy polishing silver and cleaning out bureau drawers and dusting and doing errands that they scarcely had time to exchange a word if two of them met by chance in the hall.

So it wasn't until along toward lunchtime that one or two, and finally three and four were able to gather together in Katharine and Martha's room and examine the outlook of the day.

The outlook of the day naturally hinged on the charm, and what they were going to do with it next.

"There's one thing bothers me," Martha was saying to Katharine, as Mark and then Jane joined them. "When I was only half there, where did the other half of me go?"

"Don't," said Katharine. "That's one of those questions that give you a headache just to think about. Like which came first, the chicken or the egg."

"All the same," said Mark, sitting down next to them, "it might be fun to find out."

"You mean wish ourselves there?" Katharine's eyes were round. "Wherever it is?"

"I don't want to!" said Martha. "It might be just nowhere at all! We might be just nothingness!"

"If we were, we wouldn't know it," Mark pointed out.

"But that's *worse*! Then we'd never get back at all!" Martha cried, getting excited. "I don't *want* to not know it! I don't want to be just nothingness! If we wish that, I won't come!"

"Well, you won't have to because we aren't going to!" said Jane, speaking for the first time. She walked over to the secret place and took out the charm. "It's my turn next and I don't feel like wishing. I may not make a wish for years and years. If ever." And putting the charm in her pocket, she started for the door.

"What's the matter with *you*?" said Mark, getting up to follow.

"Oh, nothing at all!" said Jane, turning on him. "Not a thing! Everything's just wonderful! Everything's just fine and dandy! Everything's just hunky-dory!"

"Well, isn't it?" asked Katharine.

"Everything's just spoiled, that's all!" Jane cried. "Everything's just utterly and completely ruined! All because some people have to tell everything they know!" And she glared at Martha.

"What did I do?" said Martha.

"As if you didn't know!" said Jane. "Here I thought we were going to have a wonderful, exciting, secret summer full of thrilling adventures, and you had to go and tell the whole thing to the first old stranger that came along!"

"You mean Mr. Smith?" said Martha, surprised. "He's not a stranger anymore. He's a friend."

"Oh, he is, is he?" said Jane. "That makes it all just lovely, doesn't it? And now I suppose we'll have grown-ups butting in and telling us what to wish all the time, and like as not wanting to borrow the charm and wasting its substance on their own devices and desires, and it's just all utterly and completely ruined!" And she went down the hall and into her own room and shut the door.

The others stared after her, amazed.

"Doesn't she like Mr. Smith?" said Martha.

"No," said Mark. "I don't think she does."

In her room Jane sat on the bed and gave way to gloom. She felt awful inside, the way you always do when you've been perfectly hateful to those you love best, and she didn't even know why she had done it. She didn't know why the mere thought of Mr. Smith upset her so—or if she did know the reason she didn't want to admit it, even to herself.

But the thing was that Jane was the only one of the four children who really remembered their father.

Martha was only a baby when their father died, and Katharine and even Mark were still very young, too young for them to recall very much about him now. But Jane remembered him clearly and with a great deal of love, and for that reason she couldn't bear the thought of Mr. Smith's coming into their lives and getting to know them better and better, and finally growing to be just like one of the family, and even trying to take the place of a father to them, which was what she was perfectly sure Mr. Smith hoped to do.

So now she sat in her room and thought and thought, and felt thoroughly miserable. Even the presence of the charm in her pocket was no comfort, because while it would serve the others right if she made a wish all by herself, the only wishes she could think of to make were horrible murderous ones, and she was old enough and nice enough to know that wishing herself invisible and going and pulling Mr. Smith's beard, or writing him a threatening letter with a pen dipped in blood wouldn't really be a bit of help or make her feel a bit better.

After a few minutes there was a knock at the door, and Mark and Katharine and Martha trooped in, looking solemn.

"We've been thinking," Mark said, "and we thought we ought to hold a Council."

"About Mr. Smith," said Martha.

"Go away," said Jane.

"You'd like him if you really got to know him," said Mark. "He was lots of fun last night."

"Humph!" said Jane.

"He was a big help when I wasn't all there," said Martha. "He's sensible about magic, not like most grown-ups at all."

"Ha!" said Jane.

"So we were thinking," said Katharine, and then trailed off, looking at Mark.

"Well?" said Jane.

"You tell her," said Katharine to Mark.

"We were thinking," said Mark, "that maybe before we make another wish we ought to go see Mr. Smith and sort of ask his advice. Just in a general way."

"*What?*" said Jane.

"*I* think we ought to take him along in the wish

with us," said Martha. "Then he could help us out again if we get in more trouble!"

"The way we always seem to," said Katharine.

"Then you could really get to know him," said Mark.

"And everything would be all right again," said Martha.

Jane was looking at them as if she couldn't believe her ears. "Has everyone in this family gone utterly and completely *insane*?" she cried. "Don't you know why he's so interested in us and nice about things? Haven't you seen the way he and Mother keep looking at each other? Do you want some old *stepfather* moving in here and changing everything?"

The others looked surprised at this, but not really terribly shocked.

"I should think he might make kind of an ideal one," said Katharine.

"It's good for a growing boy, having a man around the house," said Mark.

"I've always wished I had a father," said Martha.

Jane began to storm. "Do you really think he could ever take Father's place? Him and his old beard! Don't you know what stepfathers always turn out to be like, once the fatal deed is done? Don't you remember Mr. Murdstone? Oh!" she cried, glar-

ing round at them all. "It's no use! You don't understand! I wish . . . ."

She broke off in alarm, remembering the charm.
Then, a prey to utter recklessness, she plunged her
hand into her pocket, grasped the charm firmly, and
went on. "Yes, I do! I wish I belonged to some other
family! I wish it twice!"

Mark and Katharine and Martha gasped. This
was the worst thing that had happened yet. They
hardly dared look at Jane, for fear she might start
turning into someone else before their eyes.

But when they did look, there stood the same
brown-haired, blue-eyed, snub-nosed Jane they had
grown to know and love through the years. Nothing
seemed to have happened. Maybe nothing had. Mark
decided to find out.

"Look here, old Jane-ice," he said, putting his
hand on her arm and using a pet name that was
reserved for unusual serious moments. "You didn't
mean it, did you?"

"You let me go, you bully!" remarked a prim,
lady-like voice none of the children had ever heard
before in their lives. "You horrid big boy! I don't
like boys! And I don't like *you*!"

"Oh!" cried Martha, turning pale. "She doesn't
know us!"

"Of course she does," said Katharine. "You know *me*, don't you, dear? Kathie, that you've been through thick and thin with?"

"No. I don't know you and I don't wish to. Your frock is soiled," said the voice that, to their horror, seemed to be coming out of Jane. "My mama told me never to play with strange children."

Martha began to sniff.

"What an insanitary little girl," said the voice. "Tell her to use a handkerchief. She'll give me a germ."

"Oh, what's the matter with her?" Martha's voice rose to a wail.

"It's not her fault," Katharine said, trying to be reassuring for Martha's sake. "It's the way she's been brought up, I suppose. By that other family she belongs to, now. It *does* show what a good influence we've been, doesn't it? She was lots nicer under our tender care."

"I don't believe it," said Mark. "She's just trying to fool us, aren't you, Jane-ice?"

"Don't call me that," said the voice. "That's not my name."

"All right, then," said Mark, turning on her suddenly. "If that isn't your name, what is?"

The strange girl who looked like Jane, yet was Jane no longer, seemed startled for a moment, as if

1 3 2

she weren't quite sure of the answer. Then her face cleared.

"My mother calls me her Little Comfort," she said.

Mark made a gagging noise.

Katharine looked disgusted. "To think one of us should have come to this!" she mourned.

"It would be an errand of mercy to put the poor thing out of her misery," Mark agreed.

She-who-was-no-longer-Jane was staring around the room.

"I don't like this house," she said. "The furnishings are in poor taste. It is gaudy." Her lower lip began to tremble. "I want to go home."

"Oh, you do, do you?" said Mark. "Well, I can fix that. No sooner said than done." And he made a dive for the pocket where he knew the charm lay concealed.

But She (who was no longer Jane) pulled away, and gave him a surprisingly hard slap for such a miminy-piminy, ladylike type.

"Take that!" she cried. "You are a thief, as well as a bully!" She glared round at them all. "You are a lot of badly-brought-up children. You kidnapped me, and then tried to rob me. I'm going to tell my mother!"

And with these words, she flounced out into the

hall and started down the stairs. By the time the others had recovered from their shock and dashed after her, she was in the act of mincing out the front door.

Mark and Katharine took the stairs three at a time. Martha used the banister. But in the lower hall Miss Bick leaped forth and barred the way.

"No, you don't!" she said. "Not a soul leaves this house until the table's set for lunch!"

There was nothing the children could do about this, and nothing that they felt prepared to say. They didn't even point out that Jane had already left. As Katharine said afterwards, the way Jane was acting, right then she probably didn't *have* a soul!

But never was table set with such wild abandon, never did silver fly through the air with such great ease as it then flew. Hardly more than one precious minute had been wasted in idle drudgery before Mark and Katharine and Martha rushed out the front door and down the steps onto the sidewalk, and stood scanning the offing in all directions.

Far down Maplewood Avenue they could just make out a genteel figure in Jane's dress, picking its way along and toeing out in a way that the real Jane would have scorned to be seen doing in public. As they watched, the figure turned to the right, into Virginia Street.

And as they started to dash after it, a car drove up before the house, and Mr. Smith got out and held the door open for their mother.

"Company for lunch!" their mother called, blushing pink and looking embarrassed and pretty. "Where's Jane?"

The three children looked at each other and then quickly looked away again.

"We don't know, *exactly*," said Katharine.

"We think she's visiting somebody over on Virginia Street," said Mark, hoping that he spoke the truth, and that She (who was all that was left of Jane) had not strayed farther.

"Well, go and get her," said their mother, taking some interesting-looking packages from the car. "This is a party."

The three children looked at the ground, hopelessly.

"Or wait," their mother went on, not noticing. "You all go in the car and pick her up; that'll be quicker. I'll be breaking the news to Miss Bick about the party." And she started toward the house, her arms loaded with packages.

Mark and Katharine and Martha waited till she was safely inside. Then they turned to Mr. Smith and all started to speak at once. Then they stopped and looked at each other again.

"Shall we tell him?" Katharine asked.

"Yes." Mark nodded decisively. "There comes a time in the affairs of men, and this is it."

"I *said* we ought to, all along," said Martha. "I said he'd know what to do. This'll prove it."

And she and Mark and Katharine all piled into the front seat of the car and began telling Mr. Smith about the dread events of the morning. They didn't go into the reason for Jane's upset, though, or the way she felt about stepfathers, out of consideration for his feelings.

And Mr. Smith didn't waste time in unnecessary questions. ("Which proves," said Mark to Katharine, afterward, "that he would make an ideal step, and not Murdstone at all!") He started the motor, and the car shot down Maplewood and turned into Virginia Street.

She-who-was-no-longer-Jane was no longer to be seen.

"She must be in this block somewhere," said Katharine. "She hasn't had time to walk any farther."

"What do we do now?" said Martha.

"The question is moot," said Mark. "She could be in any one of these houses."

"We could holler 'Fire!' and everyone would come running out," suggested Katharine.

"Let's not have any more fires or running." Martha shuddered, remembering certain past experiences. "Let's knock at all the doors and ask them if they want to subscribe to the *Literary Digest.*"

"That's no good," said Mark, who had done this one summer to try to earn spending money. "All they ever say is 'No,' and shut the door."

Martha turned to Mr. Smith. "It's up to you," she said trustingly.

Mr. Smith looked pleased and touched. He also looked a little nervous, as though he were hoping he might live up to their trust. He cleared his throat.

"Well," he said, "first of all, does any of these houses look like the kind of house the family of that kind of girl would live in?"

Mark and Katharine and Martha stared up and down the block. Luckily it was a short one, with only eight houses in it, four on each side of the street. Almost all the houses looked very much like their own—comfortable, slightly shabby, family sort of houses, with an easy-to-get-along-with, lived-in look.

All but one.

The eighth house was made of cold-looking gray stone, and sat primly on an impossibly neat emerald lawn that was shut off from the street by a forbidding hedge of evergreens. A small sign on the lawn said

"Please." The walk to the front door was of bright blue gravel, edged with some boring plants that looked as though they had never blossomed and didn't intend to. There were no croquet wickets on the lawn and no bicycles or kiddy-cars sitting around, the way there were in front of most of the other houses.

"That's the one." Mark was positive. "It has to be. It looks just like her."

He and Katharine and Martha and Mr. Smith got out of the car and advanced stealthily up the street till they stood confronting the gray stone house. No one was in sight. From within came the sound of someone practicing a difficult piece upon the piano.

"That couldn't be Jane," said Martha. "She hates practice."

"I bet she doesn't now," said Mark.

"We'd better not let her see *us*," said Katharine. "She doesn't seem to like us very well any more."

"If her new family's anything like her, I don't think *they*'ll like us either," said Mark. He turned to Mr. Smith. "I guess it's still up to you, sir."

Mr. Smith cleared his throat nervously again. "All right," he said. "I'll try."

So Mark and Katharine and Martha hid behind

the evergreen hedge, and Mr. Smith, after checking to make sure that no telltale parts of them were exposed to the public gaze, squared his shoulders and marched bravely up the blue gravel walk and knocked on the front door with the imitation antique brass knocker.

When She-who-was-no-longer-Jane turned out of Maplewood into Virginia Street, she went straight to the gray stone house and up the blue gravel walk, and in at the front door. After all, this was her house and she belonged to this family now.

She went in at the front door and up the front stairs to what was now her room. There were hand-woven curtains of a cold gray at the windows, and the walls were painted in the same colorless tint. There were no colored pictures on the walls, only sepia prints of Sir Galahad and a lady called Hope. The bookshelves were full of heavy, instructive-looking books, and no toys or games, only a few sets of the helpful kind that show you how to weave linen and tool leather in six easy lessons.

She-who-was-no-longer-Jane sat down on an uncomfortable imitation antique chair and began looking at one of the instructive books. She did this as though it were perfectly natural and as though she'd been doing nothing else for years, but all the same, deep down inside her, she felt strangely empty and uncomfortable, as though she didn't belong in this prim gray room at all.

After a bit, deciding she didn't feel like being instructed just now, she put down the book and took a round, shining object from her pocket. She sat staring at it for a long while. In a dim way her mind connected it with the empty, uncomfortable feeling that seemed to hang over her, but she couldn't remember why the shiny thing made her feel lonely and unhappy.

Of course the trouble was that when she wished to belong to another family, she hadn't said a thing about not being Jane any longer. And so she had become the girl Jane would have been if she had been brought up in this cold, gray house. But down inside her somewhere, the real Jane was still struggling to exist. This is called heredity versus environment, and it is quite a struggle.

After she had been sitting by herself (or by her two selves) for a few minutes, a lady appeared in the door. She was dressed in a gown of sober gray wool.

"Why, here you are!" she cried. "Mother has been worried. She couldn't find her Little Comfort anywhere!"

"I was playing," said She-who-was-now-part-Jane-

and-part-Mother's-Little-Comfort (only from now on I think it will save time if we just think of her as She).

"Where were you playing?" said the gray lady. "You weren't in the solarium and you weren't in the patio!"

"I was around the corner. I was playing with some children."

"But we don't know anyone around the corner," said the gray lady in alarm. "Mother wants you to have fresh air and exercise, of course, but one can't be too careful about speaking to strangers! Were they nice children?"

She hesitated. "*You* wouldn't like them," She said, finally, hanging her head and looking closer at the round shining thing in her hand.

"Really, Comfort, you are not behaving like yourself today!" said the lady, reproachfully.

"I know it," said She, unhappily.

"Haven't I told you always to look at me when I am speaking to you?" the lady went on. "What is that you have in your hand?"

"I don't know. I found it."

"Let me see," said the lady. She took the shining thing in her own hand. "But this is very interesting! It seems to be some kind of ancient talisman. See, there is writing on it, but I don't recognize the language. It is not Greek or Latin. Probably it is Sanskrit. Father will translate it for us when he comes home. And now how would you like to take a nice nap until dinnertime?"

Jane and Mark and Katharine and Martha had all scorned naps for years, and the small remnant of Jane that was still there somewhere, buried under layers of Little Comfort, rose to the surface. "I wouldn't like it at all," She said.

"But you always have a nap at this hour!" cried the lady.

"Do I?" said She, her heart sinking. "Couldn't I dig some worms and go fishing instead?"

The lady looked shocked. "Why, Comfort! You know fishing is cruel, except when necessary to provide food, and we are all vegetarians here!"

"Build a block fort and have a war with toy soldiers?" suggested She, faintly.

"Why, Comfort!" cried the lady again. "There are no toy soldiers in this house! They are symbols of world militarism, and not suitable playthings! I can't think what has come over you today! It must be the influence of those bad children! No, let us go down to the drawing room and put this ancient talisman in the curio cabinet, and then you can practice your new piece till Father comes."

The remnant of Jane that still existed didn't like

seeing the round shining thing go out of her possession at all, and she didn't much want to practice a new piece either. And she had her doubts about a house in which naps were taken and bright colors were shunned, and things that were ordinary and fun were made to seem ugly and wicked. But She dejectedly followed the gray lady out of the room and down the stairway into the drawing room, which was large and cold and grey, and took her seat on the piano stool.

And it turned out that practicing on the piano, which was always sheer torment to Jane in the past, was a mere cinch now. She played away primly and perfectly, while the gray lady sat in a stiff chair of carved oak, and looked at a magazine called *The Outlook.*

This went on for what seemed like years, and the last trace of Jane was just beginning to think it might as well die away forever when there was an interruption. Someone knocked at the front door.

"Who could that be?" said the lady. "Father would use his key, and we never have visitors here."

"I bet you don't!" thought the small spark of Jane, with a last flicker of life.

The lady went to the front door and opened it. A rather small gentleman stood outside. He wore a pointed beard and a nervous expression.

"Good afternoon, madam," he said, putting one hand behind his back as though he were crossing his fingers (which he was). "I am writing a book on child psychology, and I hear you have a very intelligent daughter. I wonder if I might interview her?"

"How interesting!" cried the lady. "I have made a life study of child psychology myself!"

"You have?" said the small gentleman, looking more nervous.

"Yes. What method do you follow, the Schwartz-Metterklume or the Brontossori?"

The small gentleman looked as if he wished he were somewhere else. "I have my own method," he said. "You wouldn't have heard of it."

"But how interesting!" cried the lady. "You must come in and tell me all about it." And she led the small gentleman through the gray hall into the gray drawing room.

Outside, Katharine leaned out from her evergreen hiding place. "Psst," she said.

"Come on," said Mark, from behind his.

And followed by Martha, they crossed the emerald lawn and mounted the front steps of the house. The lady had left the front door ajar in her excitement, and standing in the hallway the children could hear everything that happened in the drawing room perfectly.

"Of course we wouldn't want any publicity," the lady was saying. "You won't use her real name in the book, will you?"

"Naturally not," said the voice of Mr. Smith (for of course the small gentleman was he). "I shall call her chapter The Jane Case."

Mark and Katharine and Martha heard a gasp, as though the name had meant something to someone in the room.

"Unless of course that is her name?" Mr. Smith's voice went on.

"Oh, no," said the voice of the lady. "We call her Comfort, but her name is Iphigenia."

"If a what?" said Katharine to Mark, in the front doorway.

"Shush," said Mark to Katharine.

"I see," came the voice of Mr. Smith, from the drawing room. "How do you do, Iphigenia? Do you believe in magic?"

"Oh no," came the voice of the lady, before She could answer. "I'm afraid your method is a bit old-fashioned. Iphigenia has never believed in magic, or anything else untrue."

1 4 5

"How sad for her," said the voice of Mr. Smith. "However, what *are* her interests? Does she collect anything, perhaps?"

"Why, yes," said the lady, before She could answer again. "She collects objects of art. Only this afternoon she brought home a rare old talisman!"

In the doorway Martha pinched Katharine. "The charm!" she hissed.

"Shush," Katharine hissed back.

"You don't say?" Mr. Smith's voice sounded excited. "I wonder if I might see if for a moment?"

"I don't see why not," came the voice of the lady. Her footsteps could be heard, crossing the room, and the suspense was more than Mark and Katharine and Martha could bear. They moved across the hall to see what was happening.

The floor of the hall was highly polished and there were some little gray hand-hooked rugs scattered about on it. Martha tripped on one of the rugs, slipped on the floor, and fell into the drawing room with a crash, just as the lady was turning from the curio cabinet with the charm in her hand and Mr. Smith was reaching out his own eager hand to take it. Mark and Katharine followed Martha into the room.

"Hello," said She, smiling at them. After half an hour in the gray house, She liked their looks better than she had at their last meeting. She turned to the gray lady. "These are the children I was playing with this afternoon."

"Well, I'm afraid they are very rude children," said the lady, recovering from her surprise. She looked at Mark and Katharine and Martha sternly. "In this house we don't walk in the front door without being asked. I think you had better go home at once. Iphigenia doesn't want to see you."

"Oh yes, she does, if she only knew it!" said Mark bravely, advancing into the room. "Let me take that charm a minute and I'll prove it. It belongs to us anyway!"

"If you mean this rare old Sanskrit talisman," said the lady, "it certainly does not. It belongs to my Iphigenia."

"She's not yours; she's ours," said Martha, getting up from the floor.

"Her name isn't what you said; it's Jane," said Katharine.

"She doesn't live here; she lives over on Maplewood," said Mark.

"Not another word," said the lady. "Such awful fibbing I never heard! You are either the worst-brought-up children I have ever seen or you are all mentally unbalanced! I'm afraid I shall have to telephone your parents!"

"No, don't do that!" said Mr. Smith, coming forward anxiously. "I'm afraid this is all my fault. I'm afraid I asked these children to come. Just a little experiment, you know. All part of my method."

"Then I don't think much of it," said the lady, getting really cross. "I don't believe you are a child psychologist at all, or if you are, you shouldn't be allowed to be! I shall write to the *Psychology Journal* and complain!"

"Very well. You're right. I'm not," said Mr. Smith, giving up. "But don't be alarmed; I can explain everything. Only it's a long story; so if you'd just let me have that charm . . ."

"So that's it!" cried the lady. "I see it all now! It's a plot! Coming here pretending to be writing a book, and all the time trying to steal our art treasures! For shame, taking advantage of these unfortunate children!"

"No, no," said Mr. Smith, becoming agitated. "This is all a mistake. That little girl isn't who you think she is at all."

"You wouldn't like her if you got to know her," put in Katharine earnestly. "You would find her a wolf in sheep's clothing."

"She's my sister, only she has what-d'you-call-'ems," said Mark.

"Hallucinations," explained Mr. Smith.

"We want to take her where they'll be kind to her," said Martha. "Jane, Jane, come on home out of this cold, slippery house!"

The remnant of Jane, down in the heart of Iphigenia, heard Martha's call. She thought how much happier she felt with Martha and Mark and Katharine, yes, and Mr. Smith, too, than she did with the gray lady. She remembered her own home and her own family, and wished she belonged to them again. She yearned to answer Martha. And she made a great effort, and forced her way to the surface and started to speak.

But before she could there was an interruption. A thin, gray gentleman appeared in the drawing room.

"Yarworth! Here you are at last!" cried the gray lady. "This criminal, aided by these delinquent children, was trying to rob our Iphigenia!"

"Dear me," said the gray gentleman, retreating slightly. "Are you sure?"

"Don't just stand there!" cried the lady. "Defend us! What will Iphigenia think of her father?"

What Iphigenia would have thought of her father will probably never be known. For at that moment Mr. Smith, having had quite enough of both Iphigenia and her parents, decided to act.

"I'm sorry to appear rude, madam, but you'll be

glad of it afterwards," he said. "At least I hope so."

And he snatched the charm from the lady's hand, took a deep breath, and wished that Jane might be twice as much Jane as she ever was.

Jane, finding herself suddenly herself again, gave a glad cry and ran, much to the surprise of Mark and Katharine and Martha, straight to Mr. Smith.

"You were wonderful," she said. "Part of me was here all along, hoping you'd save me, and you did! You were wonderful!"

"It was nothing," said Mr. Smith, modestly.

"We told you so," said Mark and Katharine to Jane.

They had run to Mr. Smith, too, and so had Martha, and now the five of them stood united, looking defiantly at the gray lady and the gray gentleman.

The lady was blinking her eyes. The gentleman was rubbing his. They looked rather like two people who have just awakened from a nightmare.

"What is the meaning of this intrusion?" demanded the gray lady. "What are you doing in our house? Go away at once!"

"This isn't your little girl, then?" asked Mr. Smith, with his arm around Jane.

The lady looked at Jane with distaste. "I never saw the horrid little thing before in my life!"

"You don't even *have* a little girl, perhaps?" went on Mr. Smith.

"Certainly not," the lady said thankfully. "So noisy and tiresome and such a strain!"

"Then if we take her away with us, it will be quite all right with you?"

"If you don't all leave this house at once, my husband will take steps! Won't you, Yarworth?" said the gray lady.

The gray gentleman took a step backwards in alarm. He did not reply.

"Thank you, madam. That's all I wanted to know," said Mr. Smith. And bowing politely, he touched the charm and made another wish.

Of course if he had asked the four children's advice, they could have told him how to word his second wish much better.

As it was, being new to magic, he didn't put in any of the things experience had taught them, like not being gone too long, and arriving back in a normal way, and their mother's not noticing anything out of the ordinary. He just wished they were twice as far as home again.

And so, a split second later, when the children's mother came into the living room and it was empty, and then suddenly Mr. Smith and the four children

151

were all sitting around it in chairs, she was more than a bit surprised.

"How funny!" she said. "I didn't see you sitting there. I didn't hear a car drive up, either."

She glanced out of the window, and it was then that Mr. Smith remembered that his car was still sitting back on Virginia Street, where he'd parked it, what seemed like ages ago.

He touched the charm in his pocket, and made a quick wish, but not quick enough. When the children's mother looked from the window, first she saw the empty street, then suddenly the car was sitting there.

She put her hand to her head and sat down suddenly.

"I really must go to the doctor about my eyes," she said. "I keep thinking I see the strangest things!"

"It's the sun," said Mr. Smith. "It's awfully strong today."

"*I*'ve been thinking I saw some awfully strange things this morning, too. Over on Virginia Street," said Mark, daringly, with a wink at Mr. Smith and Jane.

Martha giggled.

"Luncheon is served," said Miss Bick sourly from the doorway, and they all trooped in to where the festive board groaned.

The luncheon party was a great success with the four children, but their mother seemed a bit worried and preoccupied, and kept putting her hand to her forehead as if she were trying to puzzle something out, and this seemed to make Mr. Smith a bit worried, too.

The spirits of the children were so very high, however, that their mother couldn't stay upset for long. And the behavior of Jane, in particular, was enough to warm any mother's faltering heart.

She was so unselfish about second helpings, so eager to pass things without being asked, so tireless in her efforts not to accept the last extra butterscotch tart, lying luscious under its whipped cream, but to bestow it on a friend or relation, so anxious generally to show how much she loved this family above all others, that no one could believe it was the usual good old hasty hot-tempered Jane who sat there among them.

"That charm certainly does improve people, once they've been through the mill of it," Katharine whispered to Mark.

"Whispers at the table shall breakfast in the stable," said their mother.

"Kath was only saying Jane certainly was full of charm this morning," said Mark, with another daring wink at the others.

"Yes, you'd almost think she were a different person!" said Katharine, equally daring.

Martha giggled. So, I regret to say, did Mr. Smith.

"What's the joke?" said the children's mother.

"Oh, nothing," said the four children.

"I'm just feeling happy," said Mr. Smith. "This is a treat for me. I live all alone, you know, and it's years since I've been to a family party like this."

Jane looked round the room, at the colored pictures on the lemon-yellow walls and the gay printed curtains at the window and the bright rugs on the floor and the smiling faces around the table.

"This is a wonderful family to belong to," she said. "It's the best family to belong to in the whole world!"

Then she smiled at Mr. Smith.

"I think *you*'re going to think so, too," she said.

7

How It Ended

"Who gets the charm today?" said Martha, early next morning. "We've all had a turn now. Do we start over and take seconds, or should we agree on something and wish it together?"

"I think we ought to give it a day of rest," said Katharine. "After all, today's Sunday."

And once the other children thought about it, they agreed that magic on Sunday didn't seem quite right. Or at least there was a chance that it wouldn't be, and the four children were taking no further chances, now they knew how difficult the charm could be when roused.

So Katharine spent the morning reading *The Ingoldsby Legends*, which she had just discovered, and Mark built derricks with his Meccano set.

Jane humored Martha by playing dolls with her, a pursuit Jane usually scorned, but she was still feeling kindly toward her family, as a result of yesterday's adventure. Her true nature reasserted itself during the course of the game, however, and many a doll was stabbed to the heart or burned at the stake before the morning was over.

The four children all hated big noon dinners on Sunday; so when hunger reared its hideous head they just had soup and toast, and it was right after that that Mr. Smith arrived, and asked if they and their mother wouldn't like to come for a drive with him, and a picnic supper afterwards. He said he knew of a wonderful picnic place with a river and swings and a meadow and woods, and he had had six box lunches made up at Meinert's Pastry Shop.

Jane and Mark and Katharine and Martha could hardly wait to start.

"What is it that makes box lunches always sound so delicious?" Katharine wondered. "It makes you think there might be almost anything inside. Duck eggs and nectar and kinds of sandwiches nobody ever had before!"

Their mother said she had a headache and thought she'd better stay home, which didn't sound like her at all. The four children stared at her.

"You never have headaches," said Mark.

"You never want to stay home and spoil things, either," said Katharine.

"It won't be any fun without you," said Jane.

And of course after that the children's mother had to give in, and five minutes later away they went.

The picnic place proved to be all that was ideal, as Mr. Smith had said it would. Martha went picking butterfly weed in the meadow, only it seemed to be beeweed, too, and one stung her, and Katharine wandered romantically through the woods, and was almost sure she saw a snake, and Jane and Mark tried to build stepping stones across the river and fell in with all their clothes on, and altogether it was a typical happy family outing.

The box lunches turned out not to contain any duck eggs or nectar, but the sandwiches were sufficiently unusual, and there were deviled eggs and potato salad and lots of little assorted cakes that the children had fun with, deciding which ones they liked best and trying to trade off the others.

Supper was eaten round a bonfire deftly constructed by Mark and Mr. Smith, and stories were told and songs were sung, until what with one thing and another, it was long after nine o'clock when they packed themselves into the car once more, and drove home through the purple darkness.

And the four children were all so tired and happy and sunburned and sleepy that they went straight to bed with almost no ado.

Martha, as sometimes happens, was so tired that she couldn't seem to go to sleep, and she noticed that Mr. Smith didn't go home right away, but sat talking to their mother for what seemed like hours and hours.

And much later, in the middle of the night, she woke up, possibly as a result of too many cakes, and was almost sure she heard their mother crying.

This couldn't be, of course. Martha had never heard of a mother who cried, and certainly not *their* mother, so happy and strong and busy and sensible, and the pride of the Toledo *News-Bee*!

She tiptoed to the door and listened, but there

didn't seem to be any sound now. She decided with relief that she must have been mistaken, and went back to bed and to sleep.

But in the morning their mother hardly said a word at breakfast, and her cheeks looked pale and her eyes looked tired, and Martha began to wonder again.

After breakfast, when their mother had gone to work, Jane, whose new family devotion continued to shine forth, volunteered to do the dishes alone and unaided, and this brilliant example so bestirred the finer feelings of Mark and Katharine that they insisted on helping.

Martha followed them out into the kitchen, and sat watching, and wondering whether her worries about their mother were too farfetched for her to mention them.

"Does everyone realize we've had the charm a week now?" Jane was saying, scraping toast crumbs off plates and then plunging the plates in soapy water.

"Really?" said Katharine. "It seems like months, at least."

Mark began counting it out. "The fire was Tuesday and the desert was Wednesday, we met Launcelot on Thursday and went to the movies on Friday,

Jane belonged to that other family on Saturday, and we rested on Sunday."

"And today's Monday," said Jane. "The seventh day. I read somewhere that seven's a magic number. Maybe today'll be the biggest wish yet."

"When you come to think of it, no great big lasting thing has happened so far," said Mark. "We've had lots of adventures, but we're still just the same as we were before we found it."

"Our characters are improved," said Katharine, "and I think we're sort of happier."

"I don't think Mother is," said Martha.

Three faces turned to her, and, "What do you mean?" said three voices at once.

But before Martha could answer, the telephone in the hall began to ring.

Mark got there first.

"Hello?" he said. "Oh, hi." He turned to the others. "It's Mr. Smith."

"Let me," said Jane, grabbing the phone.

"Honestly," Mark complained to Katharine. "After we had all that hard work getting her to like him at all, now you'd think he were her own special property!"

"Yes," Jane was saying into the phone excitedly. "Yes. All right. We will. Yes, right away!"

She hung up, and turned from the phone, looking serious and important. "Big Council meeting!
At the bookshop in twenty minutes. Carfare will be
refunded. Can we scrape together the wherewithal?"

The week had been given over so completely to
magic experiment that allowances remained practically intact; so that was all right.

"Are we taking the charm?" Martha wanted to
know.

"Naturally! What else would an Important Council be about?" said Jane, witheringly.

Katharine fetched the charm from its hiding place,
and the four children waited for a moment when
Miss Bick's attention was elsewhere (elsewhere being
with the gas-meter man) to steal down the front
stairs, hurry out the door, and run two blocks up
Bancroft Street before waiting for the streetcar, so
she wouldn't see them from the window and take
unpleasant steps.

The ride downtown seemed endless but turned
out at last not to be, and ten minutes later found
them hurrying into the bookshop.

Mr. Smith rose from his desk, and came to greet
them. He seemed uneasy.

"Hello," he said. "You were quicker than I expected. Please sit down. I have something to tell
you."

The four children looked around, but there were piles of books on all the sitting places; so they stayed standing. Mr. Smith didn't seem to notice. He hesitated, cleared his throat, took his handkerchief out and put it away again, and looked at the floor.

"Dear me, I find this very difficult," he said. "I think perhaps first of all it might help if you stopped calling me Mr. Smith and called me Hugo."

Jane shuddered. "I *couldn't*!"

"That's a terrible name," said Mark, ever candid.

"Maybe if we shortened it?" Katharine suggested. "Hugh isn't so bad."

"I shall call him Huge," announced Martha independently. "After all, he looms huge in our future, if you-know-what is going to happen! You know, if he's going to be our—" she broke off, and uttered the last word in a piercing whisper that carried to all corners of the room—"*stepfather!*"

Mr. Smith heard the whisper, and a blush mantled his cheek.

"Then you know!" he said. "And here I was wondering how to break it to you. That's what I had to tell you. It's true. I have come to care very deeply for your mother and have asked her to be my wife."

"We thought you would," said Martha.

"Any day now," said Mark.

"We think it's wonderful," said Katharine.

"Specially me," said Jane.

"Thank you," said Mr. Smith. "You are four very pleasant children, and I should be proud and happy to be your stepfather, and you may call me Huge or anything else you like."

"*Uncle* Huge," said Mark. "It's more respectful. There is only one difficulty," said Mr. Smith.

"Won't she have you?" asked Katharine. "Is she being coy and hard to please?"

"I could go and reason with her if you like," offered Mark. "I'm quite good at it, really."

"*I* shall tell her I think she's a very lucky woman to have landed you!" said Martha.

"Please, I beg of you, do not say anything of the kind!" cried Mr. Smith in alarm, blushing again. "No. Your mother has admitted that she thinks she could care for me in return. But yesterday evening she told me definitely that her answer is no. The reason is that she believes herself to be ill. Mentally ill. I leave you to guess why."

"She's noticed things," said Jane. "Us appearing suddenly out of nowhere and things."

"That wish she half got, when she ran into you out on Bancroft Street," said Katharine.

"Me with all those diamonds and robbers," said Mark.

"I *did* hear her crying last night, then," said Martha.

"Oh, dear. Was she?" said Mr. Smith.

"That's bad," said Mark.

"And it's all our fault," said Katharine.

The four children looked solemn. Then Jane's face cleared.

"It's all right. We can fix it up," she said. "What could be simpler? We'll confess. We'll tell her the whole thing from the beginning."

"Do you think she'll believe it?" said Mr. Smith. "Remember, your mother is a very practical person."

"Stubborn, too," agreed Katharine.

"We could *show* her," suggested Mark doubtfully. "We could have the charm take her somewhere."

"That's it!" Jane's eyes were shining. "We'll let her wish—we'll give her whatever her heart desires! This will be the best deed yet! Come on, let's go over there right now!"

"Do be careful," said Mr. Smith. "Hadn't we better plan it out, first?"

But his words were wasted on the bookshop air. Jane had the charm in her hand, and rashly, excitedly, without thinking what she'd do when they got there, she wished.

The next moment they were in their mother's office.

The children's mother was Women's Club Editor of the newspaper, and that meant that she wrote all those little pieces that say which ladies are going to meetings at which other ladies' houses and what they are going to have to eat.

It wasn't a very important job, and her office was tiny, and today it was already quite filled by a fat lady who was telling their mother all about the Potluck Pageant she was planning to give for the League of Needless Women.

So that when Jane and Mark and Katharine and Martha and Mr. Smith were suddenly all there in the office, too, it made quite a crowd.

"Oh!" cried their mother, turning pale, as the five familiar figures appeared out of nowhere before her gaze. "There it is, happening again!"

"Really!" said the fat lady to Jane and Katharine and Martha, who were wedged tightly against her. "Stop shoving."

"I'm sorry, but we haven't time for you now," said Jane to the fat lady. And she wished her twice as far as where she belonged.

The lady was quite annoyed to find herself suddenly at home in her own kitchen, and later sued the newspaper for witchcraft. But she was never able to prove her case, and anyway that does not come into this story.

Back in her office, the children's mother sat staring palely at the place where the lady had been.

"It's all right," Jane told her. "We know what you're thinking, but you're wrong. We can explain everything."

"What you thought was you going crazy was just us," said Martha.

"We've got a magic charm," said Mark.

"We've had it for a week, only we didn't tell you," said Katharine. "We thought you were too old to know."

"And that night you went to see Aunt Grace and Uncle Edwin and wished you were home, *you* had it," said Jane. "And it works by halves. And that's how you happened to meet Mr. Smith. And that proves what a good charm it is, because we think he'd make a wonderful stepfather and not a bit Murdstone, and we've adopted him for our Uncle Huge, and we think you ought to marry him right away!"

Their mother looked at Mr. Smith reproachfully.

"You told them!" she said. "And now they're making all this up to make me feel better. How could you?"

"No, that isn't it at all," said Jane. "There really *is* a charm! Look." And she put the charm in their mother's hands.

"That's a nickel," said their mother.

"That's what I thought at first, too," said Jane, "but it isn't. See, it's got old ancient signs on it! Wish, why don't you? That'll prove it. For whatever your heart desires! Or wait, I'll show you how." And she touched the charm, where it lay in their mother's hand.

"I wish," she began, trying to think of something simple and harmless, yet unusual. "I wish two birds would fly in the window and speak to us."

Immediately a chickadee flew in through the window and stood on the desk.

"Hello," it said. It flew out again.

Their mother had her eyes shut tight. "Tell it to go away!" she said.

"It just did," said Martha.

Their mother opened her eyes again. "That proves it," she said. "It's just as I was afraid it was! Everything's been too much for me and my mind's given way."

"Now, now," said Mr. Smith. "You mustn't get excited." But Mark interrupted him.

"Honestly!" he said to Jane in disgust. "Making birds come in and talk to her! No wonder she thinks she's crazy! Whose heart's desire would that be? No, don't you remember how she always used to say she wanted to be City Editor of the paper some day?

Let me have that." And he took the charm from Jane.

"Careful!" said Mr. Smith.

"It's all right. I know what to say," Mark reassured him. And he wished.

The owner of the newspaper walked into the office.

"Ah, dear lady," he said. "How happy you look with your little family around you!"

Their mother turned a woebegone face upon him and said nothing.

"What part of Mother's little family is Mr. Smith?" whispered Katharine to Mark, giggling.

"Shush," said Mark.

"We are making some changes in the organization," the owner of the paper went on, "and I am glad to tell you that from this moment on you may consider yourself City Editor, at a sizeable increase in salary."

"No," said the children's mother, shaking her head stubbornly. "It isn't true. It's just some horrible crazy dream! You aren't even real. You're just a . . . a figment of my imagination!"

"Well, really!" said the owner of the paper, looking displeased. Apparently he did not like being called a figment.

"Aw, Mother," said Mark. "Don't worry; just take it. Don't you remember how you've always said you could run the paper singlehanded better than the rest of this whole dopey crowd down here does?"

"You don't say!" said the owner of the paper, coldly. "In that case, perhaps I had better withdraw my offer. Perhaps you had better look for a job somewhere else!" And he made a dignified exit.

"This is worse and worse!" moaned the children's mother. "Now I'm unemployed! And he'll tell everybody it's because I've gone raving, tearing mad, and he'll be right, because I *have*!"

"There, there," Katharine soothed her. "Mark just didn't know. He couldn't, because I'm the only one who knows what your heart's desire really is!" She turned to the others. "Mother told me once that when she was our age she always wanted to be a bareback rider." And Katharine took the charm in her hand.

"Dear me, I hardly think—" began Mr. Smith.

But before he could finish his sentence Katharine had wished, and he and the four children found themselves sitting in the front row of the grandstand inside an immense circus tent, and the ringmaster was just cracking his whip and announcing that La Gloria, the Best Bareback Rider in the World, would now perform her death-defying act.

There was a crash of cymbals, and La Gloria rode into the ring on a white horse. La Gloria was the children's mother. Only she didn't look at all like herself in pink tights and a frilly skirt. And she didn't act like herself, either.

She rode round the ring with grace and speed, and jumped her horse through hoops with spirit and style. And, what was most alarming of all to the four children, she seemed to be *enjoying* it!

"Hoop-la!" she cried. "Allez-oop! Whee!"

"Stop her!" wailed Martha. "She'll hurt herself! She'll fall!" And she jumped over the rail and ran into the middle of the ring, with Jane and Mark and Mr. Smith behind her. Forgetting the charm in her hand, Katharine ran with them. La Gloria had to rein in her horse to keep from running them down.

"Get out of the way! You're spoiling the act!" she said haughtily.

"This is awful! She doesn't know us!" cried Martha.

"Of course she does. Don't you?" said Jane.

"No, and I don't wish to!" said La Gloria. "Out of the way! The show must go on!"

"Why?" said Mark, ever willing to argue a point.

Behind them in the grandstand the audience was beginning to be restless.

"In my opinion people who interrupt other peo-

ple's entertainment should be ejected!" said a lady
in the front row.

"You're right!" said the lady sitting next to her.
"They should be ejected first and then put out!"

An angry murmur began to grow.

"Down in front!" yelled somebody.

"Get the hook!" yelled somebody else.

The ringmaster approached, cracking his whip.

Then, just as it looked as though there might be

unpleasantness, Katharine unwished, and they found themselves back in the newspaper office.

Their mother sat at her desk, a dreamy, far-away smile on her face. Katharine turned to her anxiously.

"There!" she said. "*Now* do you believe?"

Their mother's smile vanished. She looked stubborn. "That didn't happen," she said. "It was a dream."

"How do we all know about it, then?" said Katharine.

"You don't," said their mother. "You couldn't." And nothing any of the children could say would make her believe anything else. After five minutes of trying, they were all breathing hard and beginning to feel a bit desperate.

"May I point out," said Mr. Smith, at last, "that if you would only listen to me—"

But Martha interrupted him.

"Of course if you ask *me*," she said, "the trouble is, none of those wishes were any good because we didn't make her *believe* first."

The others looked at her.

"Of course," said Mark.

"Out of the mouths of babes," said Jane.

"Why didn't *we* think of that?" said Katharine. "Naturally you have to believe in magic—otherwise if it starts happening to you all sanity is despaired of!"

"Exactly," said Mr. Smith. "Now I suggest—"

But Martha had the charm in her hand.

"Oh, Mother," she said earnestly. "Mother *dear*, if you just wouldn't be so stubborn about it! I *wish* you'd believe what we keep telling you! I wish it twice!"

"I do, dear. I believe you," said their mother.

"You believe there's a magic charm?"

"Naturally, dear. If you say so, dear."

"And everything's all right and you're going to get married and live happily ever after?"

"Whatever you say, dear."

"There!" Martha turned in triumph to the others.

But Mark was looking at their mother suspiciously.

"Something's wrong here," he said. "That doesn't sound like Mother at all!"

"No, it doesn't, does it, dear?" said their mother.

"We don't want a mother that just *agrees* with everything all the time!"

"No, you don't, do you, dear?" said their mother. "I wouldn't either."

"You see what I mean?" said Mark. "Why, I bet if I said the moon was made of green cheese she'd just say, 'Yes, dear. I know, dear.' "

"Isn't it true?" said their mother. "I couldn't agree with you more, dear."

The other three were just as alarmed as Mark by now.

"This is awful!" Jane cried, turning on Martha. "You've taken Mother and turned her into some awful sappy blah character without any gumption at all! Why, Mr. Smith won't even want to marry her in this condition!"

"No, he won't, will he?" said their mother, contentedly. "I wouldn't, either."

There was a stunned silence.

"And *now*," said Mr. Smith, in a grim voice, "perhaps you will permit me to make a suggestion?"

No one had the heart to reply.

Mr. Smith took the charm from Martha's hand firmly.

"I suggest that we start over," he said, "and I suggest that we take it more slowly. And that *somebody* thinks before acting!" And he held the charm out before him solemnly, almost as if he were in church.

"I wish first that Alison may be restored to her own natural, stubborn, lovable self, and I wish this twice. But I further wish that her mind, without losing any of its natural, stubborn, lovable character, may be made open to receiving the secret of this charm, and this I also wish twice. And I thirdly wish that she may be twice relieved of the fear that has come to her through the magic of this charm, and may be twice ready to receive any boon it may grant her."

There was another silence. Then the children's mother looked round at them all, and smiled. And it was plain that these last wild minutes, ever since they had arrived in the office, had vanished from her mind.

"Hello," she said. "How nice of you all to come and surprise me."

"We came," said Mr. Smith, "to bring you a gift." And he put the charm on her desk. "This is a magic charm, and it works by halves. Ask twice for whatever you wish, and you will receive it once. It is from all of us, with our love. Now. What is your heart's desire?"

"But you know what it is," said the children's mother, not picking up the charm. "My heart's desire is to marry you and have the children love you as much as I do. And not to have to work on the paper anymore, but stay home and take care of the children instead of having to have Miss Bick. And to have the children be able to go to the country in the summers the way they've always wanted to. And to have you shave off that beard."

"Really? Don't you like it?" said Mr. Smith, in surprise. "I've grown rather attached to it, through the years. I'll hate to see it go. But for the rest of your desire, if you marry me I'll do my best to give it to you. Without the help of any charm. We won't be rich, because people who run bookshops seldom are, but summers in the country I think I can manage."

He took their mother's hand, and the two of them stood looking at each other.

"Aren't you going to wish?" said Katharine, after a bit.

"Why should we?" said their mother. "We *have* our happiness."

"Oh," said Katharine, disappointed.

The faces of the four children fell. They had never felt so let-down in all their lives. Then after a moment Katharine's face brightened.

"But it was a wish that brought you together in the first place," she said, "and it was another wish that made you meet again. It was really the charm that caused everything, in a way!"

"Maybe that's the one big, important thing it came into our lives to do," said Mark.

"You mean maybe now it's used up and won't work anymore?" said Martha, alarmed.

"Oh, and today's the seventh day, too!" cried Jane. "Maybe the magic's over!" She picked up the charm and turned to Mr. Smith. "I don't want to butt in, and I'm sure you could give Mother her heart's desire by the sweat of your manly brow alone," she said, "but just to make sure, I wish all her wishes would come true twice!"

Mr. Smith gave a cry, and clapped his hand to the place where his beard used to be. The four children agreed later that he looked very handsome without it.

Only right now they didn't notice, because right now other things were happening.

For it seemed as though the room suddenly began to shine, and there seemed to be a sound of far-off singing and a faint chiming of bells all about them. And a fragrance hung in the air that was not quite cinnamon and not quite vanilla and not quite the perfume of all the gardens in the world, but a little like all these things and something else, too. It was the scent of magic.

And their mother and Mr. Smith stood looking at each other and didn't see the shining or hear the singing or sense the fragrance because all they saw was the light of each other's eyes, and all they heard was the beating of each other's heart and all they felt was their love for each other.

By and by the shining and the singing and the fragrance died away.

"I guess that's the last wish, all right," said Mark. "It never rang bells and smelled like a perfume shop before!"

"What did you say?" said their mother.

"I said I guess that's the last wish," said Mark. "The last wish on the charm."

"What charm?" said Mr. Smith.

They had forgotten. Now that they had their heart's desire, they had no need of any other magic. They turned and went out of the office, and the four children followed them.

Jane still held the charm in her hand, but the children were as sure as they had ever been of anything in their short, full lives that with that last wish the magic had gone out of it, and that there would be no more enchanted adventures for them.

"Still," said Mark, as they reached the street, and just as though the others had spoken their thoughts aloud. "Still, we might as well test it and see. Wish something. Any old dumb thing."

"All right, I wish I had four noses," said Jane.

Everyone looked. But the usual slightly snub

one remained the only feature in the middle of the face of Jane.

"That settles that," said Mark. "Good-bye, charm." But his voice was quite cheerful.

"I guess it just came to make us happy," said Katharine. "And now we are!"

"Weren't we happy before?" asked Martha.

"Oh, sure, in a kind of way," said Mark. "The way some people are happy and some people are unhappy because they're born that way. But there were a lot of things we wanted changed, and now they're going to be!"

"No more Miss Bick!" said Katharine.

"Summers in the country," said Jane, "and a practically perfect stepfather! You know," she added, feeling suddenly rather wonderful, "it looks as if *we* got our heart's desire, too!"

But all the same, she didn't throw the old, used-up charm away. As they hurried to catch up with their mother and Mr. Smith, she stopped long enough to put it away carefully in her handbag.

She would keep it a while longer, just in case.

8

How It Began Again

And it turned out there was one more wish, after all.

The last wish was Jane's alone, and she never really knew she made it.

That night, as she was getting undressed, she found the charm in her pocket, and sat on the bed looking at it for a long time, and pondering the mystery of how it had come into their hands, and why.

And from that she went on to thinking about their mother's being married, and the changes it would bring into their lives.

She was quite contented about everything. But because she was the only one of the four children who remembered their father, she would have been more contented still if she could have felt sure that he knew about what was going to happen, and approved of it.

It had been a full day, and she was ready for sleep. Already her eyes had begun to close of their own accord. But as she put out the light and tucked the charm absentmindedly under her pillow, her last waking thought was that she wished her father were with her now, so she'd know how he felt about things.

She wasn't worrying about the charm, or working out the right fractions, as she wished it. But because there was still this one small corner in Jane that wasn't completely happy, the charm relented, and thawed out of its icy used-upness, and granted the wish, according to its well-known fashion. Immediately her father was *half* there.

He was there like a thought in her mind, assuring her that everything was all right, and exactly as he would want it, and that he was happy in their happiness.

And a wonderful feeling of peace filled the heart of Jane, and she went to sleep with a smile on her face.

In the morning she'd forgotten all about the wish. She knew only that the sun was yellow and warm, and the sky was blue, and a golden future lay ahead, and all was right with the world.

She found the charm under her pillow when she was making her bed, and put it in the top bureau drawer, reminding herself to consult with the others later about what to do with it.

But the next days were so full, what with plans for the wedding, that Jane never did get around to consulting.

And at last the wedding day came, and happy was the bride the sun shone on, and happy, too, were the four children. And after their mother and Mr. Smith had been pronounced man and wife, Mr. Smith shook hands all round, and their mother kissed them, and then off the two of them went for a week's honeymoon, and Miss Bick came and stayed with the children for the last time, and had her will with them for seven days, and biffed and banged and cleaned and complained until life became a mere burden, but there was always the comforting thought that at the end of the seven days lay freedom.

And the seven days finally were over, and their mother and Mr. Smith returned, and the four children sang "Good-bye forever!" out of the upstairs windows as Miss Bick took her departure for the last time.

And it was then that their mother told them that Mr. Smith had taken a house on a lake for the rest of the summer, where it was real country all around, and yet it was near enough for him to drive in to the bookshop every day.

So from then on all was bustle and squeak, in the words of Katharine, and if the children weren't being taken downtown to buy bathing suits and camera film and badminton birds and beach balls, they were walking to the library and choosing vacation reading or packing their nice shabby old suitcases and the nicer new ones Mr. Smith had bought them.

And it wasn't until the morning of the day before they were to leave that Jane got around to cleaning out her top bureau drawer, and found the charm again.

Immediately she summoned a Council.

"Do you suppose we ought to keep it forever, sort of In Memoriam?" she wondered.

"Put it in the curio cabinet with the other objects of art," said Katharine, giggling.

"Maybe we ought to try it again," said Martha. "Maybe it was just tired before, and now it's had a nice rest!"

"Huh-uh." Mark shook his head. "That last wish was the end. You could tell."

And the others had to agree that you could. But Martha still wasn't pacified.

"What about this, then?" she said. "It's used up for us, but how do we know it wouldn't still be perfectly good for other people?"

This was a thrilling idea.

"Sure," said Mark. "It stands to reason. It's come down through centuries with its magic unscathed—it'd take more than four paltry children to make it bite the dust!"

Jane nodded excitedly. "You mean now we pass it on to somebody else!"

"Anybody we know?" Katharine wondered.

"We could go round being sort of fairy god-mothers and granting wishes," said Martha.

Mark shook his head

"That's no good. We'd just get so we wanted to tell everybody what to wish. It'd be sort of like trying to have the charm all over again, secondhand. I think that would be kind of against the rules. It came to us out of the unknown, and I think that's where it ought to go again. I think we ought to let some utter stranger find it, and then put it out of our minds forever."

And the others had to agree that this *did* seem like the kind of noble conduct the charm would expect of them.

So it was with feelings of crusader-like righteousness that, five minutes later, the four children got off a streetcar in a part of town they didn't know at all, and stood looking around them.

Lots of people walked past, but they were all grown-ups.

"And I think it has to be a child," said Mark. "Most grown-ups wouldn't understand, unless they're wonderful ones like Mr. Smith, and you don't find types like him on every street corner."

At last they saw a little girl heading their way. The little girl had a baby with her. The baby was very young and fat, and just learning to walk, and was exceedingly slow about it. As the little girl came nearer, the four children could see that her face, while pleasant, was tired and pale.

"She looks as if she could do with some happiness," said Katharine.

The others nodded.

So Jane dropped the charm on the sidewalk, in

a place where it would glint in the sun and attract attention, and she and Mark and Katharine and Martha hid behind a rather scraggly privet hedge nearby, and waited.

"Oh, come along, Baby. Hurry up!" they heard the little girl saying. But Baby wouldn't be hurried. It walked even slower, putting each foot down carefully and then looking at it to be sure that it landed on solid ground. And the third time it looked down it saw the glint of the charm.

Before the horrified gaze of the four children, the baby picked the charm up clumsily, and looked at it. Then the worst happened. It put the charm in its mouth and swallowed.

Behind the hedge everyone gasped.

"Is it lost forever, do you think, or will it come up again?" asked Martha.

"It's a long red lane that has no turning," remarked Katharine.

"Now I suppose the *baby*'ll get a wish," said Martha. "What do you suppose it'll be?"

"Probably something horrible," said Jane, "and nobody'll know or be able to help it because it can't talk and tell them!"

"Don't worry," said Mark. "It'll probably just be about Pablum or something."

And it wasn't the baby who got the wish, after

all. For now the weary little girl, growing tired of walking so slowly, picked the baby up and began to carry it.

"Oh dear, Baby," she said. "I wish you didn't weigh so much. I wish you didn't weigh anything at all."

And because she was holding the baby who held the charm, right away the magic began to begin again.

Of course if she'd got her wish whole, the baby would have left the earth and gone shooting off into space. As it was, the charm did its usual trick, and immediately the baby weighed half as little as nothing at all, which is still very little. It left the girl's arms, bounced up toward the sky, then floated gently earthward like a piece of thistledown.

The little girl caught it, but it went bouncing up again. The little girl began to cry.

"Shall we tell her?" said Katharine.

"Wait," said Mark.

They waited. And the bouncing did its work. The third time the little girl caught the baby, something shiny flew out of its mouth and landed clinking on the sidewalk. The little girl saw the shine and heard the clink. She put the baby down, and ran to pick up the charm.

She stood looking at it. Then she looked back

at the baby, who had ceased to bounce and was sitting on the sidewalk with its thumb in its mouth.

And then, plain as day, the four children could see the little girl beginning to think, and to put two and two together. A look of wild wonder and excitement came over her face, the look of one who is about to make a magic wish.

And it was then that Mark, ever strong-minded, dragged the others away.

"Oughtn't we to tell her the secret?" said Jane. "About saying two times everything?"

"Nobody told us, did they?" said Mark. "I don't think anyone's supposed to."

He wouldn't even let the others look back as they boarded the street car.

"You never know—we might be turned into pillars of salt or something," he said. "I don't think we're supposed to know anything about it. Something tells me."

"At least we know she'll be happy in the end," said Katharine.

But Martha couldn't help wanting to know what was happening right now. When Mark wasn't watching her, she turned and looked.

The little girl and the baby had vanished, on what wild errand of adventure Martha could only guess. But she would never know. She would be left to wonder all the rest of her life.

And she wondered something else, too. After they'd ridden a few blocks, she put it into words.

"Do you suppose we'll ever have any more magic adventures?" she said. "Oh, maybe not big ones like these, but any at all? Just nice little safe ones, maybe?"

"I wonder," said Jane.

Mark and Katharine didn't say anything, but they were wondering, too.

But it was a long time before the four children knew the answer.

Turn the page to discover more exciting books in the Odyssey series.

Other books in the Odyssey series:

L. M. Boston
☐ THE CHILDREN OF GREEN
   KNOWE
☐ TREASURE OF GREEN KNOWE
☐ THE RIVER AT GREEN KNOWE
☐ AN ENEMY AT GREEN KNOWE
☐ A STRANGER AT GREEN KNOWE

Edward Eager
☐ HALF MAGIC
☐ KNIGHT'S CASTLE
☐ MAGIC BY THE LAKE
☐ MAGIC OR NOT?
☐ SEVEN-DAY MAGIC

Mary Norton
☐ THE BORROWERS

John R. Tunis
☐ THE KID FROM TOMKINSVILLE
☐ WORLD SERIES
☐ ALL-AMERICAN
☐ YEA! WILDCATS!
☐ A CITY FOR LINCOLN

Virginia Hamilton
☐ A WHITE ROMANCE
☐ JUSTICE AND HER BROTHERS
☐ DUSTLAND
☐ THE GATHERING

Look for these titles and others in the Odyssey series in your local bookstore.

Or send prepayment in the form of a check or money order to: HBJ (Operator J) 465 S. Lincoln Drive, Troy, Missouri 63379.

Or call: 1-800-543-1918 (ask for Operator J).

☐ I've enclosed my check payable to
   Harcourt Brace Jovanovich.

Charge my: ☐ Visa ☐ MasterCard
            ☐ American Express

_____
Card Expiration Date

Card #

_____
Signature

_____
Name

_____
Address

_____
City   State   Zip

Please send me _____
copy/copies @ $3.95 each

($3.95 x no. of copies) $_____

Subtotal $_____

Your state sales tax   + $_____

Shipping and handling   + $_____
($1.50 x no. of copies)
Total $_____

PRICES SUBJECT TO CHANGE